Praise for *Behind the Baton*

"As someone who worked many times over many years with Gerard Schwarz, I was always amazed with his enormous capacity for great work. Whether he was premiering new music (in which he has made an enormous contribution), or conducting the standard repertoire, the joy and natural musicality he brought to everything made every performance a memorable one. This book, *Behind the Baton*, gives us an in-depth look into the qualities that make a great conductor as well as a true servant to music."

—Horacio Gutiérrez, pianist

"Gerard Schwarz has been a towering figure in the music world for decades. Now he brings his unique insights to a brilliantly written book that spans his marvelous career. This is a must-read for anyone interested in our great art form."

—Misha Dichter, pianist

"*Behind the Baton* affords readers entrance into the mind of a great musician who has accomplished so much in our world. This book tells the remarkable story of his great championing of American music, from Howard Hanson to Jennifer Higdon."

—Bright Sheng, Leonard Bernstein Distinguished University Professor of Music, University of Michigan

Behind the Baton

Behind the Baton

AN AMERICAN ICON TALKS MUSIC

GERARD
SCHWARZ

with MAXINE FROST

AMADEUS
PRESS

AMADEUS PRESS
AN IMPRINT OF HAL LEONARD LLC

Published in 2017 by Amadeus Press
An Imprint of Hal Leonard LLC
7777 West Bluemound Road
Milwaukee, WI 53213

Trade Book Division Editorial Offices
33 Plymouth St., Montclair, NJ 07042

Printed in the United States of America

Book design by Michael Kellner

Library of Congress Cataloging-in-Publication Data is available upon request.

ISBN: 978-1-57467-476-7

www.amadeuspress.com

CONTENTS

———

CHAPTER ONE

Childhood

Growing up, I always knew my parents' story of getting out of Austria and coming to the United States. My mother, Gerta, was from Vienna, and my father, Hans—or John, as he later became known—was from Mödling, one of the city's suburbs. In the 1930s both were studying at the University of Vienna medical school. But beginning in 1938, Jews were no longer allowed to go to medical school or to any school of higher learning. One day signs went up throughout the halls of the medical building: No Jews Allowed to Attend Classes Anymore. My parents left Austria for the former Yugoslavia, now Slovenia, where my paternal grandmother had a house—it became my father's family's country house—in Rogaška Slatina, about an hour outside of Zagreb. They applied for a visa to the United States from Zagreb because my father had not only an Austrian but also a Yugoslav passport. While their applications were being processed, they headed west to Switzerland. They finished their final year of medical school at the University of Basel and got married. Then, degrees in hand, they retrieved their visas from Zagreb, purchased two tickets on the *Île de France*, and sailed for New York.

Several years earlier my paternal grandfather, Julius, just before he died, had opened a Swiss bank account, as he had felt the rise of anti-Semitism throughout Austria. This fortuitous detail is why my parents were allowed to enter Switzerland and could afford to live there for the year.

In 1939 they settled in Hoboken, New Jersey, where my two sisters, Bernice and Jeanette, and I were born. My father worked at St. Mary's

Hospital and eventually went into private practice in Weehawken, New Jersey. My parents were incredibly smart and gifted. They both played the piano, and they were great music lovers. Their children were exposed to everything—theater, opera, ballet, symphony concerts. We would go to the New York Philharmonic at Carnegie Hall and to the New York City Ballet at City Center. We all played the piano from the time we were five.

My mother often used to say, "You're the son of the doctor," which meant I had to work at a different level. My father worked from seven o'clock in the morning until eleven o'clock at night as a surgeon and family physician. I only saw him at dinnertime for half an hour. He worked very hard, as did my mother after she went back to medicine when I was eight. Before that she was simply our mother, and we were unaware that she was also a physician. My work ethic derives from their example.

When my mother returned to medicine, she did a specialty in neurology at the Veterans' Hospital in West Orange, New Jersey, and then a specialty in psychiatry at Bellevue Hospital in New York. She was a brilliant woman, but it was a difficult time for her: after being away from medicine for twelve years, she had to reintegrate medical studies into her life, then take her boards and go through certification all over again. She had forgotten a lot, and my father became her coach.

As a female doctor she was unusual in America in the 1950s, just as she had been as a female medical student in Austria in the 1930s. How many women in Austria were doing that at the time? To take an example from the music world, the Vienna Philharmonic did not have any female members then. Today they have a grand total of about six. My mother never made her decision to go into medicine into any kind of social cause. When the women's movement caught fire, she never quite got it. She thought, you just do what you do—work hard at a very high level. For her, that meant becoming a doctor and, ultimately, a psychiatrist.

My father's mother, Anna Schwarz, lived with us. She was the only living grandparent I had and was a most extraordinary and loving person. In a sense it was she who brought me up. My parents had their hands full with my sisters, and when I came along, I became my grandmother's favorite. She was happy to take over, and my mother was happy with the arrangement.

Our house was furnished in a typical Viennese style: antique furniture, portraits trimmed in gold, an abundance of porcelain knick-knacks, and a predominance of red, yellow, and—my mother's favorite color—turquoise. It was filled with warmth, history, family, and elegant clutter. We used to have family gatherings in the basement. It was quite large, and we had stained glass windows with fluorescent lights behind, so it seemed like daylight all the time. There was an organ, a huge brick fireplace, a long table that seated about twenty, and an old-fashioned bar. From the time I was about four, my father would say, "Let's go downstairs and listen to something together." He would then play me recordings of Beethoven—my favorite.

He did everything in those days—delivered babies, treated breast cancer, everything. And when you do everything, you're on call all the time. I would often make house calls with him. We would drive together to somebody's house, and he'd go in with his black bag while I sat in the car and waited for him to come back.

My father was a real patriot. He would only buy American cars and American products. He said that in 1939 America took him in, with his German accent, imperfect English, and German name, and he was always grateful to this country. There was a time when shoes weren't made in the United States, so he bought English shoes—England was okay too.

The Baseball Fanatic

We had a country house about an hour and a half away in Monmouth Beach on the Jersey shore. We stayed there all summer, from the middle of June to September. However, Monmouth Beach was anti-Semitic, something my parents didn't realize when they purchased the house. We were not allowed to join the Monmouth Beach club, where one could play tennis and swim and go to the beach, so my parents built a swimming pool. Because we did not know many people, my parents allowed each of us to bring a friend from school to stay with us for six weeks.

I loved to play baseball. My mother asked our plumber, "My son wants to play baseball—what can we do?" He told her the only place to play baseball was at the local church. So she sent me to church. The Sunday school teachers came to each of us and asked, "How many communions have you had?" Of course, at five years old, I had no idea what communion was. They said, "Oh, haven't you been brought up in the proper Christian way?" I guess not. It made me really uncomfortable. I told my mother I wouldn't go back. Eventually our house in Monmouth Beach burned down (some people said it had been deliberately set). I was in first grade at the time, and when I came home from school my mother told me about the house as soon as I walked in the door and handed me some charred baseball bats. I still remember the smell of the charred wood. It was horrible. But it turned out better for us because in Deal, where we moved after the fire, we were allowed to play tennis and go to the beach club. And we had a beautiful home, designed by Stanford White. We spent every summer there until I went to Aspen at the age of nineteen. The Deal house was sold in the 1990s.

In Weehawken, my elementary school was about a half a mile from home. I'd walk to school in the morning, walk home for lunch and back to school, and walk home again at the end of the day—twenty minutes each way. I loved my elementary school because—and this turned out to be so important for the way my life turned out—we had a chorus, a band, and an orchestra, all in this little town of Weehawken.

Our house in Weehawken, where I grew up, had doctors' offices that you reached through a trap door in our small library. The kitchen was on the second floor, and so were the bedrooms and the television. After my mother annexed two rooms of their offices, the upstairs kitchen became her dressing room; one annexed room included a much-needed extra bathroom alongside the new kitchen, and the television moved downstairs to the other. We were not allowed to watch television on weekday nights unless it was educational.

I had the smallest bedroom, but I didn't know it at the time. What did I know about bedrooms? Each of my sisters had nice-sized bedrooms, my parents had a very large bedroom, and I had a teeny little bedroom. It never dawned on me, until I went back when I was older and realized how small it was. My room was right above the front door. At night, going to sleep, I could see the lights of the cars going by through the blinds. It was my comfort zone.

In addition to our piano studies, my mother insisted we play tennis and swim. If I wanted to play baseball or anything else, that was my business, but I had to swim and I had to play tennis. I was not a fan of doing laps. When I was about nine we had a swimming coach at the Newark Athletic Club, Kurt Wurtheimer, who had been Buster Crabbe's coach. Buster became an Olympic swimmer because of Kurt, and once Kurt became my coach, I won a lot of trophies. It got to the point where I had to start traveling to swim. My mother really wanted me to and I didn't, so I dealt with the problem by somehow forgetting how to swim. My mother and I went to Mr. Wurtheimer, and suddenly I couldn't swim. They had to give me an inner tube. I would have had to start all over again, so my swimming career ended—to my relief.

Musical Beginnings

The piano was part of life in our household. My father played beautifully. When he first came to Hoboken and worked at St. Mary's Hospital, he played organ at the morning service for the nuns. My mother also played piano well. When we first started, she would practice with us every day, but eventually we practiced on our own: forty-five minutes. After ten minutes I'd say, "Oh, Mommy, I have to go to the bathroom. Mommy, I need a drink of water"—anything to get out of it. She practiced with me for about a year, then stopped. Thank God—that was rough going.

When I was seven we went to see a film version of the opera *Aida*. Sophia Loren played the title role, but the singer was Renata Tebaldi. Then came the Triumphal March toward the end, with the herald trumpets. Wow! I was hooked. At that moment I knew I wanted to play the trumpet.

I was still taking piano lessons. We had a phenomenal teacher, Doris

Humphrey. She also gave me a foundation in theory, the depth of which I realized much later.

We had a music club one Saturday a month called the Frank La Forge Music Study Club. Frank La Forge had been Mrs. Humphrey's teacher, and he was a student of someone who had studied with someone else who had studied with Johannes Brahms. I didn't mind the club, but it was Saturday morning and I had baseball games to play.

We used to play football in the street, with cars coming and going, and stickball in the schoolyard. All the kids in the neighborhood played outside the entire day. There was a ball field right above the Lincoln Tunnel where I played baseball, and right next to it was a tennis court. No one ever used it, so I used to play there. When you hit the ball out, it went into the tunnel. Thank goodness no car ever got hit.

Grossmutti

Our house had a huge attic where my mother kept all her old clothes and out-of-season clothes in mothballs. There was one little bedroom just at the top of the stairs, where Grossmutti, my grandmother, lived. As a little boy I'd sometimes get up in the middle of the night, go upstairs, and crawl into my grandmother's bed.

My mother was, frankly, tough on my grandmother, and eventually she decided to move out. So, being a very entrepreneurial woman, she bought an apartment building around the corner that had a drugstore on the ground floor. Her daughter—my father's sister, my Aunt Helen—lived with her. Helen married a pharmacist, Pat Viconte, who worked at my grandmother's pharmacy. Uncle Pat was unusual in our family: he was quiet. He had a thoughtful and gentle nature, and sometimes I would watch him work, filling prescriptions in his quiet, methodical way. I admired him very much for his assuredness in his profession, and for his artistic side: he was a superb photographer and had his own darkroom.

After Roosevelt Elementary School I went to Woodrow Wilson Junior High School, which was two blocks from our house. There was our house, there was my grandmother's building, and there was the junior high school. So I walked two blocks to the junior high school, and since my mother now was practicing at Bellevue Hospital, I would go to my grandmother's for lunch, usually chicken pot pies. A loving, giving woman, incredibly generous of spirit and heart, she died at the age of ninety-nine.

After my mother went back to work, my parents had to hire someone to take care of us. My father found a succession of nurse's aides who needed work, and they would live in my grandmother's old room. My sisters and I used to torment them. We were terrible. When I was ten my parents hired an Italian woman with minimal English named Concetta Persico. She was a doll, and we children all adored her. As with my grandmother, the more we loved someone, the more trouble they received from my mother. But all that just rolled off Percy's back.

Percy was an astounding Italian cook. Not only would she cook lavish Italian meals every night, she would relish cooking individual dishes for each of us. If I wanted pasta with meatballs, she would make it for me; if my father wanted fish, she would make it for him. She filled our house with creativity and joy, always singing in Italian while she cooked. One summer in Deal we were all gathered in the kitchen while Percy cooked. WNCN was on, playing the Stravinsky arrangement of "Happy Birthday," which distributes the pitches over a very wide range. None of us realized what it was, and suddenly Percy was singing "Happy Birthday." She was not only an unbelievably gifted chef, she was a deeply warmhearted person, with a love of music, life, and, seemingly, us. She stayed with us for many years, as we all loved her dearly, including, in the end, my mother.

First Trumpet

One night at the elementary school, all the fourth-graders were allowed to try instruments to see what they wanted to play. They had teachers on each instrument who were there to help you decide. I was still just a third-grader, but I really wanted to play the trumpet, so I went to the gymnasium at the high school and waited in line to meet with the trumpet guy, Leon Rossman.

Mr. Rossman said, "I know you. Aren't you Dr. Schwarz's son?" I told him I was.

"You want to play the trumpet?" he asked.

"Oh yes, I want to play the trumpet!" I replied.

"What grade are you in?"

"I'm in third grade."

"Come back next year."

So I waited a year, and the next year I did the same thing—waited in line to try the trumpet. I made a sound right away, but Mr. Rossman said we had to rent one at a music store. My mother was not thrilled with my choice: "Jewish Viennese children don't play the trumpet, they play the piano or the violin." Finally she acquiesced, saying, "Okay, play the trumpet, but you still have to play the piano." I said, "Of course I'll play the piano." And then she said, "But you're on your own for the trumpet. You'll have to rent it yourself."

I went to my grandmother and my uncle and my aunt and everyone I knew, and I shined shoes for everybody to make fifteen dollars to be able to rent my first trumpet for three months. Mr. Rossman became my teacher.

The same day I tried the trumpet, my best friend, Raymond Schoenrock, tried the saxophone. In Weehawken most of my friends lived in the same square block, because we were not allowed to cross the street. On our block there were mostly homes, but on a street called Park Avenue there were businesses. Mr. Gerson was the tailor. There was an itty-bitty post office. There was another shop, a candy store, and there was the bank. Raymond lived above the bank in a really nice apartment. Ray was a great friend. He was the boy who came down to our country house in Monmouth Beach for six weeks each summer. Although not a great baseball or stickball player, he was a good student and a wonderful saxophone player. He was in the first band I formed; it rehearsed (mostly popular music) in a room in our basement, which I made into my music room. Years later, once I had decided to become a musician, my father would always be able to hear what I was practicing, since his office was directly above. If he heard me improvising to jazz chords, the phone would ring, and when I answered my father would say simply, "No jazz!" and hang up.

Jeanette and Bernice paved the way for me in elementary school. When people expect you to be nice and smart, you tend to be nice and smart. My favorite teacher was the effervescent Miss Murphy, whom I had for sixth grade. There was an upright piano in our classroom that she played for us every day, sometimes singing as well. She was especially supportive of the school's musical endeavors.

Foreign-Language Records in the Morning

My father was a believer in all kinds of education. For many years we awoke each morning to French-language records blaring throughout the house. One year he switched to Hebrew records. He spoke German to us at the dinner table. My parents talked about medicine all the time in German, and my sisters and I would sit and listen; all three of us understood and spoke German quite well. Eventually my parents only spoke German when they were trying to keep something from us. But my father had done his work too well, for we understood every word they said.

Religious Study

My mother's parents were not allowed out of Austria when my parents left in 1939. In 1943 they were murdered, shot before an open grave in a concentration camp in Riga, Latvia. My mother blamed her religion for causing so much pain, right or wrong, and she was never happy about going to synagogue. My father, on the other hand, though his Jewish education pretty much ended with his bar mitzvah, was strongly committed to Jewish culture, Jewish history, and the temple.

The temple in our neighborhood was in Union City. Many Jews had emigrated to Union City and found work in the once thriving embroidery industry. Our temple was the Orthodox Temple Israel Emmanuel, where women worshipped upstairs and men downstairs. There never seemed to be enough money for any upkeep of the temple, and years later, with the population changing, the synagogue closed.

When I was nine or ten I had to get serious about my bar mitzvah, so I began taking Hebrew lessons three times a week at the Jewish Community Center of North Hudson, one block from the temple. The Community Center provided us a gathering place and a gymnasium where we played basketball. Once, on our way there, my friend Howie Karp grabbed a slice of pizza by the slice. The rabbi, Rabbi Hershman, saw us coming in and said, "Mr. Karp, is that pizza kosher?" Oops! At least there wasn't any pepperoni on it. We all loved Rabbi Hershman and his wife and children. The cantor conducted the service, which was all in Hebrew, so there were no sermons. The temple was very old, small, intimate, and beautifully designed. I had the impression that money was tight for the rabbi and cantor, but it never seemed to matter, because religion was their life.

The kids at temple argued tirelessly about whose family was more religious. Was it Mr. Wopinsky's, the jeweler's? Cantor Rosenbaum's? It definitely wasn't ours! None of the kids at temple seemed to care nearly as much about professions as they did about God and the Torah, and I felt as though I did not quite fit in. Nevertheless, my father insisted on a good religious education.

My bar mitzvah was traditional and Orthodox. I officiated in the service from nine in the morning until noon and did almost everything the cantor did. My mother and sisters wore beautiful dresses and sat upstairs, which they said they liked because they had a really good view of everything. I was so deeply moved by the experience that for some time I continued to lay *tefillin* and even wanted to be a rabbi. That lasted until baseball season.

Carnegie Hall at Eleven

In the fall of 1959 I was twelve years old and had been playing the trumpet for four years. My parents took me to Carnegie Hall to hear Leonard Bernstein conduct Dmitri Shostakovich's Symphony No. 5. The orchestra had just returned from the famous tour of the Soviet Union that Fritz Reiner had been slated to do with the Chicago Symphony. Reiner and the manager of the Chicago Symphony had been working tirelessly toward this U.S. State Department tour. It was the fall of 1959, a time when many musicians were unemployed. Orchestras had thirty-two- or thirty-four-week seasons that usually began in October. The tour represented six weeks of additional work for the musicians. Reiner made some requests that today would not seem outrageous at all. For one thing, he did not want to conduct every concert: he wanted his assistant to do some, including some of the concerts in smaller cities, which included extended bus travel.

In the meantime, Leonard Bernstein had just become music director of the New York Philharmonic, and I think that—behind the scenes—that orchestra was vying for the tour. Reiner pushed hard on some of his requests, which gave the State Department an excuse to look elsewhere. In the end, they gave the tour to the New York Philharmonic, with their new American music director, and Reiner lost his job. The Chicago Symphony musicians burned him in effigy because he had, in their eyes, cost them a month and a half's work. Bernstein requested the same terms as Reiner, and the State Department granted them all.

The Shostakovich Fifth Symphony was the centerpiece of the tour. Bernstein's interpretations were always highly individualistic, relying strongly on the conductor's own musical ideas and phrasings. Shostakovich attended the concert in Moscow and was said to have remarked, "It was a fantastic performance, but it was not what I wrote." This is especially notable at the end of the piece, which Shostakovich indicated in the score to be played at a slow tempo. After the very difficult minor-key beginning of the symphony, the work ends in a major-key, but not triumphant. Bernstein instead performed it very fast, making it sound triumphant—not Shostakovich's intent at all.

That performance of the Shostakovich symphony at Carnegie Hall by Bernstein and the New York Philharmonic on their return from the Soviet Union was life-changing for me. It was a whole world, a world I desperately wanted to live in.

Television and Radio

As a conductor, of course, the person who meant the most to me in my youth was Bernstein. He was my music director, because he had been the music director of the New York Philharmonic in the late 1950s and

'60s when I first attended concerts. I could never get enough of him, whether live in concerts or on television.

I remember when President John F. Kennedy was assassinated in 1963, Bernstein and the New York Philharmonic did a performance of Mahler's "Resurrection" Symphony for CBS in his memory. Think about it. The "Resurrection" is an hour and a half long, and they did it live on television. I can't imagine a network doing that today. And as it was on such short notice, I am sure they rehearsed very little. It may not have been the cleanest performance, but I remember vividly being glued to the television and caught up in the depth and breadth of emotion that only Bernstein could elicit from his players.

In the 1950s and '60s television and radio included the great performances of the great orchestras and the great maestros. I saw Arturo Toscanini on television. Reiner had an hourlong Chicago show most weeks on Sundays. There were very few television stations, and if one of them had classical music on, it was likely many people were watching—and listening.

Those were also the golden years for classical music on radio. There were four classical radio stations in New York: WQXR, the *New York Times* station; WNCN, which ultimately changed to a pop format; and two public stations, WBAI and WNYC. I used to hear the WQXR String Quartet live in a little auditorium in the New York Times Building. I cannot imagine a radio station today with its own string quartet, but those hourlong concerts allowed listeners and lovers of classical music like me to hear the radio broadcasts live each week. I loved radio then and I love it today. Even with modern technology, it continues to be an immense resource and opportunity to hear new artists and repertoire, not to mention unique performances that you might not otherwise happen upon.

Performing Arts High School

In elementary school I played the piano for the orchestra and often for the chorus. I also played the trumpet in the band and sometimes in the orchestra. In sixth grade, I was drafted to play in the Weehawken High School marching band. That was huge for me, including wearing the red-and-black uniform. In junior high school at Woodrow Wilson, in addition to playing with the orchestra, the band, the chorus, and the jazz band, I formed a Dixieland group that became the pep band. My father decided he wanted me to have a better academic experience, though, so after the eighth grade I left Woodrow Wilson and spent one year at the Jersey Academy, a private school in Jersey City. It was excellent academically, with smaller classes, but there was no music and no sports. After that year I pressed hard to attend Performing Arts High School. Luckily my sister Bernice, a dancer, was already attending Performing Arts. Sometimes I would practice with her in front of the mirror, holding her waist while she went through her positions.

The head of the dance department was Rachel Yocum, a physical education teacher and athlete. Her partner was Gertrude Shurr, a modern dancer who worked with Martha Graham. They became friends of my parents. In 1949 they co-wrote a book, *Modern Dance: Techniques and Teaching*, which documented Martha Graham's philosophy of movement. Liza Minnelli and Ben Vereen were among Gertrude's students. Dr. Yocum was strict, and Gertrude was like an angel.

One summer Dr. Yocum and Ms. Shurr visited us in our house in Deal, and I played tennis with Dr. Yocum. When she heard me play the trumpet, she thought I should try to go to Performing Arts. That sounded great to me, because I yearned to be surrounded by people who loved music as much as I did.

Dr. Yocum arranged for me to play for Julius Grossman, the head of the music program at Performing Arts. He told my parents, "We want him," and arranged for me to enroll. That's when my whole world changed. Not everyone loved Mr. Grossman, but I found in him a mentor and a tireless supporter. He offered me many opportunities, both in school and after I graduated.

There were two music schools in New York then: Music and Art, on 135th at Convent Avenue, and Performing Arts, on West 46th Street. Originally Performing Arts was created as a vocational school, and vocational schools were less academic than others. By the time I attended, Performing Arts was a regular high school with half our day devoted to the Arts.

Music and Art had a chorus, an orchestra, a band, and visual arts, in addition to the academics. Performing Arts was much smaller, but there were dance and drama as well as instrumental music. It had many students who went on to great careers, including Murray Perahia, who was a year ahead of me, and Pinchas Zukerman, who was a year behind. In many ways my musical foundation was built during my four phenomenal years at Performing Arts.

We were required to take private lessons, but the school did not pay for them. During my sophomore year I began studying with William Vacchiano, and I stayed with him through Juilliard. I had lessons every other Sunday morning at his house in Queens. Since I lived in New Jersey, it took me almost two hours to get there. I took a bus from New Jersey to the Port Authority, a train to Queens, then a bus on Queens Boulevard to his street, then walked the rest of the way to his house.

Youth Orchestras

By the time I was twelve I had decided to become a professional musician. In high school I practiced for hours and hours every day and played in a number of amateur orchestras: the Williamsburg Settlement Orchestra, the Third Street Orchestra, the Henry Street Settlement Orchestra, the Columbia University Orchestra, the New York Youth Symphony, the New York All-City High School Orchestra, my high school orchestra, and the Hudson Symphony—a different group every night of the week.

My friend Bernard, a fine percussionist, was the son of Reverend Gilbert Helmsley, the minister at a Protestant church three or four blocks from our house. Bernard's sister, Alberta, was an excellent trumpet player, and Reverend Helmsley would drive us to many of our rehearsals. Bernard played the timpani. He also owned the timpani, and the Helmsley station wagon was big enough for all three of us *and* the drums.

In grades eight, nine, and ten I played in the Henry Street Orchestra, which performed at a theater in the Soho area. The conductor,

Felix Popper, was a répétiteur (rehearsal pianist) for the New York City Opera. He was an old-school Viennese musician, sensitive and very knowledgeable, who specialized in the Austro-German repertoire. I played my first Felix Mendelssohn "Scottish" Symphony and Robert Schumann's Symphony No. 1 with him. Those are still highlights for me. Felix later became an administrator at the New York City Opera.

I fondly remember Helen Lindsay, the exceptionally fine first horn player and personnel manager of the Henry Street Orchestra. She ran a tight ship. She had had polio as a child and was in a wheelchair much of the time, but she also walked with crutches. I was the first trumpet and she was the first horn, and if she didn't like something I did, she would lean over and smash my foot with her crutch. We did some great repertoire—but my poor foot!

I loved playing in the Columbia University Orchestra with Howard Shannett. Howard taught at Columbia and wrote the first history of the New York Philharmonic. We did a television show with him as well as many interesting new pieces, including the premiere of a cello concerto written by a descendant of Theodore Roosevelt.

When David Epstein wanted to start the New York Youth Symphony, he posted a notice for auditions, and we all went. I remember playing all the excerpts, and he seemed very happy. I was chosen to be first trumpet, and one of my closest friends, Gene Nagy, was my second trumpet. We played everywhere together. Gene went to Juilliard, then dropped out and became a professional pool player. A really great one, too, I'm told. The New York Youth Symphony still exists. Andrew Grossman, our first horn, was an extraordinary talent. After some time with American Ballet Theatre Orchestra and the Cleveland Orchestra, Andrew became a legendary artist-manager while serving as a vice president at Columbia Artists.

Reverend Helmsley's parish house was where the North Hudson Symphony began, conducted by Arthur Rubenstein, a violinist. Gwendolyn Mansfield was the first flute. She was married to Newton Mansfield, who later became a close friend of mine in the New York Philharmonic. On Friday nights we played in the Swiss Band of Hudson County, conducted by a clarinetist, Herman Schlisserman, who had become a chiropractor when he couldn't make a living in music. He was a fine, clear conductor, who taught me so much about articulation. He helped me hear details I had not noticed before. In the Swiss Band, where I played second trumpet, the first trumpet was Hugo Besserer. I thought he sounded better than I did. My sound was clean but small. His sound was not as clean, but it was big. I knew then and there that I had to figure out a way to produce a bigger sound.

Around this time Dr. Schlisserman started a little opera company. Their conductor was an Italian, Tomasso Grasso. We did the traditional Italian operas—*Bohème*, *Traviata*—with a reduced pit orchestra and the piano playing the missing parts. This involved a huge learning curve, heightening my familiarity with this core repertoire, with a passionate conductor in Grasso. That said, I remember we sounded pretty terrible, but Grasso persisted, and thanks to him we made music.

Playing so much repertoire in all these smaller orchestras with so many different conductors was an invaluable musical education of lasting importance to me.

National Music Camp

When I was eleven years old my mother decided that I was too close to her, my grandmother, and my sisters. And because my father worked so hard and was not around much, she decided I needed to go away to camp. She sent me to the Interlochen Arts Camp in Michigan. Joe Maddy was the director, and you had to make a tape to get in. I was very nervous about it, and it was a very big deal for me when I was accepted.

When my mother put me on the train, it was the first time I had ever traveled alone—a twenty-four-hour trip to Traverse City. Once I arrived there I was very homesick. After I found my way, though, it was a remarkable experience.

No one was more surprised than I was that after my entrance audition at Interlochen, I was given first chair. Luckily I had gone to get the music ahead of time, as the first piece we played was Jean Sibelius's Second Symphony. My part was marked "Trumpet in F," and I had no idea what that meant. I hurried to my trumpet teacher, Gordon Mathie, who explained that when Sibelius was writing his symphonies they used long trumpets that were pitched in the key of F. Because I was playing a B-flat trumpet, it meant I had to transpose, which trumpet players do all the time, but I didn't know that yet. Playing the powerful Sibelius Second was my *aha!* moment, when I said to myself, "I'm going to be a musician."

My first summer at Interlochen was filled with many memorable musical moments. One was when I was chosen to conduct the theme of Howard Hanson's Second Symphony, which ended every concert at Interlochen. Our conductor, Wayne Mueller, came to me, handed me the baton, and explained what to do. My parents happened to be there that week, having rented a house nearby where my father painted. They watched me conduct, and I felt they were truly proud of me and confident in my future. My mother used to tell me that when she was pregnant with me, she had a vision of me as a conductor. But at that time conducting wasn't interesting to me; I was crazy for jazz and playing the trumpet. I went to Interlochen for two more summers and am very grateful to my mother for finding it for me.

After Interlochen, I spent my summers at our country house in Deal, New Jersey, practicing. I played nearby at the Garden State Arts Center when it was first built and became the assistant contractor. When I was seventeen and eighteen I played with some remarkable artists, including Judy Garland, Liberace, Henry Mancini, and Andy Williams. We also played for the Joffrey Ballet.

CHAPTER TWO

Freelance Trumpet Playing

When you play the piano, you press a key and make a sound. On the trumpet it's not quite so simple. Every instrument is difficult in its own way. There is nothing more difficult to play than the piano, what with the number of keys, the pedal, and the voicing. On the other hand, when you're a trumpet player, one of your biggest worries is the little spot right around the center of your lips, which controls everything. If the weather is dry that day and you smile, you might crack your upper lip. Players have to think about such minutiae. You live your life within this little area, blowing on a brass tube, and for that, remarkably, you get paid.

Growing up, I was enamored of all the great German and Austrian music—Mozart, Beethoven, Schubert, Brahms. For a time I was obsessed with Mahler, then Bruckner. One year all I listened to was Tchaikovsky. I always felt connected to Russian music—Borodin, Prokofiev, Rimsky-Korsakov, Shostakovich. And I always loved the American composers—Barber, Copland, Creston, and Diamond.

In high school, my friends and I knew the names of all the players in the major orchestras, the way kids do with baseball teams. In terms of the trumpet, I went through phases. I couldn't hear enough of Roger Voisin (1918–2008), principal of the Boston Symphony Orchestra, who was of the French school of trumpet playing. He played with Boston for thirty-eight years, retiring in 1973. After that I fell in love with Helmut Wobisch (1912–1980), the first trumpet of the Vienna Philharmonic, and his very Germanic style. And then that started to feel too dark and too heavy for me, and I switched again.

In 1963, a year after Philharmonic Hall opened at Lincoln Center, I became a subscriber to the New York Philharmonic—my home team. I idolized the first horn player, Jimmy Chambers; the first oboist, Harold Gomberg; the first flutist, John Wummer; the bassoonist Manny Zegler; and the clarinetist Stanley Drucker. John Corigliano was the concertmaster and William Lincer, the principal viola. Sol Greitzer, who later became my father-in-law, was in the viola section on the second stand. Carl Stern was the principal cellist.

Most important, I idolized my teacher, William Vacchiano. I fell in love with his playing: its thickness, warmth, and sheer beauty. I wanted to sound just like him. Bruno Walter had appointed him principal trumpet in 1942, and he was on the faculty at Juilliard from 1935 to 2002. He also taught at the Manhattan School, Mannes, Queens College, the North Carolina School of the Arts, and Columbia Teachers College.

As Vacchiano's student, I sat proudly in the last row of the third balcony at Philharmonic Hall. I never missed a concert. I became interested in some of his other students, especially Armando Ghitalla, who played primarily in the Boston Symphony Orchestra—as associate first, and then as principal. Ghitalla played in a very different style, poetic, expressive, and lyrical. He was a tremendous influence on me, and years later he and I became friends and colleagues. There were other players I also admired: Adolph "Bud" Herseth in Chicago, Gil Johnson in Philadelphia, Maurice André, and so many others. But because I was from New York, it was those New York players who I really loved.

Lincoln Center

Lincoln Center was very much a part of my life from the beginning. I first played with the New York Philharmonic when I was sixteen at Philharmonic Hall through a youth program, with William Steinberg conducting. When I was eighteen and already a professional, I played extra with the Philharmonic and the Metropolitan Opera. I played with the City Opera and the City Ballet, and I also played often with the Chamber Music Society in the Charles Wadsworth days.

My second home around this time was the New York Public Library for the Performing Arts. I was enamored of musical history, and that library is one of the most extraordinary in the world. I would spend hours and hours there. I was a theater lover as well, and I subscribed to the Lincoln Center Theater the year it was founded.

Before Vacchiano I studied with Ronald Anderson, a member of the New York City Ballet Orchestra and the American Brass Quintet. He was extremely important to my musical development. I was already first trumpet in the New York All-City High School Orchestra, but my sound was not big enough, my endurance was not what it should be, and my high register was only passable. I had to change my way of playing to get what I wanted, and he did that for me. Ronnie fixed my embouchure (mouth position), an absolutely crucial change. Without it I would never have been able to accomplish what I went on to do as a player. In addition, my interest in early music and modern music stemmed from his influence. As a member of the American Brass Quintet, he stressed the importance of different repertoire, including new and early music; and as a groupie, I became hooked.

In those years there was a great deal of musically important freelance work in the classical orchestral world, and Ronnie would often recommend me when the contractors were desperate. My first job as a freelance musician, at age sixteen, was playing with Hermann Scherchen, the great German conductor and teacher. He had written a famous textbook, the *Handbook of Conducting*, and he was conducting the Mozart Requiem with a freelance orchestra. At the last minute they needed a second trumpet, and Ronnie recommended me. It was a thrill to play second trumpet to my teacher and to play the Requiem with a man whose book I had read.

Around that same time I played at the French American Festival at Philharmonic Hall, with Igor Stravinsky in attendance. Ronnie recommended me to the Group for Contemporary Music at Columbia University, where I performed in Edgard Varèse's *Déserts*, with the composer himself in the audience. Afterward I went to Varèse's home in Greenwich Village for a reception. I felt extremely grateful to Ronnie not only for his musical guidance, but for opening up his musical world to me.

Record Collecting

My record collecting started when I was seven or eight. My father bought me a little stereo system with a turntable and two speakers. I thought it was the most beautiful system I had ever seen, a light tan color, with a woody smell that I loved. Then he enrolled me in a record club, where I received a seven-inch 33⅓ rpm record once a month. One month it would be Beethoven's Seventh, the next it would be Rimsky-Korsakov's *Scheherazade*, and the next it would be an album of Bach. Whatever it was, for a month I would listen to it over and over again. It was the most thrilling thing for me, and it cemented my lifelong love of recordings. I started my own collecting, jazz and classical, at Sam Goody's on Forty-eighth Street.

Over the years I have had the opportunity to work with many artists, but I will never forget what the harpsichordist Albert Fuller, once said: "Remember, Jerry, making a recording is making a document for the moment only." That idea is critical to recording because over your lifetime your approach to musical works changes. Of course, with each recording, my goal is always to create the greatest performance that I am able to, with the understanding that I might do it better or differently in the future.

Throughout my career I have been fortunate to have had the opportunity to record with the American Brass Quintet, the New York Philharmonic, the New York Chamber Symphony, the Los Angeles Chamber Orchestra, the Seattle Symphony, the Eastern Music Festival, and many other ensembles and orchestras throughout the world. All have been meaningful for different reasons at different times, and each one matters.

My First Solo Recording

When I was eighteen I made my first solo recording, *The Age of Splendour*. The instrumentation of the pieces, by Girolamo Frescobaldi and Giovanni Battista Fontana, on that first recording was unspecified. I never felt these works were real transcriptions, since they were not written for any particular instrument. In those days I tried to be a kind of purist, not playing real transcriptions like Maurice André did.

After hearing a recital of mine in Denver at the National Trumpet Conference, Maurice told me how much he liked my playing, but that the transcriptions he played were much better for the public. I guess he was right.

The other players on that first album were Julie Feves, a bassoonist, and Helen Katz, a harpsichordist, both classmates of mine at Juilliard. The engineer was Davey Jones. We recorded in the Rutgers Presbyterian Church on Seventy-third Street off Broadway, where I made all my Nonesuch records later on. The sound was excellent, but because of street noise we had to start recording at ten in the evening, when it was quieter.

The next recording I made was for Desto Records and Horace Grinnell, a remarkable man who loved developing new artists, was with the outstanding oboist Ronald Roseman, a member of the New York Woodwind Quintet and the Bach Aria Group. He freelanced at a time when there was a tremendous amount of work in New York. Ronnie also taught at Stony Brook and Juilliard, among other places. He was a very dear friend and later became my principal oboe at the Y Chamber Symphony, which later became the New York Chamber Symphony.

We made that recording in Judson Hall. Arthur Judson Management, which later became Columbia Artist Management, had a small concert hall in their building at 165 West Fifty-seventh Street, and it was a very good recording room. The repertoire was Tomaso Albinoni, Johann Wilhelm Hertel, and Georg Philipp Telemann. It was one of the most enjoyable recording experiences I ever had as a trumpet player. The third solo recording that I made for Desto was American music: Henry Brandt, Elliott Carter, Richard Moryl, Charles Whittenberg, and Stefan Wolpe—all friends of mine.

Juilliard

Call it youth or plain stupidity, but when I applied to Juilliard I didn't apply to any other school, which I now think was ridiculous. My father said, "Son, aren't you going to apply anywhere else?" I said no. He said, "Well, what if you don't get in?" I said, "Don't worry, Dad." Luckily,

I was accepted. During my first year at Juilliard I lived at home in Weehawken. My second year I moved to an apartment at 302 West Seventy-ninth Street between West End and Riverside. I paid $167 a month for a two-bedroom apartment.

My high school composition teacher was Paul Creston. When I turned fifteen my father insisted I study with him, and I have always been grateful for that. Back in Mödling my father had studied composition with the famed Austrian composer and professor Friedrich Wildgans.

At Juilliard I also studied with Milton Babbitt, Jacob Druckman, Vincent Persichetti, and Roger Sessions. Persichetti was a fine American composer and a fascinating teacher. He could talk about a light bulb and relate it to music. I studied electronic music with Babbitt, an austere composer but a brilliant mind. He dealt philosophically with perception in music—for example, what one is able to actually hear in very difficult contemporary music. At times composers would write music that could not be heard specifically as written. Milton was also one of the great experts on American popular song. He knew the complete Broadway American songbook and could identify all the tunes and play them on the piano. By the time I studied with Sessions he was quite old, and it seemed to me that he spent more time lighting his pipe than teaching the class. I clearly remember his insights, however, especially the harmonic implications of Mahler's Ninth Symphony. Druckman became a very good friend and in fact wrote a viola concerto for my father-in-law Sol Greitzer. He was at his best when he would go off on a musical tangent and discuss works like Györgi Ligeti's *Atmosphères* rather than the sixteenth-century counterpoint he was supposed to be teaching. I also assisted him in his orchestration class. My ear-training teacher, Renée Longy, had a comprehensive approach to the teaching of intervals, harmonies, notation, rhythmic and harmonic dictation, and sight-singing. She had developed her own system for intervals and rhythmic notation. Her comprehensive approach to the foundations of music, especially counterpoint, has proved essential throughout my life.

There was a bass trombone player at Juilliard, André Smith, who started a group called the Carnegie Brass Quintet with me and some other students: Carol Rinehart, John Cerminaro, Per Brevig, and Robert Sirinek. Carol became a soloist mostly in Europe. John became first horn in the New York Philharmonic, then the Los Angeles Philharmonic, and then the Seattle Symphony. Per became first trombone in the Met Opera Orchestra. Robert, who joined us after Carol left, became a member of the Metropolitan Orchestra. Later he became personnel manager of the Met and then orchestra manager. Before John joined the quintet, Gerald Brown was our horn player; he later joined the Peace Corps and became a conductor in South America. For me, it was gratifying to be asked by André to join and play with some of the best players at school. He took this ensemble very seriously and was determined to make it an important one. I felt terrible about leaving that December to join the American Brass Quintet, but that was a professional opportunity I couldn't turn down.

I had auditioned for the ABQ the summer before my first year at Juilliard, when I was seventeen. Though I had won the position, they were afraid I might be drafted—the war in Vietnam was going on—so they chose someone else. But by December the other trumpet player had left the quintet as well. They talked to me about my draft status and then took a chance on me. It took me seven years to get my bachelor's degree from Juilliard because I asked for extended time off to tour with the ABQ. I did not receive my master's degree at the time because of insufficient attendance: one teacher was displeased by my excused absences for performances, despite the As on all my exams.

In those days there were two degrees offered: Bachelor or Master of Science, and Bachelor or Master of Music. I had taken the Bachelor and Master of Science, which entailed a few more academic credits. When Joseph Polisi became president of Juilliard, he noticed I had nearly enough credits to receive the Master of Music degree. Because I had just conducted and recorded the two William Schuman operas at Juilliard, he was able to count them as performance credits, and I finally earned my Master of Music degree in 1990. Joseph and I were friends in high school, where we played together in the All-City High School Orchestra. He was an excellent bassoonist who went on to

Yale. His father, William Polisi, was the first bassoon of the New York Philharmonic and the NBC Symphony. Joseph is still the president of Juilliard, and we are still friends. He has been a remarkable, sensitive, and thoughtful leader for Juilliard.

When I arrived at Juilliard, all I really wanted was to get into one of the two Juilliard orchestras. I auditioned for Jean Morel, the French-American conductor of the Juilliard Orchestra. An important conducting teacher, he taught James Conlon, Dennis Russell Davies, Jorge Mester, Leonard Slatkin, and many others. At my audition, one of the excerpts he had me play was from Rimsky-Korsakov's *Le coq d'or*, and he wanted me to play all three trumpet parts. One was in F alto, and two parts were in C trumpet. I had to transpose them, and I did so perfectly. He said, "Oh, you're some acrobat?" I thought my audition had gone very well.

Then, when I arrived at school, I received my schedule—and I hadn't been accepted into either of the orchestras.

Stokowski

Since all I really wanted to do was play in an orchestra, my failure to get in one of Juilliard's was devastating. A friend of mine said, "Why don't you audition for Leopold Stokowski? He has this orchestra called the American Symphony, and they play at Carnegie Hall."

Stokowski started out as the music director of the Cincinnati Orchestra, then spent twenty-five years with the Philadelphia Orchestra. A passionate advocate of new music, he premiered Rachmaninoff's Piano Concerto No. 4 in 1926 with the Philadelphia Orchestra with the composer himself playing. Fifteen years later Eugene Ormandy, continuing in Stokowski's footsteps, conducted Philadelphia in the premiere of Rachmaninoff's revised version. Ormandy, who became the Philadelphia Orchestra's music director in 1938, retained the tradition of the magnificent sound of the Philadelphia Orchestra and its relationship with important composers. I am sure Ormandy wanted himself to be credited for that sound instead of Stokowski, but soon it became the Philadelphia sound, appropriately. When Muti arrived they tried to move away from the Philadelphia sound and instead created a public-relations campaign focused on the sounds of Mozart, Beethoven, and Brahms. The great Philadelphia was, is, and will always be known for its beautiful sound.

In 1955 Stokowski became music director of the Houston Symphony, where he performed a lot of new music. But he was not able to hire and fire at will as he had in the past, and it did not go well for him there. He left to create a new freelance orchestra in New York, the American Symphony Orchestra. Because the players were freelancers and did not work under a contract, he had the ability to hire and fire.

Stokowski became music director of the American Symphony in 1962, when he was eighty years old, and he stayed with them for another ten years. He made a conscious effort to hire women and minorities. The New York Philharmonic did not have any women until 1966, when they hired the wonderful bass player Orin O'Brien. The Berlin Philharmonic hired their first female member in 1987, and the Vienna Philharmonic did not hire their first female player until 1997. I remember Stokowski saying, "Sometimes I'm asked how I feel about having women in the orchestra. I actually prefer women in the orchestra!"

Anyone could audition for Stokowski, anytime—call him on the phone, talk to his secretary, and set it up. So I called. I was eighteen. I went to his home on Fifth Avenue in the Eighties. It was a grand apartment in the front of the building overlooking Central Park, but sparsely decorated. He brought out a big, thick book with orchestral excerpts for every instrument—a violin section, a viola section, a cello section, a bass section. Of course there was a section for the trumpet, all handwritten. The excerpts were always the same, and I knew more or less what was going to come. I played all the excerpts, and it went very well.

He said, "You must know Mozart." I said, "Yes, Maestro, I do think I know some Mozart." He said, "You must play Mozart sonatas on the piano." He was advocating that one be a thorough musician, and for that one had to know the classics. So I said, "Maestro, I know a sonata, would you like me to play it for you?"

Well, clearly, he was not looking to see if I could play it. I was supposed to say, "Yes, Maestro, wonderful idea, I'll do that." Then he talked about soft playing. That was one of my specialties, but I said, "Yes, I'll practice soft playing." I just kept saying, "Yes, yes, yes, Maestro."

The personnel manager of the American Symphony was Arthur Aaron, and he'd been a teacher of mine in high school. At night he played cello in the pit in *West Side Story*, and during the day he taught at Performing Arts. When *West Side Story* closed he became a big contractor in town. He hired a lot of orchestras, and he became the contractor for the American Symphony. Early in the 1965–1966 season the ASO needed a third trumpet, and Arthur suggested me. Stokowski looked at my audition results and agreed to take me.

So in November of my freshman year at Juilliard I was playing in the American Symphony at Carnegie Hall. Every rehearsal, every concert was on the stage of Carnegie Hall. I played with Stokowski for seven years, eventually moving up to first or co-first.

On the program of my first concert was Ernest Chausson's beautiful Symphony in B-flat, and for that I played second. The first trumpet was Teddy Weiss, and I was astounded at how lyrically he approached music. Every phrase, no matter how small, became a part of the fabric of the music. So much trumpet playing in those days was just about knocking out the notes—aggressive, short, and angular, with little phrasing. Sitting next to him, I learned the concept of thinking of your part not as *your* part, but as an essential part of the whole. What a great lesson it was at the beginning of my professional trumpet-playing life.

The Metropolitan Opera Orchestra had two terrific trumpet players—Mel Broiles and Isadore Blank. I played extra at the Met in those days and had a chance to hear Izzy often. I so admired Izzy's musicality and gorgeous sound. Most of my work at the Met was with the distinguished conductor Karl Böhm, who seemed very stern and demanding; but Felix Eiley, the personnel manager at the Met, told me that Böhm liked my playing. That meant so much to me.

Stokowski's rehearsal technique was phenomenal. He'd have four rehearsals, and in each one he went from the beginning to the end of the concert. He didn't spend the whole first rehearsal on the symphony, adding the overture at the next rehearsal, and working out the concerto at the third. He would do the complete program at each rehearsal. Every time it was the same. He conducted without a baton and was expressive and clear. Often he was a little outrageous musically, but by the time the concert came around, his way was our way.

Stokowski used only his own music, so everything was very well annotated. He made many changes in the orchestrations, even in traditional pieces. In addition, he made many unusual interpretative decisions, especially big ritardandos. What was really amazing, though, was that he allowed us to sort out our own problems. He never worked on minutiae. If the ensemble was poor or a passage wasn't in tune, he would just say, "Do better." By the third time through, it would be pretty close. By the fourth time, it was ready for the concert.

Stokowski emphasized a prominent melody and a subtle accompaniment. When I was studying with Paul Creston, he would complain about Stokowski's suppressed accompaniments. In his own music Creston often accompanied melodic material with rhythmic-harmonic ostinatos, and if the accompaniment was not played loudly enough, the piece wouldn't make sense. In 1960 Ormandy performed Creston's *Invocation and Dance* in Philadelphia, and a few weeks later Stokowski performed the same piece with the American Symphony Orchestra. Creston loved Ormandy's performance, but when Stokowski did it, Creston complained that the accompaniments were too soft, and there was one spot where the whole trombone section neglected to play at all for a few measures. Creston had heard that passage in the Philadelphia performance and couldn't imagine what happened.

He went back to look at the trombone music and saw that something had been erased. He called the librarian in Philadelphia, who explained that with any rental piece, Ormandy insisted that all his pencil markings be erased—bowings, edits, corrections. He didn't want anyone else to benefit from his work. Ormandy had heard that the trombones were missing from the Creston piece, so he had them penciled in; but the orchestra librarian erased them before the parts were returned. Stokowski never noticed the omission. He was the kind of conductor who didn't care about details.

Stokowski premiered over two thousand works by Charles Ives,

Gustav Mahler, Rachmaninoff, Arnold Schoenberg, Stravinsky, Varèse, and others. By the time I started to play in his orchestra he was having difficulty conducting challenging contemporary music. But he still had a commitment to performing new works, even if his choice of composers may not have been as astute as it had been in earlier years.

At one set of concerts Teddy Weiss was not available because of a conflict with the New York City Ballet, so I moved over to first. The first trombone player was not too happy about an eighteen-year-old kid playing first trumpet. We were rehearsing a new work that did not seem all that complicated, but it had one 5/4 bar in a section of 4/4 time. Stokowski beat through it in 4/4, so there was a beat missing every time. Finally, on the third day of this scramble, the trombone player said to me, "You have to say something." I'm thinking, No one ever talks to Stokowski. But the trombonist was really pushing me, saying that as the leader of the brass section I had to do something. So I spoke up: "Excuse me, Maestro."

There was dead silence. It seemed to me that Carnegie Hall had never been so quiet.

Finally Stokowski said, "Yes?"

"Maestro, in bar 26 I have the wrong meter. Could you tell me what the meter is supposed to be?"

"Five-four."

"Oh, thank you, Maestro."

He took a pencil and wrote in a big 5. I was so lucky to have survived that moment.

At that time I was engaged to Lillo, the mother of my two older children. I wanted her to meet Stokowski, so I said, "Come to Carnegie Hall and then after the rehearsal I'll introduce you to him."

Stokowski would often go out into Carnegie Hall after a rehearsal and stare at the empty stage. So I took Lillo over and said, "Excuse me."

"Quiet! Quiet!"

After a few minutes I again said, "Excuse me."

"Quiet! Quiet! Quiet!"

Another few minutes. "Excuse me, Maestro. I wanted you to meet my fiancée."

"You have plans?"

"Excuse me? What do you mean?"

"You have plans?"

Again, I said that I didn't understand.

"You have plans to get married?"

"Yes."

"Never get married! It's a terrible thing, it's a terrible institution! You should never, ever get married!"

"Oh. Well, thank you, Maestro!"

I had bought my parents' first home in Weehawken. I would get to rehearsals in New York around a quarter of ten for a ten o'clock rehearsal. In November I received a letter from Stokowski.

"In this cold weather," it began (it was balmy that fall), "you must properly warm up. You must get to rehearsal early and warm up your instrument so you can be ready to play. If you're not willing to do that, you will be replaced. Leopold Stokowski."

I called up Arthur Aaron, the personnel manager, and asked, "Mr. Aaron, what's this about?"

He said, "Oh, yes, well, you don't know that Stokowski gets in to rehearsal at nine o'clock, and he sits on the podium with the personnel list and checks when people arrive, to see if they are practicing their parts and warming up properly."

"But Arthur, I get up at seven in the morning and I warm up at home, and then I come to Carnegie Hall."

"Well, you'd better start practicing onstage."

So for the rest of the years I worked for Stokowski, I got to rehearsal at nine o'clock and warmed up, sitting in the back and playing long tones. Stokowski would mark me down as coming in early.

One day Stokowski came back and sat down next to me. I don't think he knew my name. Most of us had the impression that we were our instruments rather than people. He was a native English-speaker, but he used to drop his articles when he spoke. He said to me, "Play soft note."

I played a soft note. He leaned over to the bell to see if I was playing, because it was so soft he could barely hear it.

Then he said, "Play soft low note." So I played a low note very softly, and again he leaned over to the bell to hear it. Next he said, "Play soft high note." So I played a high C *pianissimo*, and again he leaned over the bell. Then he gave me a little lecture: "You have to play soft. You have to play soft in all registers. You have to learn to play soft, and to control your instrument well."

"Yes, Maestro, thank you, I will work on that." It was like the audition, when he told me I had to play Mozart sonatas.

He loved shiny instruments. Once I had this gorgeous silver trumpet with a long bell. We were doing the Beethoven Ninth and this trumpet was pitched in D, good for the Ninth. But Stokowski always preferred the B-flat trumpet because it had the richest, darkest sound. This particular long-bell D trumpet actually sounded quite good—not too bright.

Stokowski came back and said, "I like this trumpet. What is this trumpet?"

I said, "Oh, Maestro, it's a new trumpet."

"Let me hear this trumpet."

I played a few notes. He said, "I like this trumpet. Will you use this trumpet on the Beethoven?"

"Yes, Maestro."

"What key is it?"

Now I was in trouble! But I fibbed and said, "B-flat."

"Good, good. Play that trumpet."

He always wore a dark blue double-breasted pinstriped suit with a blue silk shirt and a dark blue tie. At rehearsals he'd take off the jacket and tie and conduct in his blue silk shirt. At performances he was always very formal, white tie and tails for the evening concerts and cutaways for the afternoon concerts.

He used to get angry if you did not look at him all the time, and he couldn't stand it if you wore a watch. The antithesis of an artist was a person who cared about how many minutes the breaks were. (He hated all the union rules conductors have to deal with.) So no one wore a watch. He believed in free bowing, and he would get angry if people bowed together. If someone in the violins couldn't see him, he would stop and say, "You! You there! Move! Move!" He was not an especially nice man, but he got some remarkable performances from us. I remember a particularly phenomenal concert which included excerpts from *Götterdämmerung*.

Once, when we were doing Beethoven's Ninth, Stokowski kept rehearsing the section for the four solo voices in the last movement—not only at every rehearsal, but numerous times at every rehearsal. It wasn't like him. But now that I've been a conductor for so long, I understand why he did it. It's the trickiest spot in the whole piece. The singers are singing so loudly, high or low, that they can't hear each other well, even if they are right next to each other. The reason he went over that section so many times was that he had to make sure. Getting a hard spot right once is not enough. Recently when I was doing Mozart's Requiem, there were a couple of transitions that were a little tricky—changes of tempo. I rehearsed them separately a few times to make sure everybody knew what was going to happen so that by concert time, it was comfortable.

The American Symphony did eight programs a year. We played mostly with Stokowski, although we had one or two guest conductors every year, including Böhm, Eugen Jochum, Willem van Otterloo, and William Walton.

American Brass Quintet

In December 1965 I finally played my first rehearsal with the American Brass Quintet. In the early 1960s there were two professional brass quintets, the New York Brass Quintet and the American Brass Quintet. Each group had two trumpets, a French horn, and a tenor trombone. The New York Brass Quintet had a tuba as its bass instrument and the American Brass Quintet, a bass trombone. At the first rehearsal we were doing a very hard contemporary piece by Emmanuel Ghent. The horn player and the trombone player got into a big fight about something or other having to do with the music. It was horrible, and I thought we were breaking up.

At the end of the rehearsal I said, "Oh, I'm so sorry, it's such a short time that I've been here."

They both said, "What's wrong?"

"It's over, right? You're not going to continue to work together, are you?"

"Oh, sure, in fact we're all going across the street for a cup of coffee, why don't you join us?"

I did some tremendous tours with the quintet. During my sophomore year at Juilliard, I had to take half the year off because we were doing a European tour. I saw Paris for the first time at nineteen. The following year we went to Asia, and then to Europe again. They were all long trips, eight, nine weeks, which was why it took me so long to get my bachelor's degree.

Playing chamber music trains the ear. You rehearse and hear every little detail of ensemble, of intonation, the differences of articulation, the different musical approaches. It feels like you are under a microscope together, working toward a united end. My role was usually musical— running rehearsals and leading the discussion of musical decisions. There we were a quasi-democracy: we all had equal votes, and we would discuss minutiae for what seemed like forever. Those rehearsals were fascinating in terms of personal relationships, general musical issues, and how, with everything merging, tact and thoughtfulness are paramount.

At that time I also played as a freelancer with the Metropolitan Opera, the City Ballet, the New York Philharmonic, and many smaller groups, including the Musica Aeterna Orchestra at the Metropolitan Museum. Musica Aeterna was important during my freelance years. An oboe and chamber music teacher at Juilliard who also was an important contractor, Mel Kaplan, ran Musica Aeterna. It was conducted by Fritz Waldman, a pianist, vocal coach, and conductor. One of his students was Alice Tully, a soprano, who became one of the most important philanthropists in New York and supported Waldman's orchestra. When I first joined Musica Aeterna, I knew Waldman liked the trumpets to be very discreet, so at my first rehearsal I played everything as softly as possible. He seemed pleased, and I continued in that fashion for a few more concerts. Then we did a more contemporary work with a few trumpet solos. I continued to play quite softly, and Waldman made a brief speech to the orchestra in defense of asking me to play louder. At the next rehearsal I played the solo quite softly, and again he asked me to play louder. From then on I could play my way and maintain a wonderful working relationship with him. Later, when I was nineteen or twenty, we did Copland's *Quiet City*, for trumpet, English horn, and strings. Copland attended the concert, which was where I first met him. Later I played *Quiet City* with Copland conducting in Aspen, where I got to know him much better.

During these years I played concerts with the American Symphony, and, as needed, with the Chamber Music Society at Lincoln Center. At this time I also began to conduct. I conducted for the Eliot Feld Ballet, the Erick Hawkins Dance Company, and the Chamber Music Society, usually for new music.

Freelancing was extremely difficult—I never knew what tomorrow would bring. Some days it felt as if my lip might fall off, but I always said yes to playing everywhere. I was very fortunate in those years to have had so many opportunities. I stayed focused on playing my best, but it was difficult because I worked all the time. With my busy travel schedule with the American Brass Quintet and all my additional concerts, my first marriage—to my high school girlfriend, Harriet Rubin—suffered, and after four years we divorced.

CHAPTER THREE

Erick and Lucia

Erick Hawkins grew up in Colorado and, after graduating from Harvard, studied dance in Austria. Upon his return to the United States, he studied classical ballet at the School of American Ballet. He danced with Balanchine's American Ballet and choreographed his first ballet for Ballet Caravan. He joined the Martha Graham Dance Company, the first man in the company, rising to principal dancer soon after joining. He was the preacher in the premiere of Copland's *Appalachian Spring*. Among his colleagues in Martha's company were Merce Cunningham, Pearl Lang, and Gertrude Scher.

In 1948 Martha married Erick; she thought he would make a great father because he was good-looking, intelligent, and talented. Unable to have children, however, they divorced after six years. Erick had already left her company to start his own. His movements were more subtle and more Zenlike than the extroverted Martha Graham style. Some critics noted it lacked tension. Still, he was a remarkable choreographer.

Erick worked only with live music. He also worked almost exclusively with the composer Lucia Dlugoszewski. Merce worked with John Cage, but Cage's music was all aleatoric, which meant it was composed at the moment of performance. Cage would look at the stage and do whatever he did to Merce's movements. Erick, on the other hand, created the movements first, and Lucia wrote the music second. She was frequently late completing the scores, often making the music available to us at the first performance. At one premiere in New York the curtain was delayed for an hour while we copied parts backstage.

Lucia wrote a piece called *Of Love* for brass quintet and percussion that the American Brass Quintet was premiering on Broadway at the ANTA (American National Theater and Academy) Theatre. A Broadway season was the biggest moment for any dance company. Lucia played the percussion onstage, and the brass quintet was in the pit. I sat in the conductor's chair facing the stage, and my colleagues in the quintet were right in front of me. Lucia was stage right, banging away on her percussion instruments. She kind of sang along while she played. Erick did the choreography, and Helen Frankenthaler, the American painter, designed the sets. As for costumes, everybody was naked except for G-strings.

Typically with Lucia, the piece wasn't ready on time. When opening night came, we had never rehearsed the music. The piece was in seven or eight sections, and there was a lot of improvising. It was not what we were supposed to do with Erick. Merce Cunningham and John Cage improvised, but we played written music. I had been to many rehearsals but still was not clear about when to stop. I told Erick, "I'll figure everything else out, but I have to know when it's over so we can end the piece together."

He said to me, "At the very end we're going to be upstage, bouncing up and down in contrary motion. One person will be up and another person will be down, alternating, and the whole company will be doing this across the back in a line and then you'll know it's over."

So we started out with Louie Ranger, the other trumpet player in the quintet, playing a trill on a high B. Louie used a circular breathing technique and could play a note forever. Erick asked Louie to walk down the center aisle of the theater trilling the high B. At the time Louie had very long hair that flowed as he played, creating just the dramatic effect Erick wanted.

We were getting through it pretty well; no one in the audience knew it was improvised. Lucia was banging the heck out of all her personally made instruments up there, and I was leading and trying to keep everyone on track. It was a very long piece, thirty-five or forty minutes. Lucia had requested all the tricks I could do: high notes, low notes, trills, glissandi. After a while she simultaneously banged on her instruments and sang along to whatever theatrics I was managing on the trumpet, matching my high notes exactly. Suddenly she quieted down. The dancers were upstage, in contrasting motion, and I improvised a delicate ending. We were done. There was a brief pause, and then Lucia started singing and beating on her ratchets and pieces of wood. I realized I needed to play some more. I did, and I brought it back down to end it again, with the dancers bouncing up and down, and it was over for the second time. Then Lucia started banging and singing *again*! This went on for another five minutes, which is a very long time in the theater. Finally the piece ended for real; the audience applauded, and everyone seemed happy. Afterward Erick came up to me and said, "What's wrong with you? Why didn't you end it when you were supposed to?"

Once we were doing a work by Erick and Lucia called *Black Lake*, to be premiered at the Theater of Riverside Church in Upper Manhattan. It was for ten or twelve instruments, and again, the parts weren't ready. Finally Lucia arrived with the score and no parts at seven o'clock for the eight o'clock curtain. I told everyone, "Look, just copy the music so we all have the same number of bars. You don't have to write in the right notes or the right rhythm. Just so we know where we are."

It was a forty-five-minute piece. By eight o'clock we were not anywhere near finished. I heard rhythmic applause at about eight-thirty. Forty-five minutes later Erick came out and made a speech, saying, "Sometimes it takes a little longer to make great art." We ended up improvising our way through the opening, and it went surprisingly well. Later Lucia completed *Black Lake*, and we performed it often. Working with Erick and Lucia was almost always challenging and definitely interesting.

After that I recommended Dennis Russell Davies, who took over from me. I wanted to be a great orchestral trumpet player, and conducting for Erick was taking up too much time. Erick then branched out and worked with other composers. He created dances for David Diamond's *Rounds* and for works by Alan Hovhaness, Virgil Thomson, and others.

Years later, after I had joined the New York Philharmonic, the com-

poser Stanley Silverman was advising Pierre Boulez about programming American music for the New York Philharmonic. Boulez asked
for something unusual by someone outside the mainstream of known
composers. Stanley recommended Lucia, and the Philharmonic asked
her to write a piece for their new-music series, Prospective Encounters.
Lucia was thrilled to do it and asked if it could be a trumpet concerto
for me called *Abyss and Caress*. All was agreed, and it was scheduled for
the fall of my first season with the orchestra. But then, after a short
tour and the first week of subscription concerts, the orchestra went on
strike for ten weeks. The new work by Lucia had to be rescheduled for
the spring. When Boulez looked at the score, he called me into his
study. I knew this was not the style of music he generally liked: it was
long, with extensive use of scales and gestures, and quite a thick score.
Boulez asked if I was a friend of Lucia's. I said I was. He said, "Would
you please ask her to cut two pounds from this piece?" We had a laugh,
but when I asked Lucia, she was not happy. Because of her tremendous
respect for Boulez, she did make some cuts. The performance went
exceptionally well. Raymond Ericson, of the *New York Times*, wrote:
"One thing the piece has going for it is the virtuosity demanded from
the players. The contribution of Gerard Schwarz, the trumpeter, was
of major importance and was spectacular." And Robert Kimball, at the
New York Post, wrote: "*Abyss and Caress* . . . was written in large part to
exploit the genius of New York Philharmonic co-principal trumpet,
Gerard Schwarz. And indeed, Schwarz was miraculous. The whole
performance was passionate and involved, and Boulez was a picture of
contentment."

Abyss and Caress, like *Space Is a Diamond*, a solo piece written for
me by Lucia, included many of my trick technical gestures. These unusual sounds were interesting to her and very idiomatic to me. Gunther
Schuller liked Lucia's music, and his company, Margun, published
some of her works. In 1976 he programmed *Abyss and Caress*, minus
the Boulez cuts, at Tanglewood. Gunther was happy to show the Philharmonic how the piece should have been done in its entirety.

CHAPTER FOUR

Casals versus Stokowski

One of the most influential conductors for me was Pablo Casals. I played at the Casals Festival in the 1970s when he was still conducting. He did the festival in Barcelona, and when Francisco Franco came to power, he moved it in protest to Prades, in France. Finally, he brought it to San Juan, Puerto Rico, where he ended up living. They would hire the finest musicians from around the country to play at Casals's feet, and it was incredibly meaningful and memorable. I also met Casals's wife, Marta, a superb cellist. It was the beginning of a lifelong musical and personal friendship.

The Casals Festival started out as a celebration with all Casals's greatest friends—chamber musicians and soloists from everywhere joining together. Eventually it became more orchestra oriented, with the Festival deciding it should have experienced orchestral players who knew the repertoire. Their personnel manager was my longtime friend Loren Glickman. One summer the regular first trumpet was not available, and he asked me. We stayed at the Caribe Hilton on the beach. Every morning we would rehearse, the afternoons were spent at the beach, and then we would rehearse again in the evenings.

The most amazing lesson from Casals occurred one morning when he was rehearsing us in Mendelssohn's *Hebrides Overture*. The opening of the work has a beautiful theme in the violas and cellos. Casals rehearsed the theme emphasizing a different note each time, singing how he wanted it each time. They played it many times, emphasizing the first note first, then the second note, then the third, then the fourth, then the fifth, then the last note. This exercise lasted forty-five minutes. After that, we ran through the entire overture. I was in the back playing trumpet and did not play at the beginning; I just watched and listened. When it was my turn to play something, I thought: How should I phrase? How should I play every note? What he had accomplished by focusing on those few opening bars was to make all of us think about how we should phrase each note and what direction our part played in the piece as a whole. Afterward, on the bus from the university back to the hotel, most of the musicians were highly critical of Casals: they could not believe he had spent so much time on just two bars. I said that for me, it was the greatest learning experience of my life because he had made us all focus on what was coming next—on the phrases, the music. It was a phenomenal lesson.

Around the same time I was playing with Stokowski and the American Symphony. Stokowski nuanced everything with his hands, making clear what he wanted, and he rarely talked at rehearsals, generally just playing each work from beginning to end. Stokowski's style and Casals's were complete opposites, yet both worked.

In some ways I do more of the Stokowski style than the Casals style because I believe in letting the musicians know how the piece goes. Especially with new music, it is important to go through it as much as possible so a player knows what to expect when he or she turns the page. Also, I mark my music very clearly, with all the phrasings, bowings, and articulations, so that the musical elements are there. My conducting is therefore an expansion of what is already on the page.

CHAPTER FIVE

———

The New York Philharmonic

M y lifelong dream was to play in the New York Philharmonic. When William Vacchiano retired, James Chambers, the personnel manager, contacted about a dozen players from around the country who had positions in major orchestras. Because he was a teacher of mine at Juilliard and knew my playing, he asked me to join the group, which in itself was an honor. In those days, principal positions could be decided by the music director alone—no committees—and in private. The audition was held secretly, and the only judge was the music director. When I asked Chambers what repertoire would be required, his response was, "Everything." Thinking of Boulez, I considered trying to play in a more French style, but I decided that I should present myself as I am and simply practiced every possible excerpt. It was also very important for me to practice in a large space, since I would be playing in Philharmonic Hall, not a practice studio. So I asked Reverend Helmsley, whom I had known since I was a boy, if I could practice in his church's parish house. The day of the audition I wore my best suit, a Pierre Cardin my parents had bought me in Vienna a number of years before. I brought all my trumpets and went to the stage of Philharmonic Hall. I offered the Haydn Concerto to begin. Standing alone on the stage, I played the exposition. I then stopped and looked at Boulez, and he said, "Please continue." I ended up playing the entire concerto. Then I sat down to play the excerpts, where there was music for me on the stand. He asked for all the standard repertoire and some unusual pieces as well, such as the Anton Webern Passacaglia, Op. 1, which has very simple half notes in the lower register. One of the notes, a low C–sharp, was out of tune. He instructed me to lower it, and once I did, we moved on to a number of other excerpts. Then he returned to the Webern and asked me to play the same passage, testing whether I could remember where that C-sharp belonged. Luckily, I did. After about an hour he asked me to play Bach's Second Brandenburg Concerto. After an hour of playing by myself in this large space, I felt I could not play the whole piece, so I offered the last movement, which I knew I could do. He said, "No, play from the beginning." So I played from the very beginning through the first high passage, which went well. I knew I couldn't continue, however; I stopped and told the maestro that I was a little tired, and couldn't I do the last movement?

"No, why don't you rest for a few minutes and start again."

So I sat by myself in the cavernous hall in dead silence for maybe two minutes. It seemed like two hours. I started again, got to the same spot, stopped, knowing that it would not go well, and suggested that I come back later and play the whole piece. Boulez just said, "Thank you." And I left. A few days later Chambers called me and said, "You won the audition!"

They asked me if I would consider being co-principal trumpet with Johnny Ware, who was the third and associate first trumpet. Johnny had made such a tremendous contribution to the Philharmonic for many years, and he really wanted to be principal. They said to me, "You'll spend a couple of years as co-principals, then you'll be the principal." They wanted to take the feelings of the orchestra into account because Johnny was very popular and a fine musician.

My First Rehearsal with the New York Philharmonic

For the years I was in the New York Philharmonic, I was excited about every rehearsal. I couldn't wait to experience the great music, the incomparable playing of the orchestra, and the wonderful conductors. My first rehearsal was Béla Bartók's Concerto for Orchestra. I have two memories of it. One is that during the second movement, in a very soft duet for muted trumpets, Boulez asked me to play much louder than what was written. During the break, I asked him if it was possible for the strings to play softer so that the dynamic contrasts between *piano* and *mezzo forte* in that duet would be possible. He did. In the same movement is a lovely brass chorale in A-flat. When we arrived at the A-flat major chord, I could hear that the tuba and I were not in tune. Boulez stopped the rehearsal and asked for the first trumpet and tuba to play alone. With that, the first oboe, Harold Gomberg, said loudly to Boulez: "It's the kid's first rehearsal; can't you give him a break?" At that Boulez smiled, everyone laughed, and he continued to tune the octave.

The southern tour followed that fall. Besides the Bartók, we did *La mer*, by Claude Debussy, and *Till Eulenspiegel's Merry Pranks*, by Richard Strauss. After the tour we returned to Philharmonic Hall to rehearse for the opening subscription week. The piece I was playing on that program was Strauss's *Also sprach Zarathustra*, which has a prominent first trumpet part. There is one passage, four notes ending on a high C, quite loud, with a big decrescendo to *piano*; it is very exposed. That short passage is not about how beautifully you can phrase or how deep the performer is artistically; it has to do with sound, rhythm, intonation, power, and control, and if it doesn't go well, it can ruin your career. That is the reality of being first trumpet in a major orchestra. When I arrived at the hall that night for our eight-thirty concert, I found a note in my mailbox from Johanna Fiedler in the press department to call a certain number before the performance. I imagined first that it was the *New York Times* and worked my way down through the *Tribune*, the *Post*, and the *Daily News*. Finally I said to myself, "It's probably Leighton Kerner at the *Village Voice*." I waited until seven-forty-five, went to the pay phone, put in my dime, and listened attentively to "Dial-a-Prayer." Johanna had been set up by my good friend and Principal Horn, John Cerminaro. We all had a big laugh, and luckily, the prayer worked.

At first my time in the orchestra felt like I was on vacation, and then I began to feel the pressure. When you work as a freelancer, the personnel of the orchestra or ensemble with whom you play always changes. In the Philharmonic you return each day to the same players. If it did not go well one night, the following morning you were there with the same musicians and often the same conductor. I spent a great deal of time with Boulez, and we became close friends. I used to go with him to Bell Labs in Murray Hill, New Jersey, to do some very interesting early experiments with computer music with Max Mathews. Bell Labs had an acoustic-less room, where you would sit on chicken wire in the middle of a suspended black space with the absence of light or sound, in absolute silence. I heard a recording of Philharmonic Hall with two different orchestral positions. One was the normal stage position, and one was with the orchestra sitting on the floor in front of the stage with the first rows of seats removed. Boulez used this second setup for a series of concerts that he initiated called the Rug Concerts. All the main floor seats of Philharmonic Hall were removed and the audience sat on rugs, which made the sound much more reverberant and mushy.

Boulez asked me, "Which do you like better?"

I said, "Well, the quality of the sound, I guess, in the second position is beautiful, but I don't hear the pitches very clearly. In the first version it is really clear."

This was not what he wanted to hear, but it was the truth. That was when I became very interested in acoustics. I was fortunate enough at that time to meet Cyril Harris, the renowned acoustical engineer. He had been chosen to be the acoustician for the new Avery Fisher Hall and spent a great deal of time sitting with us orchestra members: he wanted to know what it sounded like at each point onstage. The renovation of Philharmonic Hall kept the outside façade but gutted and rebuilt the inside from scratch. Cyril became a dear friend and my acoustical teacher.

After Avery Fisher Hall was completed, the Philharmonic came from Carnegie, where we had just played the Mahler Third Symphony, to play it again at the new hall. Then we did the official opening with the Brahms Violin Concerto with Nathan Milstein and the complete *Firebird* by Stravinsky. We played the first concert with Boulez in the new hall, and everyone loved it at first—though, interestingly, that opinion has changed over time. Harold Schonberg, the main *New York Times* music critic at the time, raved about how much better the sound was: "Few halls have the kind of detail . . . single instruments stood out in high relief. It was almost as if the Philharmonic were a large chamber group. In any part of the dynamic range, too, from the wispiest *pianissimo* to the most stupendous *forte*, Fisher Hall came through with extraordinary clarity. There never was any mushiness, any tonal shatter, any echo to mar the orchestral sheen." Another critic interviewed several of us, including the clarinetist Stanley Drucker; the principal percussionist, Walter Rosenberger; and me. Everybody said very positive things, but I told him we really had to adjust our playing to the hall. As Schonberg said in his opening review in the *New York Times*, "Just as a pianist with a new instrument has to spend time adjusting his fingers and ears to the new sound, so the Philharmonic— and everybody else who has appeared in the old hall—will have to readjust." The hall becomes the constant, and an orchestra has to learn how to play in it. Years later, when we built Benaroya Hall in Seattle, I worked hard with the musicians to prepare them for the enormous changes I knew were coming. And once we were in the hall, we had to be reminded continually to play in a different, more subtle way. The adjustment from Philharmonic Hall to Fisher Hall involved a similar process.

When Boulez inaugurated Fisher Hall, he began by dealing with the adjustments necessitated by the new acoustics, but he let it go too quickly. The adjustment needed more than a week or a month; it needed to continue until it felt natural.

In Philharmonic Hall I had to play very loudly to be heard, because it felt as though the sound never carried. At Fisher Hall, the sound carried so well that we had to learn how to play softly—not something that came easily to the orchestra at that time. I think that one factor that contributed to Avery Fisher Hall's failure was that the Philharmonic did not make the necessary musical adjustments and failed to fully adjust to the hall.

Carnegie Hall, where we performed during the Philharmonic Hall renovations, is one of the most important halls in the world. Playing there was incredible for the orchestra. We could feel the sound vibrating on our feet. But it is hard for those onstage to evaluate what the orchestra sounds like in the house, and it is also hard to evaluate what it sounds like in the house without anyone in it. During my years in Seattle, whether in my own rehearsals or in performances of other conductors, whenever possible I would walk all over the house to hear what the audience was hearing.

Once I joined the New York Philharmonic, all my additional playing stopped. I played mostly with Bernstein, Boulez, Bernard Haitink, and Erich Leinsdorf, and also with some phenomenal musicians. I became especially close to Leinsdorf, whom I admired tremendously. I greatly respected Boulez and often socialized with him. I also studied composition with him and was influenced by his musical insights.

I loved playing in the orchestra, but I yearned to be more involved with the music. Some of our many guest conductors did not delve deeply enough, I thought. I believed I could make a contribution. It is not that I did not love what I was doing—I loved playing—but I wanted to be more intimately involved with the music of Brahms, Beethoven, Mozart, and Haydn. I always wondered: if I had been a violinist, would I have become a conductor?

Boulez's gifts were very different from those of a traditional conductor: he was also an important composer and a spokesperson and champion for contemporary music.

"Somewhere"

In 1976 we were performing Anton Bruckner's Sixth Symphony with Bernstein. Before he began the first rehearsal he gave a little speech: "Ladies and gentlemen, I've never conducted this before. I've studied it all my life, I love it, but I've always had difficulty understanding the form." We did the first movement, then moved on to the slow movement, which begins with a beautiful section for the strings. At about the sixth bar, the second half of the first theme has five notes that are the same as the beginning of "Somewhere," from *West Side Story*. Everyone in unison said "Aaaaaah!" Bernstein had a huge smile on his face, essentially acknowledging where that idea for "Somewhere" originated. Of course, all composers are influenced by one another and on occasion borrow something from a colleague—a part of a melody, a harmonic sequence, the form, or even the basic idea of the piece.

When my dear friend Alan Benaroya first became interested in classical music, Jody and I offered to buy a subscription for him to attend six concerts in Seattle, still in the old opera house. When it came time to choose his concerts, the only thing we disagreed about was Bruckner's Sixth Symphony. I felt that Bruckner was an acquired taste and that for Alan's first subscription series maybe another program would be better. But he insisted, and after the concert he told me he loved the Bruckner. He has been a fan ever since. When I asked him why he insisted on this program, he said that I had given him "permission" not to like the Bruckner—that is, he felt he did not have to like every piece he heard. For Alan, this was very freeing.

During my third season with the orchestra there was an opening for assistant conductor, and I mentioned to Boulez that I wanted to audition. Leinsdorf had already noticed my interest and had spoken highly of me to members of the management team. For the audition, Boulez asked me to conduct the suites from Bartók's *The Miraculous Mandarin* and Stravinsky's *Chant du rossignol*. I had played both works with Boulez and knew how he did them. For the audition I conducted as Boulez would have, both musically and technically. I did one little ritard in the Stravinsky that Boulez never did. After the audition, he was extremely complimentary about my performance, with the exception of the one ritard. On the ride home after my audition, Newton Mansfield, a violinist with whom I carpooled, attacked me for conducting just like Boulez. Of course I had, I explained; that was for whom I was auditioning.

A week or so later Boulez said that the job was mine, but he had to figure out how I could be both his assistant and co-principal trumpet. Finally he told me that he had spoken to the president of the orchestra, Carlos Moseley, who said they did not want to lose me as a trumpet player. Boulez said he always took Carlos's advice and would therefore have to rescind his offer.

When I left the orchestra to become a conductor, Carlos was extremely supportive of me. He was responsible for my becoming music director of the White Mountains Festival a few years later, and we regularly talked on the phone after his retirement to South Carolina. He was a true gentleman, a fine pianist, and a great administrator with remarkable vision. He told me Bernstein's revival of Mahler in 1960, to celebrate Mahler's hundredth birthday, had been his idea. It was just one of his many visionary inspirations.

When I was in the New York Philharmonic I was always an observer. A good orchestral player has to be able to read conductors well, but that is only part of it. I studied the scores even before I became interested in becoming a conductor because I was curious about what the conductors were doing. And it was not just about the techniques specific to a particular conductor or about learning to play my part correctly; it was understanding where my part fit into the complete work. Once I decided to become a conductor, I started observing things very intensely. I learned from everything every conductor did, from their many successes as well as from their mistakes. My years as a member of the New York Philharmonic were my greatest education in conducting. I watched the conductors, saw their techniques, saw what worked, heard the words they chose. When a conductor made a suggestion, did the music get better or not? When there were problems, did the conductor solve or ignore them?

I grew up attending Bernstein's concerts in the early 1960s, and of course I never missed a Young People's Concert on television. I never dreamed I would get to work with my idol. My first experience with Bernstein was a big tour with him as our conductor laureate. We were playing his *Dybbuk Suite*, Mahler's Fifth Symphony, a Mozart piano concerto, and other works.

Dybbuk had a trumpet solo toward the beginning that was very difficult, soft and high. The real test was the opening of the Mahler Fifth. It too is a trumpet solo, and Mahler writes in the score that the triplets should be rushed, like a military fanfare. The original version, however, had no such indication, so when Bruno Walter recorded it with the New York Philharmonic in the 1950s it was performed very straight. Mahler's revised score pointed out the way the opening should be played, and the composer himself played it that way on a piano roll he made of the first movement. So I knew what Bernstein would want.

We were about to start rehearsing the Mahler. I was twenty-five and completely prepared. Bernstein hadn't been with the orchestra for a while, since he'd been on sabbatical, and after he arrived he walked through the violin section, hugging people and chatting with everybody. Finally he got up on the podium and said, "Ladies and gentlemen, I'm so happy to be back. Okay, let's begin. Last movement."

Last movement? How could he do this to me? I was ready for the first! However, that gave me a chance to play as part of the ensemble and loosen up. At last he said, "Okay, now let's do the first movement." After the big trumpet solo was over he stopped, looked back at me, and said, "What genius do we have in the orchestra now?" I never have told this story because you don't make friends by having the conductor say he thinks you're great, but I survived.

On the plane ride to New Zealand I met Bernstein at the bar. The closest I had ever been to him was sitting in the last row of Philharmonic Hall when he was conducting. Now here I was having a drink with him. The tour went exceptionally well.

John Cerminaro, the first horn, and I had been at Juilliard together, and we were exactly the same age. When George Szell, the music advisor of the Philharmonic between Bernstein and Boulez, was looking for an assistant principal horn, John was hired—at age nineteen. He left Juilliard to join the orchestra and eventually became principal. We had the most fabulous time on that tour. People said, "Look at the two twenty-five-year-olds having a ball." Yeah, we had a ball, practicing all the time. Focusing on the concerts was all we did. But it was a great trip and one of my most memorable playing experiences.

After that Bernstein, as our Conductor Laureate, worked with us six times a year. He was also very friendly with my future wife's family because her father, Sol Greitzer, was in the viola section. He was third chair, and when Boulez came, he was made principal. So Sol was principal viola and I was principal trumpet. Bernstein also loved Shirley, my future mother-in-law. Later on Lenny and I spoke on the phone regularly, even after I became music director in Seattle. Sometimes in New York I'd go over to Bernstein's apartment at the Dakota on Central Park West. We played performance tapes and talked about music, especially American music. I would play him some of the American music we were doing in Seattle. He had always been close to David

Diamond, and when I played our recording of David's Symphony No. 2, he was knocked out. He had done a reading of it in 1943 for Artur Rodziński with the New York Philharmonic, and now he told me, "I have to get back to doing American music again."A few years later he did a program he called "The Three Threes: The Copland Third, the William Schuman Third, and the Roy Harris Third Symphonies" and recorded them. And he got involved again with some of the younger American composers—Bright Sheng, Seattle Symphony's composer-in-residence, and Richard Danielpour, another of our composers-in-residence, both were played and taught by Bernstein. Toward the end of his life he did do some American music again.

I especially admired Bernstein because he was not only a conductor but also a composer, pianist, writer, and educator. All Lenny's strengths as conductor, composer, and pianist were on display on that Mahler Fifth tour. Coming offstage after he played the Mozart concerto, he said to me, "It didn't go so well, but I'm a composer and a conductor anyway." And after he received a bad review for his *Dybbuk*, he said, "Did you read that horrible review? The guy's an idiot, but I'm a pianist and a conductor anyway." Then after a bad review for the Mahler Fifth, he said, "Well, I'm a composer and a pianist anyway."

I never wanted to have to make those excuses myself. As a trumpet player, repertoire was limited in a way Bernstein's, as a pianist, was not. It was on this tour when I began to think about quitting playing the trumpet to conduct.

I learned much from Bernstein, but I probably learned the most from Leinsdorf. Coming off the stage at one of my last rehearsals as a member of the orchestra, a cellist, Avram Lavin, said to me, "Be like Leinsdorf, not Bernstein."

Haydn in the Park

In August 1977 I played the Haydn Trumpet Concerto with Leinsdorf and the New York Philharmonic during the Philharmonic's parks concerts. Over 100,000 people were in attendance for the first performance in New York's Central Park. Walking onstage before Leinsdorf and looking out onto the great lawn, which was covered with people, was quite an experience. I watched him as he stepped on to the podium and noticed a note on the only step that he had to take. As Leinsdorf began the concerto I read the note: "Elvis Presley died today. You should stop this performance and dedicate it to the memory of a man who has contributed so much to music worldwide." An interesting thought. But as I was considering whether or not I agreed with it, I almost missed my first entrance. With that, I realized that I had to focus on this important performance. The cadenza echoed through all the speakers positioned throughout the crowd. It was an exhilarating experience, and the audience went wild at the piece's conclusion. Afterward, as Leinsdorf and I exited the shell, he started screaming at the many members of the Philharmonic's staff standing near the door. He then turned to me and told me to go onstage for a second bow. When I came off he was still shouting and pointing to the numerous police officers standing backstage. Interrupting the tirade, I asked if he would join me for the next bow. He did so, and the intermission followed. It seems that a woman in a slinky red dress had entered the stage from stage left, first sat near the trumpets and then the timpani, and at last slowly crossed to the exit at stage right. Leinsdorf was saying she could have had a gun and killed him.

Leinsdorf, My Mentor

I had played two tours with Leinsdorf conducting, many subscription weeks, and the Haydn Concerto in the parks. I was also in his conducting workshop at the Philharmonic, where he was very kind and helpful to me. After I left the orchestra, I conducted for the Eliot Feld Ballet Company at City Center, of which Erich's son Gregor was on the board. Erich came to a performance of the ballet when we did Mahler's *Rückert-Lieder*. He never came backstage, but he told Eliot that he was very impressed with my conducting. He recommended me to Shelley Gold, the president of ICM Management, who became my first manager as a conductor. That was the turning point for me. After that, Leinsdorf offered me a position as his assistant at the Berlin Radio, a job he ultimately turned down.

Leinsdorf was always available to me. He approached conducting with an encyclopedic knowledge of the music and the scores he conducted, and he had a photographic memory. I came to him with questions all the time: "In the first movement of [Maurice Ravel's] *Mother Goose Suite*, I am wondering about the harmonics in the double basses. I'm not sure what octave they should be. What is correct?" Or "In the March of the Beethoven Ninth, the B-flat section in the last movement with the tenor solo, the metronome mark doesn't seem to work. What should it be?" He always had an answer, and working with him became key to how I approached my work as a conductor from then on.

Once, before leaving the orchestra, I asked him about Paul Hindemith's Op. 24 No. 1, which we were doing on a Rug Concert. I thought there was a wrong note. He started perusing the score: "The answer is always in the score." He found a directly related section and said, "No, the note is correct." To this day it is a lesson that serves me daily: the answer is, in fact, almost always in the score.

Before Henry Fogel became the orchestra manager of the New York Philharmonic, he ran a radio station in Syracuse for fifteen years, programming eighteen hours a day of classical music. Later he joined the National Symphony and then was president of the Chicago Symphony. He too was a big Leinsdorf fan. Once, Henry told me, in a rehearsal of the New York Philharmonic, the violins played so poorly that Leinsdorf insulted them, saying, "You should all go back to your teachers and your conservatories and ask for a complete refund because you play so badly, it's a disgrace!" The personnel manager ran out onstage and called an immediate break. The orchestra committee then informed Henry that Leinsdorf had to apologize. No, Henry said: "There's nothing in the contract that says Leinsdorf has to behave in a certain way. You are obligated, according to the contract, to return for tomorrow's rehearsal." The head of the committee replied, "Unless he apologizes, we won't play."

Henry told them they would have their pay docked if they didn't play. They said, "That's fine, dock us. Thursday morning, we're not going to play." Of course, Henry did not want to dock them; he wanted them to play. So Henry went up to Leinsdorf's dressing room. Leinsdorf sat facing the mirror, so he could see Henry standing in the doorway.

Leinsdorf said, "I can see you want me to apologize."

Henry said, "How did you know?"

"I can see it on your face. I'll apologize."

He went to the orchestra and said something like, "I'm a believer in civility, in behaving well, and I crossed the line. I did not behave appropriately, and I apologize." And that was the end of that. Henry became a hero because everyone thought he had convinced Leinsdorf to apologize, when all he had done was walk into the room.

Something similar happened to me with Leinsdorf. We were doing the Mahler Fifth, and the trombones cracked the same note at every rehearsal. Leinsdorf called me into his room and said, "Jerry, the trombones crack the G-sharp every time. Take care of it for me."

I said, "Of course, Maestro."

I certainly could never have gone to the trombones and said, "Don't crack this note." I figured that they had missed it enough times, that the odds were they wouldn't miss it again. At the next rehearsal, we arrived at the spot. Sure enough, they played it perfectly. Leinsdorf smiled and looked at me—but I had nothing to do with it.

Leaving on a High Note

During my third year in the Philharmonic, in 1975, we went on tour with Leinsdorf and Thomas Schippers to the Soviet Union. We were playing the Mahler Fifth again, this time at the Conservatory Hall in Moscow with Leinsdorf, and I felt it was one of my best performances with the orchestra. John Cerminaro had often told me always to make important decisions about your future after your greatest success rather than after a difficult moment. After that concert, I took a walk alone around Red Square and said to myself, "Okay, now here it is. This was a great performance in a great hall, the orchestra played beautifully, and I had played my best. I asked myself, "Is this what I want to do for the rest of my life?"

And that's when I decided it was not.

For the next two years I prepared to leave. I did not inform the orchestra for another six or eight months, but I gave them enough time to replace me. I had married the dancer Lillo Way around the time I joined the Philharmonic, and by the time I left, I had two children, Alysandra and Daniel. I expanded my teaching to the University of Connecticut and Montclair College in New Jersey, where I also conducted the orchestra, took on individual students at various colleges in New York, and continued at Juilliard.

My last year at the Philharmonic was bittersweet. I had been there for only four years. But the pull to go in a new direction felt right.

Although I had prepared for it, the period after leaving the Philharmonic was very uncertain. I had started projects and was teaching a lot, but I was not conducting nearly as much as I wanted. I remember one torturous six-week period when I did not do any conducting. I studied the scores and wondered whether it would ever happen for me.

CHAPTER SIX

———

The Waterloo Music Festival

A single event can have a profound impact on the future, yet it can slip by unnoticed until you realize what it has set in motion. It amazes me that something as simple as doing a chamber music concert in the middle of New Jersey could lead to the Waterloo Music Festival and School and the Y Chamber Symphony, determining my future as a conductor.

I was still in the New York Philharmonic. The concert was a holiday concert in the small, elegant church on the grounds of the Waterloo Village in Stanhope, New Jersey, in December 1975. I had been asked by my friend and colleague from the New York Philharmonic, the violinist Oscar Ravina, to play Bach's Second Brandenburg Concerto. Afterward, at the reception, I met Percival Leach and his partner, Louis Gualandi, who together owned the village. Percy was the more outgoing of the two and extremely charming. He was an interior designer, in a traditional English way, and his passion was his village at Waterloo. He told me they had a tradition of presenting musical events in the summer, the most important of which had been a concert with Pablo Casals a few years before. Percy spoke rapturously of his desire to fill the village with music and to create a summer music school. I told him about my experiences at the Aspen Music Festival and School, where I had taught, played, and served on the board for seven years, and said I would be honored to create his school and add music to his village. He was no doubt surprised by my response but said he was interested.

Percy and I started the Waterloo Festival in 1976. We created it on the Aspen model, with students and faculty playing in an orchestra together. I did all the administrative work to help make Waterloo into an important festival and school. Despite the terms of my contract, I wasn't paid until the third year. In a way, however, I should have paid Percy for all this did for me and for my future. This great opportunity helped pave the way for my life after the New York Philharmonic. That was the beginning of some absolutely wonderful summers for me in New Jersey's heat and humidity.

In the summer of 1973, while I was teaching trumpet at Aspen, the conductor Eleazar de Carvalho canceled his appearance conducting Sam Lipman in the very difficult Elliot Carter Piano Concerto. Gordon Hardy, the director, first asked Jorge Mester, the music director, to step in for Carvalho. Jorge could not take it on but said he'd be happy to conduct Beethoven's Sixth Symphony for the second half. Sam had been practicing this work for a year and had engaged Jacqueline Schmitt, a student of his wife, Jeaneane Dowis, to play the orchestral part for his preparation. Jeaneane had also learned to conduct the concerto perfectly, with all its extremely complicated metric modulations.

After all his hard work, Sam did not want to lose the Aspen performance. Sam called me and said, "Why don't you come over to our house and hear us run through it?"

Sam, Jacqueline, and Jeaneane did a remarkable performance. Sam said to me, "I want you to conduct this." This was three days before the first rehearsal. I looked at him and said, "Jeaneane should do it. She is phenomenal."

Sam replied, "She's not a conductor. She wouldn't know what to say to the orchestra. And you have to do it."

I told him I would take the score home, put it under my pillow that night, and hope through osmosis, I would be able to conduct the work.

Sam shook his head and said, "Stand up and let's begin."

I stood up and started sight-reading the piece, and from that moment until the performance I studied the score, eventually managing to negotiate all its metric changes. Several years earlier Jorge Mester had gone out on a limb to hire me as a nineteen-year-old to take the prestigious position of principal trumpet and teacher at Aspen. The week of the Carter, he also allowed me to do the opening work on the Carter program, Barber's *Mutations from Bach*.

The concert went so well that Sam made a recording from the live performance. This chance performance became the defining moment for me as a conductor, because after that Sam pushed me very hard to work toward my new career.

Sam and Jeaneane spent a few weeks at Waterloo that first year, and I put together a fantastic faculty—colleagues and teachers from the New York Philharmonic, the Metropolitan Opera Orchestra, the New York City Opera and Ballet, Juilliard, Yale, and other schools. Oscar Ravina became our personnel manager and concertmaster.

At Waterloo as at Aspen all the teachers were the principal players in the orchestra, and their students played in their sections. However, we also engaged experienced members of the New York Philharmonic string section, mostly violins, each one paired with a student. Not only was this a great learning experience for the string students, but we also had an orchestra that sounded pretty terrific.

At almost the age of thirty, I felt I had fallen behind my young conductor friends. I had conducted some college orchestras, including Juilliard, and some community orchestras. I had conducted a range of new music as a member of Speculum Musicae and at the Chamber Music Society of Lincoln Center. I also did some varied repertoire with the SoHo Ensemble, where I was music director from 1969 to 1975, performing at the O. K. Harris Gallery on West Broadway. But Waterloo gave me a chance to go through the standard orchestral repertoire.

I remember listening to a Toscanini rehearsal when he was conducting Richard Strauss's *Death and Transfiguration*. The beginning is a little tricky for the violas because of the rhythm, and when they started playing it wasn't together. Toscanini went crazy, screaming— not for a minute, but for many minutes. Then he said, "Okay, let's try it again." And it was fine. Then a C major chord was played horribly out of tune. He screamed again, this time for five or six minutes. And then he went back, and that time they played it in tune.

I was doing *Death and Transfiguration* that first season at the Waterloo Festival, and I had to fix the same section—the rhythms and the intonation. It took me about the same amount of time as Toscanini. I did it by actually working through each issue. Nobody screams much anymore. That was a different time.

Over the years at Waterloo I did all the Brahms symphonies; Tchaikovsky's Fourth, Fifth, and Sixth Symphonies; all Richard Strauss's tone poems; and many Mahler symphonies. I conducted works by Bartók, Beethoven, Ernest Bloch, Schumann, Sibelius, Stravinsky, and many more. I never repeated a work. It was difficult, and I didn't sleep much, especially when I added Mostly Mozart to the summer schedule. But those concerts gave me the foundation and experience I needed. I learned so much from studying and doing the actual conducting, and from working with the players at the festival. It felt like a summer intensive on the big and great orchestral works, and I was so fortunate to have some of New York's finest and most experienced musicians in the orchestra.

Especially important to me was having my dear friend and future father-in-law, Sol Greitzer, as my principal viola. He and his wife, Shirley, were very close friends of mine, and their three daughters were all students at Waterloo at different times. Shirley, a superb pianist, was also on the chamber music faculty. She later became executive director of the school and festival.

I was music director at the Waterloo Festival from 1975 to 1984. When it became impossible for me to do everything I wanted to do, Sam Lipman took over as artistic director, and I became principal conductor. That arrangement stayed in place until Sam found the festival's next music director, Yoav Talmi. I left in 1994, and unfortunately the school and festival continued for only a few more years. We had great soloists: Claudio Arrau, Marilyn Horne, Itzhak Perlman, Jean-Pierre Rampal, Nadja Salerno-Sonnenberg, and André Watts, to name just a few. We also did some interesting novelties, including the American premiere of Richard Wagner's second opera, *Das Liebesverbot*, in 1983. And we did the American premiere of Wagner's arrangement of Christoph Willibald Gluck's *Iphigénie en Aulide*.

I did Elgar's masterpiece, *The Dream of Gerontius*, and two years later, in 1990, ninety years after the work was written, I conducted its French premiere with the Orchestre National de France at the Théâtre des Champs-Élysées. We also did Percy Grainger's *The Warriors*, about which Ed Rothstein wrote in the *New York Times*: "Mr. Schwarz, who was the Music Director of the festival, was undoubtedly helped by the superior quality of the festival musicians—many of them from the New York Philharmonic. The group seemed carefully rehearsed and unusually attentive; Mr. Schwarz returned the compliment. This rapport gave Percy Grainger's *The Warriors* a crackling precision."

Over the years we performed works by Barber, Bloch, Copland, Howard Hanson, Peter Mennin, and Walter Piston, as well as many pieces by Diamond, including the world premiere of his first Suite from *Tom*. David's ballet *Tom* was based on E. E. Cummings's scenario based on Harriet Beecher Stowe's famous novel, *Uncle Tom's Cabin*, which David had read when he was nineteen. George Balanchine expressed interest in choreographing the ballet and dancing the role of Tom. The writer and impresario Lincoln Kirstein asked a number of prominent young composers to write music for it, including Virgil Thomson, Stravinsky, and Paul Bowles, but everyone declined. David asked Cummings for permission to write the music himself, and when Cummings agreed, he proceeded to write a full evening-length ballet. Plans for the production fell through and the ballet and its music were never performed, but Stokowski later asked David to write a suite based on it. David completed the *Suite from Tom*, and like the full ballet, it was never performed.

I was reading Richard S. Kennedy's book *Dreams in the Mirror: A Biography of E. E. Cummings*, and I came upon this story. The next time I saw David at Juilliard I asked him about his *Suite from Tom* and said I wanted to premiere it at Waterloo that summer. He agreed, and we did the premiere in the summer of 1981, forty-four years after it was written. It is a marvelous piece, and in 1992 I performed it again and recorded it with the Seattle Symphony.

During David's last years he was asked to write a fanfare for the opening of the remodeled Eastman Theatre in Rochester, New York, to be played by the Rochester Philharmonic. This was important to David because although he had lived most of his life in Rochester, even commuting from there to teach at Juilliard in Manhattan, they rarely played his music. I was once asked to guest conduct the Rochester Orchestra, and I agreed—as long as I could do a program of Hanson and Diamond, Rochester's own composers. They said there was no interest in Hanson or Diamond and that no one would attend the concert, so they declined, as did I. A year or so later they asked me to conduct again, this time agreeing to my program of Hanson and Diamond. The concert was very successful, especially with the audience.

David had agreed to compose the fanfare for the remodeled Eastman Theatre, but he was not writing anymore. The orchestra waited for the piece, which David never produced. They asked his close family friend, Sam Elliott, to help. When Sam asked him about the status of the piece, David said he had written three chords, and that Sam could send them along. At that point the orchestra asked if they could engage a ghostwriter to compose the fanfare. Sam asked me what I thought. I said I would be happy to write a fanfare using only David's notes. I took material from *Tom* and from his *Concerto for Small Orchestra*, and I wrote a fanfare using only notes David had actually written. David and Sam were pleased with the result.

CHAPTER SEVEN

The New York Chamber Symphony

T he 92nd Street Y, on Manhattan's Upper East Side, was founded in 1847 by German Jewish professionals and businessmen
and became a hub for all kinds of cultural and educational offerings. Its
first classical concert, held in 1938 when the Budapest String Quartet
performed a Beethoven cycle, established chamber music as a mainstay
of the Y's programming.

I had met Omus Hirshbein, director of the artistic programs at
the 92nd Street Y, at the home of Sam Lipman and Jeaneane Dowis.
They had all studied at Juilliard with the legendary piano pedagogue
Rosina Lhévinne and had also been together as students at Aspen.
Sam believed that a presenting house was ephemeral and that an
important venue like the Kaufman Concert Hall should have a resident
ensemble. He spoke to Omus about creating a chamber orchestra and
brought him to one of my concerts that first year at Waterloo. At the
time I had no idea what Omus thought of it.

The New York Chamber Soloists had done the Bach Brandenburg
concertos at Hunter College when Omus was there, and he asked me
to put together an all-star group to do the same program at the Y
in December 1976. Joseph Horowitz's review in the *New York Times*
said: "Within his chosen interpretive framework, the bright, youthful
readings Mr. Schwarz led were just about consummate. He treated
the notes with both respect and imagination—the playing was neither
stiffly metronomic on the one hand, nor fussy or capricious on the other.
There were some unconventional touches of rubato—lots of elongated
phrase endings in the Adagio of the First Concerto, for instance—but

they managed to animate and organize the flow, rather than disrupt it. The orchestra, which varied in size from about 7 to 20 members, responded with enthusiasm and finesse . . ." Speight Jenkins covered it just as enthusiastically in the *New York Post*. Both the reviews and the audience response encouraged Omus to start a resident chamber orchestra at the Y.

From the beginning, I wanted the name of our ensemble to be the New York Chamber Symphony. Since the 92nd Street Y was supporting us, they wanted us to be called the Y Chamber Symphony, which was understandable, but the 92nd Street Y did not have a national or international reputation. Nevertheless, Omus assured me we would be called the New York Chamber Symphony.

Omus engaged great soloists for our first season, among them the soprano Judith Blegen and the violinist Itzhak Perlman. We had the Kalichstein-Laredo-Robinson Trio do the Beethoven Triple Concerto and did a reprise of the Brandenburg concertos with many of the same players from our initial outing—the violinists Ani Kavafian and Syoko Aki, the violists Walter Trampler and Toby Appel, the double bassist Alvin Brehm, the harpsichordist Kenneth Cooper, and a number of wonderful New York chamber and orchestral musicians.

I thought our programming should be relatively conventional at first. When I showed David Rubin, the artists' representative at Steinway, my initial programs, he said, "These are the programs of an old man." There was nothing unusual in them, and no music of today. On his advice I included works by Bartók, Diamond, Jacob Druckman, and Webern, as well as such less frequently played works as Georges Bizet's Symphony in C and Brahms's Serenade in A Major. The bassoonist Loren Glickman helped put the orchestra together, Judith Rubin became the chairperson of the Y board, and Reynold Levy became its executive director. I asked Syoko Aki, who taught at Yale, to be our concertmaster. She and her husband, Brodus Erle, were on my violin faculty at Waterloo, and each week at Waterloo I had taken lessons from them. They opened up the world of string playing for me. To this day I mark every nuance in my score and parts. These markings create a schematic for my interpretations, which I expand on as I conduct.

Because I was a wind player, the early years of study with Brodus and Syoko's guidance were crucial to my understanding of string playing, and after Brodus died I continued to travel to Syoko's home near New Haven to take lessons before each Chamber Symphony week.

This early experience was the beginning of my understanding of what a conductor really does. Yes, the actual physical techniques of beating time and communicating with gestures to create the musical performances matter, but the work and study and musical decision making of the studying period prior to ever getting before the orchestra, is where the real work is done.

When Omus showed me the gorgeous silver brochure that came out that spring before our inaugural season, to my surprise, the name of the orchestra was printed as the Y Chamber Symphony, not the New York Chamber Symphony. Omus had simply told me what I wanted to hear and then done what the Y, which was supporting the orchestra, wanted him to do. That was just his way—to tell people what they wanted to hear. Omus was an old-fashioned impresario: he had excellent musical taste, knew great performances and great artists, and did his best to support them. He was a real gentleman, loved by those who knew him best; if you were his friend, there was nothing he wouldn't do for you.

There were two issues at the Y. First, the stage was a little small, especially when we had a nine-foot grand piano onstage. Second, the acoustics were somewhat dry and distant. The first problem would never change, but that was a minor issue. The second problem was critical. The acoustical engineer Cyril Harris, with whom I'd become friends during my days at the New York Philharmonic, lived in the neighborhood and agreed to come over and give us some ideas. He said he could design a solid shell for us that could be removed easily for nonmusical performances. He did this as a favor to me, without compensation, but asked not to be given credit. He did new halls and major refurbishments and did not want to become known for designing shells. It cost somewhere around $100,000, and Omus was able to convince Judy Rubin and the board that spending the money would turn the Kaufman Concert Hall into a fine acoustical space—which it did.

Our second season, 1978–1979, continued in the same vein with the soloists Claudio Arrau, Kyung-wha Chung, Misha Dichter, and Yo-Yo Ma. Originally Arrau wanted to do Richard Strauss's *Burleske* and Carl Maria von Weber's *Konzertstück*. I was nervous about these pieces, which I hardly knew, so I pushed Omus to see if Arrau would instead do a Beethoven concerto. Eventually Omus told me that Arrau had agreed to do the Fourth Piano Concerto.

I happened to have heard a live broadcast of Arrau performing these works that summer from Tanglewood. There were a number of ensemble problems, and I felt so relieved that we were doing Beethoven. Two weeks before the concert Omus said he had made a mistake—Arrau was going to do the Strauss and the Weber after all. I immediately called David Rubin to ask his advice, which was, "Start studying the Strauss and Weber." I ordered the scores and contacted WQXR to see if I could borrow their tape of a live broadcast from Tanglewood. They did not have it.

I had already scheduled an appointment with Arrau to go through the music, as I always do to this day. On the day of our meeting I drove to his lovely home in Queens. His wife greeted me and offered me coffee, as Arrau had not yet returned from practicing at Steinway on Fifty-seventh Street. I noticed that his piano in the living room was covered with a cloth and had photographs on the lid. It looked as though he wasn't going to play for me.

When Arrau arrived he asked for some tea, and we sat together on the couch to look at the scores. Sometimes soloists know exactly what they do and can verbalize it well; others describe their interpretations in ways that are not at all accurate. Having no choice in the matter, I diligently marked everything Arrau said. When the day of the rehearsal arrived, I was nervous and at the same time excited to work with this legendary artist. I'm happy to say Arrau played exactly as he said he would, and the rehearsal and performances went wonderfully. It was the first of many times Arrau and I worked together.

Two years later Arrau did these same pieces with me in Los Angeles, and I did not ask for a solo rehearsal for the two of us. It was one of the few times in my life that I did not have that private rehearsal. I had worked so hard for the New York performances, and I felt it would be interesting to see how they had changed—if at all. Claudio played the Strauss/Weber works in very much the same way, and after the rehearsal he could not believe how well it went. Of course, that was in part because I had marked every little nuance in our very first meeting.

In the 1980–1981 season Claudio came back to do both Beethoven's Fourth and the Fifth Piano Concertos, again giving magnificent performances. He had also been appearing with me at Mostly Mozart, and very near the end of his life he closed our Mostly Mozart season. He wanted to do the two Beethoven concertos again. Claudio's personal representative, Friede Rothe, was extremely protective of her boss and pushed very hard for these two works. I felt that two performances—one on Friday and one on Saturday, with a dress rehearsal on Friday morning— might be too much for him. I expressed my concern and said I did not think it was fair to put him through that at his age. But Friede insisted, and in the end I gave in.

During the Friday dress rehearsal Claudio played the Beethoven Fourth beautifully, but he started to show some fatigue during the Fifth. At the concert that evening the Fourth went beautifully, the Fifth less so. Then, on Saturday morning, Bill Lockwood, the manager of the festival, called me at home to say Claudio had canceled his Saturday night performance. I felt terrible for my dear friend, and now I had a real problem. It was Saturday and all the artist managers were off. We had to find a soloist, and there would be no rehearsal for a sold-out Avery Fisher Hall performance that evening.

Bill found a wonderful young pianist, Ken Noda, who could play that night, but he needed to do the Mozart Piano Concerto in D Minor, K. 466. That was a concerto the orchestra and I had done together often, and my material was well marked and bowed. I met with Ken privately in the afternoon. Ken and I were both excited about the challenge, and I knew that for the concerto the orchestra would be totally focused. We added a Mozart symphony we had recently done to replace one of Arrau's concertos. That night Ken and the orchestra played the concerto beautifully, with no rehearsal. I still treasure the memory of that performance.

Subsequent seasons at the Y expanded to five weeks, then eight. The Brandenburgs continued to be our holiday-concert tradition—five performances, always ending on New Year's Eve. Following the performance, we would go to Omus and Jessica's house on Riverside Drive for a party catered by Murray "The Sturgeon King" Bernstein, owner of Murray's Sturgeon Shop on the Upper West Side. That tradition lasted for twenty-five years.

We also did the Brandenburg series in Los Angeles, but before Christmas. What a glorious way to celebrate the holiday season. For the first few years I also played the trumpet on the Second Brandenburg Concerto until I stopped playing altogether in 1978. During that last year in Los Angeles we recorded the complete Brandenburgs for Angel records, and in the early 1980s we did a televised performance of the concert for the Bravo Network in New York.

During the 1979–1980 season with the Chamber Symphony, I did music by Aaron Copland, David Diamond, Irving Fine, Arthur Foote, and Peter Mennin. I also did an interesting arrangement for small orchestra, by Felix Greissle, of Arnold Schoenberg's *Five Pieces for Orchestra*. Szymon Goldberg became our first guest conductor, and over the years we had other distinguished guest conductors, including Eugen Jochum, Leinsdorf, and Paul Sacher, who did a program of works he had commissioned with his Basel Chamber Orchestra.

One of the highlights of our second season was the appearance of the Polish-Mexican violinist Henryk Szeryng. He used to introduce himself as an ambassador first (he was the Mexican cultural ambassador), a linguist second (he spoke seven languages), and a violinist third. I met him for the first time in December 1979 when he was doing the Beethoven Violin Concerto with us. A very elegant man, he arrived between rehearsals on Friday afternoon to play through the concerto for me onstage. Before we began he looked into the auditorium and began repeating, "Landsman"—a Yiddish word meaning "fellow countryman." When I asked him what he meant, he pointed up in the hall, where the names of David, Moses, Isaiah, Abraham, and Einstein were engraved in the dark wood near the ceiling.

We always used a stage extension when we played at Kaufmann, and because we did not have our excellent shell yet, we were constantly trying to find the optimal place for the orchestra to sit for the best acoustical results. The first thing Szeryng did was adjust the placement of the principal strings. I objected; we had been playing concerts there for over a year and had tried most positions to find which worked best.

Henryk looked at me and said, "Can't we even try this?"

I replied, "Of course we can."

His suggestions had been tried before, and we had determined that the placement he wanted was slightly inferior to the one we'd already settled on. I decided that before the next rehearsal I would put the chairs and stands back in our preferred position, and Henryk would not notice.

We began the rehearsal with the first movement of the Beethoven. The timpani strokes began the concerto, and a few measures in Szeryng stopped and complained about a spotlight in his eyes. Our stage manager, Sylvia, adjusted the light, and we began again. After a few bars he stopped again and asked for another adjustment of another light. Sylvia adjusted a different light. The third time Henryk called to Sylvia directly. I leaned over and quietly asked him if we could discuss the lights less and Beethoven a little more.

He smiled. His big issue in the first movement was for the strings not to use too much bow during the *pianissimo* passages. He had written *poco arco* in his music and looked around each time to make sure that everyone was doing it. The second movement begins with the strings alone, then the horns enter, and then the solo violin makes its first entrance. All was going well until Henryk's entrance. I looked around and saw him kneeling with a piece of chalk in his hand, marking the positions of the principal players' music stands. He suspected I would change the set-up before the next rehearsal. The third movement starts with the solo violin, followed by an orchestral response to the first two phrases and a fermata. Often conductors and soloists agree on a ritard during each of these gestures, but Szeryng and I both preferred no ritard. When we got there, to make sure we didn't slow down he conducted me with his violin—even at the concerts.

The performances with him went very well, and I invited him

to come to Mostly Mozart that summer and to Los Angeles the following season. He agreed to both. That summer he played one of the "Mozart" concertos not written by Mozart, the Violin Concerto No. 7. For our solo rehearsal I asked him to arrive at Avery Fisher Hall an hour before the rehearsal starting time to get the lighting worked out. By the time the orchestra arrived, the stage was as dimly lit as a cocktail bar. A few measures into the rehearsal I asked our principal bass, Mike Morgan, for something in a specific bar. He pulled a lighter from his pocket, flicked it close to the music, and said, "Sure, if I could only see." Everyone laughed, and Henryk let us raise the lights a little.

After the final rehearsal Henryk invited a few of the violinists; my wife, Jody; and me to his hotel suite for some cocktails and to try bows and violins. We all had a fantastic time and there was some serious drinking, especially by Szeryng. All this took place in the living-room area of his suite. After about an hour and a half he said that he would like to introduce someone to us. He opened the darkened door to the bedroom and out came his fiancée, beautifully dressed and bejeweled. She had waited in there the entire time until Henryk was ready to introduce her.

In the 1980–1981 season we had a remarkable lineup of soloists for the orchestra at the Y: Claudio Arrau, Alfred Brendel, Shura Cherkassky, Bella Davidovich, Richard Goode, and Gil Shaham. We added a baroque series and used our members as soloists: Thomas Nyfenger, flute; Ronald Roseman, oboe; Syoko Aki, violin; Jean Dane, viola; and André Emelianoff, cello. We did Bartók's *Music for Strings, Percussion, and Celesta* with the same size of orchestra that Paul Sacher had used at the premiere. I always researched the size of orchestras for specific pieces. We did Beethoven's Ninth at Alice Tully Hall one season with the same size orchestra that Beethoven had used at the premiere: fifty-five players. Essentially, the size of the orchestra needs to fit the size of the hall. That said, most composers, from Handel and Mozart to the present, would rather have larger orchestras.

We also did the William Schuman Symphony No. 5. It was my first performance of any of his symphonies, and it led to my eventually recording all these magnificent works.

That season we commissioned two works to be premiered by both the Los Angeles Chamber Orchestra and the Y Chamber Symphony: William Bergsma's *In Campo Aperto* and Leonard Rosenman's *Foci I*. Rosenman was an Oscar- and Emmy-winning film composer who also wrote for the concert stage. His concert music was a little unusual, and *Foci I* was about insects. We did the first performance of it in Los Angeles, and I was not that enthralled with it. For the New York performance I conducted the piece faster than the composer had indicated. Afterward he told me that musically the New York performance was much better than the Los Angeles one on a musical level. I certainly agreed. A few days later, however, he called me up, quite heated. After listening to the tape he had realized that the piece was five minutes shorter than it was supposed to be—I had played it much too fast.

During the 1981–1982 season we had Lynn Harrell and Yo-Yo Ma as soloists, and we did a number of premieres, including Paul Creston's *Sadhanah*, Op. 117, for cello and orchestra, commissioned by both the New York and Los Angeles orchestras. Our wonderful solo cello in New York, André Emelianoff, played it in New York, and the equally wonderful Doug Davis played it in Los Angeles. We also premiered my arrangement for full strings of Anton Webern's *Langsamer Satz* and did a memorable performance of Stravinsky's complete *Pulcinella*.

It was always a joy to find rarely performed excellent works by established composers. The 1982–1983 season was a case in point. In our eight regular subscription weeks, we played Charles Gounod's Symphony No. 2, Arthur Honegger's Symphony No. 2, Frank Martin's Concerto for Seven Wind Instruments, Mendelssohn's Symphony No. 1, and Giacomo Puccini's *Crisantemi*, Richard Strauss's Divertimento, and Stravinsky's *Apollo*. At the time only sophisticated music lovers would have known these works.

We did a number of premieres as well as our regular selection of American music. By this time our personnel was quite constant. Randall Ellis took over as our principal oboe, a position he held with great distinction throughout my tenure. Randall also became the principal at Mostly Mozart, and he came to Seattle quite often to help out our principal oboe, Bernard Shapiro. We continued to have superb soloists, including Claudio Arrau, Bella Davidovich, Alicia de Larrocha, Yo-Yo Ma, Elmar Oliveira, Dmitry Sitkovetsky, and Alexis Weissenberg.

There is a tradition of contemporary composers looking at older music through new eyes. With the orchestra we investigated these kind of arrangements by Britten, Ravel, Respighi, Strauss, and Stravinsky, among others. I suggested to the composer Hugh Aitken that he write something in this vein, and his piece *In Praise of Ockeghem* was the result. We premiered it on our opening concert that season.

Our first horn, Paul Ingraham, was unable to play the first set of concerts, so I asked the former solo horn of the Cleveland Orchestra and one of my favorite players, Mike Bloom, to join us. The main piece on the program was Schumann's Symphony No. 1. Mike played magnificently. At one point during the rehearsal I went out into the hall to check the balances. When I returned Mike asked me, "Are you going to conduct the work, or stand in the hall?" Mike was known to be temperamental, and of course he had a point, but listening in the hall is extremely valuable. I had enough respect for Mike to take his comment in stride. Mike also did some teaching for me at Waterloo.

Most horn players want to be sure the timpani aren't seated behind them, something both Mike and John Cerminaro felt very strongly about. I understood and always did my best to make sure the timpani, and for that matter any percussion, were not behind the horn section. One summer at Waterloo we were doing Aaron Copland's Symphony No. 3, and Mike was playing. At the rehearsals I had made sure no one was playing behind the horns. When we arrived for the dress rehearsal, however, we found that the stage crew had set the timpani right behind the horns. I came onstage just in time to see Mike leaving, not to return. It was very disappointing, as the situation could have been easily corrected. The silver lining was that Mike's absence created a wonderful opportunity for some of our excellent students to play principal in that concert.

At the Y we usually had two guest conductors for the main series and others for the baroque series. I always did the opening concerts, except in October 1983. We had developed a relationship with the pianist Veronica Jochum, the daughter of the renowned German conductor Eugen Jochum. I had once played under Jochum when I was in the American Symphony; he conducted a magnificent performance of Bruckner's Fifth Symphony. So I asked Veronica if she thought we might be able to get her father to work with us. For the opening of the season Veronica played the Mozart Piano Concerto in D Minor, K. 466, and Jochum conducted the Mozart Serenade, K. 525, and the Haydn Symphony No. 98. I always felt that his work with Haydn and Bruckner resulted in some of his greatest recorded performances, and I was happy that he would be doing a Haydn symphony.

Although the stage at the Y was quite small, we always managed. We used eight first violins in the main orchestra, fewer for the baroque. Jochum wanted twelve first violins and an enlarged string body throughout. I tried to explain about our hall and the acoustics there, but he would not budge—mainly because he varied the number of players in the Haydn. Stokowski did this at times: when he said "da camera" for a passage, everyone knew that it would be played with fewer strings. Jochum's concerts were a big success.

Also in the 1983 season we did the New York premiere of Gunther Schuller's Trumpet Concerto, played by the marvelous Stephen Burns. (This was the work I had commissioned when I won the Ford Foundation Award for Concert Artists, and I had played the premiere in August 1979 at the White Mountains Festival, with Gunther conducting). János Starker performed the *Konzertstück* by Ernst von Dohnányi, and we did Shostakovich's Symphony No. 14 with Alessandra Marc and John Cheek.

Omus wanted to invite Alfred Brendel to play all Beethoven's piano concertos in three concerts at Carnegie Hall and then a pair at the Y. Brendel was not thought of as a box-office artist at the time, and Omus had a tough time selling his proposal to the board. It was only because Judy Rubin supported him that they eventually agreed to the Brendel series. Our all-Beethoven series at Carnegie also included the Fifth and Eighth Symphonies and the *Coriolanus Overture*. New York's serious music lovers showed up for Brendel, and the concerts sold out. Omus was vindicated, we ran no deficit, and the audience had a great musical experience.

These were exciting concerts for us in the Chamber Symphony as well. We always felt as though we were "out of town" when we played at the Y, but performing at Carnegie Hall brought us into the mainstream. Brendel took these Beethoven works, as he did everything he played, very seriously, carefully considering every note, every detail. He had the reputation of being great at rehearsals and not as good at concerts, but that was certainly not the case with these performances. He had played through the concertos for me at our 575 West End Avenue apartment and had loved our piano, so during the month of Carnegie concerts he practiced quite often at our apartment. Brendel's appearances were some of the most memorable in the Chamber Symphony's history. After the final concert at Carnegie Hall in May 1984, John Rockwell wrote in the *New York Times* that the "exhilarating kinetic drive of [Brendel's] playing, the way Mr. Brendel managed to highlight subtly, but forcefully the score's structure, as well as the sheer skill of the finger work, proved deeply satisfying. . . . The Y Chamber Symphony has really carved out a place for itself in New York's musical life, with stylish playing in a repertory that ranges far afield from the standards offered here. And especially in such Germanic staples as this, it sounds at its very best in the cushioning warmth of Carnegie."

The season ended with the pianist Yefim Bronfman playing Mozart's Piano Concerto in C Minor, K. 459. We also did the New York premiere of Charles Tomlinson Griffes's *Notturno*.

Our 1984–1985 season opened with the French trumpet soloist Maurice André playing Haydn and Telemann. We also did the world premiere of Joan Tower's *Music for Cello*, played by André Emelianoff. I had commissioned Joseph Schwantner's *Distant Runes and Incantations* for LACO, and we gave the New York premiere of it in our second concert. I also did this piece with the Cincinnati Symphony, with the pianist Ursula Oppens as the soloist. I love Joe's music and consider him a good friend. His main champion was Leonard Slatkin. Many conductors would not program a work by a composer who was associated with another conductor, but neither Leonard nor I subscribed to that idea.

Another memorable event was Horacio Gutiérrez playing the

William Schuman Piano Concerto. When Bill Schuman suggested we do this work, I listened to a recording and came away with the impression that it was not that strong. On the other hand, Horacio— one of my favorite pianists and someone who always brings something special to every performance—really wanted to do it, so I got hold of the score. Once I began studying it, I started to see its possibilities, and in the end we scheduled three sets of performances around the same time that spring for Vancouver, British Columbia; Los Angeles; and New York. They were thrilling concerts.

The Chamber Symphony season ended with a performance of William Grant Still's *Darker America*.

Teresa Stratas

In the fall of 1985 I was introduced to the legendary soprano Teresa Stratas. She had recorded a magnificent Kurt Weill album for Nonesuch titled *The Unknown Kurt Weill*. She was now interested in recording another one, this time with orchestra. Unbeknownst to me, she had come to a number of my Mostly Mozart concerts that summer, and I learned later that they were my audition. The Weill project was mentioned to Omus Hirshbein, and he facilitated the use of the NYCS. When I met Stratas in the fall, she invited me to accompany her to Weill's *The Seven Deadly Sins* at the Brooklyn Academy, choreographed by Pina Bauch. We entered the lobby of the Academy and ran into a large crowd, so I asked her if I could go ahead, running interference. "Okay," she said, "but I promise you, this will be the last time I follow you."

At the intermission she asked me what I thought of the performance. She said it in a way that made me feel this was another test. I answered honestly that I didn't care for it. She said, "Okay, perfect. We can go now." And we did.

After that we met many times to go over the songs she was thinking of recording. We rehearsed at her apartment at the Ansonia, at Seventy-third Street and Broadway. I hadn't been in that building since my high school composition lessons with Paul Creston. We rehearsed in a circular room empty of everything except an upright piano. The room had a very high ceiling and was extremely reverberant. Her performance of each song was so convincing, I wanted her to record them all.

Teresa, Jody and I became quite close during this period, and we had some interesting times. At one point Teresa believed she was going to die from ovarian cancer; she gave us the keys to her apartment so that we could come in the next day and call 911 to remove the body. Jody and I asked my mother, the psychiatrist, what we should do, and she asked if we would feel guilty if Teresa did in fact die. We said that we would feel terrible but not guilty, so we decided to go by the apartment building and leave her keys at the desk. We saw her the next day; all was fine, and nothing was said.

In the end Teresa chose the repertoire, and we prepared for the recording, which was to take place in December at the RCA studios. Loren Glickman hired the NYCS players as well as some of the best commercial players in the city to play drum set, saxophone, and other instruments as needed. The music included some opera and some Broadway, some songs in French, some in German, and some in English. To hear her sing these songs was a real thrill: her voice's magnificence included an immense variety of colors and qualities unique to her. We met a few days before the first session for Teresa to meet the recording team and to see the studio. There she put on a cassette of an Italian pop singer with a grossly artificial, overly reverberant recorded sound and told the team that that was the quality she wanted our recording to have. It was much like the sound in her apartment.

When the first recording session was to begin, Teresa told me that she was not in good voice. She wanted me to record the orchestral part and would add hers when she was feeling better. She then went into the adjacent studio and sang into a microphone. I followed her by listening over a headset, while she was able to see me on a monitor from a remote camera; that way the interpretations would be consistent.

This went on at every session. She insisted that this was the best way because whenever she felt in good voice she could come to the studio and record, even in the middle of the night. I was extremely nervous about this because there were so many songs, and we had never performed them. We recorded the whole album that way. It was great preparation for when I recorded the Beethoven Ninth in Seattle, first with the orchestra, later with the chorus, and long after that with the soloists.

A few weeks later Teresa called to tell me that she had found a producer to help her produce her portions. She asked my opinion of him, and I told her, "He is very handsome." She hired him, and a few months later she went to the RCA studio to record. They did a few tests, she did the first song, and then she declared, "That was perfect!" The producer said, "Good, I'll turn on the machine now." The handsome producer was fired, and Bob Hurwitz, the CEO of Nonesuch Records, took over. Luckily, the recording came out beautifully. The next time I worked with Teresa was when I filled in for Seiji Ozawa and conducted Debussy's opera, *Pelléas et Mélisande*, on tour in Japan.

Thanks to the success of the Brendel and the Beethoven series at Carnegie Hall, we were invited back to do a program in the spring of the next season. By now our "regular" pianists were Emanuel Ax, Jorge Bolet, Yefim Bronfman, Shura Cherkassky, Bella Davidovich, Misha Dichter, Rudolf Firkušný, Richard Goode, Horacio Gutiérrez, Lorin Hollander, Joseph Kalichstein, Alicia de Larrocha, Peter Serkin, and Alexis Weissenberg. Each year we added at least one to the list, and in 1985–1986 these were David Bar-Illan, Grant Johannesen, and Lilian Kallir. The regular violinists were Elmar Oliveira, Nadja Salerno-Sonnenberg, and Gil Shaham; the regular cellists were Lynn Harrell, Yo-Yo Ma, and János Starker. From the orchestra we always gave solo opportunities to our concertmaster, Syoko Aki; the violist Jean Dane; the cellist André Emilianoff; the flutist Tom Nyfenger; the oboist Randall Ellis; the clarinetist David Shifrin; the horn player Paul Ingraham; and the trumpeter Neil Balm. We continued to do the Brandenburg concertos each season and at least one important choral work, usually from the baroque period. We did four world premieres during the season, works by David Stock, Hugh Aitken, Hugo Weisgall, and Stephen Albert. Stephen's beautiful *Flower of the Mountain* was sung by Lucy Shelton. She was a student of my dear friend Jan DeGaetani and was just starting her career. Lucy sang exquisitely, and to this day it is one of Stephen's most memorable works.

I had asked Hugo Weisgall, a scholar with deep knowledge of Judaism and music for the synagogue, to write something to do with a Jewish religious service. (He was also an important teacher of Bright Sheng when he first arrived in the United States.) The result was *Tekiatot* ("Shofar Sounds"), which utilized some traditional melodies from the Yom Kippur service. His music tended to be thick and difficult, but there was an integrity about it that was very appealing. This work had an offstage shofar call toward the end. The shofar, or ram's horn, is used during the High Holiday services in synagogues everywhere. I asked him if he had a player in mind, and he assured me he had a student at Queens College who played French horn and could play shofar well. At the climax of the piece, the orchestra has a dramatic silence, and the shofar blows from the wings offstage. At rehearsal you could hear the young man struggling to play the instrument, but nothing of musical value was coming out. Suddenly David Shifrin, our first clarinet, removed his mouthpiece from his clarinet and buzzed into the barrel to make a pretty remarkable shofarlike sound. The orchestra could not keep from laughing, which, luckily, the student suffering offstage could not hear or see. Then Hugo ran onto the stage, veered into the wings, and grabbed the shofar. He did not do much better. Playing the shofar is tricky. For the concerts the student did very well.

That season we also did Diamond's *Romeo and Juliet*, Panufnik's powerful *Autumn Music*, William Schuman's *Song of Orpheus*, and, with Jorge Bolet, the rarely played *Malediction* by Liszt. The program for Carnegie was the string orchestra version that I made for the Sextet from Strauss's *Capriccio*; Alexis Weissenberg playing Mozart's C Minor Concerto K. 491; Stravinsky's *Abraham and Isaac*; and the Kurt Weill *Mahagonny-Songspiel*, with a text by Bertolt Brecht. I had the idea of staging the Weill on a platform, and Michael Posnick, from Yale University, did a marvelous and subtle staging. Weissenberg played elegantly. The Strauss is always a joy for me to conduct. The Stravinsky is from his twelve-tone period, and although it sounds like Stravinsky it most likely will never have the same appeal as his more tonal works. There has been some discussion over the years about the Brecht-Weill collaboration. I love Weill's music, be it

Broadway, opera, or symphonic. That said, some say it is not terribly intellectual and therefore lacking. I remember discussing the Brecht-Weill collaboration with Pierre Boulez, who thought it was very clear that Brecht was the genius in their collaboration. Tim Page wrote a fine review of the Carnegie concert in the *New York Times* in which he observed: "Brecht's lyrics now seem skewed, cynical and false, but Weill's combination of Bergian expressionism [referring to Alban Berg], jazz, martial rhythms and his own tangy melodies retains the power to haunt."

The highlight of the 1986–1987 season was the gala in June. The Y galas generally presented a popular artist who could excite the board and sell out a performance. Our excellent board was a board not for the orchestra, but for the Y as a whole, and although we had some major supporters, such as Judy Rubin, some were less than enthusiastic about the cultural events and the expense they involved. I didn't realize how lucky I was: Omus did all the work with the board, and my responsibility was simply to put on excellent concerts. In New York, during the season, we would simply arrive at our West End Avenue apartment on Wednesday, start rehearsals on Thursday, perform concerts on Saturday and Sunday, and leave on Monday. Some weeks I would come in on the Saturday and Sunday before to do a Music Today concert on Wednesday at Merkin Hall. Once again at the Y we had our regular soloists, but this season we added my high school violinist friend Pinchas Zukerman, as well as the violinist Mark Peskanov. We also had the harpsichord soloist Tony Newman on our baroque series and the cellist Ralph Kirshbaum playing the Barber Cello Concerto.

The 92nd Street Y was celebrating the fiftieth anniversary of the performing arts at the Y, and Omus wanted something very special for this occasion, something musically serious with a connection to the organization. Our idea was to ask the Nobel Prize-winning author Elie Wiesel, who had a regular lecture series there, to write the text for a cantata with music by David Diamond. Elie read the text of "A Song for Hope" at one of his regular talks in November 1986, and then we did the world premiere of the cantata in June 1987 with a cast that included Dawn Upshaw, John Cheek, James Patterson, and Jon

Garrison. David wanted a chorus, but the stage at the Y was too small, so he included four additional singers to sing the choral part. David agreed that for future performances a full chorus should be used. Of the performance Michael Kimmelman wrote in the *New York Times*: "Mr. Diamond's achievement is in providing a score that lets the words speak for themselves, accompanying them sparely and with only fragmented melodies developed from a mournful cello solo that opens the piece. The music, through composed and lasting roughly 45 minutes, simmers with an unbroken sense of outrage and despair." It was a very meaningful performance for all involved.

On the same program, Yo-Yo played his first performance of Bruch's Kol Nidrei, as well as the cello solo in the slow movement of Brahms's Second Piano Concerto, with Joseph Kalichstein as the soloist. Yo-Yo played the Bruch beautifully, but I suggested some traditional cantorial inflections in quite a few places where he could use a portamento or a slide to more closely imitate the style of singing that inspired the work. Before we went onstage he laughed and said that the program credits should read, "Soloist, Ma, composer, Bruch, and slides by Schwarz."

We did three other world premieres: Paul Allen Levi's *Transformation of the Heart*, Nick Thorn's *Songs of Darkness, Power and Radiance*, and Barbara Kolb's *Yet that Things Go Round*. Each title was long and, I thought, hard to remember. Barbara's was the third work to be programmed. We were doing a pre-concert talk, and I explained that I preferred simple titles audiences would be able to remember, leaving the more complicated descriptions for the program notes. I asked her, why not name her piece something simple, like *Poem* or *Air*? But she felt strongly about her title. I told her the audience would not remember it, and wasn't that important? She believed, however, that they *would* remember. So we made a twenty-dollar bet. Since we had already had two premieres, I asked how many members of our pre-concert audience had been to the others. Most had attended, so I asked if any of them remembered the titles. One person remembered the title of Nick Thorn's piece. It turned out to be Nick's publisher (or possibly his copyist), but nevertheless, I handed Barbara the twenty.

The main choral works that year were Henry Purcell's *The Fairy*

Queen and Bach's *Magnificat*. We also did one of my favorites with chamber orchestra, the complete *Pulcinella* by Stravinsky. The other work I had never done with a small orchestra was Bartók's *Music for Strings, Percussion, and Celesta*. It was written for the Basel Chamber Orchestra and is extremely difficult, but with small forces the result can be even more powerful than with full strings.

As I mentioned, from the beginning I had wanted the name of our ensemble to be the New York Chamber Symphony. By the spring of 1986–1987 season, our reputation had grown, and record companies were concerned about our unusual name. Somehow, however, that spring Omus managed to change our name to the New York Chamber Symphony of the 92nd Street Y. And he did so without compromising our relationship with the Y.

The two most exciting events of the 1987–1988 season were the appearance of the violinist Nathan Milstein and the premiere of Bright Sheng's *H'un*. In addition, we did a recording of Copland's music for Angel records that included the Clarinet Concerto, *Music for the Theatre*, *Quiet City*, and *Dance Panels*. Will Crutchfield wrote in the *New York Times* in May 1988: "Gerard Schwarz and the NYCS began Sunday afternoon's concert at the 92nd Street Y by doing a service for a work most of us have underestimated, Aaron Copland's 'Dance Panels' of 1959 (revised 1962). . . . The *Pas de Trois* is eloquent in its simple melancholy, and the fast sections have an unforced rhythmic life . . . beautiful in sound and thoughtfully, elegantly conducted; dynamic shifts were strongly marked and natural-seeming and there was a lift to the rhythm that bespoke confidence."

We also did the world premiere of George Perle's Cello Concerto. We performed many other works by American composers as well: Samuel Barber, Elliott Carter, Irving Fine, Vincent Persichetti, and Stephen Albert.

Milstein played the Bruch Violin Concerto No 1. He was near the end of his career by this time but still played magnificently. When I ran into Emanuel Ax a few weeks before the series with Milstein, I asked him if he had any thoughts on working with him. Manny, who early in his career had accompanied Milstein on some tours, said,

"Look out for the second performance!" In the Heifetz and Milstein era many soloists felt that conductors were necessary evils.

Our rehearsals went fine, and so did the first concert. Manny's warning came back to me at the Sunday concert, where suddenly it seemed Milstein was trying to trip me up. He played many important ensemble moments quite differently than we had rehearsed, and each time he looked at me to see if I was able to catch him. Thank goodness I was on my guard and well prepared, and I caught him at every sudden change. I almost felt that he would have been happier if I had made some mistakes.

On the second half we did Persichetti's beautiful work for trumpet and strings, *The Hollow Men*, after the T. S. Elliot poem. Neil Balm, our principal trumpet, played it beautifully, and I was happy to present this excellent work, which is so rarely programmed on orchestral concerts. After the concert Wanda Horowitz, the wife of Vladimir Horowitz and the daughter of Toscanini, came backstage to tell me how disrespectful it was to have a second soloist on the program with Milstein. I hadn't thought of the ten-minute Persichetti as a solo work.

H'un was the first work I ever commissioned from Bright Sheng. I had already performed some of his music on my Music Today series at Merkin Hall, and I was extremely excited by what he was doing as a composer. He seemed to be able to combine American/European and Eastern/Chinese traditions in a very organic way, and his voice was clear and unique. *H'un* was translated as *Lacerations*, and it concerned Bright's interpretations and remembrances of the Cultural Revolution, which he had lived through in China.

When I received the score, I was in shock. It didn't have any of the beautiful melodies he had previously written. His melodic material was always a special combination of East and West and helped define his voice. This new work was angry, dissonant, and tortured. It was also very long. I was worried that it wouldn't be successful. I wanted this to be a great start to what I was sure would become an important career, and we discussed the piece extensively. Bright explained that the subject of his work was so horrific, it couldn't be represented with anything but the most severe music. I said it was too long, but he said he wanted me to try it first; later we could make some cuts if needed.

At the first rehearsal, I explained to the orchestra what the piece was about. They gave it their best, but the intensity was hard to sustain and very taxing. Bright then agreed that the piece needed to be cut. He and our librarian, Richard Lee, worked very hard for the rest of that day and night and made the work what it is today.

H'un was such a success that every major orchestra in the United States played it, and Kurt Masur and the New York Philharmonic featured it on a European tour. I played it often and recorded it twice. I also programmed it a number of times with the NYCS to try to keep it in the repertoire. Bright showed it to Bernstein, who also thought it was remarkable.

Our major choral work for that season was Handel's ode *Alexander's Feast*. The editing I did on that piece was quite extensive. I remember vividly being up through the night, completing the extensive ornamentation I use while my wife, Jody, slept. After the concert she said she already knew all the ornamentation. When I asked her how, she said, "I must have absorbed it in my sleep."

The 1988–1989 season opened with Bernstein's *Trouble in Tahiti*. During the season we were also performing the world premiere of Bernstein's *Arias and Barcarolles* as orchestrated by Bright Sheng. Harold Shapero was to do a new work, and we scheduled two wonderful works with narrator: a repeat of Beethoven's complete *Egmont* from our first season, narrated by Werner Klemperer, and *Le bourgeois gentilhomme* by Richard Strauss, with José Ferrer narrating the poet Richard Wilbur's English text. The French cellist Paul Tortelier was a highlight for me among so many soloists. Fifteen years earlier I had heard him play the Tchaikovsky *Rococo Variations* at the Casals Festival in Puerto Rico. Since there was no trumpet in the Tchaikovsky, I stood in the wings next to Casals and his wife, Marta. Casals and Tortelier had some disagreements about politics, and this was their first meeting in many years. After the performance Casals was very complimentary. When I first worked with Paul in Scotland, I reminded him of the story, and he was so happy there had been someone to witness that exchange. For this

NYCS set of concerts he did the Tchaikovsky and the Gabriel Fauré *Elegy*. We also did the Ferruccio Busoni Violin Concerto for the first time, with Jaime Laredo as the soloist.

Our daughter, Gabriella, was born around our opening week, so for one of the very few times in my life, I canceled a performance. We were very lucky to engage David Zinman to do those concerts.

I first heard Strauss's *Le bourgeois gentillhomme* when I was a member of the New York Philharmonic, when Leinsdorf programmed it. Leinsdorf had commissioned the renowned American poet Richard Wilbur to write the connecting text, and it was premiered by the Boston Symphony when Leinsdorf was the music director. I fell in love with the Strauss then and there and have programmed it whenever possible. That said, it is a very hard work to schedule because the complete incidental music calls for a male chorus, three vocal soloists, a narrator, and a relatively small orchestra that nonetheless includes five percussionists.

Bernstein's *Arias and Barcarolles* was originally for mezzo-soprano, baritone, and piano four-hands. At the time Bright Sheng was studying with Bernstein and was given permission to make a version of this charming work for strings and percussion. Bernstein sent one of his assistants to represent him at the run-through, before the first rehearsal. All was going well until the assistant started to criticize some of the freedoms I was taking: he wanted me to play the work metronomically. Eventually I was able to assure him that Lenny would approve, because he rarely conducted anything metronomically. Our two soloists, Susan Graham and Kurt Ollmann, sang wonderfully through it all. After the performance I sent Lenny a tape, and he called me to rave about it. His only complaint was that he felt Susan was too operatic: he thought it should be sung more simply, almost in a Broadway style. The next time I saw Lenny he greeted me with a smile and said, "So I hear from my assistant that you think I am too free with my tempos!" A year later we recorded it in Seattle with Jane Bunnell and Dale Duesing. Lenny called again to tell me how much he loved it and said he hoped he could conduct it one day as well. Unfortunately, he died before that could happen.

Harold Shapero's work was interesting. He wrote a Symphony for Classical Orchestra in 1947, at the age of twenty-seven that made a tremendous sensation. He wrote very little after 1950 and never seemed to fulfill all the great expectations of his early work. He allowed me to do a string orchestra version of three movements of his String Quartet (1941), and at that time I asked him to compose a new work for the orchestra. He agreed. I found him to be brilliant and charming but sometimes sharp-tongued. In the end he gave us *Three Hebrew Songs*, which he had been working on for quite a while and which were really nothing new. Still, it was a joy to get to know him.

During the 1989–1990 season we did three world premieres: Richard Danielpour's *Metamorphosis*, William Thomas McKinley's *New York Overture*, and Andrzej Panufnik's *Harmony*, a poem for chamber orchestra. Panufnik also recorded his *Arbor Cosmica* with the orchestra at that time. Our choral work was Handel's *Acis and Galatea*, and we did the New York premiere of the complete ballet *Nobilissima Visione*, by Hindemith. That work was only known in the suite form for large orchestra. I believe the original, for small orchestra, is a greater work. Sometimes complete ballets have a great deal of filler for the stage changes or costume changes—the complete *Mother Goose* of Ravel, the complete *Three-Cornered Hat* of Falla, even the complete *Firebird* of Stravinsky come to mind. Then there are works like this Hindemith or the Strauss *Le bourgeois gentilhomme*, which are even better in the complete versions. During my final year as music director in Seattle I was able to record the complete Hindemith.

I have always tried to engage the finest conductors as guests. There are so many orchestras around the world and relatively few outstanding conductors. During the 1990–1991 season Erich Leinsdorf agreed to conduct the NYCS. We had become close over the years, and he saw an opportunity to do some Bach cantatas, which he was generally unable to program. His concert with us consisted of Cantatas Nos. 140, 155, 82, and 42, and we had excellent soloists: the soprano Benita Valente, the tenor John Aler, and the bass Hermann Prey.

The other interesting guest was Paul Sacher, who, as the music director of the Basel Chamber Orchestra, commissioned many works from such twentieth-century masters such as Bartók, Stravinsky, and Bohuslav Martinů. Among the works he did with us were Bartók's

Music for Strings, Piano, and Celesta and Stravinsky's Concerto in D, both of them his commissions.

I have always agreed with Serge Koussevitsky that when you play a new work you believe has a real future, you should repeat it as soon as possible—even every few years. Koussevitsky did this with Stravinsky's *Symphony of Psalms* and many other works. During this season we repeated Bright Sheng's *H'un* and Handel's *Judas Maccabaeus*. We also gave the world premiere of Lowell Liebermann's tone poem *The Domain of Arnheim*.

Our 1991–1992 season again had extraordinary soloists, including Bronfman, Perlman, Shaham, and Joshua Bell. My interest in composer arrangements continued with the Britten arrangement of the second movement of the Mahler Symphony No. 3, the title taken from the movement's original title, which Mahler later withdrew: *What the Wild Flowers Tell Me*. We also did the Webern arrangement of Six German Dances by Schubert. I had done his arrangement of the Ricercar from Bach's *Musical Offering* a number of times on the same program with the Schoenberg String Quartet Concerto, after Handel. I had found a letter from Webern to the conductor Hermann Scherchen describing in detail how to perform all the many tempo indications Webern suggested. I also found an old recording of Webern conducting these Schubert dances with a German radio orchestra in the 1930s. The rubatos were gloriously excessive, similar to how I had done the dances earlier and recorded them as well.

We did our regular series of American works by Copland, Creston, Diamond, Albert, and Sheng, and three world premieres of works by Lukas Foss, Henri Lazaroff, and Aaron Jay Kernis. I had done a few pieces of Aaron's with my Music Today Ensemble at Merkin and felt he was a composer with a promising future. During his early years his music might have been overly difficult, but his gift was apparent from the beginning. This season we did his *Symphony in Waves*. The St. Paul Chamber Orchestra did the world premiere, and we were doing the New York premiere and recorded it. It was very difficult, especially for the horns, but a powerful work. Aaron continues to be one of our most important composers. On the more traditional side, we did the

Honegger Fourth Symphony and the Martinů Double Concerto for two string orchestras, timpani, and piano, both commissioned by Paul Sacher for the Basel Chamber Orchestra and both excellent works. I remember playing the Honegger Fifth Symphony with Stokowski and the American Symphony. I often did his Second Symphony and recorded it as well. Martinů is another excellent composer who is too rarely played. I adore his symphonies and have a wonderful memory of doing his Third Symphony with the Czech Philharmonic in 2005. On the same concert I also did Diamond's Fourth Symphony, both works written during the same year and premiered by the Boston Symphony. It was Koussevitsky who commissioned Martinů to write a symphony a year while he lived in the United States, beginning with his First Symphony. Koussevitsky premiered six of his symphonies between 1942 and 1946. David knew Martinů during this time, and in fact one summer, while Martinů lived out of the city, David stayed in his New York apartment. David, knowing of my love of these works, gave me a miniature score of Martinů's Fourth and Fifth Symphonies signed by Martinů to David "with great admiration." Martinů was an important teacher as well during his time in the United States; among his students was Alan Hovhaness.

Our premieres for the 1992–1993 season included Leo Smit's *Alabaster Chambers* and the New York premiere of Albert's Cello Concerto, played by Yo-Yo Ma. We opened the season with the complete Mendelssohn *Midsummer Night's Dream*, with narration by Christopher Plummer. That season we received the ASCAP Award for commitment to new music as well as three Grammy nominations.

The highlights of the 1993–1994 season were a performance of Beethoven's First and Ninth Symphonies at Carnegie Hall, the world premiere of Diamond's *The Death of Peter Whiffle*, the New York premiere of Kernis's *Musica Celestis*, and a six-movement suite I arranged from Panufnik's *Arbor Cosmica*. Panufnik and I had corresponded a great deal about it. The only stumbling block was the key relationships among the complete work's twelve movements, and in the end Andrzej was happy with my solutions. The shorter length is much easier to program yet still marvelously effective. *Musica*

Celestis, a string orchestra version of the second movement of Kernis's String Quartet (1990), became a favorite of mine. I have performed it often and recorded it originally for a project with Starbucks, now out on Naxos.

During the previous season I had asked Nadja Salerno-Sonnenberg to play and conduct for a week of concerts. She did an impressive job, and for the 1994–1995 season I expanded that idea to have Vladimir Feltsman, Shlomo Mintz, and Vladimir Spivakov do the same. We did the New York premiere of three outstanding works: Ellen Taaffe Zwilich's Concerto for Violin and Cello, John Harbison's *The Most Often Used Chords*, and excerpts from Sheng's *Song of Majnun*.

Two sensational pianists new to the major concert scene appeared with us for the first time in the 1995–1996 season: Hélène Grimaud and Awadagin Pratt. We did the Gounod Symphony No. 2, a rarely played yet remarkable work; lots of American music; and the world premieres of Augusta Read Thomas's *5 Haiku* for piano and orchestra and Vivian Fung's *Flares*. Gusty has had a remarkable career already and is gifted in so many ways. Vivian was a student of Diamond's, and through that connection I did her lovely work. I think it was a good beginning for her, and she has continued to have a great success.

Omus made the 92nd Street Y into an important cultural center for New York. Yes, they had a wonderful history, but nothing like what Omus brought to them and to New York. He was incredibly charming but there were times when he didn't run his world at the Y in a traditionally businesslike way. Luckily he had Linda Greenberg assisting him for many years and then the remarkable Jackie Taylor. Yet there were always board members who thought that because of Omus they were spending too many resources on music and not enough on areas such as the health club. As long as the leadership understood the remarkable work that Omus was doing, everything went well, but when the leadership changed and they were less interested in classical music, things became quite difficult for him. After the 1995–1996 season Omus left the Y. The 92nd Street Y continues to be a very special place in the city, but their musical offerings, good as they are, are nothing like what they once were. As

Left to right: Bernice, me, Jeanette, and my mother, ca. 1951, in outfits my mother made for us. Personal collection.

A painting of my grandmother by the Austrian painter Franz von Matsch. In 1913 Matsch was riding the trolley in Vienna when he saw my grandmother and asked my grandfather if he could paint a portrait of her. He agreed, and after the painting was finished, my grandfather bought it. The painting ended up in my grandmother's family home in Rogaška Slatina, Slovenia. In 1969, I was playing a concert with the American Brass Quintet at the biennale of new music in Zagreb, and on a day off I went to my grandmother's home. My father had asked me to go and get the painting. My grandmother's sister was still in her beautiful home, but under Communism it had been converted into a four-family residence. I was given the painting, and when I returned home my father gave it to me. It now hangs in our New York apartment, where it is a treasure. Personal collection.

With my grandmother Anna, 1950.
Personal collection.

Fred Miller (English horn), Kun-Woo Paik (piano), and me rehearsing in 1964 for
a performance at Performing Arts High School, playing my arrangement of some
Copland works that was used for the spring dance department performance. Both
Fred and Kun-Woo have gone on to important careers in music, and we continue
to be friends. Personal collection.

With Boulez when I was in the New York Philharmonic; I loved him and learned a great deal from him during our years together (1972–1977). Behind us is the personnel manager and former first horn, James Chambers, who made it possible for me to audition for the orchestra in 1972. Photograph courtesy of the New York Philharmonic Archives.

The French soloist Maurice André played with me in New York, Seattle, and other orchestras. He was a great player and a wonderful friend. With the pipe is Allen Dean, whom I replaced in the American Brass Quintet when he moved to the New York Brass Quintet. Also shown is Roger Voisin, one of the idols of my formative years, a chamber music coach of mine at Tanglewood, and the first trumpet of the Boston Symphony for many years. Photograph by Charles Colin.

Playing the Haydn Concerto with Boulez and the New York Philharmonic in 1973 in
Philharmonic Hall. The principal cellist, Lorne Munroe, is to Boulez's right.
Photograph courtesy of the New York Philharmonic Archives.

In Seattle with Van
Cliburn, 2005. Van was
larger than life. He had
gone to Juilliard with my
mother-in-law, Shirley
Greitzer, and both studied
with Rosina Lhévinne. He
was always wonderful to be
with, and his performances
of the Tchaikovsky First
and Grieg Concertos were
memorable. Photograph
by Larey McDaniel.

A performance of the Haydn Trumpet Concerto at the Aspen Music Festival, ca. 1974, conducted by Herbert Blomstedt. Beginning at the age of twenty, I spent seven years on the faculty at Aspen. I was also the chairman of the music committee and therefore the musicians' representative on the board. What a remarkable education this was for me! I will always be grateful to the conductor Jorge Mester for giving me that opportunity. Photograph by Steve Pettit.

With Leonard Bernstein and John Cerminaro after a performance of Mahler's Fifth Symphony in Australia in 1976. Those concerts were among the most memorable of my Philharmonic years. Photograph by Bert Bial, courtesy of the New York Philharmonic Archives.

With Bernstein at the Siplett winery in Australia in 1976; orchestra violist Barry Lear is in the background. We were playing American football using a soccer ball. Lenny was having a great time and playing very aggressively! Photograph by Bert Bial, courtesy of the New York Philharmonic Archives.

With Pierre Boulez, Paul Zukofsky, and Milton Babbitt, ca. 1976. Paul and I were good friends and worked together on some projects involving new music and education. Milton was a dear friend and a teacher of mine while I was a student at Juilliard. Photograph by Bert Bial, courtesy of the New York Philharmonic Archives.

With the Los Angeles Chamber Orchestra at the Ambassador Auditorium, Pasadena, California, 1978. Photograph 2017 © Martin Reichenthal.

At the Waterloo Music Festival with the pianist Alexis Weissenberg and my future in-laws, Sol and Shirley Greitzer, in 1979. Personal collection.

Publicity photograph, one of a series done at the beginning of my conducting career in 1979. Photograph © 2017 Jack Mitchell.

Conducting the Los Angeles Chamber Orchestra in Carnegie Hall in 1980. This tour brought us to the Lake Placid Olympics and was our first appearance in Carnegie. Photograph 2017 © Martin Reichenthal.

In front of Carnegie Hall for the debut of the Los Angeles Chamber Orchestra, 1980. *Left to right*: Ed Birdwell, the executive director of the orchestra and former horn player with the American Brass Quintet; Paul Shure, concertmaster; Bonnie Douglas, associate concertmaster; and Paul's wife. Photograph by Nancy Birdwell.

With Alysandra
and Daniel in 1980.
Personal collection.

A recording session of Beethoven's Symphony No. 6 with the Y Chamber Symphony (New York Chamber Symphony) at Manhattan's Masonic Temple Auditorium, 1981. Amelia Haygood was the executive producer, and the team of Marc Aubert and Joanna Nickrenz were the co-producers. Most of my Nonesuch and Delos recordings were produced by Marc and Jo. Photograph courtesy of Delos.

Omus departed, so did the orchestra, with Omus as our executive director and vice president. It was almost like starting from scratch. We organized a board led by the brilliant psychoanalyst Ernest Kafka, and we had some wonderful members. We reduced our season to six weeks and moved to Alice Tully Hall. The acoustics were perfect for our size orchestra and the audience was strong. Of course, everything changed financially, because we no longer had the support of the Y.

Fund-raising became a major issue, yet our style of programming and engagement of soloists remained the same. We repeated Albert's *Flower of the Mountain* and did premieres by Danielpour, Diamond, Lutosławski, and Kernis. Our choral works were the Haydn *Missa Brevis* and Schubert's *Lazarus*, a beautiful and very touching work.

We opened the 1997–1998 season with the Beethoven Ninth and did new works by Teddy Shapiro, Barbara Kolb, Sheng, and Diamond. That season the leader of the Serious Music Division at ASCAP, Fran Richard, held a composition competition for composers under thirty-five and asked me to be a judge and to perform the winning work in Seattle. I agreed, and that spring I went to the ASCAP offices with a group of about fifteen composers to choose the winner. There were three everyone liked and a fourth, Michael Hersch, whom only I liked. At the time his music was strongly influenced by Shostakovich, but it had something unique as well. The other judges did not agree with me, and that put us in a difficult situation, since I was the one who was to program and conduct the piece. Fran really wanted us to come to an agreement, but that was not to be. Jesse Rosen, who had just accepted the position of general manager in Seattle, got involved, and he and Fran came up with a solution. We would do all three composers' pieces that everyone agreed on, on successive concerts in Seattle: one on Sunday, one on Monday, and one on Tuesday. Fran managed to find a little additional funding so we could also give a prize to Hersch for a new work to be premiered with the NYCS. I was overjoyed to be able to premiere works by four gifted young composers. Allan Kozinn wrote in the *New York Times*:

Gerard Schwarz' advocacy of American music goes back to the

start of his conducting career . . . Early on, his tastes in new music were fairly omnivorous: his lamented Music of Today series mixed the difficult and the accessible, often showing that the distance between them was not so vast. In recent years . . he seems to have narrowed his focus . . . delving more deeply into the neo-Classical and neo-Romantic repertories. Three works in that style—two certified oldies and a world premiere—shared the first half of his program with the New York Chamber Symphony.

During the 1998–1999 season we also did the premiere of David Stock's *A Little Miracle* with the amazing mezzo Vivica Genaux as the soloist. It is an extremely moving work, which I subsequently did in Seattle and recorded in Berlin. And my friend the pianist Eugene Istomin appeared with us during the season. We first worked together in the late 1970s at Waterloo and then with the San Francisco Symphony. In San Francisco we were part of a Mozart festival, and as always he was playing beautifully. At that concert, just before the performance was to begin, the stage manager mentioned to us that the microphones were for the radio broadcast—we were not to be distracted by their presence. Whenever performances are recorded, the artists are always informed and asked to agree.

For some reason, however, the San Francisco management had not informed us about the radio broadcast. Eugene always played so perfectly that one would think it should never have mattered to him, but he went crazy. He refused to go onstage, saying that this was not a recording session but a concert. I felt really bad for the poor stage manager, as he was just the messenger. It took me some time to calm Eugene down, and in the end he performed just beautifully.

The opening concert of the 1999–2000 season started with Busoni's Concertino for Clarinet with our extraordinary principal clarinetist, Jon Manasse. He became our first clarinet player during the previous season, and I should mention that he is married to Jody's sister Pamela. Next came selections from Mahler's *Des Knaben Wunderhorn* with Angelika Kirchschlager, who had sung with me as Octavian in Strauss's *Der Rosenkavalier* in a 1997 Seattle Opera Production. After the intermission we did the Pfitzner *Kleine Sinfonie*, then ended with the Schubert Fifth Symphony. During the season Lauren Flanigan sang a new work by Deborah Drattell, *Lost Lover*, and we also did the premiere of Phillip Lasser's *Circle of Dreams*. Itzhak Perlman guest conducted for the first time.

For the 2000–2001 season we did new works by Daniel Brewbaker, Henri Lazarof, Aaron Kernis, and Andrew Stein. We also did a special concert in memory of our friend Alan Hovhaness. Judy Mendenhall, our solo flutist, played Sheng's *Flute Moon*. We also did Bruch's marvelous Third Symphony.

I decided that after twenty-five years I would make this my last season with the orchestra. My commitments in Seattle and Liverpool, where I was conducting my first season, were heavy, and I was hoping to travel less. It always seemed that every time I felt I was settling in, I had to make another trip. As I told Allan Kozinn of the *New York Times* in February 2001: "I feel that I've gotten the orchestra to where I want it to be. It has its season at Alice Tully Hall, it is without debt, and it has a strong audience. My problem is not the time spent conducting. That's the easy part. It's finding the time to do all the other work that a music director has to do—administrative work, working with the board and the staff—and at this point in my life I don't have the time."

CHAPTER EIGHT

The Los Angeles Chamber Orchestra

When the Los Angeles Chamber Orchestra was founded in 1968, Neville Marriner was engaged as their first music director. Then music director of the Academy of St. Martin in the Fields, he was an excellent choice to help create this marvelous new ensemble. He and his wife, Molly, couldn't wait to come to warm, sunny Los Angeles four or five times a year and stay at Richard Colburn's estate in Beverly Hills. Dick was a very successful businessman as well as an amateur violist with a fine string-instrument collection. He was also the main supporter of the orchestra.

Neville continued as music director for ten years. Eventually Molly stopped coming to Los Angeles, and Neville was so busy guest conducting and conducting his London orchestra that he decided to leave. Ed Birdwell, the horn player from the American Brass Quintet, was now the executive director of LACO. He thought that with my experience at Waterloo and in New York, I might be a good fit for the orchestra and invited me to guest conduct.

My guest week was played at the Mark Taper Forum at the Music Center, which was a theater for plays. Its acoustics were of course dry so audiences could hear the actors clearly; but classical music needs a little reverberation to add warmth and beauty, a continuation of the sound. To add to the problem, the sets for the plays were always left onstage, and the orchestra had to play around them.

When you guest conduct, it's usually a good idea to follow the lead of the music director. I never change the seating of the orchestra, for instance. Two questions came to me from the stage manager before the performance. First, he asked me if, in accordance with Mr. Marriner's custom, I would like a shot of cognac before the concert. I declined. Then he asked me if I would like the same amplification that Mr. Marriner always used; apparently he used to amplify the sound slightly to add some reverberation to the dry acoustics. I trusted Neville and said yes.

I don't remember what the play was, but there was a toilet on the set, and the horns were sitting near it. The program included Bach's Brandenburg Concerto No. 1, the thirteen-instrument version of Copland's *Appalachian Spring*, Hugo Wolf's *Italian Serenade* in the chamber orchestra version, and Mozart's Symphony No. 33.

The next day I was in the airport, about to fly home, when I was paged. It was an old friend of mine, Buell Neidlinger, a very fine bass player and quite a character. He'd had a fight with LACO and had not played my concert because he was suing them. He gave me a tirade over the phone, told me I should not take the job, and went on and on about how horrible they were. But when Ed Birdwell offered me the job, I accepted.

That was the beginning of eight delightful years in Los Angeles. I loved the orchestra and the board, and I made some dear friends. At first I lived in Dick Colburn's pool house in Beverly Hills, but eventually I stayed with my friends Tony Jackson and Marylyn Savage in Pasadena. When I first came to the Los Angeles Chamber Orchestra, the men wore traditional concert attire, but the women wore an array of gowns in different colors and patterns. Part of the reason orchestras wear traditional concert attire is to be less distracting to the music, so I asked the women to wear black for our concerts. This upset my associate concertmaster, Bonnie Douglas, as she liked wearing gowns and had a number of beautiful ones. I pointed out that she could wear them when she appeared as a soloist, which she often did.

The NYCS and LACO were different, and I tried to take the best from each and build on it. LACO had a lyrical quality, as reflected in the principal strings, while the NYCS had a more intense sound. I tried to bring some of Los Angeles's elegance to New York, and some of New York's intensity to Los Angeles. Of course I would never compare the orchestras or for that matter discuss one with the other. The rehearsals in Los Angeles were very interesting because the concertmaster, Paul Shure, talked quite a bit, and I wasn't used to that. For the most part, though, he simply confirmed my ideas.

The personnel of the orchestra were a tangle of interrelationships. Shure's wife, Bonnie Douglas, was the assistant concertmaster. The principal viola, Janet Lakatos, and principal cello, Doug Davis, were a couple, and when we appointed Ilkka Talvi to be the principal second, his wife, Judy Allers, sat on the first stand with him. To complicate matters even more, Ilkka's future second wife, Marjorie Kransberg, was also in his section. The wind players were all-stars, led by Allan Vogel, the first oboe. Dave Shostac, a classmate of mine at Juilliard, was the first flute, David Shifrin was the first clarinet, and Ken Mundy was the first bassoon. After the first season I appointed Robin Graham as first horn. Robin was married to my dear friend John Cerminaro, who was then principal horn of the Los Angeles Philharmonic. They were all fine players. In another interesting coincidence, Bonnie came from Seattle, and when she and Paul retired from Los Angeles studio life, they moved back to Seattle. Ilkka was for many years the concertmaster of the Seattle Symphony. Marjorie became Ilkka's wife and the concertmaster of the Pacific Northwest Ballet and the Northwest Chamber Orchestra. David Shifrin moved to New York and played for a time with the New York Chamber Symphony. When Doug Davis retired, he also moved to the Pacific Northwest and played some principal cello for me in Seattle while we were looking for a new principal. Robin and John divorced, and Robin became principal with the Cincinnati Symphony; she married Bob Elias, who, for a short time during my last year at LACO was our executive director. There's still more: my composer friend Henri Lazarof, who taught at UCLA, married Janice Taper, Mark Taper's daughter. When we were building Benaroya Hall in Seattle, Janice gave a gift to name the auditorium the Mark Taper Foundation Auditorium. Deborah Rutter worked for the Los Angeles Philharmonic, and after my time in Los Angeles she became the executive director of LACO. She then became the executive director of the Seattle Symphony with me for ten years. The music world is a small one.

Ed Birdwell chose the Wilshire Ebell Theatre as our new home for my first season as music director. Although the acoustics were not perfect, the Wilshire Ebell had an important history in Los Angeles.

I always tried to give a feeling for the direction of the season at the opening concerts. For the 1978–1979 season opening, I programmed Diamond's *Rounds*, a Vivaldi violin concerto, and Ravel's *Tzigane*, played by the young violinist Elmar Oliveira, who had recently won the gold medal at the International Tchaikovsky Competition in Moscow. After intermission we did Debussy's *Sacred and Profane Dances*, played by another young soloist, Nancy Allen, followed by the Schubert Fifth Symphony. The program presaged the direction of our season: American music by one of our great living composers, two highly gifted young soloists, and a traditional major work for chamber orchestra. And that was the kind of programming I did throughout my eight years in Los Angeles. After the opening series I went to Ed and Nancy Birdwell's home for dinner. That night was Carlo Maria Giulini's opening concert as music director of the Los Angeles Philharmonic, a post he held from 1978 to 1984. I had played with him in New York, when he did a matchless Bruckner Ninth. The orchestra had not played the symphony in quite a long time, and at the first rehearsal, it fell apart and we had to stop. The first oboe, Harold Gomberg, stood up and asked Giulini if he could be clearer—more like Mr. Reiner used to be. That stopped the rehearsal dead in its tracks. Giulini said simply, "I'm sorry, Mr. Gomberg, but I am not such a good conductor"—and won the orchestra's heart.

At those concerts Giulini fell in love with John Cerminaro's horn playing. After I left the New York Philharmonic and Zubin Mehta had taken over as music director, Giulini and the executive director of the L.A. Philharmonic made Cerminaro an offer that he accepted, and John moved to L.A. Ed, Nancy, and I heard the live radio broadcast of the L.A. Philharmonic's opening concert with their new music director. The one thing I remember during that broadcast was that the intermission featured a discussion between Ernest Fleischmann, the executive director of the orchestra, and Martin Bernheimer, the chief critic of the *Los Angeles Times*. I was floored when I heard

Ernest ask Martin what he thought Maestro Giulini's strengths and weaknesses were. Asking this very important and distinguished critic about the new music director's weaknesses? Clearly Ernest, who had worked so hard to get Giulini to come to Los Angeles, was already working against him. The orchestra loved Giulini, and in his seventh and final season he asked the orchestra for their help. The players couldn't understand, and only after his departure was announced did they realize that Giulini was asking them to help him stay on as music director. Years later André Previn told me that before accepting the music director position in Los Angeles, he met Giulini in Europe. Giulini warned him about Ernest, but André, who had grown up in Los Angeles, felt he could handle Ernest. In the end, though, André's L.A. story was not dissimilar to Giulini's.

During that first season with LACO we began traveling to play concerts south of Los Angeles, and we also started a chamber music series. Eventually we played concerts in Santa Barbara, San Diego, El Cajon, Irvine, La Jolla, Palm Springs, Orange County, Santa Ana, and the Redlands, as well as at Claremont College and Royce at UCLA. In my second season we began our residency at Ambassador College and did our first tour to the East Coast, including Carnegie Hall. Ambassador College was a bit controversial. They were associated with the Worldwide Church of God, and Ambassador Auditorium was the meeting-place for their services. But the college had a long and important commitment to classical music; in fact, the hall opened in 1974 with Giulini conducting the Vienna Symphony. Now LACO finally had a real home. We had our offices there, we could rehearse there either onstage or in a rehearsal room on campus, and the church elders never interfered with our programming. Whenever we did any work with a text, we had to submit the text, but no one ever objected to anything. They also provided us some very important financial support.

We started doing the Brandenburg concertos in December 1979 and maintained that tradition, as I was doing in New York. Two things put the orchestra on the map: the many recordings we were doing for Nonesuch and Delos, and the East Coast tour in February 1980. The tour repertoire included Haydn's Symphonies Nos. 89 and 96, excerpts from Handel's *Water Music*, Edvard Greig's *Holberg Suite*, the Bach Double Concerto for Violin and Oboe, Beethoven's First Piano Concerto, Bill Conti's *Kinesis*, and Mozart's Piano Concerto in E-flat Major, K. 271. We first played concerts in Los Angeles, Claremont College, Palm Springs, and the East County Performing Arts Center. Then we went to Toronto; Montreal; Lake Placid; Montclair, New Jersey; the 92nd Street Y; the University of New Hampshire; Dartmouth College; Carnegie Hall; and the Kennedy Center. We did the premiere of Bill Conti's piece at the Winter Olympics in Lake Placid; it was broadcast on NPR.

One day in 1977 Jacques Leiser, a manager who worked with a number of Soviet artists, asked me to come to his office to hear a pianist with whom I was unfamiliar play a recital that had been recorded live in Italy. She had given a stellar performance of Frédéric Chopin's Sonata No. 2, and I immediately wanted to work with her. After the meeting I went to Juilliard, where I was teaching that day, and ran into a student, Dmitry Sitkovetsky, a very talented violinist. I asked him if he knew the pianist Bella Davidovich. He laughed and said, "Yes, she's my mother!" I laughed too, thinking he was joking. Later that day I saw him again and said, "Seriously, who is Bella Davidovich?" He said, "Seriously, she really is my mother." Dmitry is now a famous soloist and conductor, and he and I have been close friends ever since that day at Juilliard in 1977. That was also the beginning of a long and delightful relationship with Bella, and it was how we ended up together at Carnegie Hall that season for her New York orchestral debut.

The concert with the orchestra at Carnegie Hall was memorable. Bella played extraordinarily and the orchestra soloists in the Bach shone. The chief critic of the *New York Times*, Harold Schonberg, wrote: "Normally chamber orchestras are not big business, but there is something in Mr. Schwarz that seems to evoke real excitement in his followers. . . . The Los Angeles Chamber Orchestra is a cohesive group with good tone and an obvious involvement with what it is doing. Mr. Schwarz is a spirited conductor with a fine ear . . . with talent on this order there is no place for him but up." The headline in the *New York Post* was "Los Angeles can be proud."

The tour was a highlight of my years with LACO. In addition, the great advantage of having two chamber orchestras was the possibility of repeating repertoire and working together to commission new works. Soloists could also be given more exposure so artists like Yo-Yo Ma, Szeryng, Arrau, Oliveira, Salerno-Sonnenberg, Gary Graffman, Sitkovetsky, Firkušný, Ax, Gutiérrez, Johannesen, and others could appear in both places. Carol Rosenberger appeared often, as did Elly Ameling. Helmuth Rilling, a regular guest conductor, did a South American tour of Bach's Mass in B Minor with the orchestra. We shared new works by Creston, Starer, Bergsma, Stock, Schwantner, Rosenman, and Kraft, often doing the world premiere in L.A. followed by the New York premiere. I particularly remember one program during my final season on which I did Mendelssohn's First Symphony. When it was premiered, Mendelssohn had not completed the Scherzo, so he orchestrated the one from his Octet for Strings and used it as the Scherzo for the first performance. After writing the Scherzo as it exists in the work today, he took the Scherzo from the octet and had it stand alone as a short work for small orchestra. I thought it would be interesting to program them together: first do the octet Scherzo, and then the First Symphony. That is what I did, but the program annotator did not mention the connection between the two works. When the review came out in the *Los Angeles Times*, the critic was very critical of my uncharacteristic orchestration of the octet Scherzo!

During those years there was only one recurring issue: finances. As a chamber orchestra we were always the little guy compared to the Philharmonic, and most of the important donors supported the activities at the Music Center. There wasn't one season when we could relax even a little bit, and each year we seemed to be on the brink of folding. Ernest Fleischmann once wrote about developing an orchestra community of 150 players that would perform a variety of genres and style: new music, chamber music, opera, ballet, and so forth. I therefore met with Ernest to talk about merging the two orchestras to create this dream orchestra. We would maintain a certain degree of independence, but he would oversee the complete operation. In the end, he said that although he was intrigued, he thought the Philharmonic musicians would not like the idea.

By 1985 I was music director of Lincoln Center's Mostly Mozart Festival, the Waterloo Festival, the NYCS, LACO, and the Seattle Symphony, which I had started conducting in 1983: three orchestras, two summer festivals, and a lot of guest conducting.

I had a great deal of energy, but with all the administrative work required, something had to go. I loved working with all the gifted musicians of LACO. I liked the board members and had many close friends. When Seattle came into the picture, though, I thought I should give up one chamber orchestra. They were both excellent, and I loved conducting them, but in the end I decided to give up LACO. Eventually I gave up the Waterloo Festival as well—two festivals simultaneously were too much.

The LACO board was not happy about my leaving. During my last year I helped the orchestra become involved with the newly founded Los Angeles Opera, and the players asked me to help them choose the next music director. They wanted Christof Perick, and they thought the board was interested in Neville's concertmaster of the Academy, Iona Brown. Dick Colburn thought having a violinist/leader, rather than a conductor, would create more of the desired separation between LACO and the Philharmonic. Iona didn't conduct, so she was their choice.

Delos

During my first season as music director of LACO, we programmed a chamber music series at the Wilshire Ebell Theatre. In the audience were Amelia S. Haygood, of the Los Angeles–based record company Delos, and Carol Rosenberger, a pianist who did most of the label's artistic advising. I played the trumpet in one of those concerts in January 1979, among my last as an instrumentalist. Amelia and Carol wanted to make some recordings of my trumpet playing. Though touched by their interest, I had to tell them I planned to stop playing soon and wouldn't be playing any concerts to support disc sales. But they persisted. If they believed in something musically, the business aspect always came second.

Amelia Haygood, who died in 2007, was the president of Delos and also a psychologist. She was a remarkable person. The talented pianist Carol Rosenberger was equally involved in the company.

We made two recordings of trumpet music: *The Classic Trumpet Concertos of Haydn and Hummel* and *The Sound of Trumpets*. For the latter, which consisted of baroque repertoire, I formed the New York Trumpet Ensemble; and the orchestra for both was the 92nd Street Y Chamber Symphony. We recorded at the Masonic Temple Auditorium on Twenty-third Street.

Our concerto recording was the first digital recording made in New York with Soundstream of Salt Lake City. Ellen Taaffe Zwilich was our producer, and my dear friend from high school Fred Miller assisted. I did not realize the importance of the event, but many critics and music writers were listening to and analyzing this new digital system. My feeling—and it has not changed to this day—was that the most important element of a successful recording, from an engineering standpoint, was the microphones used and the placement of those microphones.

Ronnie Roseman's gorgeous oboe playing and the work of the flutist Tom Nyfenger really stood out on those recordings, as did the work, on *The Sound of Trumpets*, of Neil Balm, Ed Carroll, Mark Gould, Raymond Mase, James Miller, Robert Sirinek, and Norman Smith. Soon after, Delos began recording me regularly with LACO. We did works by Beethoven, Dvořák, Handel, Mozart, Prokofiev, Shostakovich, Stravinsky, and Vivaldi. One of the most memorable was the complete Handel's *Water Music*. I wrote these crazy ornaments for the first oboe, Allan Vogel, on a flight from New York to Los Angeles. I also wrote ornaments for our first horn, Robin Graham, and eventually for everyone else.

In 1978 my friend the violinist Elmar Oliveira, who won the gold medal at the Sixth Tchaikovsky International Competition in Moscow, and Amelia and Carol wanted to record the Vivaldi *Four Seasons* with him. We were scheduled to do the recording at Little Bridges at Claremont College in Ontario, California. When Elmar arrived at JFK airport, he saw the word "Ontario" and thought it was Ontario,

Canada. He said that he was going to Los Angeles and changed his flight to LAX in Los Angeles, which made him an hour and a half late for the session. We were well rehearsed when he finally arrived, and his playing was so phenomenal that we'd lost no time. It remains one of my favorite recordings of the *Four Seasons*. The other recording I'm very proud of is the collaboration we did for PBS of Stravinsky's *L'histoire du soldat* (The Soldier's Tale) with the animator Robert Blechman in 1982. Carol Rosenberger was and still is a superb artist. Because of a childhood illness she was not able to have a rigorous performing career, but we made many recordings together. She recorded the Beethoven Fourth Piano Concerto, Falla's *Nights in the Gardens of Spain*, Richard Strauss's *Burlesque*, Shostakovich's First Concerto, some Haydn concertos, and Howard Hanson's Piano Concerto.

Nonesuch

When I was in high school, Nonesuch Records was my favorite label besides Columbia. Columbia was the label that recorded the New York Philharmonic, Cleveland, and Philadelphia. But Nonesuch LPs sold for a dollar. They had many English imports and some very interesting performances. A young music enthusiast could buy some wonderful recordings for only a dollar.

When I met Tracey Sterne, the head of Nonesuch in New York, we became friends. She liked my trumpet playing, but later, when I became a conductor, she lost interest. She didn't care about conductors; she was interested in instrumentalists, singers, and repertoire. At the time Gil Kalish was her pianist, Jan DeGaetani her mezzo-soprano, and William Bolcom her composer. Bill and his wife, the singer Joan Morris, did some fantastic recordings of popular songs, mostly from what's now called the American Songbook. Arthur Weisberg did a fabulous series of new-music recordings for chamber ensemble. Those recordings received a great deal of critical attention and strongly influenced the contemporary music scene. Nonesuch was one of only two labels—the other was CRI—that did such excellent performances of important new music.

My early award-winning record, *Cornet Favorites*, was made under

Tracey's auspices. I remember how I persuaded her to do it. We were having a party at my house in New Jersey, and Bill Bolcom and Tracey were there. Toward the end of the evening Bill and I read through some terrific pieces of Americana by Herbert L. Clarke. Everyone just loved the music, especially Bill. Tracey was all for recording it, and that was the beginning of *Cornet Favorites* and later *Cousins*.

When Nonesuch was sold to Elektra Asylum, the big pop label, Jack Holzman moved operations to Los Angeles. Tracey ended up leaving, and Jack hired his brother Keith to run Nonesuch. The critics, who loved Tracey, immediately attacked Nonesuch, and the label had to try to do something of significance to redeem itself. They hired me and LACO to make a series of recordings for them. We did about twenty, and I'm really proud of them all. Disappointingly, however, very few were ever released on CD.

CHAPTER NINE

New–Music Ensembles

My teacher before William Vacchiano was Ronald Anderson. I owe so much to him in terms of my trumpet playing, but equally important was his influence in guiding me to study and understand new music and early music. In the early 1960s the important new music ensemble was the Group for Contemporary Music at Columbia University, directed by Harvey Sollberger, a flutist and composer, and the pianist and composer Charles Wuorinen. Ronnie was their trumpet player, and on occasion they would ask me to join them when they needed a second trumpet. I played with the Group in the Lincoln Center French American Festival for both Varèse and Stravinsky.

In 1967 we were playing Chou Wen-chung's *Pien*, a chamber work with a major piano solo and an ensemble of fifteen players. Harvey Sollberger was the conductor and Charles Wuorinen, the solo pianist. We were paid only a small honorarium, so the rehearsals were scheduled around the players' individual professional commitments. With so many musicians involved, we usually rehearsed at eleven o'clock in the evening or even later. We probably spent a month rehearsing the piece bar by bar. It was very tedious, but everyone seemed totally committed.

Both trumpet parts had primarily single notes rather than phrases, with many mute changes. Finally we did a run-through of the whole work. It was difficult to remember what had happened at the beginning of the rehearsal period, and after my panic about playing all these isolated notes with the difficult mute changes, we arrived at the end of the piece. I didn't have much of an idea of what had happened, but I was very happy to have gotten through my part without any accidents. Just then Ronnie leaned over to me and said, "Great piece!" I was stunned. How could he tell? I'd been so busy just trying to get through my part!

That experience increased my desire to do more contemporary music, which ultimately led to my involvement with both Speculum Musicae and Music Today.

Speculum Musicae

New-music ensembles were popping up everywhere. The most successful was the Contemporary Chamber Ensemble (CCE), co-founded by Wuorinen and Arthur Weisberg in 1961. Weisberg, the group's conductor, was a remarkable bassoonist and a terrific conductor of complex contemporary music. The group established a residency at Rutgers University, toured the world, gave more than a hundred world premieres, and recorded for Nonesuch Records.

In the 1960s and early '70s new music was being written mainly for ensembles rather than orchestras, and most of the important American composers were writing for the CCE. Some friends of mine wanted to start their own group as a kind of outgrowth of the Group of Contemporary Music. They also wanted it to be flexible enough to make touring possible, and any member who was interested would be allowed to conduct.

So Speculum Musicae ("mirror of music") was founded in 1971, led by pianist Ursula Oppens, violinist Rolf Schulte, cellist Fred Sherry, clarinetist Virgil Blackwell, and percussionist Richard Fitz. Another group of musicians would be added as needed. After winning an audition for Susan Wadsworth and Young Concert Artists, Speculum Musicae started touring and getting important exposure in New York.

Speculum Musicae became known for its playing of composers from the academic avant-garde, such as Wuorinen and Carter. By this time I had joined the New York Philharmonic, but I continued to work with Speculum Musicae as my Philharmonic schedule permitted. I was given Luigi Dallapiccola's *Piccola musica notturna* to conduct with the group, and I later conducted it in Israel, New York, and Los Angeles.

I also conducted Carter's Double Concerto for piano, harpsichord, and sixteen players divided into two chamber orchestras of eight players each. Ursula played the piano solo, and Paul Jacobs played the harpsichord. I had already conducted Carter's Piano Concerto in Aspen, so I was familiar with all the difficult conductor-related issues in his music, but there was a new challenge in store.

There is one sixty-four-measure section in Carter's Double Concerto where you have to conduct three in one hand against four in the other, with the beginning of each bar coordinated. I asked Pierre Boulez, "How do I do this and turn the pages?" He told me to make a cheat sheet consisting of a series of cues that could fit on two pages. I would rehearse two pages at a time, but for the run-through and the concert I used the cheat sheet of rhythmic, dynamic, and orchestration cues. It worked great, and I still have the cheat sheet.

Two years later Boulez was conducting the Double Concerto with the New York Philharmonic. He told me he had heard from Elliott about how wonderful my performance was. He had one question: How did I do the sixty-four measures of three against four? I told him the story, and he was amused—he had forgotten he'd suggested I make a cue sheet. He asked me if he could borrow it. When he returned it, I asked him how he liked it, and he said he'd had only one problem—when I wrote the abbreviation "TT" for tenor trombone, he was confused, since he used "TT" for tam-tam, or gong. We had a laugh about it, but from then on I always used "TT" for tam-tam and "pos" (the abbreviation for *Posaune*, the German word for trombone) for tenor trombone.

I once said to Leonard Bernstein, "When it's all said and done, as great a conductor as you are, we are all servants of the composers. The composers are the real geniuses. We're the artists who reproduce what those creative artists write. I think you should forget about conducting and just focus on your great, great, music because you are a great composer."

Bernstein argued with me; he said that new music was headed down a very treacherous path. Although he declared the symphony dead, he had grown up in the 1940s, when new music meant the accessible works of William Schuman, David Diamond, Aaron Copland, and Roy Harris. Bernstein himself still wrote in a tonal, accessible way, even though he freely made use of new techniques and styles, such as serialism, aleatorism, and jazz, to express his ideas. It was his belief that even though unusual imaginative ideas had their place, music had to be grounded. It was hard for him to understand how serial and aleatoric music would contribute to great and meaningful art, and where he would fit into music history.

I was in the audience for Bernstein's appearances at his Avant-Garde Festival with the Philharmonic in January 1964. For half of every program he would perform unusual music by Larry Austin, Morton Subotnik, John Cage, and others. I think the festival demonstrated clearly that even though these styles were championed by a number of modern composers, they did not represent the right direction for music.

Peter Mennin, a fine composer and once the president of Juilliard, said to me: "It doesn't matter what style you write in. Write any way you want. You can write with serial techniques or tonal music. It's a question of personality. When I listen to or look at a work, and if the composer has a distinctive style of writing, then it's successful as far as I'm concerned. It doesn't matter to me what style that is."

Every one of the great composers, whether Sibelius or Richard Strauss or Wagner, has a distinctive style or voice. This does not mean that Strauss's *Rosenkavalier* is the same as his *Elektra*, but both are in his voice. The music of the internationalists—those without a strong nationalistic bent—and of those composers who utilize extended aleatoric and serial elements, tends to lack that distinctive voice. I believe works with individual voice and grounded musical emotions will have an extended life span, because this emotional connection is what we all crave from music.

The Birth of Music Today

By the late 1970s I had the idea of creating a new-music ensemble that I would conduct, one that would not be aligned with any particular style of contemporary music. I wanted to stay in touch with what was going on with the younger generation of composers and at the same time do older twentieth-century works that might be hard to program for a more traditional symphonic audience.

A friend suggested I create the Schwarz Concerts, similar to what Serge Koussevitsky had done in Paris in 1920–1924 when he created the Grands Concerts Symphoniques Koussevitsky. He played two concerts a year of new music by composers such as Honegger, Prokofiev, Ravel, Alexandre Tansman, Ernst Toch, and Stravinsky. I agreed to the project, and decided on the title "Music Today" to reflect not only the music being written today, but the performance today of all twentieth-century music.

I will always be grateful to Lydia Kontos for establishing this series. I conducted three programs each season at Merkin Hall at the Hebrew Arts Center for Music and Dance on Sixty-seventh Street in Manhattan. André Emelianoff assisted me in all the programming. We had a core ensemble drawn mostly from the NYCS, as well as many guest soloists and extra musicians. Jonathan Haas and Neil Balm helped in every other way, not only by playing the percussion and trumpet parts flawlessly but by making musical suggestions and dealing with personnel issues.

Music Today's debut concert, in September 1981, featured a premiere by Edward Barnes, a recent Juilliard graduate, and other works by established contemporary composers. Edward played the piano in his Concerto for Piano, Percussion and Strings, inspired by passages from a Sam Shepard play. We also did Wallingford Riegger's *Study in Sonority*, for ten violins, and Milton Babbitt's *Correspondences*, for strings and synthesized tape. We concluded with Schoenberg's string-orchestra version of his Second String Quartet with the soprano Margaret Chalker.

Other highlights of Music Today: we celebrated the 100th anniversary of Percy Grainger's birth; we did the New York premiere of Stephen Albert's half-hour song cycle *Into Eclipse* prior to his winning the Pulitzer Prize for the work; we premiered and recorded George Perle's Serenade No. 3, which was nominated for a Grammy Award; we did the premiere of Stephen Albert's *Treestone*; we celebrated

George Perle's seventieth birthday and premiered Bernard Rands's prizewinning *Canti del sol* in the chamber version; and we programmed a series to celebrate the centennial of the birth of Heitor Villa-Lobos.

Around this time I was introduced to the music of Andrzej Panufnik. In 1982 I was conducting in London when Bernard Jacobson and Janice Suskind, from Boosey and Hawkes, asked me if I might be interested in doing a work of his that had never been performed. They gave me a score, and I became a huge fan. We premiered Panufnik's *Arbor Cosmica* for twelve strings in November 1984. Of that concert, John Rockwell wrote in the *New York Times*: "Over the last three seasons, Gerard Schwarz's Music Today at the Abraham Goodman House, has established itself as one of the most interesting, non-polemical new-music series in town. This season's first concert, Wednesday night, handsomely reaffirmed that distinction. The most newsworthy item on the program was a world premiere, of *Arbor Cosmica*, by the seventy-year-old Andrzej Panufnik . . . what counts is quality and Mr. Panufnik's would seem to have that virtue; certainly *Arbor Cosmica* did." The rest of the program consisted of George Perle's Concertino (1979), played by Richard Goode; William Schuman's 1980 concert version of his score for Martha Graham, *Night Journey* (1947); and Aaron Jay Kernis's *Morningsongs* (1983). Over the years we also premiered works by Richard Danielpour, Jacob Druckman, Lukas Foss, Gerald Levinson, Cliff Martinez, William Mayer, George Rochberg, Christopher Rouse, Joseph Schwantner, George Tsontakis, Richard Wernick, and Ellen Taaffe Zwilich, among others. It was at one of our first concerts that I met the young Chinese composer Bright Sheng, who later became composer-in-residence at the Seattle Symphony and composer-in-residence at the New York City Ballet. Bright is now the Leonard Bernstein Distinguished University Professor of Composition at the University of Michigan–Ann Arbor.

By 1989, however, I could no longer keep up with the demands of the project. I turned it over to André Emelianoff, who became Music Today's music advisor, and Jon Haas and Neil Balm, who managed it.

CHAPTER TEN

Mostly Mozart

The New York Philharmonic used Philharmonic Hall at Lincoln Center from October through June, but it was vacant in July and August. This was a financial burden, and because one of the primary mandates of the Center was to "encourage, sponsor or facilitate performances," William Schuman, the Center's president, wanted classical music performed there during the summer. He believed that many music lovers, both local and visiting, would attend concerts if they were popular and well marketed. He had a number of allies in the quest: Schuyler Chapin, the Lincoln Center programming director; William Lockwood, his young assistant; and two independent producers, Jay K. Hoffman and George F. Schutz. The first successful test was in the summer of 1963, when they produced a short festival, August Fanfare, that led to Midsummer Serenades: A Mozart Festival in August 1966. The attraction was Mozart, affordability (tickets were $3.00), and informality. The festival grew from four weeks to seven weeks; changed its name to Mostly Mozart; expanded the repertoire to include Haydn, Schubert, and Beethoven; and served an audience that loved classical music and embraced the spirit of a festival that did not challenge them with a broad repertoire.

The lack of a music director left all the decision making in the hands of Lockwood, and Loren Glickman, the personnel manager and first bassoon. Loren was a fine musician and an excellent personnel manager for the festival, and he gave Bill some wonderful advice. Bill knew music and artists and had a knack for marketing. The orchestra had excellent musicians, but neither Bill nor Loren could help in terms of performance. Though in the beginning the festival concerts were very well received by the audience and press, eventually the reviews focused on the repetitive, narrow programming and on the fact that the orchestra did not always have a high level of ensemble playing.

In 1978 Bill Lockwood, by that time the director of programming, invited me to play-conduct at the Mostly Mozart Festival. Instrumentalists like me or Pinchas Zukerman would play a concerto and conduct the remainder of the program. On my first concert I played the Haydn Trumpet Concerto, and the main work was Mozart's Symphony No. 39.

At the same time the White Mountains Festival in New Hampshire was looking for a music director. Carlos Moseley, president of the New York Philharmonic, recommended me to David Dana, chairman of the White Mountains Festival board. and with Carlos's enthusiastic endorsement I was appointed music director.

I continued to conduct Mostly Mozart, including the opening of the 1980 season, for the next few years. Donal Henahan, of the *New York Times*, wrote: "Mr. Schwarz, with about 40 players under his control at every moment, led a splendid performance of Mozart's *Jupiter Symphony* that was both precise and robust, not the easiest qualities to meld persuasively. . . . Mr. Schwarz had definite ideas about balancing the instrumental choirs that promoted a lucid shining sound."

Mostly Mozart continued as a very popular festival, brilliantly marketed and with an excellent orchestra. However, there was no music director to give the orchestra a musical personality. The orchestra generally received mediocre reviews, though the audience didn't seem to care. They did the same pieces over and over again, and the audience didn't mind that either. In 1982, however, the remarkable Martin Segal, chairman of the board at Lincoln Center and a brilliant campaigner for the arts, went to Bill and said, "Bill, we have to do better. We need a music director."

Being chosen for Mostly Mozart was an extraordinary opportunity for me. Of course, most talented conductors have many opportunities when they are starting out. When you are thirty, everyone thinks you are going to be the next Leonard Bernstein. When you are forty, someone else is going to be the next Bernstein. I am not sure how I was selected, but it helped that I was a New Yorker. I knew the Mostly Mozart people, and I knew the players. I knew what it would take to make them into a cohesive orchestra, and I was curious about repertoire. But it was a lot of responsibility for a young conductor. In 1982 I accepted the title of Music Advisor, and in 1984 my title was changed to Music Director. Mostly Mozart was always a part of Lincoln Center, Inc., so no one ever discussed the possibility of our becoming a constituent. Unlike the other organizations I was involved in, which obligated me to do fund-raising, Lincoln Center provided the resources for all our needs. On the other hand, if we wanted to do something more than the seven weeks in New York and the one week in Washington, it had to pay for itself. Our task was to occupy the hall and to present popular programs. There was never any ambition for us to do more, like touring or recording, unless it could pay for itself without incurring a deficit or requiring fund-raising.

The Philharmonic was happy to have us there because it lessened the portion of the deficit for which they were responsible. We kept Fisher Hall busy in the summer, and we seemed to be bringing in a new audience who did not usually attend classical concerts. I thought the casual atmosphere and the reasonable ticket prices were major contributors to the makeup of the audience and the remarkable attendance numbers.

The transition to having a music director was a somewhat sensitive one. I became much more involved with choosing the soloists, programs, conductors, and personnel in the orchestra. That was difficult for Loren, because until I came along he had not had to report to anyone but Bill. Loren was an excellent musician with a good ear, and he knew a great deal. He was also a very loyal person, and he had his favorites. It was tricky for me at first to make the necessary moves to improve the orchestra, but in the end Loren, Bill, and I developed an excellent working relationship.

My first contract was for five years. You can't do much in less; you need to stay and commit yourself. If you don't have a real musical vision, that is a different issue; but making an artistic impact takes time.

Marty wanted the whole atmosphere of the festival to change—to be invigorated with new ideas. Bill supported the changes in the orchestra but wasn't wild about the expansion into more challenging repertoire. Loren supported the repertoire changes but didn't like my involvement with personnel. Heidi Waleson wrote in the *New York Times Magazine*, "In 1982, the 16-year-old Mostly Mozart Festival was in trouble, with critics talking about poor playing and morale, and increasingly stale programming." That was how things stood when I began my tenure in 1982.

When I began rehearsing, we dealt not only with the overall musical conception of the work at hand, but also with the crucial elements of ensemble, rhythm, intonation, balance, string quality, and phrasing. I believe that the musical concept and the sound quality of the orchestra affect everything, and I felt that if the orchestra embraced my concept of a sound––dark, warm, rich—and followed my concept of the piece—the musical details of the phrase markings and the varied articulations and bowings—we could create a cohesive ensemble and an awareness of excellence. If I presented the road map, we could get there together.

Since each season began with my conducting for two weeks, one at the Kennedy Center in Washington, D.C., and the opening week in New York, I could set the tone for musical expectations for the whole season. Over time we attracted many fine musicians. The reviews improved, and people were starting to appreciate the orchestra. They asked for more money—and received it. They became a tenured orchestra and won better conditions for themselves and more control over their professional lives. Loren would say it became less homey, less familial, and more of a job. The musicians called it more professional. Musicians tend to want to rehearse less, but the Mostly Mozart orchestra was always a hard-working orchestra. Festivals are not like full-time positions—you anticipate working harder.

The other important element was expanding the programming within the confines of the Mostly Mozart Festival concept. You want to stimulate the audience, which means you don't play only the chestnuts. On the other hand, the chestnuts need to be played. There is a strong argument for playing this repertoire. The last few times we did Beethoven's Ninth Symphony in Seattle, I discovered that many people in the audience had never heard it live before. At Interlochen I conducted the World Youth Symphony Orchestra, which is made up of young musicians ages fifteen to nineteen, in the Brahms Second Symphony, and I asked how many had ever heard it before, live or recorded. Maybe 20 percent raised their hands. There is so much music to hear that no one can have heard it all, and a fifteen-year-old might easily have missed the Brahms Second. Whatever piece you play, on any concert, it could be someone's first time hearing it.

You have to continue to play the standard repertoire. Orchestras are not museums. In a museum you walk in and look at a painting, often for less than a minute per painting. But if we do not play a particular symphony, it does not get heard in the concert hall. You can hear a recording, which is a great experience; but it is not a live concert.

My job was to make the Mostly Mozart orchestra a first-class orchestra and to invigorate the repertoire. We would do things that were interesting, so that people who wanted to hear something other than the bread and butter of the Mozart repertoire could do so. I could expand our core repertoire considerably if the audience was there. In a way, our success with the audience was a problem because the administrators expected an average attendance of 90 percent of seats sold. When I first came to the festival, they had done only ten or twelve of Mozart's twenty-seven piano concertos. I wanted to do all of them, as well as all the symphonies, all the less familiar operas, the Masonic music, and other important works.

My whole first season was chock-full of beloved chestnuts, but I also programmed a lot of other music, such as Joseph Haydn's opera *L'infedelta delusa*. On another program we did Luigi Cherubini's Symphony in D. Cherubini was a contemporary of Beethoven's, and Beethoven considered Cherubini's Requiem to be the greatest work in that genre ever written. We also did Sergei Prokofiev's *Classical Symphony*, a twentieth-century tribute to the music of the classical era; Mozart's opera *Zaide*; and Brahms's Serenade No. 1 in D Major. We did music by J. C. Bach and C. P. E. Bach, works that had greatly influenced Mozart. We did Tchaikovsky's Orchestral Suite No. 4, better known as *Mozartiana*. All the pieces fell within the framework of Mozart—music by composers whom he influenced and by composers who influenced him. And whenever we wanted to make sure of ticket sales, we did a Vivaldi special. In 1984 we did for the first time Richard Strauss's extraordinary arrangement of Mozart's opera seria *Idomeneo*.

We were playing six concerts a week with four different programs that featured interesting music and great soloists and chamber music groups. Mozart wrote some charming serenades to be played outdoors that we started performing at pre-concerts on the plaza. We did our week at the Kennedy Center, playing many of the same programs, and we held an outdoor dress rehearsal every year. We began playing children's concerts and giving Meet the Artists suppers. To give another perspective on the Mozart season, we also introduced early-instrument ensembles.

We systematically went through all the Mozart symphonies, all the piano concertos, many of the early operas, and all the Mozart arrangements of Handel. When I told Bill I wanted to do the *Messiah* in the Mozart version, he was skeptical. "*Messiah* in the summertime?" I told him it was part of what Mozart did, and that his Handel arrangements should be represented.

Then I said that we had to do it in German.

"How can you do *Messiah* in German?"

"*Messiah* has to be in German because the Mozart version was done in German." That was the whole idea when Baron Gottfried van Swieten commissioned these arrangements: he wanted the great works of Handel to be understood by a large German-speaking audience. Mozart actually changed the rhythms to fit the German language and reorchestrated it in a classical rather than a baroque style, so there was no way to do his version except in German. So Bill went to John Nelson, an old friend of mine who had conducted Mostly Mozart numerous times, and asked his opinion. John said, "How can you do *Messiah* in German? Out of the question." Then he asked Joseph Flummerfelt, from the Westminster Choir, what he thought. Joe said, "How can you do *Messiah* in German?"

Bill came back to me and said, "See? Your colleagues say we can't do this in German." I told him, "Bill, we cannot do the Mozart version in English. Besides, the audience will not know it is in German until they arrive."

Bill was so angry with me that the ad in the *New York Times* said, "Handel's *Messiah*, Mozart version, sung in German." Our two performances of Handel's *Messiah* in German, arranged by Mozart, sold out.

I tried to inaugurate a series on Sunday afternoon that would be less expensive, and I wanted to do a young artists series and a chamber music series at Alice Tully Hall. We did do a bit of that, but it never became a regular part of the festival. I also pushed hard for staged opera. Every year we performed a seldom-heard opera, such as Mozart's *Mitridate, re di Ponto*; *Il re pastore*; *Apollo et Hyacinthus*; *La finta semplice*; *Bastien und Bastienne*; *Ascanio in Alba*; *Lucio Silla*; *La finta giardiniera*; *Thamos, König in Ägypten*; *Zaide*; and *Der Schauspieldirektor*. But I wanted to stage one of the great operas a year. The argument against it was that New York already had the City Opera and the Met—did we really need to be doing opera as well? When City Opera had a season in the summer, I could see that, but once they left the summer season, there was no other opera going on except for what the Met was doing in the parks.

What I wanted to do was an educational program with professionals and students. There would be two casts for whichever opera we were doing, a principal cast and a secondary cast. The secondary cast would be young singers learning from more experienced singers, and the ticket prices for performances with the young singers would be less expensive. The program would also include teaching sessions with the more experienced singers. The same would happen with the director and the assistant director, with the lighting designer and the assistant, and with the costume director and the assistant. There would be a student seminar orchestra, drawn from college students throughout the country, playing for the opera. I selected *La clemenza di Tito*. Julie Taymor agreed to direct, and I had a great cast on hold.

Joseph Polisi, the president of Juilliard, was very much in favor of it, but the idea died because Beverly Sills, who was the chairperson of the

Lincoln Center board, did not support it. What a lost opportunity! It would have been fabulous to do a staged opera at Juilliard's wonderful Peter Sharp Theater.

Early on in my tenure at Mostly Mozart we had an opening for a timpanist. The contract in those days allowed me to choose anyone I liked, so I chose a wonderful musician and timpanist, Mike Crusoe, my timpanist in Seattle. The decision caused some problems with our local players in New York and, by extension, their union. Bill Lockwood asked me many times if it was absolutely necessary to hire Mike. My response was always the same: he was the best musical choice. The union's unhappiness grew. Bill told me that they were planning a protest at our opening night; couldn't I change my mind? When Mike arrived for the first rehearsal, everyone seemed surprised to see that he was African American. Bill asked me why I had not told him, and my answer was simple: the issue was his musicianship, not his race. Interesting that all the threatened protests were abandoned.

In 1985, for Handel's 300th birthday, we did *Alexander's Feast* in the Mozart version and some additional early-instrument programs. We also did Luigi Boccherini for the first time. We did a concert called Mozart in Paris, part of the France Salutes New York Festival. We did all the music Mozart wrote when he was in Paris—*Les petits riens*, the Concerto for Flute and Harp, and the Symphony No. 31 in D ("Paris").

We also had an event called Mozart and the Dance, featuring the New York Baroque Dance Ensemble. We did some things with the Lar Lubovitch Dance Company, and Neville Marriner came with the Academy of St. Martin in the Fields Orchestra. For our Winds Spectacular we did Mozart's Serenade for Thirteen Winds (also known as the "Gran Partita") and Handel's *Royal Fireworks Music*, with fifty wind players. We also did Mozart's version of Handel's oratorio *Acis and Galatea*.

One of my favorite events was the Haydn Week, which we did in 1988. In the middle of that week we did a Haydn marathon, beginning at two in the afternoon and going to ten or eleven at night. We performed vocal works, chamber music, solo piano pieces, and vocal quartets. Kurt Masur came with the Israel Philharmonic for an all-Haydn program with Heinrich Schiff, and we did the *Lord Nelson Mass* with some great soloists—Dawn Upshaw, Jane Bunnell, Vinson Cole, and Jan Opalach. The program notes were written by the renowned Haydn scholar H. C. Robbins Landon, who also hosted the marathon.

Cecilia Bartoli made her American debut with Mostly Mozart in 1990, singing selections from Mozart's *La clemenza di Tito* and Rossini's *La donna del lago*. The Chicago Symphony winds also came, and we had the Canadian Brass, joined by ten assisting principal brass players from the New York Philharmonic and the Boston Symphony, in a big brass spectacular.

It became our tradition at Mostly Mozart to offer programs that offered our audiences something unusual in addition to our standard fare. As Anthony Tommasini wrote in the *New York Times* in August 1997: "That Mozart was a savvy professional-for-hire, was made clear by the festival Music Director, Gerard Schwarz, who conducted an ebullient overture to *La Villanella Rapita*, an opera by Mozart's contemporary, Francesco Bianchi, followed by two extensive scenes composed by Mozart for a subsequent production of that same Bianchi opera. . . . Mr. Schwarz concluded with a shapely and stylish performance of Symphony No. 35 in D, the *Haffner*."

Bill had very strong opinions about guest artists. We didn't stop using the artists Bill liked—James Galway and Jean-Pierre Rampal, for instance—but we added to them. Whenever I worked with someone I really liked in Seattle or Los Angeles or at the NYCS, I'd invite them to Mostly Mozart. We featured such emerging artists as Joshua Bell, Stephen Hough, Midori, and Nadja Salerno-Sonnenberg. At times we used the pre-concert programs as a kind of audition: we would invite a new artist to do one of our pre-concerts, and if we liked them we'd engage them for the following year.

Mostly Mozart was the best-selling event at Lincoln Center. But as we became more innovative, we always had to keep an eye on ticket sales. I wanted to do the Schoenberg Concerto for String Quartet, which I did in 2000 with the Tokyo Quartet. It's based on Handel, and it isn't your usual Schoenberg. The program included Handel's

Concerto Grosso Op. 6 No. 9, Webern's arrangement of the Ricercar from Bach's *The Musical Offering*, and the Schoenberg concerto. We had a rough time selling this fabulous program. You never want to do anything the audience is going to hate. But if people aren't familiar with something, they tend to avoid the concert not because they don't like the music, but because they don't know it.

We always thought we were getting a younger, less affluent, more casual audience because of the way we were marketing the festival, which was completely different from the way classical music is usually promoted. One summer Marty Segal decided to do a major analysis of the audience. It turned out we were getting essentially the same audience at Mostly Mozart who attended the Philharmonic or the Met. So we raised our prices.

The Tokyo Project

At the time Ronald Wilford, the president of Columbia Artists Management and one of the great conductor managers, was my manager, together with Judie Janowski. Around this time a new hall opened in the Shibuya section of Tokyo. Tokyo is a huge city, which has sections, somewhat like New York City's boroughs. The difference is that in New York most cultural life is centered in Manhattan, whereas Tokyo has a little cultural center in each district.

In the Shibuya district, a department store called the Tokyu Department Store wanted to include a cultural center—good for business and good for the area. They built a big complex alongside their flagship store, with a large concert hall, a museum, a movie house, a theater, and a traditional theater for kabuki. Orchard Hall opened with the musicians and singers of the Bayreuth Festival doing *Lohengrin*, with Giuseppe Sinopoli conducting. Because the Bayreuth Festival ensemble had never traveled, it was incredibly complicated—"like moving the entire city," in Ronald's words.

After the first year Tokyu approached my manager and asked for another festival. Ronald suggested they present Mostly Mozart in Tokyo. He had to arrange a marriage between Lincoln Center and Orchard Hall at Tokyu Bunkamura, and we had to make certain it would not create a deficit. At first there was skepticism. Although Bill Lockwood's father was a professor of Asian studies at Princeton, Bill had never been to Japan. George Weissman, the chairman of Lincoln Center, had some issues as he was stationed in Pearl Harbor during the Second World War. Ronald had George meet with the CEO of the Tokyu Group. They connected over their love of cigarettes, as George had been the head of Philip Morris. It was not simple, but Ronald prevailed. It was thrilling to watch it all work out.

We planned to do a two-week season at Bunkamura for three years, starting in 1991; it continued for nine years. We brought most of the programs and important soloists from New York. There was a different program each night, with a rehearsal in the afternoon just before the performance. One year Alexis Weissenberg canceled just prior to the performance. We had other pianists there for other concerts, however, so Lilian Kallir went on without a rehearsal and played a magical performance of the Mozart Concerto No. 19 in F, K. 459. It was a phenomenal musical time for the festival and for all of us involved. Ronald Wilford came for quite a few years and attended every concert; we all had great times together.

Diamond in Tokyo

Beethoven's Ninth Symphony is the most popular classical work in Japan. It's usually performed between Christmas and New Year's Eve, and in Tokyo alone there are probably fifty performances of it each year. In 1996, when the Mostly Mozart Festival had its annual summer residency in Tokyo, we scheduled the Beethoven Ninth, and our hosts at Tokyu Bunkamura decided to commission a work by David Diamond to precede it. The result was his *Ode*, to be premiered at the festival that year. With its subtle quotes of the Japanese national anthem, it preceded the beloved Ninth with a lovely local flavor.

David decided to come for all the festival's nine concerts and also the rehearsals. A great music lover who loved being part of it all, he attended everything. However, we did not begin to rehearse David's *Ode* until the end of the second week of our residency. As we approached the premiere, he became more and more agitated. Then, at his first rehearsal, he made some suggestions about the interpretation in a disagreeable tone. It was one of the few times we ever argued. I told him, "David, we're going to rehearse your *Ode*, and it will be perfect, it will be a great performance, I promise you. I have to alloted time for each piece, so that each piece receives the proper attention, as each matters." By the second rehearsal he had calmed down.

For that performance of the Beethoven Ninth I had an outstanding quartet of soloists— Carol Vaness, Nancy Maultsby, Vinson Cole, and Clayton Brainerd. I usually place the soloists in front of the orchestra, but this time they were in the back, in the front row of the chorus. I prefer to have the chorus enter at the beginning of the performance, staying seated until their entrance in the last movement, and have the soloists enter after the second movement while the orchestra does a little tuning, with the hope that they enter discreetly, to no applause, so there is no disruption of the symphony's flow.

When I looked at the stage before I entered, I noticed that the chorus—all one hundred singers—was missing. I had told the stage manager I wanted the chorus on from the beginning. He assumed that since the soloists were coming on after the second movement, the chorus could do the same. It is hard to avoid some disruption when the soloists enter mid-work, but for the entire chorus to file onstage in the middle of the piece would be too much.

"I'm sorry," I said, "but I want the chorus on now. I would rather wait five minutes now than have the whole piece interrupted by this tremendous stage change after the second movement. Please tell them to put their ties on."

We also did New York State tours with the orchestra, sponsored by New York Telephone. For four years we did programs throughout the state in smaller venues with soloists such as Horacio Gutiérez, Ken Noda, and Young Uck Kim. We also made our debuts at the festivals of Tanglewood and Ravinia, and at the Friends of the Arts Festival on Long Island.

At the end of the 1991 season, we did a concert of the last three Mozart symphonies as the culmination of the bicentennial observation that Lincoln Center mounted for Mozart's death. In the August 26, 1991,

New York Newsday, Tim Page wrote a review and evaluation of my work to date titled "Gerard Schwarz Leads Elegant, Propulsive Mozart":

> This writer recently raised the question of whether it was possible to play too much Mozart—whether the vast amount of his music that has been programmed and recorded in this bicentennial year, might perhaps be too much of a good thing.
>
> On Saturday night at Avery Fisher Hall, Gerard Schwarz and the Mostly Mozart Festival Orchestra offered stunning proof that there are works that are indeed inexhaustible, at least when played with the elegance, propulsion and technical command that distinguished the last festival concert of the year.
>
> Schwarz seems to me an underrated conductor. To be sure, he is generally credited with building the Mostly Mozart orchestra from a fairly lackluster ensemble into the splendidly disciplined group it is today. But one notes a continuing disinclination, among critics and listeners, to take the extra step and recognize him for what he has become—i.e. a first-class Mozartean.
>
> There are several reasons for this hesitancy, I think. To begin with, Schwarz has as they say, "Grown up in public." Having made his initial mark as a dazzlingly brilliant trumpeter while in his early 20s, he was already famous in musical circles before he ever picked up the baton. Experience has taught us to be suspicious of the restless "star" soloist in search of new conquests; for every Vladimir Ashkenazy (who is at least as fine a conductor as he is a pianist) there are a dozen or more pretenders to the podium, engaged time and again because of their instrumental skills, which, unfortunately, do not translate into effective leadership of an orchestra.
>
> Second, Schwarz was, in his early years as a conductor, all but ubiquitous. At one point, he was the Music Director of the New York Chamber Symphony of the 92nd St Y, The Seattle Symphony, The Los Angeles Chamber Orchestra, the Mostly Mozart Festival, and the Music Today series at Merkin Concert Hall—simultaneously. It was an exhaustive, rigorous—and highly diversified—seasoning, but the market was just flooded with Gerard Schwarz.

Still, I'll go out on a limb and call Saturday's concert the most sustained exciting presentation of Mozart's orchestral music I've heard this year (and I've heard lots of them). Schwarz has evolved his own distinctive conception of Mozart's style: His readings are marked by sinuous clarity, directness of emotional argument and a refusal to dawdle (that does not, however, preclude disciplined, caloric, luxuriance in the slower movements). To those attuned to the ruminative Mozart interpretations of an earlier generation, Schwarz' readings may occasionally sound driven; to those who favor the clipped dance rhythms of the "early musickers," it is likely that Saturday's concert seemed overly subjective and romanticized. As a listener who believes in many ways to approach a masterpiece (or, rather, a trio of masterpieces: Mozart's last three symphonies) I found Schwarz' performances eminently satisfying.

There were many felicitous details throughout the evening, but the finale from the "Jupiter" symphony calls out for special attention. This wonderfully expressive and affirmative music is also a formal miracle: a sustained, intricate, five-part counterpoint exercise, perfectly accomplished. Schwarz and the Mostly Mozart Orchestra offered a fleet, joyous performance that exulted in its own virtuosity from the first rustle of the strings to the last thunder of the tympani.

Live from Lincoln Center

When I was growing up, there wasn't much on television, but every once in a while on a Sunday night you could catch the Chicago Symphony. And of course, I never missed a Young People's Concert with the New York Philharmonic and Leonard Bernstein.

As a member of the Philharmonic I participated in the last Young People's Concert with the New York Philharmonic when CBS tried to keep it going with Michael Tilson Thomas. Then, in 1976, the cellist John Goberman came before the Philharmonic and asked us to participate in the first *Live from Lincoln Center* program. I knew John from our days as freelance musicians in New York. I also knew the work of his father, Max Goberman, who had conducted a wonderful series of Haydn symphony recordings I owned, as well as a great deal of Vivaldi.

Hot lights seemed to be a big problem for the television recordings. However, John had new cameras that did not require any additional lighting. The fees were small, and everyone was to be paid the same. For me, to be on television, radio, or a recording was very important. The orchestra eventually agreed, and the first program, conducted by André Previn, with Van Cliburn as soloist, included Strauss's *Ein Heldenleben* and the Grieg Piano Concerto. The program was being done for PBS, which became the new outlet for great music.

During my twenty years at the helm of Mostly Mozart, we did twelve *Live from Lincoln Center* shows. It was always a joy to work with Goberman. He wanted to create outstanding shows with wide audience appeal, which we did with conservative programming and important soloists: the violinists Bell, Perlman, Shaham, and Zukerman; the pianists Ax, Cherkassky, Feltsman, Gutiérrez, Larrocha, and Watts; the flutist James Galway; and many singers. We even had Werner Klemperer narrate a complete performance of Mozart's singspiel *Der Schauspieldirektor* (*The Impresario*). These programs, with one exception, were always on opening night, and I believe this had a positive effect on ticket sales for the rest of the season. The one time we televised our final concert, ticket sales were slow for the beginning of the season. It was almost as if the television broadcast announced to the audience we were at Fisher Hall and the season had begun. Our most successful broadcast in terms of television audience was my last, in 2001. The program featured Emanuel Ax playing the Mozart Concerto No. 22, K. 482, on the first half, and then, after intermission, we did the Mozart Requiem (as completed by his student Franz Süssmayr), followed by his exquisite *Ave verum corpus*. The superb soloists—Uta Selbig, Florence Quivar, Michael Schade, and Richard Zeller—and chorus produced a performance that was nominated for a prime-time Emmy.

John Goberman spent a great deal of time and effort to make the intermissions interesting. They were never scripted, but they were thoroughly discussed. Of course, Bill Lockwood played a key role in these talks and always advocated for a broadcast. This was not automatic as priority was given to the New York Philharmonic, along with the Metropolitan Opera, the Chamber Music Society, the New York City Ballet, and other ensembles that are constituent ensembles of Lincoln Centers. Mostly Mozart was not a constituent. The programs were always very exciting for the orchestra, the soloists, and me, and certainly they were high-pressure events. Kirk Browning was the director of most if not all of my shows; he was truly a great artist. John Goberman and I remain good friends, and he has given me some wonderful advice and guidance for my current All-Star Orchestra TV/Educational project.

Mostly Mozart: Fighting for its Life

In 1993, midway through my tenure at Mostly Mozart, there was a major change. We had had the second highest income in our twenty-seven seasons and sold an average of 90 percent in Avery Fisher Hall for our thirty-nine concerts. Jane Moss had taken over the position of executive director of programming after Bill Lockwood's remarkable tenure ended in 1992. Jane loves everything new and cutting-edge, so it was no surprise that she tried to initiate a Lincoln Center Festival that leaned in that direction. She felt the best time to do this was during Mostly Mozart and that the main venue should be Fisher Hall, which would entirely eliminate the Mostly Mozart Festival.

I am not at all critical of Jane's desires, since I too am a believer in furthering the repertoire with great new music, theater, and dance. My problem was with the need to displace Mostly Mozart to accomplish this goal. In the spring of 1994 Edward Rothstein wrote an article in the *New York Times* headlined, "Can This Be the End of Mostly Mozart? Talks Are in Progress." In it he claimed that "discussions are taking place at Lincoln Center that could eliminate the Festival completely."

At the time I was in Tokyo, conducting the Tokyo Philharmonic, and to say I was surprised is an understatement. Mostly Mozart was a great success and reached a large and appreciative audience. We gave such artists as Bartoli and Galway their New York debuts. We played great music that filled a void in the city, especially during that time of year. Jane convinced Nat Leventhal that a new Lincoln Center Festival should begin in the summer of 1995, and they engaged the New York Philharmonic to play for two weeks in their regular hall in what should have been the middle of the Mostly Mozart Festival. Ed Rothstein spoke to me in Tokyo, and I was quoted in the *New York Times* as saying that I would be "shocked" to see the Philharmonic displace Mostly Mozart, despite the orchestra's contractual right: "I don't think Kurt Masur would do such a thing."

After I got off the phone with Ed, I called Marty Segal, then Jerome Greene and Peter J. Sharp, our two major supporters. They all agreed that a musically successful festival based on Mozart, which attracted a large and enthusiastic audience for Lincoln Center and New York City, deserved to continue. Marty took charge and was able to salvage the following 1995 season by having Mostly Mozart perform in Avery Fisher Hall on either side of the Philharmonic's weeks. When I returned to New York from Tokyo, Kurt Masur and I spoke, and he was very supportive of Mostly Mozart.

Of the opening night of that summer's 1994 Mostly Mozart Festival, Ed Rothstein wrote in the *New York Times*: "As if eager to assert its vitality in the face of uncertainty, the Mostly Mozart Festival Orchestra, under its Music Director, Gerard Schwarz, presented one of the best opening night concerts in several years. . . . The playing was well rehearsed and the orchestral sound warm and focused; the graciousness of confident musicianship was heard throughout. The concert can serve as a model of how fresh ideas can still be found in a summerlong set of variations on Mozartean themes."

The season that next summer was divided into two parts, with the New York Philharmonic playing for two weeks in the middle. After that a compromise was reached: there would be a Lincoln Center Festival in July, and Mostly Mozart would be reduced to four weeks in August. It was the perfect solution: the city's cultural life could easily accommodate both festivals. Interestingly, even though the Lincoln Center Festival was Jane Moss's idea, Lincoln Center moved Jane to the directorship of Mostly Mozart.

I remained music director of Mostly Mozart until 2001. Some

of the repertoire highlights from 1996 on were Mozart's *Davidde penitente* and *Coronation Mass*; a week devoted to Mozart in Prague; Haydn's *Creation* and all his string quartets; excerpts from Weber's *Der Freischütz*; Schumann's *Das Paradies und die Peri*; and Richard Strauss's *Divertimento*.

Our Tokyo residency continued through the 1999 season. In 1999 I decided that after my twentieth season in 2001 I would leave my position to spend more time composing, which I had just begun again, and quite frankly to have a little time off in the summer. In October 1999 Allan Kozinn wrote in the *New York Times*: "In a move that Lincoln Center officials say caught them by surprise, Gerard Schwarz has said that he will relinquish the music directorship of the Mostly Mozart Festival when his contract ends in 2001. Mr. Leventhal said yesterday that he was 'Surprised and also disappointed, because we were coming off a really strong season, in which the orchestra was playing, by all accounts, better than ever.' . . . In a letter . . . , Mr. Leventhal asked Mr. Schwarz to accept the title Conductor Emeritus, 'To signify what I am confident will be your continued association with Lincoln Center for many years to come.'"

After I left, Jane took the Mostly Mozart Festival in many new and interesting directions, expanding its theme to encompass cutting-edge new music. That said, the Mostly Mozart Festival continues to this day, something of which I am very proud.

CHAPTER ELEVEN

———

The Liverpool Years: 2001–2006

W e spent five remarkable years in Liverpool, where we had a comfortable flat in the center of town near the Town Hall, made many lasting friendships, and played some incredible concerts. I felt an immediate rapport with the orchestra when I first conducted them in 1995. Among the works that I did before becoming the music director were Beethoven's Ninth Symphony, Shostakovich's Tenth Symphony, Strauss's *Sinfonia Domestica*, Sibelius's Second Symphony, and the Adagio from Mahler's unfinished Tenth Symphony. The press were very supportive. In February 2000, after my appointment as music director was announced, Gerald Larner wrote in the *Times* of London:

> Gerard Schwarz is already familiar in Liverpool from the series of concerts he gave with the RLPO just under a year ago. His appointment . . . will be particularly welcome to those who heard him secure such vivid playing from the orchestra in Strauss's *Sinfonia Domestica*. . . . Not the least impressive aspect of the Liverpool performance was the abundance of picturesque detail and the accomplishment of the orchestra in colouring it and phrasing it so expressively while at the same time balancing the textures with such consistent clarity. His long-term structural purpose was evident from the start and he sustained it with a rare combination of calculation, determination and inspiration. Schwarz and the RLPO clearly have faith in each other, which in an extremity like this is of immense value in securing a fearless and authoritative performance.

And Pauline Fairclough wrote in the *Guardian* in March 2001 for a program of the Adagio from Mahler's Tenth Symphony, his *Kindertotenlieder*, and Sibelius's Second Symphony: "It was apparent from the outset that nothing was being taken for granted: not until you see and hear every member of the strings playing with equal intensity do you realize what a rare event it is. A rich, homogenous tone was the stunning result. Schwarz does not over-exert himself on the podium and the result is the sound of an orchestra at ease with their conductor and basking in the sheer joy of playing."

From these early days until I stepped down, I always felt that the driving force behind the orchestra was the phenomenally artistic visionary Sandra Parr. Over the years she held many titles in the artistic department. She had and has tremendous knowledge and excellent taste. Her husband is a tremendously gifted clarinetist, and they have fantastic twin daughters.

When I was appointed to be their music director, the chief executive was Antony Lewis Crosby and the chairman of the board was Peter Johnson. They made an excellent team, and both had a vision of the orchestra's future. In general, American music directors are more involved with all the activities of the orchestra than their European colleagues. The European style is for the music director to concern himself only with concerts; the rest is left to the administration. Liverpool, however, wanted an American-style music director, which meant they wanted me to help with all the programs, guest artists, and conductors, and to be actively involved with the development of the orchestra. I was kind of hoping for a more European-style level of involvement, but I certainly understood the orchestra's position and accepted it. I felt that Antony, Peter, Sandra, and I could do some excellent work together. Unfortunately, Antony left before I began, and his departure meant that many of our plans never materialized. Peter was always fantastic, but was under tremendous pressure with respect to the orchestra's finances. As Lynn Walker wrote in *The Independent* in February 2000: "Schwarz . . . whose concerts last year won critical acclaim will be music director rather than principal conductor. By putting his stamp on all areas of the orchestra's work he will perhaps give it the sense of direction it has lacked since Sir Charles Groves' tenure ended in 1977." The headline of Stephen Moss's article in the *Guardian* read, "Can Gerard Schwarz save the Royal Liverpool Philharmonic?" In the article he wrote that "Liverpool is seeking a conductor who offers vision as well as sound."

My first concert as music director was on September 12, 2001. We were doing some Mahler songs and his Second Symphony. Our daughter Gabriella had had her bat mitzvah in Seattle the previous Saturday, September 8, and it was an absolutely wonderful day in every way. Gaby chanted so beautifully and was so poised in both her reading from the Torah and her thoughtful speech. We had a joyous celebration afterward, but it was the very touching and spiritual Saturday service that remains in my memory. Family and friends came from all over the world, and the party continued on Sunday morning with a brunch for the family and the out-of-town guests.

Later on Sunday I left for London and Liverpool to do my opening subscription week. We began rehearsals on the evening of the tenth, and during a break in the afternoon rehearsal on the eleventh Sandra, looking extremely worried, told me that a couple of planes had flown into the World Trade Center in New York. I didn't understand at first, and then, like everyone else in the world, realized that thousands of men and women had been murdered while simply doing their daily work. That event fundamentally changed the world. The Mahler never seemed more appropriate, with its subject matter of death and the afterlife. I immediately called Jody and asked about my sister, Jeanette, who worked in the financial district. Luckily, because she was traveling with my father from Seattle on Monday, she had planned to go in to work late on that Tuesday and therefore was safe. Because I am Jewish and American, Liverpool had to have extra security for the performances during these first weeks of the season. I did Mahler's Symphony No. 2, "Resurrection," again in June of that season in Seattle and dedicated the performance to the victims, observing a long memorial break after the first movement.

The second week of the season included Stravinsky's *Rite of Spring* as well as his early short work *Scherzo fantastique.* I also programmed

Panufnik's Third Symphony and Alexander Asteriades' arrangement of Mahler's Piano Quartet. After the second week in Liverpool the travel restrictions were lifted, and I was able to return to Seattle.

Liverpool was the first British orchestra to produce its own recordings through their cooperative record company, RLPO Live. The main orchestra member/director was the oboist Jonathan Small, who held the title of executive director. Jonathan, representing the orchestra, wanted me to do the late nineteenth- and early twentieth-century German and Austrian repertoire, particularly all the Mahler symphonies and Strauss tone poems. Under Sir Charles Groves, the orchestra's principal conductor from 1963 to 1977, Liverpool was the first British orchestra to mount a complete Mahler cycle. The first recording that we did together was Strauss's tone poem *Eine Alpensinfonie* (*An Alpine Symphony*), followed in March 2001 by *Don Quixote*, with Lynn Harrell as the cello soloist, in October 2001. *Don Quixote* also has a very prominent role for the solo viola and a somewhat smaller one for solo violin; they were played by the orchestra's principal violist David Greenlees and concertmaster Malcolm Stewart. We were all very pleased with this recording. Lynn played his role of Don Quixote as a great opera singer portraying a role on the stage. His cello was simply a vehicle to that end, and he played every phrase and every gesture as if he were Don Quixote. David and Malcolm were both excellent, and this was an auspicious beginning to a marvelous recording collaboration with the orchestra. I was always very happy to have the microphones in place, because the concert event had an additional excitement. All the other conditions were excellent as well. The Philharmonic Hall was and is a superb recording venue. The producer, Michael Ogonovsky, and sound engineer, David Pigott—both members of the horn section—were first-rate as well. They were a pleasure to work with and had a strong musical commitment to the final result. I had suggested to Jonathan that they engage an important booklet notes writer, so they asked Michael Kennedy. By the time we did the live recording of the Strauss, the strings were producing the rich, vibrant, dark sound I always strive for. Our recordings were first released on the Danish label Classico and then on Avie, Artek, and Naxos.

I was interested in expanding the orchestra's educational scope, so we added the Musically Speaking series, which had been so successful in Seattle, on Sunday afternoons. It began to attract a nice audience, and we were able to repeat some works, something the orchestra had not done at home. We did some other repeat performances with the idea that some audience members attended depending on the day of the week and the time. We traveled all over the north of England and became the Classic FM radio station's Orchestra of the North. This led to some useful exposure on Classic FM, which broadcasts throughout the country.

During that first season I programmed with the idea that the threads started would continue: American music like Diamond's Fourth Symphony, English music like Walton's Symphony No. 2, and some new works like Daniel Brewbaker's *Fields of Vision*, David Horne's *Ignition* with Evelyn Glennie, and Bolcom's Flute Concerto with James Galway. We also began a focus on Max Bruch, the music director from 1880 to 1883, and brought some of my other favorite soloists to Liverpool, such as the violinist Nadja Salerno-Sonnenberg and the pianist Alexander Toradze.

The culmination of my first season was a performance at the Proms in London. The program was Panufnik's *Sinfonia Sacra*; the Prelude and "Liebestod" from Wagner's *Tristan und Isolde*; Strauss's Symphonic Fantasy from *Die Frau ohne Schatten*; and Siegfried's Rhine Journey, Siegfried's Funeral Music, and Brünnhilde's Immolation Scene from Wagner's *Götterdämmerung*; the soloist, Jane Eaglen, sang magnificently. Everyone talks about the atmosphere at the Proms, but nothing can adequately describe being there. The audience's excitement and appreciation were memorable. After the concert Paul McCartney and his wife came back to visit. We all know that he is from Liverpool, but I hadn't known that he was a Wagner fan. After the concert he spent an hour with us, and our friends from New York, Michele and Giuseppe Torroni, were especially touched when Paul sang "Michelle." We stayed till the hall closed down.

Liverpool, Season 2: 2002–2003

We began the 2002–2003 season with an all-English program of Walton and Edward Elgar. The highlights of the season for me were performances of Josef Bohuslav Forester's *Cyrano de Bergerac*, Silvestre Revueltas's *Sensemayá*, and our first Mahler recording, his Third Symphony. We also continued our Strauss recordings with the Duett-Concertino and *Sinfonia Domestica*, and we did Panufnik's Concertino for Timpani, Percussion and Strings with Ian Wright and Graham Johns as the excellent soloists. Both were longtime members of the orchestra, and when I first arrived in Liverpool Graham told me that I had been a part of one of his great early experiences as a student going to an orchestral concert. He had sat directly behind me when Bernstein and the New York Philharmonic were on tour doing the Mahler Fifth in Australia in 1975. Joshua Bell came and did the premiere of Behzad Ranjbaran's outstanding Violin Concerto.

Max Bruch is primarily known for his works for violin and his *Kol Nidrei* for cello and orchestra, but during his lifetime he was better known for his oratorios and other choral works. We did his *Song of the Bell*, a magnificent work that I repeated in Seattle a few months later. We also did his Third Violin Concerto, which is one of seven works he wrote for violin and orchestra, and though not quite as good as the very popular First Concerto, it is still wonderful. We also performed and recorded Mahler's First Symphony and Shostakovich's Thirteenth, with Gideon Saks as the bass soloist. We did two performances in Liverpool, and as usual with live recording, I listened to the first performance to see what we needed to improve for the second performance; I expected Gideon to arrive early so we could discuss it. I programmed Bright Sheng's *H'un* (*Lacerations*) to open the program so that we would have two composers' musical statements about horrific acts of the recent past. Before the concert Sandra Parr told me that Gideon, who lived in Manchester—about forty-five minutes away by car—was going to be late because of a problem with his train. I told Sandra to tell him to take a cab and I would pay for it. He didn't have enough money, so Sandra waited for him by the stage door with the cash to pay the driver.

Liverpool, Season 3: 2003–2004

Our themes continued with American music, English music, and Panufnik and Bruch. We performed and recorded the Mahler Sixth and the Strauss Oboe Concerto with Jonathan Small as the superb soloist. The two most interesting projects of the season were a Bernstein recording and a recording for the *Mail on Sunday* (the *Daily Mail*'s Sunday version). The newspaper, which was giving away CDs, asked us to do a CD of popular classics. All their giveaways had been of popular music; this was the only time they did classical music. We recorded the first movement of Beethoven's Fifth Symphony; Mozart's Symphony No. 39, Minuet movement; Fauré's *Pavane* in F-sharp Minor; the Prelude and Dance of the Swans from Tchaikovsky's *Swan Lake*; Grieg's "Morning Song" from *Peer Gynt*; Johann Strauss Jr.'s *Blue Danube Waltzes*; the second movement of Dvořák's Symphony No. 9, "From the New World"; the Bourée and Hornpipe from Handel's *Water Music*; and the Toreador Song from Bizet's *Carmen*. On a single day in February, 2.8 million copies of that CD were distributed! Great music was given to so many people who may not have been exposed to classical music before.

Our Bernstein recording was done for the Milken Archive. This recording was especially meaningful to me because it brought together so many dear friends from different points in my musical life, and because of my love and respect for Leonard Bernstein as both a person and a composer. Neil Levin's article in the program booklet brought the text of his *Kaddish* to life. Working with Neil on this project was truly inspirational, as was the leadership of Paul Schwendener in bringing this recording and all the Milken Archive recordings to life. The orchestra played with intensity, sensitivity, and technical skill. Willard White performed the narration of the Third Symphony sensitively and without amplification, like the work of a great actor on the stage. Yvonne Kenny sang with haunting expressiveness, and the recorded sound, with my regular team of Ogonovsky and Pigott, was excellent.

During my years in Liverpool I had a wonderful personal and working relationship with the director of the Philharmonic Choir, Ian Tracy, a great choir leader and organist. For *Chichester Psalms*, the boy soprano was Michael Small, the son of our solo oboist.

Three of our closest friends in Liverpool are Rex and Shirley Makin and their son Robin. I still read Rex's weekly column in the Liverpool *Echo*. He and Robin head an important law firm in England. Rex and Shirley are noted philanthropists and supported this recording financially. Jody and I would often go to their beautiful home to have Shabbat dinner on Friday nights and hear remarkable stories about Liverpool. We would also, on occasion, attend services at the Princes Road Synagogue, a very beautiful and very spiritual place where one can see and feel the history of the Jewish community in Liverpool. The many reviews for the Bernstein CD were excellent. Philip Clark wrote in *Gramophone*: "Gerard Schwarz conveys the unfolding drama with strategic clarity. The orchestra and voices sound as if they're taking pleasure in Bernstein's highly inventive scoring, running the spectrum of his jazzy big-band swagger and post-Darmstadt atonal works with ease." Jerry Dubins wrote in the January–February 2006 issue of *Fanfare*: "Kudos to all involved, not least of whom is Gerard Schwarz, a conductor who, in my experience, never seems to set a foot wrong." And *All-Service* published an article on November 21, 2005 that opined: "Schwarz's reading of Symphony No. 3 is the most moving I have ever heard. I think it shows that perhaps we have yet to fully appreciate what Bernstein did as a classical composer."

The season ended with a concert to celebrate the 100th anniversary of the Liverpool Cathedral. It was an unusual program, featuring Carl Orff's *Carmina Burana* and sections from Anton Bruckner's Mass in E Minor, interspersed with movements from Olivier Messiaen's *L'ascension*.

Liverpool, Season 4: 2004–2005

The orchestra's solo cellist was Jonathan Aasgaard, an outstanding artist. He performed Bloch's *Schelomo* at a concert in November as the beginning of a project he called "From Jewish Life." The recording, on the Avie label, also includes Bloch's *Prayer*, Bruch's *Kol Nidrei*, David Diamond's *Kaddish*, and my *In Memoriam*. I could not have asked for a better colleague and a better musician to be in this important position. In July we again appeared at the Proms, and this time the concert was also televised. The most important part of the program was Ralph Vaughan Williams's *Sea Symphony* (Symphony No. 1). Leila Josefowicz played Bruch's Violin Concerto No. 1, and we began with Mendelssohn's *Hebrides Overture*.

Liverpool, Season 5: 2005–2006

This was my final season with the orchestra as music director. I enjoyed my time there immensely. The travel from Seattle was at times challenging, but the musical results were always wonderful and worthwhile. I can't say that my departure was my choice. I had worked very hard to try to lift the orchestra up, both musically and institutionally. I had pushed the staff, orchestra, and board to try to reach a new level, both artistically and in terms of funding and general management. It's clear from listening to our recordings, usually done live, that the musical result was outstanding. The programming was always interesting and my commitment to the orchestra was very strong. But the team that engaged me changed, and things were different. Some wonderful new people came into leadership positions, especially Peter Toyne, who succeeded Peter Johnson as chairman of the board. His push for broad, clear growth as an institution was too much for many in the organization, especially the chief executive and the board chair that followed. In the end, the players never embraced the American music director model that the previous team had wanted, and without the support of the staff leadership and the board leadership, it was an untenable model.

Also, for some, change is difficult. John Rockwell had an interesting take on the situation. In an August 2004 New York Times article titled, "A Hard Time for Americans in Britain's Disheveled Music World," he wrote about Leonard Slatkin's departure from the BBC Symphony Orchestra after four years and my 2006 departure from Liverpool after five years. He wondered if there was some sort of "lingering anti-Americanism at work here . . . or [anti-]Jewish Americans" since both Leonard and I are Jewish. He mentioned that one London critic " . . . spoke speculatively of a certain residual, genteel anti-Semitism in Britain. In Britain, one problem has been the resistance, by management and musicians alike, to the American model of the music director . . . " Slatkin told Rockwell that he was not able to participate in hiring musicians and in programming. He rarely was able to suggest soloists even for his own concerts. Rockwell wrote about the orchestral musicians in England wanting to govern themselves "overtly or covertly." He went on to suggest that such difficulties were also my problem in Liverpool and explained that I " . . . rejected an offer to extend his [my] contract but only as a guest conductor. According to many London critics, British orchestras are adept sight-readers and can rip off a plausible performance at the first rehearsal. But they apparently balk, by and large, at the hard work, directed from the podium." Rockwell writes about the challenges of being a music director in England much better than I could.

CHAPTER TWELVE

Family Life

At the time of this writing Jody and I have been married for thirty-two years. I'm very lucky to have had such an extraordinary partner for all this time. There are no words to describe how remarkable our relationship has been from the start, and how it continues with love, respect, admiration, and trust. When I joined the New York Philharmonic in 1972, Jody was thirteen years old, and her father, Sol Greitzer, was the principal viola. He had been in the NBC Symphony with Arturo Toscanini before that, an opportunity he'd been able to take advantage of because of Milton Katims, who later became the music director of the Seattle Symphony. At that time Milton was associate principal viola of the NBC Symphony, and when there was an opening, Milton recommended Sol to Toscanini. I have a picture in my studio of Milton sitting on the first stand and my father-in-law sitting on the last stand. Later my father-in-law joined the New York Philharmonic and moved to the second stand. Boulez appointed him principal in 1972.

That year, 1972, was a hard one for the orchestra. They went on a ten-week strike a few weeks after I joined. This was when I met the Greitzers. Our families became fast friends; Sol was a great musician and a generous man. He always had a warm smile for his family, and in most cases everyone else as well. He was sensitive but could be very strong in the face of any injustice.

Shirley Greitzer, my mother-in-law, was from Dallas. She had graduated from high school at the age of fourteen and spent a few years at Southern Methodist University before entering Juilliard at sixteen, where she studied with the grande dame of piano teachers, Rosina Lhévinne. Shirley was a terrific pianist and much later directed placement at Juilliard. Sol and Shirley joined our Waterloo Festival and School faculty, and that was when I noticed what a good chamber music coach she was. Sol had a great class of students at Waterloo, and he led the orchestra's viola section. He also did some conducting and played and coached chamber music. All three Greitzer girls, Deborah, Jody, and Pamela, attended Waterloo as students, and we were very close.

Jody was and is gorgeous and brilliant, with an effervescent personality, and furthermore she is an outstanding flutist and musician. When she was a senior at the High School of Music and Art in New York, her sister Debbie was at Juilliard studying bassoon. Jody had been accepted at a number of Ivy League schools and decided to attend Barnard College, but just before her first year she changed her mind and decided to attend Juilliard instead. Her summers were spent in Aspen at the music festival, and Shirley became the executive director at the Waterloo Festival.

In Shirley I finally had someone at Waterloo who was not only thorough and intelligent, but who really knew music. She needed some administrative help, so after Jody graduated with her master's from Juilliard, she worked part-time at the Waterloo Festival. At that time Jody was playing in several chamber groups, doing children's concerts through the Lincoln Center Institute and freelancing in New York, and was engaged to the violinist Robert McDuffie.

By the fall of 1982 I was divorced and Jody had ended her engagement. My mother had always said that if you want to know what your wife will be like in the future, look at her mother. She also felt that the more you have in common, the more likely the marriage would last. Jody's parents and mine had long, happy marriages. But I was thirty-five and had two children; Jody was just twenty-three. So I asked Shirley if I could date her daughter. She replied, "It's not up to me. Ask her yourself." After three or four months I finally got up the courage to ask her out. Early in 1983 I invited Shirley and Sol to my apartment at 575 West End Avenue for some Chinese take-out. I didn't cook, but I was pretty good at ordering in. I knew Jody was around, and I asked Shirley to invite her girls to join us. To my delight, Jody came. We all had a lovely evening, and after everyone had left and I finished cleaning up, I finally called Jody. After a lot of hemming and hawing she agreed to have dinner with me but did not want anyone she knew to see us together. That meant we needed to go to the East Side for dinner. It was a very strange beginning. Once she realized I was interested in a serious relationship, she relaxed a little, but she still was reluctant to tell her father about us. By the following November I had asked her to marry me, and eventually I told Sol.

During the 1983–1984 season in Seattle I was considering taking the position of music director and asked Jody if she could see herself living there. The Seattle Symphony's executive director, Mark Walker, and his wife, Ludmila, invited Jody to stay with them. In November 1983 Jody flew out of a snowstorm blanketed New York City. She arrived in Seattle to mild weather, sunny skies, and the brilliant greenery that gives Seattle its sobriquet, "The Emerald City." Jody fell in love with the city.

In June 1984 we started planning a large wedding, even though that was not quite what I wanted. I was working, traveling, and studying a great deal, so I told Jody, "Look, I really want to get married, and I don't want to wait until September. I have this date free, June 23, right before the summer begins. Can we see if everyone in the family is available? Then we can have the wedding at the apartment."

It turned out that everyone was available. We drove out to my parents' doctor's office and my father took blood from us both (a blood test was required for a marriage license in New York State). I flew out to Seattle, and Jody took care of all the details.

We needed a huppah (a marriage canopy) for the ceremony, so Jody opened the yellow pages and saw a listing for an outfit on the Lower East Side called "Rent-a-Huppah." She called and said, "Excuse me, I'd like to rent a huppah." The man on the other end of the phone said, "What kind of huppah would you like? I mean we have huppahs in silver, wood, brass. You tell me what kind of huppah you want, and I get you one." As it turned out, the rabbi brought his own. Jody's family rabbi, Ronald Millstein, was available the following Saturday evening.

Jody bought rings at Jerry Blickman Precious Jewels (the Blickmans were old family friends of ours). She also hired a phenomenal florist to put peonies (her favorite flower) everywhere. That Friday I took a red-eye back from the West Coast. Jody picked me up at JFK Airport, and we drove straight to the marriage license bureau in Queens near the airport. I had a lunch to get to right away with Donal Henahan, who was doing a Mostly Mozart preview article for the *New York Times*, so we raced back to the city. The following evening, after sundown on June 23, 1984, we were married with every member of our family present: my parents; my sisters and their families; Jody's parents and sisters; my two children, seven-year-old Daniel and ten-year-old Alysandra; and a friend of Jody's, Nadine Asin. Four family members held the huppah. It was the most meaningful and most heartfelt wedding I had ever witnessed. We celebrated with caviar, champagne, and cake, and it was all perfect in every way.

That September I began all my seasons—with LACO, the NYCS, and the Seattle Symphony Orchestra. The first concerts were with LACO and had some conflicts with the Jewish High Holidays. In Seattle we eventually worked to avoid those holidays, but that practice had not yet begun. Jody came to Seattle ahead of me to worship, and I arrived a few days later. We were not sure how to make arrangements for all this, so I called the symphony office, and they suggested that Jody contact Gladys Rubinstein. Gladys's husband, Sam, was a lifetime board member. They were very committed to the arts in Seattle and were real music lovers. Gladys took Jody in as if she were her daughter, and from that moment on the two of them were as close as could be. Neither Sam nor Gladys was religious, but Gladys made Jody feel totally comfortable and succeeded in making us feel as though they attended synagogue regularly. They became like family to us, and when our two children were born, the Rubinsteins became their godparents.

Welcoming the Kids

After five years as a duo, we were thrilled to find out we were having a child. It seemed like the whole city took part in our excitement. We loved dealing with all the details of the baby's new room and figuring out who would help when we returned from the hospital.

I was rehearsing the second subscription concert of the 1988–1989 season, which included Schumann's Symphony No. 1, the Symphonic Fragment from Richard Strauss's *Josephslegende*, and Shostakovich's Piano Concerto No. 1, with Joseph Kalichstein as the soloist. That Friday I was with Jody at Swedish Hospital in Seattle, and our associate conductor, Christopher Kendall, was taking the rehearsal of the Schumann. Gabriella was born early in the morning, and all seemed well. After a few hours Jody told me to go to rehearsal, since there was nothing more for me to do.

I was in heaven and went back to the Opera House to continue rehearsing the Schumann. Forty-five minutes later I was told to return to the hospital: Jody had internal bleeding and had lost a great deal of blood. It was touch and go for several days. Two dear friends, Andrea Selig and Gladys Rubinstein, were with us most of the time, and five days later Jody was out of intensive care and out of danger.

We kept our New York apartment until 2001. I was still working often in New York, and our families still lived there. My older children, Alysandra and Daniel, lived with their mother in New Jersey. Both Alysandra, born in 1973, and Daniel, born in 1977, had known Jody from the time they were born, as our families were friends. Jody became a very supportive stepmother to them. The kids loved her, and we spent a great deal of time with them during each New York trip. Ultimately they both came to live with us in Seattle and attended high school there.

Alysandra attended the Lakeside School and then Barnard, where she majored in English and minored in dance. She returned to Seattle to the University of Washington, where she went to medical school and did her surgical residency. Both my parents were doctors, and my daughter has carried on that tradition. She later finished her surgical residency at the University of Wisconsin and now practices general surgery in Milwaukee, where she and her husband, Dave Lal, a pediatric surgeon, live with our grandchildren, Aidan and Layton. I am very proud of Alysandra for her dedication to her profession, and for how she balances her successful career and dedication to her patients while being a fantastic mother to Aidan and Layton and a devoted wife to Dave. It is a joy for me to see the same kind of dedication that my parents had to their patients in Alysandra as well. Layton plays the piano now, and Aidan plays the trumpet. Both boys are a testimony to her and Dave's wonderful parenting.

Daniel, an artist and musician, attended high school at the Bush School in Seattle, then enrolled at the University of Washington, where he studied classical bass with Barry Lieberman. Daniel is incredibly talented. He plays in several bands, including a country band; he runs an artistic T-shirt business, and he does amazing metal sculpture. For my fiftieth birthday he presented me with a marvelously intricate and beautiful metal music stand, which is now in New York with us. Daniel lives and works in Seattle. I am very proud of how devoted he is to all his ventures. He is a deeply loyal and caring person.

In our early years together, Jody and I loved living in downtown Seattle. She was born in Dallas but grew up in Queens, where she had had a very long commute to the High School of Music and Art. When she attended Juilliard, she moved to an apartment on Seventieth Street. She loved being in the middle of everything, and she taught me to love it as well. When I became music director of the Seattle Symphony in 1985, we bought a condo downtown at First Avenue and Virginia, at a time when few people lived downtown. The fact that our building was mostly empty did not really register until people began moving to the city. At first we could park anywhere, as the garage was basically empty. Two years later the garage was full. We were just above Pike Place Market, which Alysandra and Dan also loved and where we shopped most days. At that time the neighborhood was a little questionable, especially at night, but we did not mind. Our apartment was a duplex with a beautiful view of Puget Sound from our balcony. We had two bedrooms and a loft space, so there was plenty of room for Alysandra and Dan when they visited.

We did not move anything from our New York apartment, so we had to buy everything new. Jody worked with the designer Melinda Dreyer. Everything else—dishes, cutlery, glasses, kitchen items, towels, sheets, beds—was purchased at a local department store, Frederick

& Nelson. Most of it was delivered the day we took possession of the condo, except for the dining room chairs. Around that time the symphony development department decided we should give a catered dinner party for the major supporters of the orchestra. Jody was given the contact information to do the inviting. We had not met any of the guests except the Rubinsteins.

The event was to begin with cocktails at seven, followed by dinner at eight. Seven came around, and we were still waiting for Joe McDonnal, the caterer, to bring the food and the rented dining chairs. At last he arrived with his team carrying the chairs and the food. We all had drinks at seven-thirty instead, and nobody seemed to mind. All the couples who attended that night became our very close friends over the years. Jody was only in her mid-twenties at the time, and although she had the sophistication of someone much older and more experienced, the pressures on her were very great in those formative years of the orchestra. But in a sense, she had grown up in and around the New York Philharmonic, so this environment was second nature to her. Everyone loved her, especially the development department.

We continued to go everywhere together even after our first child was born. Gabriella was an excellent traveler. The first European trip we took was to Paris, and Gaby behaved perfectly—probably because she had the perfect mother. Two years later Jody became pregnant again, and Julian was born in 1991. There was a little drama this time as well: our doctor arrived late and almost missed the birth. In the end it all went smoothly, and soon we were traveling with a double stroller. We purchased the apartment next door to us in Seattle, combining the two so our four children could have their own rooms. In New York we moved to a larger, four-bedroom apartment in the same building on West End Avenue.

Eventually we wanted even more space in Seattle, so we bought a house in the Queen Anne neighborhood, a historic home built in 1903. We then put the wall back up between our combined condo and sold the two units separately. In those years, whenever I did a piece by David Diamond, he would stay with us. David didn't realize our condo had once been two separate apartments. The day we put the wall up between the two apartments, David was still sleeping, and I had not told him what we were doing. Barely awake, he came upstairs in his pajamas and robe, ran into a wall, and then saw a door he did not know existed. Flabbergasted, he opened the door, went out into the hall, and rang the other doorbell to be let inside. A few days later, while we were at a rehearsal, the movers packed up and moved David's belongings along with the rest of the family's. We had to go through all our boxes to find the one that held David's clothes. To the day he died, he insisted he was still missing one tie.

At this time the Seattle Symphony had embarked on the campaign to build Benaroya Hall. Our home quickly became a hub for dinner parties, cocktail parties, musical soirées, opening-night galas, and the annual Maestro Circle dinner party. Often Jody cooked for small soirées, but the larger events were catered by Russell Lowell and his team, who made the complicated logistics of setting up a catering kitchen— sometimes in our garage and sometimes extended in our backyard kitchen—seem easy. Because we had the space to seat 100 people at a formal dinner, it was a gorgeous personal place to entertain and host events for the many people in the community who cared deeply about the future of the symphony.

Gabriella and Julian attended Seattle Country Day School nearby. They both participated in neighborhood baseball, softball, and swimming. They both played the piano, and in addition, Gabriella played the violin and Julian, the cello. They each played in the Seattle Youth Symphony. We attended Temple de Hirsch Sinai, where the children attended Hebrew School and where their bat and bar mitzvahs were held. Soon Gabriella and Julian followed their sister, Alysandra, and attended the Lakeside School, where all three received the most inspirational and aggressively academic education imaginable. Most mornings I cooked breakfast and drove the children to school. We were lucky to be able to live and work in such a wonderful city, to grow together and to be a part of the community. For all of us, it felt like a luxury. Music directors in most cities last ten to fifteen years at most. My twenty-eight-year tenure in Seattle afforded us a very happy family life. Our house was often point central for all our children and their friends, and our friends. There were pool parties and dinners. Halloween always saw 400-plus trick-or-treaters, and visitors often heard Julian playing the organ upstairs.

I confess that a great stress reliever for me, in addition to skiing, was mowing our lawn. Luckily most of our grounds were shrubbery of varying sorts, mostly flowering plants like rhododendrons, azaleas, camellias, roses, and magnolia trees. The lawn in the front and the back combined was quite small. I had fond childhood memories of mowing the lawn with my father in New Jersey. I couldn't quite convince any of our children to enjoy it as much I did, but I found it quite relaxing. Once a neighboring gardener asked me if I wanted to go into business with him—he thought I did a good job. I thanked him for the compliment but declined his offer, explaining that I wasn't a professional.

For most of our years in our house in Seattle we had a wheaten terrier named Constanze, or Stanzy for short. She would sit next to me for hours as I studied in my office. I would pet her, then she would move onto one of the chairs in my office, and then she would return. This went on for hours. She did not like most modern music, so if I turned on anything after Stravinsky, she would leave. We all miss her.

Gabriella went on to attend George Washington University in Washington, D.C., where she majored in political science and minored in journalism. I always felt her proclivities were influenced by our Seattle mornings spent comparing and contrasting the four newspapers that arrived daily. While in Washington, Gabriella interned at many news organizations, including CQ Politics, Fox News, and, finally, CNN, where she was hired during her senior year. She went on to hold many positions at the network: producing for *State of the Union*, writing for the political ticker as an associate producer, then as producer, and eventually as White House producer for Jessica Yellin. While there she received an Emmy for election night 2012. Gabriella traveled all over the world—Israel, Ramallah, Jordan, Myanmar, Thailand, Cambodia, South Africa, Tanzania, Senegal, Costa Rica, Mexico, Ireland, Berlin, and throughout the United States—covering President Obama through his reelection. A highlight for me was attending the White

House Christmas party for the press as Gabriella's plus-one, where we took a photo with the president and first lady. Mrs. Obama has spoken out on the importance of the arts in children's lives, a cause I am thrilled she has championed. Today Gabriella is the news editor at Flipboard in Palo Alto, California. I am extraordinarily proud of all her accomplishments. She is a multitalented young woman—brilliant, charming, and intuitive, with a real zest for life in our complicated world. Her ability to understand and digest the news is something to behold. Her writing and reporting are the fairest I have ever seen, with an understanding of context and history. She lights up all of our lives.

Julian attended the Colburn School in Los Angeles for two years. He then transferred to the Juilliard School, where he earned his bachelor's degree in May 2014 and his master's in May 2016. Julian is the eighth member of our family to attend Juilliard, and the first of the third generation of Juilliard attendees in our family, a succession that began with his grandparents Sol and Shirley Greitzer. Julian won first prize in the 2013 Schoenfeld International Cello Competition in Hong Kong and has since embarked on a very successful solo concert career. I am thrilled and always moved when we work together, as we have on numerous occasions. There is no prouder moment for me than when I am on the podium conducting for him. He premiered Sam Jones's Cello Concerto with me in Seattle, and then again with the All-Star Orchestra; we have done the Elgar Cello Concerto in Australia, Shostakovich's First Cello Concerto in Seattle, Dvořák's and Saint-Saëns's Cello Concertos in Hartford, Strauss's *Don Quixote* in Charlotte, and Brahms's Double Concerto and Dvořák's Cello Concerto at the Eastern Music Festival. His concert engagements are numerous—many more beyond those we are able to coordinate together. Julian's knowledge of music is remarkable, and he has the ability to speak on any subject convincingly and succinctly. I always marvel at his capacity for memorization, playing full recitals with at times very complicated music. In addition, he is a great tennis player. When we are both at home in New York, we play tennis often. He usually beats me these days.

Jody and I moved back to New York in June 2012 after my last season as music director of the Seattle Symphony. We reside now on the Upper East Side, and I travel from here now. Jody played flute a great deal in Seattle, including with the Seattle Chamber Music Festival, the Seattle Opera, the Seattle Symphony, and many other groups, but she has now been writing fiction for many years. She is currently enrolled in graduate school at Sarah Lawrence College pursuing a master's of fine arts in writing. She is completing a novel about the music world.

CHAPTER THIRTEEN

The Seattle Years

My predecessor at the Seattle Symphony was Rainer Miedel, a German conductor, who died of cancer at the age of forty-five. His widow, Cordelia Miedel, is a fine cellist who taught at the University of Puget Sound. Before that our music director was Milton Katims. Before Milton, there were so many—the most famous was Sir Thomas Beecham.

Henry Hadley, the Seattle Symphony music director from 1909 to 1911, was a superb composer, and he must have been a fine conductor. He left in 1911 to start the San Francisco Symphony and became their first music director. In the 1920s the Seattle Symphony had a female music director, Mary Davenport-Engberg. She was thought to be among the first female music directors in the country.

Milton Katims was the conductor who really put the orchestra on the map. Milton was a famous viola player, and a very fine one. He played in the NBC Symphony on the first stand with Carleton Cooley, as Cooley's number 2 viola. Milton also guest conducted the NBC Symphony. He was very close not only to Toscanini, who loved him, but also to Isaac Stern, Alexander Schneider, Pablo Casals, and others in that group.

It was Stern who suggested Milton for the position of Seattle Symphony's music director in 1952. Milton elevated the orchestra. He brought in great soloists at the beginning of their careers such as Horacio Gutiérrez and Yo-Yo Ma, and they had some important early opportunities as a result. Milton created a Sunday series to feature those emerging young artists, was very involved with education, and was an active member of the community. The orchestra's profile was raised considerably under Milton.

After Milton left, Rainer Miedel did some terrific work with the orchestra. He improved it by adding many excellent players and doing some good fundamental work with the musicians.

Looking for an Orchestra

During the 1980–1981 season I was quite busy as the music director of two festivals and two chamber orchestras. I was hoping to become involved with a large orchestra and possibly reduce some of my other activities. Luckily, a number of orchestras were interested in me at that time. In the spring of 1981, while guest conducting the Kansas City Philharmonic, I became friends with their executive director, Mark Walker, who shortly afterward became the executive director of the Seattle Symphony. During that season Rainer became very ill and was unable to conduct some concerts in March. Mark asked me to come to guest conduct. The program was a concert of concertos to be performed by members of the orchestra, and Mark encouraged me to change the program with one exception, the Mozart Clarinet Concerto, which would be performed by their longtime solo clarinetist, Ronald Phillips. Phillips was retiring at the end of the season after fifty-six years in the orchestra.

The program I suggested included Stravinsky's *Song of the Nightingale* and Schumann's First Symphony, as well as the Mozart. The last time Ronald had performed the concerto was with Thomas Beecham, and he had a small pocket score with all Beecham's suggestions. I was quite amazed at how well Ronald played, and of course he was a wonderful gentleman; our friendship lasted for many years until his death in 2004. The concert went well. Miedel, whose cancer was quite advanced, decided to step down at that time, and Walker asked me to step in as music advisor. He indicated that as in Kansas City, he would like me to consider being music director, but they had to go through a proper search. I was not sure if I had any interest because of the orchestra's serious financial problems, but I was happy to help out and accepted the music advisor position. During that season I was able to do only a few weeks. Rainer died in March 1983. For the remainder of the 1983–1984 season I took over many of Rainer's programs, beginning the season in September with Mahler's Symphony No. 1 and ending it in May with his Symphony No. 2, "Resurrection." It was a great deal of Mahler for such a short subscription season, but I was thrilled to do them. Over the years I have conducted the Seattle Symphony in these masterpieces fifteen times.

At the time the personnel of the orchestra was in flux. The concertmaster, Karl-Ove Mannberg, was only part-time: his wife was happy to have Karl-Ove come for six weeks a year, but she did not want to live in Seattle. The first trumpet had just left for Boston, and we had a guest during that season who had studied with me at Juilliard, Eddie Carroll. The first flute, Scott Goff, had been a classmate of mine when we were both students at Juilliard. I knew the first horn, Bob Bonnevie, from the Casals festival. The musicians on the committee to choose the next music director were both leaders of the orchestra—the first cellist, Ray Davis, and the principal second violin, Janet Baunton. They both had gorgeous sounds and were very thoughtful musicians. When I did my initial guest conducting I was quite taken with the cello section and their unified approach. Janet's husband, the principal percussionist, Randy Baunton, was also a remarkable player and the brilliant leader of the orchestra committee. No matter what Randy played, he made it sound beautiful.

At the end of the 1983–1984 season Mark asked me to become the music director. I enjoyed working with the orchestra, but the orchestra's precarious finances led me to turn him down. Mark pushed hard, though, and eventually we agreed to change my title to principal conductor and see how things went. During the 1984–1985 season I was beginning to see tremendous growth in the orchestra. There are two basic ways a new leader can work with an organization: make changes to establish your loyal group of new people, or work with the individuals who are already in place. I always believed in the second way and felt that as long as the musicians were working hard, I would do my best to work with them. There are music directors who "clean house," and over the years I have been offered music directorships that might have required that. In all my years in Seattle, however, I only fired four players. Some people have criticized me for that kind of loyalty, but it was and is the way I work. Of course there were many retirements during those years and a very few cases of reseating, but we all wanted the best possible musical results. Most of the players rose to the challenges, and we seemed to be on the same path musically.

During the 1984–1985 season Mark again asked me to become the music director and said that the reason they were not raising as much money as necessary was because the position hadn't been filled. I knew this probably was not true, but by this point I had fallen in love with the orchestra and wanted to agree. Jody and I had married in June of 1984, and if I were going to accept this position, Jody would need to be part of the decision. When Jody had visited prior to our marriage, one of the first dinners we had that week was with two board members and their spouses, Dave and Joyce Grauman, and Dave and Jane Davis. Both men were surgeons, and all four of these people were knowledgeable music lovers who became among our first friends in Seattle. Jane was fascinating, a huge art collector with a remarkable twentieth-century American art collection. We loved them all, and we thought, if this is representative of what Seattle was like, Seattle was a community we could adore. After marrying in June 1984, we became Seattle residents at the beginning of my first season as music director. The two other very important people integral to my decision were Charles Odegard, chairman of the Seattle Symphony board and president of the University of Washington, and Hans Lehmann, a physician who was a longtime board member and a close friend of Milton Katims.

I accepted the Music Director position. Now the real work began.

Buying Into the Dream

The main question I asked before accepting the position of music director was: what do the board, orchestra, and staff want the orchestra to look like in the future? An orchestra might simply want to serve the community and play good concerts but may not be specifically interested in becoming a great orchestra. Having an aspiration to become great puts pressure on everyone. The orchestra has to push itself; so does the conductor, and so does the staff. The musical events become much more significant. The preparation is more intense, and all levels, from management to the board, must buy into the dream.

I was once asked to consider accepting a different music director post, and I asked the staff and board what kind of orchestra they wanted. They weren't interested in pushing the artistic level and were quite happy with the generally serviceable and occasionally excellent concerts the orchestra was giving. Everything was comfortable, and everyone seemed content. This was during my early days of being a conductor, and all I wanted to do was to be involved with a great orchestra and give great concerts for a large and appreciative audience. The status quo was not interesting to me. That was more than thirty years ago, and that particular orchestra has remained the same. It's still a good orchestra, and they are serving their community well.

In Seattle everyone—the board, the staff, and the orchestra's leadership—answered the question the same way: they wanted to be a great orchestra. Was there a 100 percent buy-in? Some players probably were not interested in working so hard, but the players' organization leaders strongly supported this vision. We also needed to change the community's perception of the orchestra. We had to go from answering such questions as "why do we need an orchestra?" to creating a sense of the orchestra as the city's jewel. I felt like everyone was on the same page, and we rolled up our sleeves and began to work very hard.

In the beginning we had only twelve weeks of regular subscription concerts. It was hard to get artistic momentum with so many weeks between performances of the regular repertoire. We played for the ballet and the opera, and we all shared one hall, the Seattle Opera House. It had opened in 1962 and was a converted arena. Interestingly, even though it was rebuilt for the symphony, it was called the Opera House.

A few years after the symphony's move to its new home they started the Seattle Opera, and the opera started the Pacific Northwest Ballet. Mark Walker was unhappy about spending so much time in the pit, and he did not like the atmosphere of the Seattle Center—it was mostly an amusement park then. In 1985 he began looking for a new place for us to play, and in 1998, we finally opened: Benaroya Hall.

When the orchestra musicians played for the opera or the ballet, they were employed by those organizations, so in essence they had three employers. The opera and the ballet used about two-thirds of the players. When I asked what the other members did, I was told they stayed home but were paid—contractually, anyway—by the orchestra, while those used in the opera or ballet were paid by those organizations. This was an opportunity to expand the remaining players' activities. I developed a new-music series, a baroque series, and a classical series, as I felt these would help develop the orchestra's ensemble, musical phrasing, and detail of execution. I also started doing Handel's *Messiah* at Christmastime. Working in smaller groups concentrated our needs and increased our communication. We eventually added a chamber music series, and we started making recordings. All of this had a huge impact on the quality of the orchestra. We also brought the orchestra out into the community by playing in a variety of venues.

The Audience Knows

The orchestra not only wanted to be better, it wanted to be great, and that was crucial. At the time the players complained about the schedule and that they were not paid well enough. I believed that if we focused on playing better concerts, everything would improve. The artistic level would rise, more people would attend concerts, we would be able to raise more money, and this would hopefully translate monetarily as well for them.

And that's what happened (though not quite as quickly as I had hoped)—all because of the quality of their music making. The audience knows the difference. If the concert is dull or not well played, the audience may not return. Why should they? They can stay home and listen to their CDs. But if something exciting is going on, and they hear the ensemble getting better and better, you will not be able to keep them away. When an audience sees the people onstage caring about what they are doing and playing their best, they want to be a part of it, and they return often.

My approach has always been to try to focus on problems one at a time. One year I spent a part of some rehearsals tuning the double basses. I did the same with the trombones, coaching Bach chorales prior to the rehearsal. The first violin section had some consistent intonation issues. We had to work hard on that, since it affected the quality of the sound as a whole. To achieve a dark, warm string sound, we had to first fix the intonation and then work together on the unanimity of bow strokes, bow distribution, and bow speed. We also performed in a hall that was not very clear. We only had one rehearsal on the opera-house stage. An orchestra needs to rehearse in the hall that is their home as much as possible. The only advantage was that the rehearsal room was dry, and therefore we could hear the problems well.

There were two things I stressed early on that work in tandem: breathing and moving together as an orchestra. If you watch European orchestras, they move together. Most American orchestras are trained not to move, not to distract, when in fact moving together shows the phrasings, the subtleties of the music. If you move physically together and breathe together, you phrase together as one, and the musical vision becomes clear. It is not just that the conductor gives you the sign, but it is the concertmaster then reinforces that sign, and so on down the line and throughout the orchestra.

Once, when I was in the New York Philharmonic, we were on tour at the Lucerne Festival. One night the Berlin Philharmonic played, and the following night the New York Philharmonic played. My close friend Philip Jones, a thoughtful and exceptional musician, came to both concerts and commented on the musical involvement of the Berlin orchestra and the lack of involvement from the New York orchestra. He then commented that the exception was when we were playing *An American in Paris* by George Gershwin. Then we were as physically involved as the Berlin orchestra was when they played Brahms. In my early years in Seattle, we worked on moving and breathing together and being as involved as possible with all repertoire.

In addition, I tried to improve the way we sounded in the opera house. We tried different variations. I had the orchestra play out in front of the proscenium. After I raised the pit and moved the orchestra forward, the strings immediately sounded better. I then added some reflectors on the stage. The hall was multipurpose, with a shell around the orchestra when we played. I tried to secure the shell so it would not vibrate and absorb all the bass notes rather than projecting them. Such issues are accomplished in a matter not of weeks but of years. Every year we dealt with more and more of them.

During the 1984–1985 season we performed mostly in the Seattle Opera House, but it was often busy, as it was used by many other groups. We still had a few weeks of concerts scheduled with no place to play. Mark Walker wanted to try doing some concerts away from the Seattle Center, so we decided to hold performances at the Fifth Avenue Theatre, doing Mozart and Haydn weeks, and a light classics series as well.

In the early 1980s downtown Seattle was not the vibrant place it is today, and some symphonygoers felt it wasn't safe. We needed a little time to get patrons to feel comfortable about coming to hear us at the Fifth Avenue Theatre.

We also began a new-music series at the Nippon Kan Theater in the international district and a baroque series at the Moore Theater downtown. We also did a Beethoven Festival at Meany Theater at the University of Washington.

That year we did a special single concert on a Sunday afternoon. It was the first time I worked with Mstislav Rostropovich. We began that program with some excerpts from Tchaikovsky's *Swan Lake* that I had done at Waterloo a few years earlier, and after intermission we did the Dvořák Cello Concerto. Slava gave a spectacular performance. It was the first of many that we did together in Seattle, each a memorable occasion.

Slava often had dinner at our home after his concerts. On one occasion the other guest was David Tonkonogui, a wonderful cellist in the orchestra and our son's teacher. Julian was six or seven, and Slava asked him to play before dinner. Afterward Slava said, "Please, Julian, don't practice too much, I still have a few good years left!"

That year we also continued our Mahler cycle with the Third Symphony and presented our first piano recital with Vladimir Ashkenazy.

My dear friend Bella Davidovich played Rachmaninoff's *Rhapsody on a Theme of Paganini*, and Alicia de Larrocha played César Franck's *Symphonic Variations* and Manuel de Falla's *Nights in the Gardens of Spain*. I was especially excited to present her to our audience after the successes we had had in New York at Mostly Mozart. Alicia played magnificently and without histrionics. She would simply walk onstage and play with artistry and care. It surprised me that the house at that set of concerts was not full, but Seattle did not know Alicia yet. Fame in one city does not necessarily transfer to another. After those performances, Alicia's concerts always sold out, and she became a Seattle favorite.

On another program I did the Mendelssohn *Lobgesang* (published after his death as the Symphony No. 2), and Emanuel Ax played Beethoven's Piano Concerto No. 3. Manny was a good friend from Mostly Mozart and the NYCS. He played beautifully as always. The *Lobgesang* struck all of us as such a masterpiece, too rarely performed.

We continued with our Festival at the Fifth Avenue Theatre for a second year. Sometimes new ideas, or in this case new venues, need time to take hold, to give audiences a chance to understand them and to succeed. Our soloists for the second year at the Fifth Avenue Mozart and Haydn weeks were with the pianists Eugene Istomin, Malcolm Frager, and Jeffery Siegel, and the violinist Young Uck Kim. For the light classics I did an all-Tchaikovsky program; the remaining programs were conducted by Franz Allers, Henry Mancini, and Morton Gould. Henry was a soft-spoken and highly intelligent performer, as well as a prolific film composer. I had worked with him when I was eighteen at the Garden State Arts Center in New Jersey when that facility first opened. I met Morton Gould when I was in the American Brass Quintet, and I played on some of his television sessions. Later on the Seattle Symphony and I recorded a whole album of his works: *Formations*, the Concerto Grosso for Four Violins, excerpts from the *Cinerama Holiday Suite*, excerpts from his score for the CBS documentary *World War I*, the Symphonette No. 2, excerpts from his score for the NBC miniseries *Holocaust*, and *Festive Music*. Morton had a great sense of humor, and was an important supporter of American music, especially as president of the American Society of Composers, Authors and Publishers (ASCAP) from 1986 to 1994.

The two most important changes during the 1985–1986 season were my taking the title of music director, and the appointment of Stephen Albert as our composer-in-residence. I met Stephen when I performed his *Into Eclipse* on my new-music series, Music Today, at Merkin Hall in New York City. My dear friend André Emelianoff was helping me with programming the series and suggested Stephen. It was because of this piece that I met Christopher Kendall, who conducted the premiere of the chamber version with his Twentieth Century Consort in Washington, D.C. Eventually Christopher became my assistant conductor in Seattle and went on to have a distinguished career in music education at the University of Maryland and the University of Michigan.

It was at the performance I led in March 1984 that I fell in love with Stephen's voice as a composer. The musicologist Mary Lou Humphrey described him for his publisher, G. Schirmer, as a "feisty, outspoken man of great integrity, uncompromising ideals, enormous warmth and fierce loyalty." This was all true. While most composers made their livelihood from teaching, Stephen felt that teaching the music of others would get in the way of his own creativity. He made a very nice income as a dealer of rare stamps, a life he kept separate from his music world.

After the Music Today performance I asked Stephen to become our composer-in-residence in Seattle, a post he accepted and held from 1985 to 1988. Stephen was generally unknown, and the Seattle music community thought I was doing something very strange, but I had confidence in him. A few months later Stephen won the Pulitzer Prize for his First Symphony, *RiverRun*. We eventually premiered nine of his works.

During the 1985–1986 season I programmed Stephen's *RiverRun* on the same program as the Dvořák Piano Concerto with Rudolf Firkušný. When one of our local critics criticized my collaboration on the concerto, Stephen called him on the phone and complained. The critic said that I did not look at the soloist enough. Of course this has nothing to do with the musical result, but it was a lesson that, for some people, the visuals really matter.

Stephen was always brutally honest. After a performance of mine of the Brahms Third Symphony he said nothing, which I assumed meant he did not care for it. The next night we did the second performance of the work, and he came backstage to say how great it was, and that it was so much better than the previous night. The following day I told Stephen that the performances were quite similar, except for one cracked note in the French horn toward the beginning of the piece on the first night. I felt the mistake had colored his opinion of the whole performance. He disagreed, so I gave him tapes of both performances. He listened to them, and a few days later he told me I was right. I try never to focus on individual mistakes like that. That said, they can alter one's perception of a performance.

I had a similar experience one summer with my principal horn at Mostly Mozart, Paul Ingraham. Even the greatest horn players can easily crack a note once in a while. One summer we were doing some excerpts from Beethoven's opera, *Fidelio*. I wanted to do the main tenor and soprano arias with more lyric voices than the Wagnerian types usually used. After all, in Beethoven's time there was no such thing as a *Heldentenor*.

We engaged two great artists, Carol Vaness and Vinson Cole. In the first performance the French horn cracked a note at the beginning of Carol's big aria. It was a magnificent performance overall. But the *New York Times* critic could neither forgive nor forget the fluffed note and gave the orchestra a bad review for what otherwise was a wonderful performance.

I continued to do a fair amount of guest conducting during the 1985–1986 season. On one occasion Marshall Turkin, manager of the Pittsburgh Symphony, asked me to guest conduct for a week and to suggest a composer for a work they wanted to commission for their retiring concertmaster, Fritz Siegal. I recommended Stephen Albert, and the result was *In Concordiam*, for violin and orchestra. Stephen was present at the first rehearsal of his piece. As I often do with a first-rehearsal reading of a new work, I run through it to allow the orchestra to get an overall understanding of the piece. Often the mistakes in the first run-through fix themselves as the players become better acquainted with the work. Because Stephen was quite a character and could be very outspoken and direct toward musicians, I asked him to remain quiet at the first rehearsal. We could meet afterward and make sure his concerns were addressed. I explained this to Fritz and requested that he put off asking Stephen's opinion until after the first rehearsal.

Fritz had prepared very well and played the work flawlessly from the first reading, but of course the orchestra needed to be rehearsed at certain points and to become familiar with the work as a whole. Fritz had agreed not to say anything, but at the end of the reading he looked out to Stephen in the audience and asked him for comments. Stephen jumped up and ran down to the front of the stage and gave a dissertation to the orchestra. I could not be impolite to the composer in front of this fine orchestra, so we all waited patiently as Stephen went through the piece bar by bar.

In Concordiam was a terrific piece and received a splendid premiere. However, I felt the ending was a bit thin in terms of orchestration, with only the solo violin and a very few accompanying instruments playing. After the premiere I told Stephen my concerns. He agreed and rewrote the ending. As a thank-you, he gave me two versions of the last page of the piece, one before my suggestions and one after, with all the additional notes written in red ink. I treasure that memento to this day.

At this time Stephen was living primarily in Boston; however, he would come to Seattle for twelve or fourteen weeks during the season. I did a Musically Speaking concert in January 1986 called, "What Is Color in Music?" The works under consideration were Debussy's *Jeux*, Prokofiev's Second Violin Concerto, and orchestral excerpts from Wagner's *Götterdämmerung*. I had the idea that Stephen could write a sequence of chords for me and simply orchestrate them differently using the various sections of the orchestra—woodwinds, brass, percussion, and strings. Then, if he had time, he could do it with a little more variety. I was also going to use the "Farben" movement from Schoenberg's *Five Pieces for Orchestra*, then discuss the Debussy.

The concert was on Sunday afternoon. I called Stephen in Boston on Friday to ask if he could do the orchestrations, and he said he could. When he arrived on Sunday with the music, he had an exquisite sequence of chords orchestrated as I had requested and had written a heroic melody to go with it. It was perfect for the educational purpose, and it made a wonderful musical statement. Stephen was onstage at this concert, and I asked him to describe his compositional process to the audience. His explanation charmed our audience.

The following year Stephen was writing *Anthems and Processionals* for the orchestra as part of his Meet the Composer residency. He asked me to return the manuscript of the chords used for that Musically Speaking concert. He then used it for the opening of his new work, which we premiered in March 1988.

During the 1985–1986 season we once again engaged a stellar line-up of guest piano soloists: Jorge Bolet, Grant Johannesen, Rudolf Firkušný, Yefim Bronfman, Horacio Gutiérrez (twice—once for the Brahms Second Concerto, and again during our Mozart festival with the Piano Concerto in F Major, K. 459), Lilian Kallir, Alexis Weissenberg, Lorin Hollander, and David Bar-Illan. I was building a following for Nadja Salerno-Sonnenberg, who returned after her success in the 1983–1984 season. János Starker did the great but rarely played Hindemith Cello Concerto, and Franco Gulli performed the Alban Berg Violin Concerto (my first time conducting that work). Henri Lazarof wrote his *Poème* as a wedding gift for Jody and me, and we premiered it in March. I still believe it to be one of his finest works.

I began the season featuring the orchestra with works by Ravel, Copland, and Brahms. During the season I did my first performance of Stravinsky's *Symphony of Psalms* and Mahler's Ninth Symphony. We continued our festival at the Fifth Avenue Theater with three Mainly Mozart concerts and four Summer Light Classics concerts. I did a Spanish-influenced program with pieces by Emmanuel Chabrier, Manuel da Falla, Joaquín Rodrigo, Nicolai Rimsky-Korsakov's *Capriccio espagnol*, and Copland's *Danzón cubano*. Gunther Schuller conducted an evening of American music including works by Scott Joplin, Charles Tomlinson Griffes, and George Whitefield Chadwick. Franz Allers did a Viennese evening, and Gerhardt Zimmermann did an all-Gershwin concert.

Engaging good guest conductors is always a challenge. Soloists can come in for a few days and play recitals or orchestral engagements, but conductors generally need to spend a full week, and sometimes they'll have concerns about the quality of the ensemble. In general I believe in the adage, "There are no bad orchestras, only bad conductors."

That said, at times a conductor may not have a rapport with the orchestra, no matter how good each is. When I was in the New York Philharmonic I had a conversation with the general manager, Herb Weissenstein, about this very topic. He was thrilled that the Philharmonic had a relationship with three great conductors: Boulez, Bernstein, and Leinsdorf. We knew their styles and expectations, and very often that led to exceptional performances of the repertoire they excelled in.

It was hard to lure guest conductors to faraway Seattle, and I was always trying to engage the best ones. In 1987–1988 we started to have some success when we engaged Sergiu Comissiona, Mark Elder, Neeme Järvi, Yan Pascal Tortelier, Hermann Michael, and Maxim Shostakovich. We also did five-weeks of pops programming each season with the director Norman Leyden. The audience loved Norman, who took his job very seriously: he had his own music and arrangements and made his own programs.

We also had some superlative pianists. Jorge Bolet, with whom I first worked at the Waterloo Festival, became a regular in Seattle. John Browning was a dear friend who went to Juilliard with my in-laws. Horacio Gutiérrez had appeared with us twice in the previous season and by now was a real Seattle favorite. András Schiff, Alexander Toradze, Emanuel Ax, Alexis Weissenberg, and the Hungarian American pianist Béla Síki, who taught at the University of Washington, also appeared with us. Henryk Szeryng, the legendary violinist, was now appearing with me whenever it could be arranged, and we had a fantastic group of cellists. Lynn Harrell had been featured in the previous two seasons, as had János Starker, and this season Paul Tortelier and Nathaniel Rosen joined us as well.

As we always had a wonderful volunteer chorale in Seattle, which was administered somewhat independently. I would try to include a variety of repertoire for them during the regular Seattle Symphony season. In 1986–1987 we did the Beethoven *Missa solemnis* and the following season, the Brahms *German Requiem*. Both were memorable performances. We did a special concert with Leontyne Price, and she returned for a recital. Kiri Te Kanawa also gave a recital.

When our executive director, Mark Walker, left, Ed Birdwell became our vice president and executive director. Ed played horn in the American Brass Quintet when I was a member, and we were very close friends. I always felt he would be a great arts administrator and helped him in that regard at the Aspen Music Festival. We worked together again after he left the quintet and Aspen to become executive director of LACO. Ed later took positions with Carnegie Hall and the Boston Symphony, then headed the music program at the National Endowment for the Arts. I loved Ed and his wonderful wife, Nancy.

Recordings: Delos

When I first became music director of the Seattle Symphony, Amelia Haygood and Carol Rosenberger at Delos said, "When the orchestra's ready, we'd like to record the Seattle Symphony." It took about three years before I felt it was time. We decided to record a CD of Wagner because at that time the orchestra was doing Wagner's *Ring* cycle every summer with the Seattle Opera. In those days, everywhere I went music lovers identified Seattle with the *Ring*. I therefore thought starting to record with Wagner was a natural entry point. It was standard repertoire, which meant we might be judged by critics alongside other orchestras more famous than ours, but because it was repertoire we were known for, we thought it might not attract the kind of criticism we could have faced with other standard repertoire.

It is hard to evaluate an orchestra without hearing it in standard repertoire. People will say, "Oh, they do Takemitsu wonderfully, but can they do Beethoven or Brahms well?" Then again, it is dangerous to record music that does not need to be recorded. Wagner excerpts seemed like the right balance. Delos sent us their famous engineer, John Eargle, to head the production team.

In those days, it was unusual for orchestras other than the most famous to record the standard repertoire. Certainly, the New York

Philharmonic or Boston Symphony could, but Seattle? Why would anyone buy a recording of Seattle doing Brahms, when you could buy the Berlin Philharmonic? In the early days of my tenure there, we were thought of as a second-tier orchestra. That perception began to change with our first Wagner recordings. Their critical success led us to become known as "America's Wagner orchestra." It was a terrific beginning. The next step was mapping out our own repertoire. That is when we began our American music cycle project, starting with the works of Howard Hanson. When Amelia heard a performance of the Hanson Second Symphony in Seattle, she not only loved the piece but wanted to record it. I told her that generally critics didn't like this kind of music. She didn't care; she wanted me to do the complete symphonies. I was very nervous about that, because if I was going to schedule performances of all seven symphonies, I had to be sure that she would follow through even after seeing some mediocre reviews. And follow through she did. Yes, the concert reviews in both Seattle and Los Angeles were not stellar for Hanson, but Amelia's instincts were correct, and both the sales and CD reviews were excellent.

This was an exciting year for recording. Our first CDs had been very well received. During this season we recorded Hanson's Symphony No. 1; Gershwin's *An American in Paris*; Walter Piston's Symphony No. 2; a complete recording of Bartók's ballet *The Miraculous Mandarin*; Zoltán Kodály's *Háry János*; Tchaikovsky's Symphony No. 2; Schumann's Symphony No. 1 as well as his Overture, Scherzo, and Finale and *Konzertstück* for Four Horns; and Richard Strauss's *Sinfonia Domestica* and *Josephslegende*.

I chose one composer as a guest conductor each season, and this season we had Krzysztof Penderecki. Robert Shaw also came to do Mendelssohn's *Elijah*. We premiered works by Fred Lerdahl and James Willey and continued our commitment to American music with Albert, Diamond, Griffes, Hanson, Piston, and Wallingford Riegger. And we had some great guest artists: Marilyn Horne, Alicia de Larrocha, and Isaac Stern. One of my favorite pianists, Shura Cherkassky, had recently appeared with me in New York and Los Angeles. The only date that worked for him coincided with a week when I was in

Europe. Each season the assistant conductor did a subscription week, so I arranged for Shura to play with Christopher Kendall.

Christopher knew Shura's reputation for playing very freely and thanked me sarcastically. I told him not to worry. Shura had recently done the Chopin Piano Concerto No. 2 with me in New York, and I gave him a tape to study. A few weeks later Christopher came to me, very pleased, and said he had memorized Shura's performance. I had waited for that moment. I told Christopher that I had another tape, one from the second performance. The next day Christopher went crazy: the performance was entirely different. Shura never did the same performance two days in a row. In the end, Christopher did magnificent performances with Shura, and Shura loved him.

Shura and I had done a tour with the Chopin Piano Concerto No. 1 with LACO a few years back, and each of the five performances was different. Generally I do not care for that, but with Shura I never minded. You think of an interpretation both emotionally and intellectually, and from that framework you hope to create something special. His playing was so natural and so musical, and from the opening bars you could see where his interpretation was going to go. Before each performance Shura would ask me to make sure to look at him. If I didn't, he would do something musically to get my attention. I learned that the only time he needed me to look at him was when the piano part was not too difficult. At those times he would look up at me.

That season we expanded to eighteen subscription weeks, and the orchestra no longer played for the Pacific Northwest Ballet.

We had some important administrative changes in the late 1980s. When I was with the NYCS I had engaged Pat Takahashi to be my librarian. After one year I received a call from Robert Shaw, who apologized—he was taking Pat to Atlanta. Pat married the clarinetist William Blayney, and I fondly remember guest conducting Atlanta when Pat and Bill's son, Tom, was born. When we were finally able to get a designated librarian position in Seattle, I stole Pat back from Atlanta and brought her and her family to Seattle. It is impossible to overstate how much that appointment has meant to me over the years, both personally and professionally.

The 1987–1988 season again began with an all-orchestral program: Bedřich Smetana's *The Moldau*, Piston's Fourth Symphony, and Dvořák's Ninth Symphony. Our recording project with Delos was now in full swing, and the orchestra was growing artistically to meet the challenges of producing high-level recordings.

I thought it was very important to travel with the orchestra. Musically, touring helps an orchestra focus. Orchestras that do not travel much see touring as fun and a time to connect with their colleagues while not having the day-to-day issues that always come up at home. Touring was a bad word with the many members of the Seattle board, since many had been disappointed by the orchestra's 1980 European tour, which was of course before my time. They seemed pleased with the artistic results but were concerned about the financial results. I believed we could get good fees in southern California because of my history with many of the presenters and that, if we were able to break even, people would be more open to touring in the future. My friends in Southern California came through, and the tour was a success, artistically, socially, and financially. There was an excellent preview article by John Henken in the *Los Angeles Times* for the tour: I was quoted as saying: "People don't know us. Coming to a major center like Los Angeles is important for us." Henken continued: "The problem of his orchestra's identity is a real one for Schwarz, who humorously reported receiving a 'who-do-you-think-you-are?' challenge from a journalist, regarding the current tour. The tour itself is part of Schwarz's answer to such questions . . . Schwarz had a close relationship with his players here, and that, he says, is true of his work now with the larger ensemble in Seattle. 'I feel like we're all looking for the same thing, for the same reasons. There's an unanimity of opinion, to make music on the highest level we can.'"

During this season we began our Hanson symphony series with his Second Symphony and *Elegy*. A highlight for me was doing Percy Grainger's *The Warriors*, a work I also did with the Sydney Symphony a few years later.

We began our Stravinsky recording cycle with *Petrushka* and *Scherzo fantastique*. At the last session we still had forty-five minutes of recording time left over, so we did a splendid rendition of his *Fireworks*. I was so proud that the orchestra was able to record this short but difficult work in such a brief period of time, without a prior performance.

During the season we also performed and recorded Wagner's Prelude to Acts 1 and 3 and Good Friday Spell from *Parsifal*. I adore this music. I first heard the *Parsifal* suite with Leinsdorf conducting the New York Philharmonic when I was in the orchestra. After the concert I went to his dressing room to congratulate him and chatted with his manager, Shelly Gold. Shelly asked me what I thought about the Wagner, and I told him how remarkable and beautiful the suite was. The suite takes about forty-five minutes, and it is all slow-moving music. Shelly said, "You and Erich are the only two people in the hall who liked it!" He said it was a very important piece for Erich, but boring for the public. I did not agree about the boring part.

Bella Davidovich made her debut with us in 1986–1987, and her son, Dmitry Sitkovetsky, made his in 1987–1988. Another one of my favorite programs was the penultimate program of the season, when Emanuel Ax played the Beethoven Fourth Piano Concerto on the second half of the program. The first half consisted of two favorites of mine: Hans Pfitzner's *Three Preludes from Palestrina* and Alexander Scriabin's *Poem of Ecstasy*. We ended the season with Mahler's Fourth Symphony, continuing our Mahler performance cycle.

Our Trip to Moscow

Through my friend Dmitry Sitkovetsky I was invited to spend a few weeks in Moscow during Christmas and New Year's Eve in 1989. Politically this was a very interesting time, as new freedoms were beginning for the Russian people. Jody, Gabriella, and I were traveling from London, where I had been guest conducting. Because I was doing David Diamond's Symphony No. 4 at one of the concerts in Moscow, David was meeting us in Moscow.

The first question that came up was where to stay. I had been in Moscow in 1976 with the New York Philharmonic, but this was Jody's first trip. We had a choice of a hotel suite or an apartment in the artists' building. A friend of Dima's offered us his mother's apartment, since she was lecturing in Paris. We thought it would be very interesting to live as residents of Moscow rather than as tourists. Dima was staying in the same building on the same floor with his Uncle Vitaly.

Gaby was fourteen months old. We asked if they could arrange for a crib for her, thinking that a portable one would be easy enough to obtain. Well, we found out that was a major issue. Cribs like that were not as common in Russia as they are in the United States. Vitaly and his son traveled far out of town to find one, and it then needed to be assembled. The pieces of the crib didn't quite fit, so they had to spend hours making it work.

We had come well prepared, not knowing what we would find. We had a large box of disposable diapers, two cases of bottled water, peanut butter and crackers, cheeses, fruit, and other food items. The whole Sitkovetsky family laughed at us, especially about the water. Dima often came down the hall for water.

Moscow was snowy and icy cold. The building had a staff of older women guarding the entrance, making sure all was well. The apartment was small and crowded, but it worked for us, even though Jody and I had to share a twin bed. Life became quite simple. The highlight of the day was sitting in the small kitchen at a table near the window, listening to *Midnight in Moscow* on the radio.

Dima had suggested an all-Beethoven program for the Moscow Philharmonic, including the Violin Concerto, and some American music featuring Barber's Violin Concerto for the Radio Orchestra. With the Philharmonic there would be two concerts, so the overture and concerto were the same for both; the Fifth Symphony would be on one and the Sixth on the other. For the Radio Orchestra program we began with Diamond's Symphony No. 4, then the Barber Violin Concerto. After the intermission we did Tchaikovsky's Symphony No. 2, the "Little Russian." Dima played both concertos commandingly, but the orchestras were quite different. The Philharmonic was more Old World and the Radio Orchestra more technically proficient. The Philharmonic concerts were very moving. You could feel the joy and seriousness of their approach.

We played at the beautiful hall at the Moscow Conservatory, and the audience was extremely receptive. Before beginning the rehearsals with the Radio Orchestra, I was told that they were very nervous about the Barber and Diamond pieces. Surprisingly they read them both excellently, and the result sounded similar to that from a fine American orchestra.

I was surprised that the orchestra did not know the Tchaikovsky symphony and did not care for it. Like orchestras around the world they rarely played the first three Tchaikovsky symphonies, and because they played so much Tchaikovsky in general, they did not take the "Little Russian" very seriously. I had to work hard to create a good performance of the piece and to convince the musicians of its worth. In the end it all went very well.

I was paid in rubles and of course had no use for them. I tried to give the stacks of currency to Dima's Uncle Vitaly, but he turned them down and showed me a closet full of them, with little value. U.S. dollars were the most highly valued currency at the time.

We hired a wonderful woman as a babysitter for Gaby when we were out during the evening: she had been Dima's nanny. When we returned to the apartment after the first concert, she was terribly upset. She had tried to wash one of the disposable diapers, but it just got heavier and heavier, so she hung it in the bathroom to dry, which of course it didn't. Once we explained they were disposable, she felt better. We wanted to give her something special when we left and asked what she would like. All she wanted was the extra diapers.

How Could We Have an Influence?

For most of the twentieth century, only a few orchestras beside the New York Philharmonic and the New York Symphony played concerts in New York. Since New York was the musical capital of the country, the Boston Symphony and the Philadelphia Orchestra began playing regularly at Carnegie Hall. When a conductor such as Serge Koussevitsky wanted to bring an important work he had premiered in Boston to the attention of the music world, he would bring it to New York. He did this with the Bartók Concerto for Orchestra.

The New York Music Critics Circle Award was very valuable for any new work. The city was the home of the most important critics, managers, and magazines of the classical music world, and anything of any significance pretty much had to happen there. It's interesting that the printed score of Bartók's Concerto for Orchestra says that the premiere was on December 1, 1944, in New York at Carnegie Hall. But in fact the world premiere was in Boston on that date, and the first New York performance took place on January 10, 1945. Little attention was paid to the piece until it was performed in New York.

In Seattle we didn't have the budget to bring important works or new ideas to New York. If we wanted to influence repertoire, we had to go in another direction: recording. We did have local radio broadcasts each season and did five television shows during my tenure, but I would have done four or five television shows annually if we could have afforded it. Generally the ratings were not high enough to make it worthwhile for the stations, even if the musicians' costs were covered. We once thought that the reason public television was important was to do quality programming that did not rely on ratings. Classical music would never receive the ratings of pop music, and it was always difficult to convince public television stations that classical music was important, beyond *Live from Lincoln Center* and *Great Performers*. Toward the end of my years in Seattle that situation changed for the better with new leadership at KCTS, Seattle's PBS station. They have also been important supporters of my current All-Star Orchestra project.

Two things are essential in recording: having the desire to record, and having someone who wants to record you. Once they want to record you, you have to decide on the repertoire. This may involve some persuasion. "Oh, you're going to do Bach's 'Goldberg' Variations? Why would anybody want another version of the 'Goldberg' Variations?" Of course, sometimes they do.

I knew if we played better and more people came to the concerts, we would get more support. You also have to demonstrate that the orchestra is part of the community. In my early years in Seattle, people would say, "Why do we need a good orchestra? Who cares? We certainly don't need a great orchestra. What's the difference? Is this relevant to our community?"

Those were the kinds of questions I had to answer in 1983, 1984, and 1985. Eventually people stopped asking them, but it took time. Staying in Seattle for so many years meant that I had time to accomplish things that would have been impossible otherwise. You become part of the community, which means people support you. And it was as part of the community that we were able, at the Seeds of Compassion conference in 2008, to bring together a chorus of six hundred singers and instrumentalists to perform the last movement of Beethoven's Ninth for the Dalai Lama and Desmond Tutu.

Finding Our *Nutcracker*

Symphony orchestras try to come up with some repertoire that will essentially be their *Nutcracker*. Ballet companies throughout the country make an important part of their budget from that masterpiece. They do so many performances that they turn a profit, and it helps their bottom line.

Symphony orchestras do not have a *Nutcracker*, but I always tried to think of works Seattle could do that would have the same financial effect. *Messiah* became one, and we did five performances of it a year that usually sold out—so 12,500 people heard this masterpiece of Handel annually. Over the years we did this with the Beethoven Ninth Symphony as well. We found that the Mozart Requiem fits into that category, as well as Orff's *Carmina Burana* and Vivaldi's *Four Seasons*. I have conducted *Messiah* over fifty times and the Beethoven Ninth over sixty times; each one is important, and each one is thrilling.

At the beginning of the 1988–1989 season I was interviewed by Melinda Bargreen of the *Seattle Times*. One of her questions had to do with the terrible problem we were having with scheduling in the opera house. The three major arts institutions were doing quite well and needed to have more time in the hall; it was clear that one of us had to look for a new home. Since the Opera House worked better for the ballet and opera, it made sense for us to be the one to look for a new home. We consulted Cyril Harris about both the Fifth

Avenue Theater and the Paramount Theater. His opinion was that the Paramount could not work acoustically but that the Fifth Avenue Theater could be made to work by reducing the size of the balcony and greatly reducing the number of seats under the overhang. He also suggested tightening the stage and exits for loss of sound. However, the Fifth Avenue had a Chinese decor that could not be touched, and it would have given us only about 1,800 seats—a far cry from the more than 3,000 at the opera house. Under those circumstances, Cyril did not want to be involved with the project. Sam Stroum, our chairman, was interested in buying the Paramount, so Christopher Kendall and I went to Portland to listen to a similar hall that had been renovated for the Oregon Symphony. We returned and reported to Sam that Cyril was correct: it would not be a good idea to renovate the Paramount. When Melinda Bargreen questioned me about a new home for the orchestra, I told her of our community's great need. She published the story in the Sunday edition, and Sam called me that morning. He though Melinda's article was terrible and was upset that I had spoken to her about a new hall when we had such pressing financial needs. From now on, he said, I should only be talking about endowment, not a new concert hall. He was the boss, so I told him I would do just that.

Musically the season was very exciting. Both Isaac Stern and Marilyn Horne gave recitals, and our orchestral soloists were once again outstanding: Cherkassky, Davidovich, Firkušný, Freire, Hollander, Kalichstein, Larrocha, Salerno-Sonnenberg, Suk, Vaness, and others. Penderecki was a guest conductor, and Diamond helped with one of my Musically Speaking concerts on which we performed his Fourth Symphony. We also did premieres by Lerdahl and Willey and works by other Americans: Piston, Hanson, Albert, and Gershwin. Robert Shaw came to do Mendelssohn's *Elijah*, and we continued to do a great deal of recording of Bartók, Diamond, Grieg, Kodály, Schumann, Strauss, and Tchaikovsky.

The 1989–1990 season was a terrific one for me. I received the Ditson Conductor Award from Columbia University, did Mozart's *The Marriage of Figaro* with the Seattle Opera, my fourth production with them, and I conducted major orchestras in Paris, Bamberg, Frankfurt, and Moscow, as well as a semistaged production of Stravinsky's *Chant du rossignal* at the Kirov in St. Petersburg. The many recording projects in Seattle continued, and I began a series of Haydn recordings for Delos with the Scottish Chamber Orchestra. Two recordings for my old company Nonesuch were nominated for a Grammy: the music of George Perle with the Music Today ensemble, and a CD of Kurt Weill with Teresa Stratas and the NYCS. The highlights for me in Seattle were an all-orchestral program to start the season that included Diamond's magnificent Second Symphony, Respighi's orchestration of Bach's Passacaglia in C Minor—both of which we recorded—and Brahms's Second Symphony. During the season we did our first Elgar Symphony No. 1, a work rarely programmed by American orchestras. I did the Verdi Requiem with a guest choir director, George Fiore, who would become our new director. Again we programmed works by many American composers—Barber, Diamond, Hanson, Hovhaness, Jonathan Kramer, Mennin, Paine, Piston, Schwantner, and Sheng. We also did two world premieres, one of Dan Asia's, Symphony No. 1, and the other of Lazarof's *Tableaux* with the piano soloist Garrick Ohlsson. We continued our composer-conductor concerts with Panufnik conducting his own Nocturne and Symphony No. 8, as well as music by his favorite, Mozart. Our Mainly Mozart series continued, but we moved it to Meany Hall at the University of Washington and collaborated with their music school. One of our soloists during the season was Yo-Yo Ma. He performed the Édouard Lalo Cello Concerto as well as the world premiere of David Diamond's *Kaddish for Cello and Orchestra*.

David Diamond and Yo-Yo had met during the Diamond *Song of Hope*/Bruch *Kol Nidrei* program with the NYCS in 1987. I asked David if he would write a kaddish for cello, and asked Yo-Yo if he would perform it. This led to the premiere of Diamond's *Kaddish* for cello and orchestra in April 1990. However, Columbia Records, which had Yo-Yo under contract, would not allow him to record it with us for Delos, so my dear friend János Starker recorded it.

The 1990–1991 season created some wonderful musical memories for me. We did the Busoni Piano Concerto with one of my best friends from high school, Kun Woo Paik. Kun Woo and I often played together in small recitals while we were both at Juilliard. After he graduated he moved to London for further study and ended up marrying a famous Korean actress, Yoon Jeong-hee, and living outside of Paris. When we did the Busoni, an audience member sent me a note: he had recognized Kun Woo's wife and suggested that I introduce her to the audience before beginning the concerto. We also performed two of my favorite choral works, Elgar's *Dream of Gerontius* and Mendelssohn's *Lobgesang*. We continued our Bruckner cycle by doing the magnificent Symphony No. 8, and were finally to the point where we could repeat a Mahler symphony, so we did the Symphony No. 1 again. Our composer-conductor this season was my dear friend Gunther Schuller, and we continued to record a great deal, including American music by Albert, Creston, Diamond, Hanson, Hovhaness, and Piston. Our first volume of Hanson received three Grammy nominations and, surprising everyone, stayed on the Billboard Classical Top Twenty Chart for forty-one weeks! We also recorded the complete *Daphnis et Chloé* by Ravel. Our three small orchestra series, Basically Baroque, Mainly Mozart, and American Music, were doing quite well. Finding venues at which to present these concerts was a challenge, but they were always interesting and musically rewarding.

We added some guest conductors to the Pops series, did our eighteen subscription weeks, continued our live radio broadcasts on Classical KING FM, and continued to record for Delos. In 1990 our recordings received five Grammy nominations.

In 1990–1991 we also started a lecture series called The Creative Impulse, which I hosted with creative artists, mostly composers. We talked about art and its future as well as its importance in the city, the state, the country, and our civilization in general. We asked questions about what art was and who the arbiter of art should be. We presented one of the lectures in an art gallery where a metal garbage pail, painted green, hung on the wall. I asked the composer Richard Danielpour if he thought it was art. He was very careful, but in the end he called it "entertaining."

We opened the 1991–1992 season with Mahler's Symphony No. 3. I was reminded of the first time I heard this masterpiece live at

Carnegie Hall, when the Boston Symphony performed it in 1961 with their concertmaster and assistant conductor Richard Bergen conducting. It was a very small audience: the work was basically unknown to the general public, and Bernstein's Mahler revival had just begun. That performance helped create in me a deep love of his music.

Our second subscription program featured Hanson's Symphony No. 5, Danielpour's Symphony No. 3, and Tchaikovsky's Violin Concerto with Gil Shaham. This was typical of those days, yet I'm surprised that we were able to do these programs so successfully. The American music was not modern in a severe way, but to most in our audience it must have been unknown. Of course, by this time we had done so much American music that to our audiences, Hanson was as traditional as Copland.

We did William Schuman's *Judith*, our second recording of his music after doing the Fifth Symphony the year before. It led to our recording project of all Schuman's symphonies, a project that has meant so much to me personally and artistically. Because Paul Creston had been my main composition teacher when I was in high school, I was overjoyed to record his Symphony No. 3. We also did Hanson's Symphony No. 5 and his Piano Concerto with Carol Rosenberger. We invited the Juilliard Quartet back to do Louis Spohr's Concerto and Piston's Concerto, which we also recorded. Jessye Norman and Ivo Pogorelich did recitals, and the composer Toru Takemitsu joined us for a Musically Speaking concert in which we performed his piece *A Flock Descends into the Pentagonal Garden*. We ended the season with Hanson's Seventh and Beethoven's Ninth Symphonies.

It was imperative that we increase our revenue, so we presented four recitals: Zukerman and Perlman, Salerno-Sonnenberg with Cecile Licad, Yo-Yo Ma with Jeffrey Kahane, and Kathleen Battle. We also began a new tradition that lasted at least until I left, which was to stage one of our five Pop programs without the orchestra, something we called "stand-alone." Ed Birdwell left as our executive director for personal reasons and MaryAnn Champion, our board president, took over. Ron Woodard, who was the president of the Boeing Commercial Airplane Group, became our chairman. It was Ron who brought us into the era of Benaroya Hall; he was a remarkable leader for the organization at this crucial point. We won an Emmy for our TV program "A Romantic Evening" for KCTS, and the station also recorded our first Musically Speaking program of the season, making two hour-long shows from the material.

Jody and I were very close to the great actor Werner Klemperer and his partner and soon-to-be-wife, Kim Hamilton. Werner, the son of the legendary conductor Otto Klemperer, was an avid music lover. he would come to many of my rehearsals and concerts in New York at the Ninety-second Street Y, Fisher Hall, and Alice Tully Hall. He always requested a score and would follow along during rehearsals and concerts. Werner and I worked together whenever possible. To open this 1992–1993 season, he narrated the complete *Egmont*, a narration, based on Goethe's original tragedy, linked Beethoven's music with the story line from the play. The rest of the program was André Watts's performance of Beethoven's Fourth Piano Concerto. André is an extraordinary man and a very great artist; over the years I have probably performed with him more than any other pianist, beginning with the Waterloo Festival in 1976.

We also had János Starker with us again, as we did just about every year. This season he played the Ernst von Dohnányi *Konzertstück* for cello and orchestra, which we also recorded. Emanuel Ax and Misha Dichter were with us again, as they were most seasons, and at Mostly Mozart as well. Peter Serkin did the Max Reger Piano Concerto. Peter played the traditional repertoire but was also very interested in works on the periphery of the standards, and he was deeply interested in the Reger. I wanted to delve more deeply into this composer's oeuvre, but he is a composer that has never resonated with me—at least not yet.

Continuing with the idea of establishing certain musical programmatic traditions during this holiday season, and with the strong encouragement of Mel and Roz Poll, both dear friends—Mel is an excellent tenor, and Roz is a committed volunteer for the arts and a manager—I programmed Handel's oratorio *Judas Maccabaeus* in both New York and Seattle. Roz was convinced that this could become a yearly occurrence, not only because of the quality of the music, but because of the story line as it relates to the Jewish holiday of Hanukkah. The staff was not convinced we could fill our opera house with this work. They were right.

We did Diamond's Symphony No. 8 and John Corigliano's Symphony No. 1. John also joined me for our discussion of his work on our Musically Speaking concert. Bright Sheng became our new composer-in-residence this season. We did a suite from his opera *The Song of Majnun*, and he started the Young Composers Workshop. The workshop taught gifted beginning composers; most were in their junior and senior years in high school, but some were younger. Instruction in composition over a period of three or four months culminated in a concert of chamber music with Seattle Symphony musicians. This workshop continues to this day. After Bright left the orchestra, Sam Jones, my longest-serving composer-in-residence, taught these talented young composers.

Among the most interesting pieces of the season was Ernest Bloch's symphony *America: An Epic Rhapsody*. Bloch was born in Geneva, Switzerland, in 1880 and came to the United States in 1916, where he composed and taught until 1930, at which time he returned to Switzerland with a grant that enabled him to compose without having to teach. He returned to the United States again in 1939. In 1927 the magazine *Musical America* held a competition for American composers to write a work on an American theme. It was judged by Boston's Koussevitzky, Philadelphia's Stokowski, New York's Damrosch, Chicago's Frederick Stock, and San Francisco's Alfred Hertz, and the winner would receive $3,000. The work would be premiered simultaneously by those five orchestras and would be performed the following season by most of the American professional orchestras. Bloch, who had become a citizen by the time he composed the winning work in 1926, started the score by quoting Walt Whitman: "O America, because you build for mankind, I build for you." At the end of the work Bloch wrote an anthem to be sung by the audience during the performance; he hoped it would become our national anthem. The anthem is quoted often throughout the last movement, and I thought that if the audience had the anthem written out with Bloch's text, it might be possible to have them join in with the assembled chorus onstage at our performance. I decided to try this out at my Sunday afternoon Musically Speaking concert in a program that would be repeated on the following two nights. Program notes with musical examples were typical at one time; however, many people don't read music. But I decided, why not? I inserted the anthem into the program, and prior to the performance I explained to the audience that at the end of this forty-five-minute symphony we would all sing this anthem together. I was able to rehearse with the standing audience at the Musically Speaking concert. I first played the anthem with the orchestra and chorus onstage and then rehearsed with the audience. I told the audience that I would give them a warning and then, at the appropriate moment, ask them to stand, and I would conduct them. It went off without a hitch. They seemed as thrilled as I was at hearing 3,000 people sing Bloch's anthem. But what would happen on Monday and Tuesday nights? I decided to put an insert in the program again with the music and words, preceded by an explanation of what was going to happen. I told the audience they would hear the melody many times during the last movement and that our chorus would be spread throughout the hall to help. At the appropriate time I would turn around and we would all sing the anthem together. Remarkably, the audience was terrific both nights.

We started to add special concerts, similar to the old light classics and the like that we thought would attract a large audience. One was a Tchaikovsky Spectacular: the *Romeo and Juliet Overture*, the Piano Concerto No. 1, *Marche slave*, and the *1812 Overture*. It was a success, and in subsequent seasons we would add a special single performance with either the soloist or the program, guaranteeing a large audience. We did the Mahler Symphony No. 7; the only one we had not yet programmed was the Symphony No. 8 ("Symphony of a Thousand"). We ended with a lovely program: Copland's rarely played *Symphonic Ode* and his Piano Concerto (with Lorin Hollander), excerpts from Prokofiev's *Cinderella*, and, to end the program, Ravel's Suite No. 2 from his *Daphnis et Chloé Suite*.

This was the orchestra's ninetieth-anniversary season. I described my feelings about it in the program:

When I think about music, I think about a wealth of extraordinary masterpieces, works of art, many of which have become monuments of the orchestral repertoire over a period of three hundred years. When I look to our 90th anniversary season, I am amazed that this orchestra has had such an incredible history. We have performed under some of the greatest composers of the twentieth century who joined the Seattle Symphony as guest conductors. Think of it: Stravinsky, Hindemith, Hanson, and Copland.

When I put this season together, I wanted to create a feeling for what was going on musically ninety years ago, one of the most exciting times in musical history, as well as to continue to look to the future. 1903 was the culmination of the great romantic period with the new voice of the twentieth century. We were about to see the emergence of Russian-French-American composer Igor Stravinsky, who in the second decade of the new century changed the direction of musical composition. To pick a handful of representative pieces from the 1903–1904 season was difficult. But peppered throughout our 90th season we will perform Elgar, Sibelius, Ives, Mahler, Liadov, Glazunov, and other prominent composers who were actively composing at the turn of the century. Yet, as with every season, we look forward to our own time. Therefore, to commemorate our 90th season, three works have been written for us by McKinley, Sheng, and Tsontakis. Two of our other favorite living composers will also be joining us: David Diamond, for a performance of *This Sacred Ground*, based on the Gettysburg address, and Alan Hovhaness, for a performance of his signature piece, *Mysterious Mountain*.

To open the season we begin with an extraordinary overture written by Elgar in 1903, *In the South*, which is more of a tone poem by this English composer.

William Thomas McKinley, a remarkably prolific composer from Boston, joins in our 90th season celebration, with a world premiere of his Concerto for Orchestra No. 2, written for the Seattle Symphony that year.

One of Seattle's favorite violinists, Elmar Oliveira, joins us for two works by composers who were very active in the early part of this century: Ravel, and Chausson. Concluding that concert, we will perform Dvořák's exquisitely beautiful Symphony #6.

Our 90th season also marks the 150th year since the birth of Edvard Grieg. We will be honoring his jubilaeum throughout our season by performing his noteworthy compositions.

One of the most exciting series for me each season is our six Musically Speaking performances on Sunday afternoons. These concerts give us all an opportunity to delve a little deeper into the magnificent music that the symphony performs.

It is my hope that our Musically Speaking series will help us to further understand the musical voice of these great composers and possibly make it easier for their works to *speak* to us.

It was a very special season in other ways as well. Perhaps most significant was the appointment of Deborah Rutter as our executive director. I met Deborah during the winter of the previous season, when I was conducting the Los Angeles Philharmonic; she had left the Philharmonic to become the executive director of LACO. We had an excellent meeting, and afterward I spoke to Ron Woodard and the search committee to support her as our next executive director. I thought she would be fantastic, with her experience in Los Angeles with the Philharmonic and the Chamber Orchestra, her extensive knowledge of music, and her business acumen as a graduate of the business school at Stanford.

We once again opened the season featuring the orchestra with an all-orchestral program: Elgar's *In the South*, Hanson's *Lux Aeterna*, excerpts from Grieg's *Peer Gynt*, and, after intermission, Tchaikovsky's Symphony No. 6. We also did a suite of Sibelius tone poems, lovely works that are not often programmed: *Lemminkäinen's Return*, *Pohjola's Daughter*, *Night Ride and Sunrise*, and the popular *Valse triste*, written in 1903. After the success of the prior seasons' recital series, we initiated a Distinguished Artists Series with recitals by Isaac Stern; Yefim Bronfman; Frederica von Stade; Pamela Frank and Peter Serkin; Mstislav Rostropovich and Lambert Orkis; and Jessye

Norman. We also started a series called Popular Culture, which included the remarkable Bobby McFerrin. The pianist Awadagin Pratt made his debut with the orchestra. Besides being a great musician, he is a fine athlete and wanted to play some basketball while in Seattle, so some of the musicians in the orchestra put together a game for him. I wasn't wild about this: it is easy to hurt a hand or finger in a basketball game. Monday's concert went very well. But on Tuesday Awadagin came to my dressing room just before the concert with his right arm in a sling. When he saw the look of horror on my face, he started laughing—it was a joke!

As a great admirer of the music of Richard Strauss, I had always wanted to perform his *Taillefer*, written in 1903. Strauss was asked to compose a piece for the University of Heidelberg's centenary celebration, and in return he would receive an honorary doctorate. With university resources available he could write a twenty-minute piece for 120 musicians, plus three soloists and large chorus. The orchestra is almost the size of Schoenberg's *Gurre-Lieder*, but the work is much shorter. I really wanted to do it for the ninetieth anniversary, but hiring all those soloists and extra players was impossible. If I did a choral work on the second half, the soloist and chorus would be taken care of—but what about all the extra musicians, probably a minimum of forty extra? The only option was to do it in conjunction with the excellent Seattle Youth Symphony. What a great experience it would be for the students. I asked the orchestra if they would permit the Youth Symphony to play with us. (Generally orchestras do not allow nonprofessionals to be used as extra players.) I said that I would love it if they could make an exception in this case, but if not, I would understand completely. The musicians agreed, and the program had the *Taillefer* on the first half and Beethoven's *Missa solemnis* on the second. We enlarged our own chorus by adding the Seattle University Chorale, and it was a most remarkable experience for everyone onstage. The season ended with Mahler's Symphony No. 6, written in 1903.

We were now full speed ahead for our new concert space, Benaroya Hall. That year I received Musical America's Conductor of the Year award. It was the third time it was given, and I was the first American to receive it. I also began my relationship with the Tokyo Philharmonic and Orchard Hall, going there three times a year for two weeks of concerts on each trip.

I believed that if the orchestra was to perform in a venue or on a series, I should conduct and perform with them. With that in mind, I conducted the opening Pops concert this season with an all-Gershwin concert featuring the great jazz singer Ernestine Anderson. We again began our regular subscription season with an all-orchestra program: Brahms's Serenade No. 1 and the Bartók Concerto for Orchestra, which we had recorded a few years prior. Our second series included Mahler's Symphony No. 4. On the same program Alessandra Marc sang Richard Strauss's *Four Last Songs*, and we began with his *Till Eulenspiegel's Merry Pranks*. Alessandra had just done some Wagner and the Mahler in Tokyo with the Tokyo Philharmonic the previous season. At the time she didn't know the Mahler and asked to have the music sent to her, which we did—four times. She kept misplacing it. When she finally listened to it she said, "Kathleen Battle sings this, not a big soprano like me." But I felt that in that low range her voice would be perfect. The soprano part is more in the mezzo range, and the quality of voice should be childlike. I felt that a big voice like hers could be perfect for this work. I pushed pretty hard, and in the end it went beautifully.

The other memorable moment of this concert was bringing in John Cerminaro to play first horn. Our regular horn, Bob Bonnevie, was sick, so I asked John if he could come in as a guest. I remember being in the rehearsal room at the opera house when John played his first solo toward the beginning of Mahler's Fourth Symphony. Jan Baunton, our principal second violin, said to me while the music was going on, "Who is making that incredible sound?" An incredible sound it was. This was the beginning of a long and wonderful musical relationship between John and our orchestra. There were some rough patches, as there always are in a family, but what an artist he was and is, and how he helped change the level of our orchestra. His exacting work ethic influenced everyone. He was always extremely well prepared and arrived early to acclimate himself, to focus, to concentrate, to be there for

Drawing for the 1983 Mostly Mozart Festival by Al Hirschfeld, published in the *New York Times*. Pictured are oboist Heinz Holliger, flutist Jean-Pierre Rampal, violinist Henrik Schering, cellist Yo-Yo Ma, violinist Pinchas Zukerman, and pianists Alicia de Larrocha and Bella Davidovich. Photograph © The Al Hirschfeld Foundation. www.AlHirschfeldFoundation.org.

Nadja Salerno-Sonnenberg at the Waterloo Festival tent in New Jersey, ca. 1982. This was the beginning of her wonderful career and one of the first times we worked together. Photograph by Sol Greitzer.

At the Seventy-ninth Street entrance of Riverside Park. This was used for promotion of the Mostly Mozart festival in 1983. Photograph © 1981 Jack Vartoogian/FrontRowPhotos.

At Jody's and my wedding, 1984. *Back row, left to right*: my mother, Gerta; my father, John; Jody; Rabbi Milstein; Jody's father, Sol Greitzer, my brother-in-law Sandy Grossman; Jody's mother, Shirley Greitzer; and me. *Front, left to right*: my son Daniel, my niece Allegra Grossman, and my daughter Alysandra. Photograph by Brian Grossman.

Jody and me, around the time of our wedding, in 1984. Personal collection.

This photograph of Jody, Gabriella, and me was taken by a wonderful photographer of children, Camilla Panufnik, at the beautiful home she had shared with her late husband, the great Polish-English composer Andrzej Panufnik, in Twickenham, England, 1989. Photograph by Camilla Jessel Panufnik.

At Alysandra's bat mitzvah in 1985. *From left, front row*: John, Gerta, me, Daniel, Alysandra, Jody, Bernice, and Sandy Grossman. *Back row*: Jeanette and Bob Young. Personal collection.

Andrzej Panufnik at the 92nd street Y when we did his *Autumn Music* in 1985. Andrzej and his wonderful wife, Camilla, were very close friends. I continue to be very excited by his marvelous music. Photograph by Camilla Jessel Panufnik.

With Dizzy Gillespie, 1985. I was fortunate to know a few of the jazz greats during my trumpet-playing years. Photograph by Charles Colin.

Carol Rosenberger, 1991. I worked with Carol in her capacity both as an artistic adviser with Delos and as a superb piano soloist with a number of my orchestras over the years. She now runs Delos. Photograph by Johan Elbers, courtesy of Delos Productions, Inc.

A reception during the Mostly Mozart Festival in Tokyo, 1993. *Left to right*: pianist Lilian Kallir, mezzo-soprano Cecilia Bartoli, me, violinist Chee-Yun, and bass-baritone Samuel Ramey. I conducted Cecilia's New York debut at the festival. Personal collection.

Peter Serkin after a performance with the Seattle Symphony of the Max Reger Piano Concerto, 1992. Serkin is a remarkably thoughtful and proficient pianist. Photograph by Larey McDaniel.

In Seattle with Amelia Haygood, who led Delos's American music recording project. She began the series with the symphonies of Howard Hanson and went on to feature many others, including Alan Hovhaness, pictured here. That series had a great impact on the reemergence of interest of the great music of the American symphonists from the middle of the twentieth century. Photograph courtesy of Delos Productions, Inc.

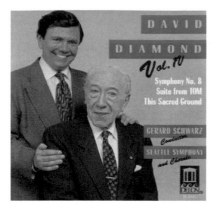

I have had wonderful partners, first Delos and then Naxos, to bring twentieth-century American music to greater prominence, including Barber, Carter Creston, Diamond, Fine, Foote, Griffes, Hanson, Mennin, Piston, and Taylor. This CD cover above is the fourth volume of the David Diamond series. Personal collection.

Left to right: my sisters, Jeanette and Bernice, and my father, ca. 1995. Bernice lives in Short Hills, New Jersey, and we would often spend family time together at her beautiful home. Personal collection.

In Seattle with Vladimir Feltsman, ca. 1995. I met Vlodya when he first arrived in the United States in 1987, and in the years since we have collaborated on a wide range of his extensive repertoire. He is a great artist and a wonderful friend. Photograph by Larey McDaniel.

Jody, Gabriella, Julian, and me at home in Seattle, 1998. Photograph by Mike Urban.

There were two flutists who often came to Mostly Mozart, Jean-Pierre Rampal and James Galway, ca 1995. This was a photo from the opening series of concerts with Galway at Fisher Hall. I first met Jimmy when he was first flute with the Berlin Philharmonic and would come to visit our New York Philharmonic principal, Julius Baker. Not only was he an exceptional player, but even when he was still in the orchestra he had a clear vision of his future as the major soloist he became. Photograph by Alexander Agor.

Yo-Yo Ma, 1998. I started working with Yo-Yo in the late 1970s, playing most of the major repertoire for cello as well as some new music, such as David Diamond's *Kaddish* and Richard Danielpour's Cello Concerto. Photograph by Larey McDaniel.

Hélène Grimaud at the very beginning of her career, 1998. She was so fresh and fascinating, both musically and because of her love of wolves, which led her to move to a state that allowed pet wolves. Photograph by Larey McDaniel.

When Nelson Mandela came to Seattle to speak in 1999, I had the opportunity to give him a conducting lesson: he was going to conduct the orchestra and many schoolchildren, including Gabriella and Julian, in South Africa's new national anthem. He agreed to do it only if I would stand next to him and help out if necessary. He did a beautiful job. Photograph by Harley Soltes/The Seattle Times.

Conducting a rehearsal of the Czech Philharmonic and Prague Philharmonic Choir in Ernst Toch's *Cantata of the Bitter Herbs* at the Rudolfinum in Prague, 2000. The program included Milhaud's *Sérvice sacré*, both released on Naxos. ©2016 The Milken Family Foundation, courtesy of the Milken Archive of Jewish Music.

Renée Fleming with the composer Behzad Ranjbaran at the premiere of his *Songs of Eternity*, Seattle, 2002. I premiered his Violin Concerto with Joshua Bell in Liverpool in 2003. Both were very successful.
Photograph by Ben VanHouten.

Jody, Gabriella, Julian, and me in Sun Valley, Idaho, during the Christmas break in 2003. Skiing at this resort was a wonderful family tradition of ours. Photograph by Otto Lang.

Pat Takahashi, 2003. She is a very dear friend and a great librarian. Much of my success is owed to the remarkable work that she has always done for me, first in New York and then in Seattle. Photograph by Larey McDaniel.

Jody and me with Jack and Becky Benaroya in Seattle's Temple De Hirsh Sinai in 2004. Photograph by Robin Layton.

the music. John took every rehearsal and every concert seriously, and his attitude was adopted by many of the orchestra members. He was not only a great artist and a great player, but he helped build the quality of the orchestra.

On our third series we did the world premiere of David Stock's *Power Play*; Albert Roussel's Symphony No. 2, a great work very rarely played; and the Tchaikovsky Violin Concerto with Akiko Suwanai. This was her first appearance with us, and at twenty-two she had already won the Tchaikovsky Competition in Moscow. She played gorgeously, and I will never understand why she did not become one of the music world's superstars. On the next series, I did the Glazunov Symphony No. 6, an extraordinary work rarely performed in the United States. Even with all this unusual music, the audience continued to grow. I felt we had developed a real sense of trust and hope for the future of the orchestra, the community, and classical music. On the next series we did the Tchaikovsky Symphony No. 4 and the world premiere of Henri Lazarof's Choral Symphony No. 3. The Lazarof was a long and very difficult piece for chorus, orchestra, and alto and bass soloists. The chorus part was extremely challenging, and they worked for months. Sheila Nadler and Terry Cook were the excellent soloists. The piece was a huge challenge for everyone—especially the audience. So far I had only programmed new music that the audience generally liked and at times loved, but this forty-five-minute symphony did not touch them the way others had.

As I mentioned earlier, Milton Katims was very important to the growth and success of our orchestra during his twenty-two years as music director. I was finally able to invite him to guest conduct after the fund-raiser that he had done for us a few years before. Joshua Bell was the soloist, and Milton did Barber's *Medea's Meditation and Dance of Vengeance* and the Brahms Symphony No. 4. With this concert all the issues of Milton's past were finally laid to rest.

Deborah Rutter, Jody, and I, in full fund-raising mode, were helped by so many in the community. The Seattle Music Teachers Association even got involved, having their piano students sell practice time to raise money. Their success allowed us to buy an additional Steinway grand piano for the new hall, which we named "Kids for Keys." It had a darker, more colorful sound than our other Steinway and made for a marvelous option for our soloists. This was the season that we decided to move the future hall to the downtown site where it is today.

I continued to work through the Shostakovich symphonies this season with the Eleventh. Up to that point I had only conducted the First and the Fifth, so I decided to study them all, doing one each season (with a couple of exceptions). I also did Shostakovich's Symphony No. 13 in New York with the Chamber Symphony. The last concert of the season usually featured a major choral work, and this time we did *The Damnation of Faust* by Berlioz.

The 1995–1996 season was an exciting one. The first order of business was to find a new director for the chorus. I have always tried to bring musicians into the orchestra family who would bring something special to the organization, whether as a player, an assistant conductor, or the choral director. For the last fourteen years we had two wonderful choral directors, and since the chorus is a volunteer organization with a relatively small budget, we always had difficulty filling the position of conductor, which was part-time. During the 1994–1995 season Gregory Vancil was the interim director, and we had a number of very gifted guests. Then a kind of miracle happened. Abraham Kaplan, a distinguished professor at the University of Washington, said he might be interested. Abe prepared many of the choruses for Bernstein at the New York Philharmonic and even advised Bernstein when he was composing his *Chichester Psalms*. He also followed Robert Shaw as the director of the Collegiate Chorale in New York and wrote a seminal book on choral conducting. When we met again (I had known him since my trumpet-playing days in New York), Abe said that he would love to do it, but there were a number of conditions. He wanted to go over all the repertoire with me, including standard works such as Handel's *Messiah*; he wanted his title to be associate conductor for choral activities rather than assistant conductor; and he wanted the chorus to have its own concert, supported by the Seattle Symphony. In other words, he wanted to create a great chorus. I loved his plan, and we began. Abe was a perfectionist, and our very detailed meetings about repertoire were always interesting. He demanded much of his singers and auditioned everyone, keeping only the most qualified members.

Abe chose to clean house and make difficult decisions right away. But his approach was met with tremendous opposition. The chorus was even more of a family than the orchestra: they were volunteers who sang because of their love of music and for the social atmosphere created by that love. I asked him if he would consider going a little more slowly, but his answer was always an artistic one, and I had agreed to support him. Deborah also had her concerns, but we stood by Abe through some very difficult times. A mezzo he eliminated was married to a prominent sports writer for one of our local newspapers, so Abe's every move and performance was scrutinized by the press. A campaign against him ensued. I loved Abe and supported him as well as I could. Although his decisions were right musically, they may have come too quickly for our volunteer chorus. Musically, however, he did an exemplary job, and it was always a joy for me to discuss the vocal scores with him. Abe stayed with the symphony for five seasons, making great strides with the chorus and important contributions to our performances.

There were a few other important additions. David Diamond became our honorary composer-in-residence. Also, John Cerminaro became the guest principal first horn. When I first arrived in Seattle, Carla Johnson was the artistic administrator and orchestra manager; she was always a joy to work with, with a mischievous sense of humor. As we started to grow, she gave up the position of orchestra manager and worked primarily on artistic areas. She had left the season before, and Toby Tolokan took her place. I respected Toby and loved working with him.

The opening concert of the season was an all-orchestral one, with the David Diamond *Romeo and Juliet* and the world premiere of Sheng's Four Pieces for Orchestra. After intermission we did Dvořák's Notturno in B for Strings, and we ended with Leoš Janáček's *Sinfonietta*.

The Key Arena

In October the new basketball arena, the Key Arena, was opening. The owner of the Seattle SuperSonics, Barry Ackerley, asked me if the symphony could play for the opening. He wanted the first event to be not a basketball game, but a community-oriented concert. I loved the idea and after a number of meetings, he decided on Peabo Bryson as the popular guest soloist and José Carreras as the classical guest. The orchestra was beginning to be a real community asset and this kind of exposure was wonderful for us and for classical music. It was decided that I would do the first half with the orchestra and that the second half would be Bryson and Carreras. I programmed the Overture to Glinka's *Ruslan and Ludmilla*, the "Jupiter" movement from Holst's suite *The Planets*, Tchaikovsky's *1812 Overture* with the University of Washington Husky Marching Band as special guests marching in uniform, and ended with John Philip Sousa's *Stars and Stripes Forever*, conducted by the coach of the basketball team, George Karl, and joined by the Sonics' Gary Payton, Detlef Schremph, Sam Perkins, and Michael Cage in the percussion section. The orchestra's percussionists, led by Randy Baunton, came with me to the team's practice facility to teach the very enthusiastic players to play various instruments and to teach George to conduct. Everyone had a great time, and the sold-out arena of 17,000 went wild for the symphony and Sonics alike.

A highlight that year was the performance and recording of Panufnik's Symphony No. 3. It is a real masterpiece, and it became the main work on an all-Panufnik recording made for JVC's new record company. To this day it is one of my favorite CDs, but unfortunately the JVC record company did not last long, and I have not been able to have the CD released on another label. We did Walton's Symphony No. 1 and Bolcom's Symphony No. 4 and Hovhaness's *Magnificat* with our chorus and soloists. We also premiered Bill Kraft's *Symphony of Sorrows* and Robert Starer's Double Piano Concerto, played by Misha and Cipa Dichter. All the other series continued very successfully—Musically Speaking, Pops, Popular Culture, Discover Music, and Distinguished Artists—with Galway, Gutiérrez, Jerry Hadley, Thomas Hampson, Larrocha, and Mutter as soloists. We also had the Basically Baroque series, Light Classics, and Mornings with the Symphony, and we played for the Seattle Opera.

In November the design of our new performance space was unveiled, and the building was named Benaroya Hall. Our building team was in place and excitement was growing. Two of my favorite pianists were playing that season, Ivan Moravec and Eugene Istomin. Gene was celebrating his seventieth birthday with a cross-country tour. Part of the idea was to travel with his own piano and piano technician. It is easy to understand what a joy that could be for a pianist, instead of hoping for the best with unknown instruments when you arrive at a concert hall. Most important halls have a few pianos to choose from, but there is nothing like the comfort of playing on your own instrument. As a young soloist Gene recorded many albums and later collaborated with Isaac Stern and Leonard Rose in a trio. Now he wanted to record his favorite Mozart concertos and asked if I would conduct them with him and the Seattle Symphony. I agreed, and a date was set for his arrival on the West Coast.

Gene wanted to have his own definitive recording of two Mozart concertos, K. 467 and K. 459. He wanted everything to be perfect—the orchestra, the recording room, and the recording company. He chose an audiophile company and asked that the recording take place at the St. Thomas Center, a little way outside of town. We had three sessions scheduled, one on Monday afternoon and two on Tuesday. At a small dinner for Gene at our home on Sunday night, he told me that in the slow movement of K. 467 the strings needed to sound more beautiful than those of the Vienna Philharmonic. I said we would try.

When we arrived at the venue, the special engineer was setting up his handmade microphones, which were placed not directly on the floor but on foam boxes, so that there would be no extra vibrations. My regular engineer, Al Swanson, was acting as his assistant. The owner and president of the company was present, as were the piano technician Gene had brought from New York and my longtime producer, Adam Stern. I don't think Gene ever made a mistake, and his piano sounded fantastic, its sound bright but beautiful. Though I had performed these concertos many times with the orchestra, we had not done them recently. During the first reading, every time there was the slightest problem Gene would look unhappy, and he would occasionally say something. Some of the orchestra members noticed it and were displeased. However, we did the first take of the first movement of K. 467 and, with very few exceptions, it went very beautifully.

We took a break and went to an adjacent room to listen to the sound. This did not go well at all. No matter how great the microphones might be, the most important thing in recording is their placement, clearly the engineer was not experienced enough to know this. Gene was very upset: he told the owner of the company there was no clarity, there was no brilliance to his sound, and the overall sound was too reverberant. Gene did not hold back at all and was quite undiplomatic with the owner of the company, who reacted with equal strength. Gene said there was no brilliance to his sound. The owner responded that this was the sound that his company wanted. Gene blew up: "*Your* sound? You are supposed to record *my* sound!" Thinking they were going to come to blows, I took Gene aside and told him that we should finish the concerto—I would fix it later, when we did the final mix. (I really didn't know how, but it seemed better to continue than to cancel the session and waste all this time and money.)

The next issue was that Gene wanted to start not at ten the next morning as we were scheduled, but at noon. I told him I would ask the orchestra if we could start at eleven. Musicians, like everyone else, have their own lives outside the orchestra, and I didn't have much hope that they would acquiesce, especially after Gene's comments during the first run-through. Sure enough, the orchestra refused, which upset him further. If he had asked us a few weeks earlier, there would have been no problem. We finished the afternoon, completing the concerto with the inferior sound quality. That evening I received a call from Gene's wife, our longtime friend Marta. I told her that Gene's concerns were absolutely justified and that I would make it work somehow.

I called Al Swanson and asked him what time he was arriving in the morning. About eight, he said. I asked him to whisper in the engineer's ear a better placement for the microphones and told him I would arrive at eight-thirty to see how it was going. If the engineer was agreeable, then I would not interfere, but if not, I would insist on some changes. When I arrived it was clear that all was under control, and Al was working miracles that I hoped would solve the audio problem. We now started with the other concerto, K. 491. Again Gene played beautifully, and after the first run-through of the first movement we went back to listen. Thank goodness, it sounded wonderful. We finished the concerto in the morning session and now had a third session with nothing left to record, so I said to everyone that it would be nice to go through yesterday's concerto, since we were so well in sync now. We might even get some better material to use with yesterday's session. Of course, I knew how unlikely it was that anything from that first day could be used. Luckily, we ended up recording K. 467 a second time in its entirety with the new microphone setup. Nearly everything was perfect the first time through, and I was able to discreetly fix any small problems without any comment. The results were terrific, and that recording remains one of my favorites.

During this season we also inaugurated a new series dedicated to the music of contemporary composers, and we won a first-place ASCAP Award for Programming of Contemporary Music. We also had received this award in 1994.

Everything in these last two seasons in the Opera House was about looking forward, yet I felt we needed some real excitement to mark our farewell. That came in the form of celebrating Howard Hanson's one hundredth anniversary with a concert performance of his only opera, *Merry Mount*, from 1934. This work had been a great success when first performed by the Metropolitan Opera. We had a very strong cast, and it was a triumph. It was recorded Live for Naxos. The following season we did a concert performance of the marvelous Stravinsky opera *Le rossignol*. We celebrated the twentieth anniversary of the chorale, and we announced a five-year grant to do a new-music series that we called New to Seattle. Because of space problems, we did that series at the Intiman Playhouse, a theater space. We did a Schubert anniversary series at the ACT Theater, and we celebrated David Diamond's eightieth birthday. Our recording of Mozart with Eugene Istomin was released.

For the 1997–1998 season, we did do some looking back on our thirty-two years in the opera house, beginning with an opening-night gala with Van Cliburn. We also premiered works by three young composers across three concerts.

The Building of Benaroya Hall

From the moment I arrived as music advisor to the Seattle Symphony in 1983, the executive director who brought me to the city, Mark Walker, had talked about the need for a new hall for the orchestra. Within a few years he had decided that we could move the orchestra to the Fifth Avenue Theatre. The Fifth Avenue was rarely used in those days, and for only $10 million it could have been made into a concert hall with about eighteen hundred seats. The theater was part of a large portion of the city center owned by the University of Washington and managed by Unico Properties. By the mid-1980s it was apparent that the symphony would need a new home. But when Mark began negotiating in earnest with Unico, he discovered that their management agreement with the university would end in 2010, so they could not agree to anything past that date. With that the foray into the Fifth Avenue Theatre as our home ended.

The issue of the terrible scheduling problems of the opera house continued, as did the mediocre acoustics for orchestral performance. In the fall of 1987 Charles Osborn, of the Leo Kreielsheimer Foundation, entered our lives. The foundation owned property directly across Mercer Street from the opera house. Charlie had offered it to the art museum a few years earlier, but the museum decided to build downtown instead. Osborn loved the Seattle Center and did not like downtown Seattle, so he thought this site might be a good fit for the symphony. We were in no position financially to commit to building a hall or to fund a study to see if a concert hall would fit on the site, so Osborn hired the architectural firm of Loschky, Marquardt and Nesholm (LMN) to do a site-feasibility study and, if that worked out, a preliminary design. Charlie knew that we could not be part of this work because of the symphony's finances, but he kept us apprised of the progress. He asked me to recommend an acoustician; I suggested Cyril Harris. This led to the establishment of the team that eventually built Benaroya Hall. I knew Cyril from the renovation of Philharmonic Hall at New York's Lincoln Center to become Fisher Hall in 1972–1974. Cyril would often sit with me in the trumpet section; we became friends, and he taught me about acoustics. He designed the acoustics for the Metropolitan Opera House at Lincoln Center, Symphony Hall in Minneapolis, Powell Hall in St. Louis, the Opera House and Concert Hall at the Kennedy Center, Abravanel Hall in Salt Lake City, and the Krannert Center at the University of Illinois, among many others. The choice of Cyril was somewhat controversial, because Fisher Hall was not the total success that his previous halls had been. But Charlie did not question my choice, and Cyril began an association with us that continued through the opening of Benaroya Hall in 1998. By the spring of 1988 it was determined that the hall would fit on the site, and we were given three years to commit to using it.

The biggest issue with the site was that it was a tight fit for a concert hall. This ruled out additional parking and a huge lobby, but most important, the traffic problems were extremely difficult on Mercer Street already, even without another performance venue. I have always believed that the concert experience begins when you arrive at the hall and ends after you depart, whether by car or public transportation. In Seattle, at the Seattle Center, there was not public transportation. People arrived by car, and the parking and traffic problems before and especially after a performance were terrible.

We were hoping for public as well as private funds to support the hall, so Mayor Charles Royer formed a twenty-one-member concert-hall task force led by John Mangels, the respected CEO of Rainier Bank. At the final meeting of his group we were invited to see and discuss all the possibilities. On the Seattle Center grounds there is a large football stadium called Memorial Stadium that is owned and managed by the school district. At that meeting the director of the center, Virginia Anderson, unveiled a beautiful design of the concert hall on the stadium site: there was plenty of room, and visually it was very impressive. But there were two big problems: the school district was willing to give the site to the Center only if the Center could find a comparable site for the stadium in the downtown area, and the new plan was much more expensive than the Kreielsheimer site. Neither of these issues could be resolved. At the meeting John asked me what my first choice would be for a site. I told him that all I cared about was getting a symphonic hall for the orchestra, and the site was not my major concern. I did not want to make any demands; I wanted it to be clear that the hall needed to be the focus. He pushed me, asking: all else being equal, where would I like the hall to be? I answered, "Downtown!" I said I had always felt that a city could be identified by its cultural institutions, and its buildings should be in the center of city life, and that it was healthy to spread the arts facilities around; and since the Seattle Center had the Opera House and two theaters for plays, building a symphony hall downtown near the Seattle Art Museum would be ideal. That was one of those moments I will never forget. Clearly, my answer was both unexpected and unwelcome.

At this point we had our team in place, with Ed Birdwell as the executive director and Sam Stroum and Dick Cooley leading the board. The site of the Kreielsheimer parcel was chosen, and we had many people supporting the project, led by Peter Donnelly and Dwight Gee of the Corporate Council for the Arts. The State of Washington was going to give capital arts projects $14.6 million throughout the state, with the Seattle Symphony getting the largest and first gift of $8.1 million. The project for a symphony hall seemed on its way, with the cost only being the remaining $54 million, which we would have to raise. The orchestra board and the city and county political leaders decided to propose a bond issue for a $95 million city and county measure to fund parks, community centers, and Seattle Center improvements; it was slated for a vote in May 1991. We took the lead on this and raised $750,000 to fund the effort for the election. Ed had been with the orchestra for five years, and with his vast experience as the director of the music program of the National Endowment of the Arts, he was the perfect man to lead. It all seemed to be going well, and we were finally on a positive trajectory concerning our difficult finances. But, I asked Ed, what would happen if the bond issue failed? He replied, "We will close down." The measure failed.

It is hard to explain what that loss did to our organization—especially the staff. Raising the $750,000 was difficult, and now we were in real financial trouble. Ed had some health issues and resigned, so our board president, MaryAnn Champion, took over while we looked for a new executive director. The other important addition to our organization was the appointment of Ron Woodard from Boeing as the new chairman of the board. Ron brought in Edmond Williams, also from Boeing, to develop a strategic plan to deal with our deficit. We had had remarkable leaders with Stroum and Cooley, and now we had MaryAnn and Ron. MaryAnn did a remarkable job for ten very difficult months. Ron, who became president of the Boeing Commercial Airplane Group, was a great leader and a brilliant man. With the great artistic and audience growth we were experiencing, things once again started to look up.

We asked Cyril Harris to once again look at the Paramount and the Fifth Avenue Theatre. The Fifth Avenue was too small. As for the Paramount, he told us what we would have to do to make that theater work but that if we decided on it he would have to withdraw. This became a little complicated, because Sam Stroum was considering purchasing the Paramount for our use.

I had to go to Portland to listen to their orchestra in a Paramount-style hall and report back to Sam. Eventually I was able to convince him that the Paramount was the wrong choice for us. During this trying time I remained focused on the music making and the orchestra's artistic growth. The administrators and board conducted a long search for Ed Birdwell's replacement, and with all of our support, Deborah Rutter joined our team.

Deborah came into a very interesting and at times challenging situation. On the plus side, the orchestra was playing beautifully. Our audience was strong and supportive, and the repertoire was interesting. We had some excellent board members and staff members. On the negative side, we were constantly in financial trouble. I don't believe that Deborah had been told how precarious the situation was. One could feel her rolling up her sleeves and getting to work.

In March 1993, just five months after her arrival, Jody and I were invited to a party on a Sunday at the home of our very close friends Jack and Becky Benaroya. Jack told me that he had a problem and asked if we could have lunch the next day at the Rainier Club. Jack was never one for small talk. If he had something on his mind, he would get right to the point. He told me that he was interested in giving $10–15 million either to the symphony for the new hall, which he had read about in Melinda Bargreen's the *Seattle Times* article, or to the University of Washington. He asked me what I thought. I immediately answered, "Give $15 million to the symphony!" I can still see his smile. We immediately started to talk about details. I explained to him that his gift would get the concert hall project really started, but that we had serious financial issues that had to be dealt with. I asked him if he would consider giving us the money immediately so that we could use it as an endowment until we were ready to spend it on the new hall. He said that he would think about it and get back to me.

Jack wanted to keep all this confidential (with the exception, of course, of Deborah, Jody, and his wife, Becky) until the details were worked out. He discussed it with his longtime adviser Bob Ash, who asked Jack what would happen to his gift if we were not able to raise the additional money necessary and the concert hall project did not become a reality—a legitimate concern. Together they decided to give the $15 million in three stages: the first third when we broke ground, the second third when we were halfway done, and the final third when the project was completed. In the meantime he would give the orchestra $800,000 a year, which was better than we could expect from endowment interest.

Two aspects of the gift were the most important: the money itself, and having the Benaroya family helping with the project. Up until this time Jack and Becky had always made their philanthropic gifts anonymously. It was very important for us to have Jack accept credit and help with the fund-raising. I really wanted the Benaroya name on the building, and eventually we were able to convince him that we needed his public endorsement. Sam and Gladys Rubinstein, too, did not want any recognition, but we told them how important having their name on the music director's suite would mean, and they agreed. The same was true of Craig and Joan Watjen, who also wanted their gift of the hall's organ to be anonymous. They eventually agreed to the naming of the Watjen Concert Organ.

Word started to get out that the symphony had a major gift for the hall, but the only ones who knew who it was or any of the details were Jody, Deborah, and I. After a few months it was clear that it needed to be made public. The night before the announcement we had a dinner at our downtown condo for the Woodards, the Stroums, the Benaroyas, the Champions, and Deborah. We asked Jack and Becky's favorite chef, Saleh Joudeh, to prepare their favorite dishes. With the excitement of a child I told everyone who had made the gift. It was a very special night for everyone.

The announcement the next day was thrilling. The staff did not know the details, nor the orchestra, nor the major players in the Seattle artistic scene. Of course the money was very important, but even more important was the message that it sent about the orchestra's financial future. This was the most significant of its many defining moments in recent years. Now people could feel confident that we had a secure financial future. Deborah engaged brilliantly with the elected officials, and we had tremendous support from the mayor, the city council, the county council, and the state.

In June 1993 City Councilman Tom Weeks and Deputy Mayor Bob Watt asked us about the possibility of a downtown site. One possibility was an empty block between Second and Third Avenues and University and Union Streets. The site was called the Marathon Block, and although it was zoned to be used by the Toronto-based development group for a pair of office buildings, economic issues in Seattle stalled the construction. This large block was a small hill or knoll with an entrance to the underground bus tunnel and an unoccupied Jones building on one corner. Charles Osborn had recently died, and Don Johnson had taken over as the director of the Kreielsheimer foundation. They continued to be extremely supportive under Don's leadership. Deborah and I were very careful not to react to the possibility of a downtown site. However, if the mayor and leaders of the city were interested, we of course would listen. From the start of this exercise we said that if there was to be any chance of a move downtown it would have to have the financial support of the city, since we could not increase our portion of the proposed $125 million budget.

Our very brilliant and thoughtful mayor, Norm Rice, realized that if downtown Seattle was to be a vibrant part of the city, the concert hall needed to be downtown. The Seattle Center had the Bagley Wright Theater, the Opera House, and the Intiman Theater, but the downtown core had only the Seattle Art Museum and a small, dying residential and retail core. By this time everyone knew my dream was to have the hall downtown, but I was grateful to Kreielsheimer and felt pulled in both directions. I agreed with Deborah that we had to let the future site unfold whichever way it would. Many close friends were extremely hostile to downtown and even feared going there at night. Patrons were worried not only about safety, but also about parking and traffic issues. Don Johnson was extremely concerned that we would even consider the possibility. I was at a reception when Norm Rice tapped me on the shoulder and said, "Don't worry, Jerry, you're going to get your concert hall downtown!"

Norm's main purpose at this time was to revive the downtown core, and the Seattle Symphony fit right into his plan. He had already gotten Nordstrom to agree to take over the former department store space of Frederick & Nelson. Some months before, Jody had attended a dinner at which John Nordstrom told her, "If Norm thinks we are moving into the Frederick's building without him opening Pine Street, he is kidding himself." But Norm pushed forward a vote to open up the then all-pedestrian Pine Street to traffic, the absence of which was hurting retail in the center of town. Lo and behold, Pine Street opened, and Nordstrom agreed to renovate and move. Meanwhile Jeff Smulian had agreed to the Pacific Place Project across from the new Nordstrom building, and an above-the-street elevated passageway between them would remain. Norm's jigsaw puzzle was working, and having the symphony downtown would anchor the southern end of the city with the art museum.

The downtown site was 38 percent larger—a huge benefit for us. We put together a committee to investigate it from every vantage point with Bagley Wright, a major patron of the arts in town, and the brilliant lawyer Ralph Palumbo serving as co-chairs. Jody and I had had a remarkable weekend the summer before with Bagley and his wife,

Virginia, at the magnificent island home of two of Seattle's most important and brilliant citizens, Jon and Judy Runstad. At dinner, the idea of the hall's being downtown was the major topic of discussion, and it became a defining moment for the support and involvement of these two couples. Don Johnson thought it was a setup, since Bagley had been a staunch supporter of the art museum's going downtown rather than to the Seattle Center site. They looked into parking, which was abundant near the Marathon block, especially at night, when most of the concerts would take place. They analyzed the safety issues with the police department and discovered that downtown was as safe as the Seattle Center. They worked with LMN architects to make sure that the site, which was on a rather steep incline, would work. They looked into traffic flow from the freeways and bus travel to the site. In July 1994 they recommended going with the downtown site if the financials could be worked out. It would be more expensive to build downtown because of the size of the lot, and the fact that the land had not been donated. We also had to deal with the Jones building, which would have to be bought and demolished. The city had to be a major player in this decision, and they came through. In November the city council voted unanimously to support the downtown site for Benaroya Hall. At this time, in a huge sign of support and civic dedication, Howard Wright and Jon Runstad, who owned the Jones building, announced they would demolish it and gift the land to the city for Benaroya Hall. The city would own the building, and we would build and manage it.

Of course there were some disagreements. I wanted five levels of parking under the building, for two reasons: it would best for our patrons, and it could be an important income stream for years to come. The city council thought everyone should come by bus. In the end we had two levels of parking for 430 cars. The next year was thrilling as the design of the complex took shape. The lead architect, Mark Reddington; the representative partner of LMN, Judd Marquardt; the acoustic engineer, Cyril Harris; and Deborah, Jody, and I worked through many ideas.

The fund-raising was very exciting. Each time we met with prospective donors, we told the story of this incredible dream for us and for the city. The architectural plans were making big strides, and it seemed that with each meeting there was more to show. This was also a time for opportunities for our donors, and Deborah and I met with Craig and Joan Watjen to talk about a major gift.

Jody and I had met the Watjens at a few Mariner baseball games in the suite of the president of the club and his wife, Chuck and Susan Armstrong. Susan was a member of the symphony board and had been a member of the Los Angeles Philharmonic board. Real music lovers, she and Chuck were great hosts during the games. Whenever I met Craig, who had a small ownership in the club, he seemed more interested in talking about music than baseball. It turned out Craig was a professional clarinetist who had graduated from Juilliard and attended Tanglewood in the summers. An early Microsoft employee, by this time he had left the company and was pursuing other venture interests. He told me he wanted to make a small contribution to the Benaroya Hall, and I told him it was too early. I assured him I would bring him to the LMN office when the plans were more advanced.

When Craig and Joan finally came to the LMN offices, they were excited by what they saw. He also asked many probing questions, and we agreed to meet in a few weeks to talk about specifics. Deborah and I felt that the opportunity that would be best for the Watjens, because of Craig's close connection to music, was the organ. I was insistent that we have the organ, for three basic reasons: first, to be able to play the orchestral music that uses the organ without having to use an electric instrument, which is inferior to a pipe organ; secondly, I knew it would help the musicians to hear each other onstage because of the different-sized reflective surfaces that the exposed pipes would create; and thirdly, because such a beautiful instrument would help define our hall visually.

There were two problems. For one thing, organs were expensive; and for another, Cyril had never built a hall with a visible organ and was reluctant to do so. I explained my reasoning to the executive committee of the board, and they supported me in a kind of showdown with Cyril. Our schedules did not overlap much during that time, so I stopped by his hotel for an hour on my way to the airport as I was leaving for

Europe and Cyril had just arrived from New York. I hoped all my reasons would work with Cyril, since he was the one I had learned most of them from. At the Kennedy Center concert hall he had an organ behind a wall that would only be opened when the instrument was being used. He suggested that arrangement, but I did not want to compromise. The back wall of the stage would need to be divided into three sections, with the outer sections open only when the organ was being used but the center section, where the keyboard was located, always open. I thought that this would allow some of the volume from the brass section to be lost rather than reflected into the house. Up to now Cyril's halls reflected all the sound into the auditorium. That is generally a positive attribute, but with powerful American brass sections the result was at times too loud. In the end he agreed, and we put the organ in our plan.

When we met with Craig and Joan at the symphony offices we had already floated the idea of the organ. Craig did extensive research about concert pipe organs and listened attentively as Deborah and I explained this need for the hall and the opportunity for them. The price for the size of organ that would be sufficient for such works as the Saint-Saëns Organ Symphony was about $1 million, but an organ with the ability to play all the repertoire, including music from the baroque period forward, would be double that. After our presentation Craig simply said, "I'll take the big one!"

Organists and organ builders all over the country became involved; I received more correspondence about that decision than any other. We decided, in accordance with the wishes of most, that the instrument have the traditional tracker action. I had also looked into the possibility of having a second, remote console that would make it easier for the organist to follow the conductor, but that expense could not be justified, and our local advisor, Carole Terry, from the University of Washington, thought it unnecessary. We did a major search for a builder, with Craig serving as the leader in this decision. After an exhaustive search we chose the C. B. Fisk Company of Gloucester, Massachusetts. They were very busy and could not have the organ ready for five years, which would put its opening in 2000. That was a major concern for me, but

Steve Dieck, our partner at the company, said that he could have all the exterior pipes completed by the opening of the hall in 1997. I pushed very hard for a 1997 opening, thinking that it would probably be 1998; but if I did not push, who knew when it would be?

I had lunch with Ernest Fleischmann when I was in Los Angeles conducting the orchestra in 1994. He asked me when Benaroya Hall was due to be completed. I told him 1997, but I expected 1998. At the time Disney Hall was at the same stage, and Ernest said we would never have our hall in that time frame, but they would have theirs. Disney Hall opened in 2003; Benaroya Hall opened in 1998.

When the Fisk organ was completed, it had 4,489 pipes, and it was wonderfully successful. I had been carefully studying all Cyril's halls during this time. I remember conducting in Powell Hall in St. Louis. I was told that when the renovation was completed, the players had difficulty hearing each other onstage, and the hall was too reverberant. That can be easily fixed by lowering the ceiling, which Cyril did, by about ten feet. When I went into the fly space above the ceiling during my investigation, I found two ceilings—the original one and a second, identical one ten feet lower. Cyril did some diagrams for us of the heights and shapes of the ceilings of the best halls around the world. Of course, the width and length of the hall have a great deal to do with the results, as well as the general shape. While I was in St. Louis, our architect, Mark Reddington, joined me, and we went from there to see Cyril's first large hall, the Krannert Center for the Performing Arts at the University of Illinois.

The Krannert Center had one very interesting feature for us. At this point our new hall was to have around 2,000 seats. This was a problem for concert revenue. A sold-out concert at the old opera house meant 3,000 tickets; in the new hall we could sell only two-thirds as many. What I noticed at the Krannert Center was that their second balcony had many more seats than their first balcony. The relationship of the width of a balcony compared to the height below the balcony needs to be 1 to 1. So if the balcony was ten feet wide, the space between it and the floor below would need to be ten feet as well. In the Krannert Center the lobby was below the second balcony. That meant that their first balcony would be the required ratio but the second balcony could be extended farther back, since there were no seats below that extension. Many concertgoers will tell you that the best seats in the house are those farthest from the stage. I told Mark Reddington, our architect, that this might be a chance for us to add seats. Cyril always had the final word; Mark knew that although the design had to be magnificent, the acoustics were the most important element in a concert hall. Luckily, Cyril thought it was a splendid idea, and we were able to add 500 additional seats to the original 2,000.

Our fund-raising team was a great group, and we had a lot of fun together. It consisted of the artistic vision and need, the architecture and acoustics, the financial plan, and then the ask. I did the artistic part, Mark did the building (if he was not available, Judd did this) and Deborah did the close. When she was not available the task fell to Karen Rothko-Wynn, our development director, or Nan Garrison, our former development director and fund-raising consultant. We probably did this twice a week for four years at friends' homes, and very often at our Queen Anne home, on which occasions Jody became a major player; we would often have a dinner as well. After these five years of hosting dinners about once a week, we took an entertaining-at-home break for several months.

Jody and I had worked with Jon and Judy Runstad to help with the Jones building. Jon also advised us about materials for the public spaces. With the larger space we could include a recital hall. Some people thought we should not do the recital hall, because the symphony did not specifically need a small hall. My feeling was that the city needed a first-class hall for chamber music.

Boeing was very generous to us, thanks to Ron Woodard. For the hall project they lent us two project managers: Bob Wickline, who was with us from start to finish, and Andrew Clapham, who was with us for the final three years. Bob was the man who had to make sure that the building was on time and on budget. He was incredible, but at times frustrating, especially on specific issues. I don't know how we could have done it without him, but the way he looked over that budget was something to see. There were always three issues that were projected as "on," but only if additional money could be raised: the organ, the recital hall, and the water element on Second Avenue. The first two were mine, and the third was Bob's. The organ became part of the plan early on, but the recital hall was a different story. It seemed to me that most of the board was not convinced that we needed it. We finally had the defining moment with Woodard, Wickline, and myself. Bob made his case: forget about the small hall. I countered that although the orchestra did not need a small hall, the city needed it, for cultural reasons. After the meeting Woodard looked at Bob and said, "Make it happen." And that was that.

The money for the recital hall was given by the remarkable Linda Nordstrom in honor of her mother, Illsley Ball Nordstrom. The look of the hall was something that concerned me. Benaroya Hall was to be covered in dark wood from a single African mahogany tree, giving it a warm glow, but the recital hall was to be plaster. Of course, most halls are primarily plaster, but the thin veneer of wood in the big hall gives it a visual warmth that is really important—especially for a large concert hall. I wanted to cover the plaster in the recital hall with that same mahogany. Unfortunately, we couldn't afford it. That hall had a few compromises already. I wanted 800 seats so that we could present chamber music without creating a financial deficit. That was reduced to 540 seats, and the sound isolation would not be as complete as in the big hall, again because of the expense.

Jon Runstad was on the design committee and knew of my worries. He and Judy had given an additional gift to correct the stone to be used in the Boeing Gallery floor across the main entrance on Third Avenue. The estimate had come in at $50,000 more than it actually cost, so Jon suggested that we use the extra money to put the mahogany on the recital hall's back wall. What a generous gift!

Cyril, a perfectionist, was always wonderful to work with but uncompromising in his beliefs. He used to say that the Marathon Block was the worst place we could have chosen to build a hall. Under the little slope in that block were the Burlington Northern and Santa Fe Railroad tracks, with many trains roaring by on a daily basis. We were also adjacent to the Downtown Seattle Transit Tunnel. Cyril knew of some companies that built rubber isolation bearings that the hall could sit on. The first company said they thought it would work but couldn't guarantee complete isolation. Cyril fired them and hired another firm that would guarantee the result, with the building sitting on 310 rubber pads. It worked.

At the same time Cyril was finishing all the detail work on the acoustics, he gave us our options for the seats. Cyril believed that for seat colors there were only two choices, gold or red. In the end, the decor committee agreed on a honey gold for the seats, which complemented the warm mahogany on the side walls. They chose tan carpeting by Jack Lenor Larsen, a Seattle native, and tan paint. Jody told Mark Reddington, "When people come here to this beautiful sanctuary of music, I want them to feel as if they are wrapped in the warm color of honey, so they never want to leave."

Two of our most important artistic leaders in Seattle, Bagley and Virginia Wright, had initially expressed the desire to choose an internationally renowned architect for Benaroya Hall. In the end they were very pleased with Mark Reddington's work. I suggested that we instead commission a painting by an internationally famous artist for the hall lobby and asked the Wrights to help choose the artist. We considered two painters: Robert Rauschenberg and David Hockney, both of whom had connections to music. In the end they commissioned Rauschenberg to do the large work that hangs over the entrance to the auditorium.

Late in the process my friend Dale Chihuly told me he would like to make some decorative chandeliers for the hall. Dale's idea was to hang five chandeliers in the lobby area facing the Rauschenberg. I knew the Wrights liked Dale's work, but I felt that his chandeliers would detract from Rauschenberg's work, which the Wrights had commissioned. I arranged a meeting with Dale, Parks Anderson, who was Dale's most trusted advisor, and Mark Reddington, who was to take the lead. The idea was to put one chandelier at either end of the Boeing Gallery, which was a public space and would be seen by many more people. This was the only time Mark failed me. When we arrived at the moment in the discussion, he did not offer our plan, and instead, Dale and

Parks left thinking they were to produce the five chandeliers to face the Rauschenberg!

We did finally make the change and Dale agreed to the Boeing Gallery, where the Chihuly chandeliers hang today. Jack and Becky Benaroya, with whom Dale was very close, had one of the world's premiere glass collections, which had started with their introduction to Dale and the Pilchuck Glass School, and they commissioned Dale to create the remarkable chandeliers.

By this time Jack and Becky had committed much more than the original $15 million, even though we never asked them for anything. Jack always made his own decisions about gifts. That happened later in the project when, in a meeting, Jack was informed that there would be concrete all along the north side of the building (the Union Street side), from Second Avenue to Third Avenue. Jack started shaking his head; he felt we were turning our back on part of the city. Not only did he insist on upgrading the materials to the same golden Kasota stone used on the rest of the building, but he paid for it as well. He also wanted an inspirational saying to be carved into the stone. We found the quote from Aaron Copland that graces the north wall: "So long as the human spirit survives on this planet, music in some living form will accompany and sustain it and give it expressive meaning."

When Dale completed his magnificent works on either end of the Boeing Company Gallery, I noticed that an entrance door to the recital hall at the north end of the gallery partially covered the glass. I was worried that the chandelier would not be properly seen for the opening concerts and asked the LMN team to correct it. They said they would—but only after the opening, which was fast approaching. So I asked Jack to have a look, and he made sure it was fixed in time for the opening. We were able to fund the water element that Bob Wickline wanted, and it added to the beauty of the site. Patsy Collins, a great supporter of the arts in Seattle and the owner of KING Broadcasting at that time, added a war memorial on the west side of the building on Second Avenue to commemorate the 8,000 Washington State residents who have died in wars since World War II.

Opening Week 1998

For the last few years we had all been anticipating this opening week. We wanted to have an event for each area of music that we served, from our regular full-orchestra subscription concerts to the pop concerts, recitals, small-orchestra repertoire, new music, education, and community involvement. We also thought we could create a few gala concerts that could help our budget for the season.

Most important was the opening night—the first time the public would hear the orchestra in the new hall. For the program I wanted a soloist who would be both musically rewarding and grand. We asked Jessye Norman if she would sing the Immolation Scene from Wagner's *Götterdämmerung*. I thought we could perform a second half of excerpts from this opera that would tie into our history and early recordings, and at the same time would show off the orchestra and, of course, the hall. For the first half we needed a new work. The obvious choice for me was David Diamond, who wrote *A Gala Celebration* in honor of the orchestra and the Benaroya family. To highlight the strings, I programmed my arrangement for string orchestra of Anton von Webern's gorgeous *Langsamer Satz*. To show off the winds and brass, we programmed Stravinsky's *Firebird* Suite (1919), one of the works conducted by Stravinsky with our orchestra when the Opera House opened in 1962.

Over these last four years Jack Benaroya would occasionally ask me about the acoustics in the main hall, which had been named the S. Mark Taper Foundation Auditorium, and I would always assure him that they would be great. As the opening approached, he would question me more and more frequently, and I started to get nervous. How could I be so sure? What if we made a mistake? Early in September I called a quartet of brass players and asked them to play a few notes in the hall. I also asked our harpist to do the same. Jack, Deborah, Jody, Cyril, and a few others joined me for this little experiment. The instruments sounded fantastic, top to bottom. Then I asked them to spread out on the stage to see if they could continue to play with good ensemble while relying only on their ears while separated. That experiment also went well. Then I asked the harp to play at many different dynamic levels and walked all over the hall, including the third balcony. Even when she played as softly as possible, I still heard her clearly from the back row.

We had arranged to do two free pre-opening concerts, so that we could play in the hall with a full audience. One concert would be for all the men and women who built the hall, and one would be for the family and friends of the staff, orchestra, board and volunteers. I wanted to conduct one work and have Adam Stern, my assistant, lead the rest so that I could walk around our new hall and listen. It was an amazing experience. The hall was sensational from every section. Of course the sound was a little more direct up close, becoming a little dryer and a little more blended farther back, but from every vantage it was truly beautiful, warm, clear, and rich. As much as I had warned the orchestra that the hall was going to be clear and live, I knew we had work to do. Every little imperfection of intonation could be heard, and every change of color was there to behold, and we could play as soft as we liked. I believe that it is one of the finest halls in the world and that it helped our orchestra grow artistically.

My approach throughout this building process was simply to watch the committee's work and not interfere unless I had to. (When the committee dealing with the recital hall made their decision about seat colors, for example, they decided to have alternating colors for each seat, giving it a kind of checkerboard design. I stepped in, imagining how it would look if the hall was not full.)

We began our opening night program with a short pre-concert to involve students from the local schools, colleges, and youth orchestras, Henri Lazarof's *Celebration for Four Brass Choirs*, with brass players situated throughout the hall. The opening concert was recorded for our local public television station, KCTS. Melinda Bargreen wrote in the *Seattle Times* on September 14:

> The most momentous weekend in the 105-year history of the Seattle Symphony has come and gone. . . .
> The first impressions: the big hall is gorgeous to the eye and to the

ear. The recital hall, a little more utilitarian in design, also delivers a big sound with abundant clarity. . . .

And then there was the orchestra, just as Schwarz had promised—heard in a way it's never been heard in the Opera House. The hall delivers a tremendous volume of sound, but it also is well-defined sound, allowing the listener to "hear into" the orchestra as never before."

And Bernard Holland wrote in the *New York Times*: "The acoustics designed by Cyril Harris seem exceptionally good. One hears the different orchestra sections with clarity, and already the floorboards resonate nicely. Having been witness at the inauguration of several dry, dead halls in recent years, I find this one a pleasant surprise."

Richard Campbell was the critic for the *Seattle Post-Intelligencer* during my Seattle years. For his opening night review he wrote about the excellent architecture and audience amenities—"but if the sound is pale or timid, wild or uneven or just plain mediocre, the hall is simply not a success. There were few doubts opening night that Benaroya would take its place among the best of dozens of concert halls around the globe. . . . Every note, the softest roll of the timpani or the hush of the lower strings, has presence . . . Gerard Schwarz . . . was a principal force behind Benaroya. It was he who dictated the kind of acoustics the hall would have: less opulence, greater clarity, sympathetic ambience. . . . The bravos were well-deserved." On the afternoon of Sunday, September 13, we opened the Illsley Ball Nordstrom Recital Hall with Mozart's last three symphonies. Although the recital hall is a little drier than the big hall, it was perfect for the Mozart—clean and clear even though quite exposed. It is a sensational hall. The great violinist Kyung-wha Chung was playing a recital in Benaroya hall the next night. She came to the concert and loved the hall. Furthermore, she said that playing in the recital hall would be of great artistic value for the players. I agreed. Kyung-wha's very musical family emigrated from Korea to Seattle when she was a teenager, and she and her talented siblings all grew up there. Her recital of Schubert, Bartók, and Schumann with the pianist Itamar Golan proved that Benaroya Hall was exceptional for recitals as well.

On Tuesday we presented a jazz program at Benaroya titled "An Evening with Chuck Mangione." On Wednesday we presented a composer-in-residence retrospective in the recital hall as part of the Music of Our Time series. We did two world premieres, David Stock's Viola Concerto and Samuel Jones's *Janus*, as well as Richard Danielpour's *First Light*, which I had premiered with Music Today in 1988. We also did Bright Sheng's *Postcards*, a work whose New York premiere I had conducted in April 1998. Stephen Albert's beautiful *Flower of the Mountain*, which I premiered in 1986, was on the program, and we performed David Diamond's *A Gala Celebration* on opening night. David is represented at every performance in the hall to this day: he wrote the music played on all kinds of bells to call the audience back after intermission, and we recorded it with our percussion section. We had hoped to have David's work as the music for Benaroya Hall and Sam Jones's similar work for chimes alone for the Nordstrom Recital Hall. Unfortunately, our public-address system could not accommodate both, so Sam's music has never been used.

On Friday we did a special concert with Yo-Yo Ma. The program was Barber's *Music for a Scene from Shelley*; the world premiere of Sheng's cello concerto *Spring Dreams*; and, after intermission, Richard Strauss's *Don Quixote*. I first heard Bright's *Spring Dreams* when it was premiered with Yo-Yo and a traditional Chinese-instrument orchestra. I loved the piece and suggested Bright arrange it as a traditional cello concerto, which he did.

On Saturday we held a Kids' Day at Benaroya Hall, with four children's concerts in the recital hall and in the evening a pops show with Gladys Knight. Adam Stern conducted music by Gould and Gershwin, and Benjamin Wright conducted for Gladys Knight. On Sunday we did the Day of Music, which was free to all and lasted from eleven in the morning till eight in the evening and used both halls, the lobbies, and outdoor space, with all types of music and many members of the community performing.

The next week was our opening subscription week, and André

Watts was playing MacDowell's Piano Concerto No 2. We began with Beethoven's *Leonore Overture* No. 3 and ended with Mahler's Symphony No. 1. The Mahler was on the first program that I conducted with the orchestra as music advisor in 1983 and again in 1991, so it was the perfect piece for this important event.

I had a great respect for Jessye Norman, though prior to the hall's opening night I had only worked with her once, when we did the Schoenberg *Guerre-Lieder* in Los Angeles. Because we were televising the opening concert, her contract gave her the right to approve the general camera work after the dress rehearsal and to approve the final product before a delayed broadcast. Randy Brinson from KCTS showed her his work after the dress rehearsal. When I asked him how she liked it, he said she thought it was all right, but in a few spots she requested changes. Such as? I asked. He replied, "During the big bass trumpet solo, when she was not even singing, she wanted the camera on her and not on the bass trumpet." She wanted the camera on her pretty much the entire time. After the concert Randy edited the material and sent it to Jessye, who had a few weeks to approve it. The weeks passed with no response. Then, shortly before the local broadcast, she sent KCTS a note saying that she did not want the show to be aired. Of course it was much too late to cancel the show. Her lawyer then sued in her home state of South Carolina. KCTS had the suit moved to Washington State, no representative of Jessye's ever appeared, the case was thrown out of court, and the program won an Emmy.

Once our first season in our new home began, every day was thrilling. I still have that same feeling every time I enter the magnificent hall. Our concerts were Thursdays through Sundays, and we were able to add a visiting orchestra series, some remarkable specials with artists such as Mstislav Rostropovich, a chamber orchestra series on which we performed all six of Mozart's 1784 piano concertos, new music, baroque music, light classics, a recital series, pop culture, pops concerts, many varieties of children's concerts for all ages, and continuing educational concerts. Vladimir Feltsman and Vladimir Spivikov did programs on which they both played and conducted. During this season my former manager from Columbia Artists, Larry Tucker, joined the staff as orchestra manager. Charles Simonyi gave $1 million to endow the solo horn position for John Cerminaro so that John was no longer a guest principal, but simply the principal horn.

One of the highlights for me was Gil Shaham playing Erich Wolfgang Korngold's Violin Concerto. Written for Jascha Heifetz, the work is problematic with respect to the balance between the violin and the orchestra. Korngold was known for his work in Hollywood, and it seemed to me that the piece had been written to be played into a microphone, after which the recording engineer could fix any balance problems. I was determined to make the materials work without having to constantly ask the orchestra to play softer. I asked our librarian, Pat Takahashi, to white out most of the dynamics and change them to my new ones. When Gil arrived, he was amazed at how good the balance was and asked me about it. When I told him what I had done, he asked me if he could borrow the set of parts for his performances the following week with the New York Philharmonic. Of course I said yes.

After the success of Hanson's only opera, *Merry Mount*, we did a concert performance of Deems Taylor's *Peter Ibbetson*. We had recorded Taylor's *Through the Looking Glass* a few years earlier, and I truly love his music. I studied both of his operas and decided I preferred *Peter Ibbetson* to *The King's Henchman*. We had a great cast: Lauren Flanigan, Anthony Dean Griffey, Richard Zeller, and Charles Austin. The reviews were excellent, and our live recording came out very well. I was hoping the recording would lead to some staged performances, but so far it has not. Rebecca Paller wrote in the August 2009 issue of *Opera News*: "Conductor Gerard Schwarz and the Seattle Symphony perform with such conviction and technical accuracy that it's hard to imagine a better reading of the score, and the members of the Seattle Symphony Chorale sound sublime in the French folk tunes in Act III." Joseph Newsome wrote in *Voix des arts* in July 1999:

> The Seattle Symphony again confirm their standing among America's finest symphonic ensembles, playing with unperturbed excellence that illuminates Taylor's generally uncomplicated but

learned orchestrations. The woodwinds make an especially strong showing, seizing every opportunity for melodic eloquence with relish. Presiding over the performance is the Symphony's Music Director Gerard Schwarz whose considerable operatic experience is apparent in his coordination of choral, orchestral, and solo vocal forces. Maestro Schwarz's approach draws out the grandeur of the orchestra interludes but also allows plenty of space in which lyrical phrases are allowed to expand romantically without risking sluggishness.

I asked János Starker to do the world premiere of Alan Hovhaness's Cello Concerto. But János felt that it might be a little simple, so I asked Alan if he would be open to some suggestions to make it more interesting for both the cellist and the audience. He said he would be happy to hear from János, and the collaboration worked very well. A close friend of theirs and mine, Dennis Russell Davies, conducted the performance. We also did a symphony by Hugh Aitken, which was well received.

That was a very different reaction than I received when we premiered Henri Lazarof's *In Celebration*, the Symphony No. 4. The work is for large chorus and orchestra with texts from Haydn's *Creation*, Milton's *Paradise Lost*, Coleridge's *The Aeolian Harp*; Ecclesiastes 3:3–4, and Psalm 98. The work was very difficult for the audience, and I received many letters of complaint, something that had rarely happened before. The president of the board, Dorothy Fluke, even called me to complain about how unhappy the board was with it. It became difficult for me to program Henri's music after that and the similar experience of his Symphony No. 3.

I had recorded many of Henri's pieces, and in July 1998 we did his *Kaddish* for Naxos and the Milken Archive with the Berlin Radio Symphony Orchestra. The short work went very well. In Berlin in 2005 we recorded his Double Concerto with the same orchestra and team headed by the producer Wolfram Nehls. Later Henri heard a recital played by our son Julian. Very impressed with his sound and musicianship, Henri wrote a concerto for him. But I could not program it in Seattle and so far it has remained unperformed. The memories of the audience and board are long.

The most important debut this season was bringing Marvin Hamlisch to conduct a pops program. I loved Marvin on many levels, and Larry Tucker did too. Marvin had a great success and soon became the director of our pops series, a position he held for the rest of my tenure as music director.

Our second season in Benaroya Hall, 1999–2000, again began with the Day of Music. More than thirty ensembles from all over the metropolitan area and in every discipline of the performing arts participated. We were feeling more and more comfortable with the new acoustics, though the adjustment was taking longer than I'd anticipated. Almost all the personnel, board, staff and orchestra remained the same. We began two new traditions that lasted throughout my tenure: performing Handel's *Messiah* before Christmas, and doing the Beethoven Ninth between Christmas and New Year's.

After one performance of the Beethoven Ninth I was signing CDs of our recording of the work. A few people came up to me and said they had never heard the Beethoven Ninth live, and some—not only fifteen-year-olds, but also adults—said they had never been to a symphony concert before. One man said, "It was unbelievable. I was on the edge of my seat the whole evening!" A critic once told me he was disappointed hearing the same symphony every year at Mostly Mozart. It was never the same one, but I understood his point. My response was simple: there are many people who have never heard the "Jupiter" Symphony before. There are many who have never heard it live, and there are many members of the audience who have never been to a concert at all. A critic who goes to concerts four or five days a week hears everything, but the audience does not. In a city of almost nine million people, hundreds of thousands have never heard the "Jupiter" Symphony before. It is our responsibility as musicians to both perform new repertoire and continue to offer the great classics.

Have Tuba, Will Travel—with Hot Dogs

At the end of the 1999–2000 season in Seattle, our longtime tuba player resigned. We needed someone right away: the opening concerts of the 2000–2001 season included Stravinsky's *Petrushka* and Strauss's *Also sprach Zarathustra*. In July I called John Cerminaro, who was teaching in Aspen, to ask him if there was anyone there who might be able to fill in for a year. He told me about the tuba fellowship winner at Aspen that summer, Chris Olka, who had just graduated from Juilliard. Chris was interested in the job, and John oversaw his taped audition. We offered him the yearlong position.

Chris and his wife, Kim, had already returned home to New Jersey by the time we called him on a Friday to ask if he could be in Seattle for a rehearsal at ten o'clock Tuesday morning. Without thinking, he said yes, then got in the car and started driving—in a tropical storm. Eighteen inches of rain hit the East Coast. Chris planned to stop at a bank to get some cash for gas, but when he arrived in Milwaukee, the storm had closed all the banks, and the ATMs were not working. His mother wired him money from Florida, but because of the weather there was a delay and he had to wait eight hours to receive it. When he finally received it, he bought a six-pack of hot dogs for ninety-nine cents and drove almost nonstop to Seattle. He arrived at one o'clock in the morning on Tuesday and made it to the rehearsal. At the time I had no idea what he had gone through. Chris's first rehearsal that day was with *Petrushka*. You can only make a first impression once, and what a great impression he made! Chris had no place to practice, so he practiced in the park until the police said he was disturbing the peace. Then he practiced in the loading dock of the hall, until he was told that he could be heard in the recital hall. I finally found a practice room for him, and his first season went very well.

I was in love with his playing and his great attitude, and I was also very fond of his gifted wife, Kim Russ, a pianist. It turned out that when my mother-in-law, Shirley Greitzer, had been the director of the Juilliard placement bureau, she helped Kim and Chris a great deal. They didn't realize Shirley was my mother-in-law.

After a year in the orchestra, it was time for Chris to audition for the permanent position. It is usually difficult to win a position if you have already played with an orchestra for any length of time. The committee members are always told to make their judgments based on what they hear for those twenty or thirty minutes on that particular day, but it is sometimes hard to shelve your preconceptions. There were three excellent tuba players in the finals, and in the end we all felt that Chris was the best.

John, Carmen, Michael, and André

John Delo is a retired Microsoft employee. He and his wife, Carmen, loved music and mapped their life out according to local symphony, opera, and ballet schedules. They were also ballroom dancers and had a ballroom in their home in Bellevue, Washington. They had an apartment in London and another in Vienna, so the concerts in those cities also played a part in their overall schedules. A few years ago Carmen contracted a horrible degenerative disease. First she could no longer dance, and then she could no longer walk. They moved into the city and John would take her in her wheelchair to performances in Seattle, Vienna, and London.

She was a beautiful woman and always wore a bow in her hair. They used to sit in the front row at the old Opera House. In the new hall they disliked the front row, so they sat in the third row. They became friends from afar with Michael Miropolsky, our assistant principal second violin. They would just come to the concert and look at Michael, and Michael would look at them, and they would nod. That went on for many years. They finally met when John and Carmen made a gift to endow his chair.

Just a few months before Carmen died she was having a great deal of difficulty keeping her head up. We were performing a concert with André Watts, and the second half was Beethoven's Fifth Piano Concerto. André played it just exquisitely—a very special, spiritual performance. Suddenly, Carmen raised her head.

By then she was staying in a nursing home, so John dropped her off at Horizon House after the concert. Carmen died that night after the concert. She was found kneeling in a prayer position at the foot of her bed.

When I arrived in Seattle, the symphony had 5,000 subscribers.

Now we had 40,000. As always, during the 1999–2000 season we did many works by American composers, including an all-Copland program to celebrate the 100th anniversary of his birth, a premiere by Theodore Shapiro, and an all-American program by the National Symphony under Leonard Slatkin. I asked Bright Sheng to conduct one of the Music of Our Time concerts. He programmed John Adams's Chamber Symphony, a very difficult work. Bright had to push the players pretty hard, and they were upset with the amount of work required. The players thought they should be paid additional money, and asked for a meeting with me. I listened and of course sympathized but explained that some concerts were easier than others. The week before, for instance, we had played an all-Beethoven program that required very little preparation. At times we must put in many hours, and at other times very few. Part of the contract with the players requires the music to be available at least four weeks in advance, so they have the opportunity to practice hard works over a period of time. In the end everyone understood.

We did Stravinsky's *Oedipus Rex* with his *Rite of Spring*. We also did my first performance of Shostakovich's Symphony No. 15. This is one of the few I had yet to conduct. As always, I studied very hard, but I had some trouble with the last movement. For about half of the movement there are no real dynamic changes at all, just soft and softer. This isn't uncommon in his works, so I decided to phrase everything and add nuances of dynamics and slight tempo fluctuations. At the first rehearsal of the last movement I became unhappy with my decision. At the next rehearsal I decided to play it exactly as Shostakovich wrote it, basically *non-espressivo*, and for about 146 measures simply soft. It was spectacular.

Years earlier I had done a work by William Bergsma on the Music of Our Time series at the Nippon Kan Theater. When I was in the New York Philharmonic we did Roy Harris's Symphony No. 3 with Bernstein on tour in Europe, and a few months later did the same work with Leinsdorf. It was fascinating to see how stagnant the symphony felt under Leinsdorf. Leinsdorf used to say, "I'm not from the school of the *ritardando*," and he generally conducted with little tempo fluctuation. Bernstein, on the other hand, manipulated the tempo a great deal, especially in American music, and his interpretation of the Harris symphony was much more vivid and expressive. It was an important lesson for me. I liked Bergsma's symphony, but I interpreted it as I had usually done for Diamond and other music of that era. After the dress rehearsal Bill came to the front of the stage and said that it was wonderful but then added, "Please don't do me any favors. Just play it as I wrote it." I did, but I still feel the piece would have been better with more nuance.

About five years after we did the Shostakovich 15th, I wanted to program it again. When the executive director at the time looked over the programs for the season, he asked me to remove the 15th, afraid that it would deter a large audience. When I am asked to do this I always agree. There is a great deal of music out there, and no one work is that important. I asked him which Shostakovich symphony he would like me to program, and he suggested any with a single digit.

The big event for this 1999–2000 season was the dedication of the organ. The instrument had not been ready for the 1998 opening, so in another grand occasion we dedicated the Watjen Concert Organ in July 2000. From small baroque works through the major orchestral and concerto organ works of the twentieth century, the magnificence of its sound and the delicacy of its possibilities were on display. Carole Terry, our resident organist and professor at the University of Washington, had worked hard with the Fisk team and Craig and Joan Watjen to design this instrument. It has 4,490 pipes, 62 voices and 83 ranks, and Fisk has named it Op. 114. The American Guild of Organists had their convention in Seattle at the same time as the dedication, and we invited some great organists for the occasion. The first program featured works by Bach, Handel, Haydn, Franck, and Alexandre Guilmant, along with the world premiere of Diamond's Symphony No. 10. David had started the symphony for us in 1989 but interrupted it to compose his Symphony No. 11 for Kurt Masur and the New York Philharmonic. David then returned to the Tenth. He had completed the first and second movements and at my suggestion included a very important organ part in the third and fourth movements. The new symphony was very difficult, but it was magnificent.

The second program included Piston's Prelude and Allegro and Copland's Symphony for Organ and Orchestra on the first half, and Francis Poulenc's Organ Concerto and Guilmant's Symphony No. 1 on the second half. The third concert was made possible by the AGO, which is committed to building the repertoire of new music for the organ. They have a tradition of commissioning works for their conventions and for this one chose those we premiered at this concert: Naji Hakim's *Seattle Concerto* and *In Fullness of Time* by Robert Sirota. After premiering the Sirota I decided to try to program it again in the season after next. We initiated the organ recital series the following season.

The main personnel change during 2000–2001 was the appointment of George Fiore as our chorus director. I had worked with George at the Seattle Opera and found him to be a stellar colleague, with a fine concept of sound and text.

This was also the year that violinist Maria Larionoff became the associate concertmaster. Choosing Maria was a difficult decision, because our numbers 3 and 4 first violinists also auditioned for the position. (At this time the musicians' contract stated that for any new titled position, we must first audition orchestra members who wanted to apply.) I put together a committee of all the principal string players and everyone agreed that not only did Maria play the best of the three, but that she would be an excellent choice no matter who else might audition. Quite simply, her playing was magnificent in every way. The easy way out would be to choose none of the three, but the correct decision was to give the position to Maria, which I did. I have always tried to make such decisions solely on the basis of artistic quality. Usually people get over such disappointments, but these two players never did. The unsuccessful players were quite angry and did not take my decision well. In fact, they never forgave me, and one of them even threatened me: "You will rue the day you did this."

The Delos Separation

We made many recordings for Delos that won awards, and the CDs sold very well. The Grammy-winning engineer John Eargle did most of our initial engineering, and Delos engaged excellent writers for the liner notes. Everything they did was of the highest quality. However, they were not necessarily as good at the business side.

In the late 1980s record companies were still paying orchestras to record. They would also pay royalties. Delos had some difficulty keeping up with all the bookkeeping. Investigating sales to make sure proper royalties are sent is part of every recording contract, a provision that had led to multimillion-dollar settlements for such artists as Leonard Bernstein and Mitch Miller with Columbia Records. Delos was a small company that was doing well, but they certainly were not spending money freely. They made some tremendous deals with the Seattle Symphony that were good for the orchestra but not so much for Delos. In the end Delos was not able to meet their royalty commitments.

This never bothered me. So they didn't pay their bills or issue royalty statements in a timely fashion; they championed our orchestra, did everything artistic at the highest level, brought some great American music to a broader audience, and in the process helped our orchestra grow in quality and renown.

Nevertheless, after looking into Delos's books, the Seattle Symphony's administration had many of these recordings returned. That meant Delos would no longer offer them—we would own them outright. Therefore many of our sensational recordings became suddenly unavailable or out of print. If you wanted to buy our version of Bartók's *Miraculous Mandarin* or Stravinsky's *Chant du rossignol*, or Handel's *Acis and Galatea*, or the Bach transcriptions by Elgar and Respighi, you were out of luck. All these great recordings were in our symphony offices instead of on the shelves. Furthermore, this was very hurtful to the two remarkable women at Delos, Carol Rosenberger and Amelia Haygood, who had stood by us, been there for us, and made these recordings possible. I never understood what good came of having them unavailable.

Delos was my company, and I was always grateful to them for their tremendous support. I was terribly sorry that they lost our recordings. Eventually Klaus Heymann of Naxos Records created the Seattle Symphony Collection and reissued all our Delos recordings. When I spoke to Klaus before the release he said, "I haven't listened to them all, but the orchestra is so much better now than it was then. Are these older recordings of the highest quality?" I said, "Absolutely." "How did you do that?" he asked. I replied, "We just took twice as long to record things because we had to make more corrections then."

Today the Seattle Symphony can record a Brahms symphony in a few hours, whereas in the early days it would take three sessions. Of the hundreds of CDs that I have made, I can think of maybe three that I am unhappy with. A critic once wrote about the Delos reissues that even in those early years, the sound of the orchestra was much the same as it is now. I believe that is correct. The concept of sound was always paramount in our approach; it was the technical issues that were the ones most in need of improvement.

I have always loved beginning the season with some standard repertoire that helps solidify the sound of the orchestra. For the 2001–2002 season we began with a four-concert Beethoven festival. Hearing any great composer with a series like that focuses one's perceptions of that composer. When I was in the New York Philharmonic, we did a series of Mahler concerts at Carnegie Hall with Leinsdorf, Levine, and Boulez. As much as I love Mahler's music, at the time I saw the flaws in the music much more clearly. Of course, with Beethoven there seemed to be no flaws.

We opened our Learning Center this season. This was particularly exciting for Deborah and me, since only the Chicago Symphony had anything like this, and we thought that the center could be an important addition to our educational work.

I had always been interested in doing a yearly festival of some sort focused on music of a single region, country, or historical period. The first, highlighting music from the Pacific Rim—China, Japan, Korea, the Philippines, Taiwan, and Vietnam—occurred toward the end of this season. Bright Sheng was my co-director. Bright worked very hard to look at Asian music's influence on American music and to represent a broad variety of works. We also programmed music from the United States, Australia, and Canada that demonstrated an Asian influence. The highlights, for me, were Takemitsu's *From me flows what you call Time*, played by the percussion ensemble Nexus, and Bright Sheng's *Nauking! Nauking!*, played by the virtuoso pipa player Wu Man.

The next season, 2002–2003, was our centennial, and we opened with a gala featuring Renée Fleming singing—among other selections—the world premiere of Behzad Ranjbaran's *Songs of Eternity*. We also premiered a work for percussion and orchestra by Margaret Brouwer, with Evelyn Glennie as the soloist. Furthermore, we commissioned six new works—by John Harbison, Daniel Brewbaker, Bright Sheng, David Stock, Chen Yi, and Samuel Jones. That season I received an ASCAP special award for my championing of American music, and the Pacific Northwest Branch of the National Association of Arts and Sciences gave me its first IMPACT award for lifetime achievement.

We also undertook our first tour to Carnegie Hall. Because of the expense, the board had wanted to cancel it. However, Deborah and I believed strongly that it would be very important for the orchestra, especially during our 100th anniversary. Choosing a tour program was difficult, but in the end I decided to do Sibelius's Symphony No. 2, written in 1903, as the main work. I originally wanted to do Strauss's *Sinfonia Domestica* because it was written in the same year and premiered at Carnegie Hall, but Carnegie Hall's artistic department thought the Sibelius would be better for ticket sales. Bright Sheng's *The Phoenix* was to have its New York premiere as well. It is written for dramatic soprano and orchestra, so I asked my dear friend Jane Eaglen to do the honors. She was not well-known in the new-music world, but she is a phenomenal musician, and I felt she would bring something special to his work. To say that Bright is very particular is an understatement. Bright and Jane got along well, but Jane felt that Bright didn't know how to write for her kind of voice, and Bright felt that she wasn't necessarily suited to his kind of music. It was a tightrope for me, but in the end I thought Jane was sensational, if not in a typical new-music style. It reminds me of the premiere that I did with Frederica von Stade at the Lincoln Center Chamber Music Society of a new work by Peter Mennin called *Voices*. Flicka had some trouble with the pitches at first, but Peter said he was excited about her ability to perform, the beautiful quality of her voice, and her personality onstage. He was less concerned with her accuracy. I agreed with Peter. In the end, she also had the pitches in hand.

When the Philadelphia Orchestra came to Seattle with Riccardo Muti a number of years before, they had programmed excerpts from *Turandot* by Ferruccio Busoni. I loved this piece and Busoni's language, and I programmed some excerpts for the tour as well. One of my favorite pianists, Horacio Gutiérrez, played Rachmaninoff's Fourth Piano Concerto on some of the concerts. For the Carnegie Hall concert, we did Strauss's *Death and Transfiguration*, Bright's *The Phoenix*, and Sibelius's Symphony No. 2. The audience was very large and enthusiastic, and for an encore we did a movement of the Busoni suite. Ara Guzalamien, who was Carnegie's artistic person, laughed and said he suspected this was the first time an orchestral work by Busoni was ever played as an encore at the hall!

Jeremy Eichler wrote in the *New York Times*:

> The conductor Gerard Schwarz, familiar to New York audiences after the decades spent at the helms of the Mostly Mozart Festival and the New York Chamber Symphony. But Mr. Schwarz's long-standing commitment has been to the Seattle Symphony. . . . Mr. Schwarz's investment in Seattle, since 1985, has helped the orchestra thrive. Its artistic growth was evidenced by its Carnegie program ... the group's sound is full and rich, and the musicians play for Mr. Schwarz with palpable commitment. The outer movements of the Sibelius were broadly contoured and dramatically delivered. . . . The Strauss had generous volume and theatrical sweep."

The tour was a tremendous success, and in the end we raised $600,000 more than we needed. When we drew up the budget for the following season, the board complained that we had no tour to help balance the budget! We also made a tour to Florida with Truls Mork and did the first of a number of Washington State tours aiming at underserved cities and towns.

My favorite concert of the season was Schumann's *Das Paradies und die Peri* with a great cast that included Ute Selbig, Kristine Jepson, Hans Peter Blochwitz, and Richard Paul Fink. Also during that season we presented Yo-Yo Ma both with his Silk Road Ensemble and as a soloist in four concerts. With the orchestra Yo-Yo did Peter Lieberson's *Six Realms* for amplified cello and orchestra—not a very audience-friendly work, but Yo-Yo is one of those artists who constantly push their own boundaries.

Our special festival series, Viva la Musica, continued that spring. I wanted to do music from south of the border, so Sam Jones and I spent a great deal of time looking at scores and listening to tapes. We found some excellent works, many by composers I had never heard of, such as a great cantata—*Florentino, el que canto con el Diablo*—by the Venezuelan composer Antonio Estévez. For a good cross-section of styles, we chose works by Carlos Chávez, Máximo Flügelman, Alberto Ginastera, Osvaldo Golijov, Amadeo Roldán, Carlos Surinach, and others.

There was an important choral tradition in England and Germany during the last half of the nineteenth century. That music is rarely played in the United States, but we did a superb oratorio by Max Bruch called *The Song of the Bell*. One of our many great soloists that season was Van Cliburn, who played Grieg's Piano Concerto. Van and my mother-in-law and father-in-law attended Juilliard at the same time. Shirley and Van were both from Dallas, and they studied with the same teacher, Rosina Lhévinne. We had a party for Van at our house after one of his concerts, and he insisted on phoning Shirley despite the late hour. She was delighted! Van was a sweet and most charming gentleman.

Toward the end of the season Deborah decided to take a leadership position with the Chicago Symphony. Our former chairman, Jerry Grinstein, who was a good friend of an important member of the board in Chicago, had been asked about Deborah. He told me that he would like to give this gentleman a thoughtful response and very confidentially asked me my opinion of her and whether I thought she would be a good fit for Chicago. I gave her my highest recommendation. She had done a wonderful job for ten years in Seattle, and I felt that the move would be perfect for Deborah and Chicago. Patty Sabee became acting executive director; she had been with us for many years and was outstanding in every position she had held, so the transition was seamless. I thought Patty would be an excellent choice and made my opinion known, but in the end it was a board decision.

One would think that, after the opening of the hall in 1998, the dedication of the organ in 2000, the centennial season of 2003, the continuing festivals, and the artistic growth of the orchestra, things might begin to calm down—but that was not the case. We celebrated my twentieth year during the 2004–2005 season, completed the premieres of our centennial commissions, chose a new executive director, began the search for a new concertmaster, and debuted the first year of our Made in America festival. The opening gala told many parts of the story: six soloists, each playing or singing a short work or movement, and a very unusual work called *Jubilee Variations* written for the fiftieth anniversary of the Cincinnati Symphony. Their music director, Eugene Goossens, wrote a theme and asked ten American composers—Creston, Copland, Taylor, Hanson, Schuman, Piston, Harris, Anis Fuleihan, Bernard Rogers, and Ernest Bloch—to compose one variation each, giving them the key and the mood or type of movement. Goossens wrote the finale, and the piece is sensational.

At the end of the season a good friend of ours, Charles Simonyi, gave the orchestra $10 million. Charles is one of the most remarkable and brilliant men I have ever known. He is among my closest friends, and he truly knows and loves music. His gift at this particular time in the history of the orchestra was crucial, and the director of his foundation, Susan Hutchison, was instrumental in making it happen. At the same time Ron Woodard and MaryAnn Champion rejoined the board as chairman and president respectively, and Susan also joined the board, which chose Paul Meecham to succeed Deborah. I think the world of Paul. He is a wonderful gentleman with a great knowledge of music and excellent taste. He stayed only a few years before going to the Baltimore Symphony, but they were terrific years.

We premiered works by Paul Schoenfield, Gabriela Frank, and David Schiff. When Paul Schoenfield was in Seattle for his premiere, we invited him to dinner. However, Paul kept kosher. He said he would be happy having Cheerios, raw vegetables, and a can of tuna on a paper plate. I discussed the matter with Jody, then called Paul back: "If

Jody could guarantee a 100 percent kosher meal, could you eat with us?" He said yes. So Jody bought new pans and utensils and got some salmon from a fishmonger who had a kosher knife, and she used a kosher gourmet shop for the soup starter and the dessert. Ron Woodard had already called to say he would be taking advantage of his standing invitation to dinner on Monday nights. That night we all ate our very first kosher meal off paper plates with plastic knives and forks in our dining room. We had many laughs about this delightful evening.

During the season we did the complete *Manfred* by Schumann, with a text by Lord Byron. The narrator, John Kuether, and I edited the text. Also during the season we auditioned fifteen violinists for the concertmaster position. They were all excellent, and we invited a number of them to come back and lead the orchestra the following season. The auditions were quite involved and included orchestral repertoire, solo repertoire, and chamber music. This decision was mine, but I invited the whole orchestra to come to the auditions and to send me their opinions.

On the family front, Julian had his bar mitzvah in May, and our close friends Aggie Gund and Daniel Shapiro gave $50,000 in his honor to the education endowment fund of the orchestra, as they had done two years before for Gabriella's bat mitzvah.

David Diamond, one of America's greatest composers and such a dear friend who was almost a member of our family, died on June 13 at the age of eighty-nine. We dedicated our performance of Verdi's Requiem to him at the end of the season. He had been our honorary composer-in-residence since 1995.

The most exciting event of the season was the Made in America Festival, Part 1. It featured music by some of the most important American composers of the recent past: Samuel Barber, William Bergsma, Leonard Bernstein, Elliott Carter, Carlos Chávez, Aaron Copland, Paul Creston, David Diamond, Irving Fine, Morton Gould, Charles Griffes, Howard Hanson, Roy Harris, Alan Hovhaness, Charles Ives, Peter Mennin, Vincent Persichetti, Walter Piston, Wallingford Riegger, Ned Rorem, William Schuman, Roger Sessions, Randall Thompson, and Virgil Thomson. Part 2 would be devoted to living composers, especially the younger generation. David Diamond was able to attend the concerts that featured his music just weeks before his death. When I think about the music of this past century, especially the period from 1925 to 1960, it strikes me that Americans were in the forefront.

In 2004 I was appointed to the National Council on the Arts, which was headed by Dana Gioia, a brilliant writer, poet, and critic. I don't know anyone who knows as much as he does about all the arts. The agency had become quite bloated, appointments to it having turned into rewards for the president's campaign supporters or for a spouse or partner who needed an honor. Dana brought the Council back to its original concept, with a membership made up of fewer than twenty artists and knowledgeable supporters from different disciplines. Every member had to undergo an FBI investigation, and some of our neighbors in Seattle asked if I was in trouble, because the FBI was knocking on their doors and asking questions of them. I was very proud of this honor, and of the opportunity in some small way to help our country. I never thought of this as being political in any way. I do not align myself with any party, and I try to stay out of political discussions, though I care deeply about the future of our country. I saw this as an artistic appointment, not a political one. Dana wanted me on the council because of my knowledge of music, and in a sense I became the music expert on the council. I had no idea that anyone would think ill of me because President George W. Bush, a Republican, had appointed me. I was clearly wrong, but then I have often been guilty of this kind of naiveté. I would have been equally happy and honored had Barack Obama appointed me, and I was thrilled to be sworn in by Supreme Court Justice Sandra Day O'Connor. My years on the Council were fascinating, and I learned much about the breadth and depth of artistic activity all over the country.

Recording William Schuman

One of my last projects in Seattle was recording the complete symphonies of William Schuman. He had been the president of the Juilliard School and the president of Lincoln Center. Joseph Polisi, the current president of Juilliard, a close friend of Schuman's, and the author of an excellent biography on the composer, introduced the idea to Schuman's son, Tony, who helped make the initial funding possible. Naxos's Klaus Heymann was extremely enthusiastic about the project as well. William Schuman rejected his first two symphonies, and his son did not want us to record them since his father disliked them. I decided to look at them anyway during a trip to Washington, D.C.

After reviewing Schuman's early manuscripts at the Library of Congress, I agreed with his decision to withdraw the works. We began our series with Schuman's Symphony No. 3 and concluded with his Symphony No. 10. The reviews of the series were uniformly excellent. Lawrence Johnson wrote in the March 2010 issue of *Gramophone*: "The Sixth stands as one of Schuman's most impressive achievements. It's a tough, flinty work but Schwarz draws a quite sensational performance from the Seattle musicians, even besting the Ormandy/Philadelphia account, the somber eloquence coming through with great impact. [As for] the *Prayers in a Time of War* (1943). . . . Schwarz and the Seattle players deliver a moving, beautifully played performance." Merlin Patterson wrote in the November 2010 issue of *Fanfare* after the release of Symphonies Nos. 6 and 8: "They bring the cycle, now on Naxos, to a magnificent conclusion with brilliant performances of two of the composer's most challenging works, thus completing one of the most significant series of recordings in recent memory." Each of Schuman's symphonies is very different from the others. It is sad to see how few of these symphonies (with the exception of the Third, which Bernstein used to program together with Harris's Third and Copland's Third) are played today.

Especially because of his important associations with Juilliard and Lincoln Center, Schuman's symphonies should be played regularly in New York by the New York Philharmonic. Of course, he is not the only neglected contemporary American composer. It is nice to see how much new and experimental music is being programmed, but these great composers of our recent past deserve to be heard each season. Bill was in attendance when I performed and recorded (live) his two operas *A Question of Taste*, and *The Mighty Casey*. My first recording for what became the complete symphony cycle was of his *Variations* on *"America," New England Triptych*, Symphony for Strings (Symphony No. 5), and *Judith*. After hearing the recording he wrote: "The performance has so many superlative elements that I would do the overall excellence of the rendition an injustice by citing the special places that appeal particularly to the composers' soul. It is rare indeed to have the combination of intellectual depth, technical superiority and emotional involvement to the degree that any composer would hope for. Jerry achieves these desiderata in a seemingly effortless way. What he has accomplished with that orchestra is outstanding."

Naxos released the first recording of our Schuman series—his Fourth and Ninth Symphonies—during the 2005–2006 season. Naxos, through the Milken Archive, also released our recording of Robert Beaser's *Heavenly Feast*, another excellent work by a composer who is not programmed often enough, as well as our recording of two rarely performed works by Shostakovich, *The Execution of Stepan Razin* and the tone poem *October*. We had scheduled three festivals this season: Mozart, for the 250th anniversary of his birth; Shostakovich, for the 100th anniversary of his birth; and Made in America, Part 2. To me, celebrating the anniversaries of the most famous composers is important mainly as a marketing tool and rarely has programmatic significance. Neither Mozart nor Shostakovich needs any help. The Eastern Music Festival's celebration, in 2015, of the 100th anniversary of David Diamond's birth seems to have been the only such commemoration for this important composer.

The 2005–2006 season also marked the beginning of a new series of doing Bach cantatas as companion works on the annual Beethoven's Ninth programs. These masterpieces are rarely performed, with the exception of solo cantatas such as *Ich habe genug*. I chose only the cantatas written for Christmas or New Year's, and I continued this tradition for quite a number of years.

Mikhail Pletnev came this season with the Russian National Orchestra, and we performed a concert with both orchestras onstage together. The program was the Fifth Symphonies of Shostakovich and Tchaikovsky. I would conduct the Shostakovich with Seattle principals, and Pletnev would do the Tchaikovsky with Russian principals. We had one rehearsal. Pletnev did not want to conduct the rehearsal, so I rehearsed all the tempo changes and critical transitions in both pieces. The sound of this huge orchestra was extraordinary, and everyone enjoyed the experience, even though it was more a show than an artistic achievement. Luckily, I have never had any physical problems with conducting, but working with such an enormous orchestra was very challenging for my arms!

As always, we did a number of new works during this season, but the most important piece was the Tuba Concerto, featuring Chris Olka as the soloist, by our composer-in-residence, Samuel Jones. This technically difficult piece was commissioned by Sandra Crowder in memory of her late husband, James. He was an amateur tuba player and a Boeing engineer. Musically, his love was Wagner, and Sam was able to bring all these elements together brilliantly in the third movement. This was the first of a series of concertos Sam wrote for the Seattle Symphony and the All-Star Orchestra, including concertos for the horn, the trombone, the cello, and the violin.

Another important event for me was a television broadcast on our public station of one of our subscription weeks, which included Shostakovich's Symphony No. 8. It was recorded live but edited to include some interesting commentary and visuals. John Forsen did the executive producing, and we won an Emmy for this show.

Adam Stern had been first our assistant conductor and then our associate conductor, staying with us for a total of nine years. After he left we decided we should find a young conductor and give him or her a lot of experience for two or possibly three years, then move on. For the upcoming season we chose Carolyn Kuan, and that choice turned out to be wonderful. She had the curiosity and talent necessary for the assistant conductor position. Carolyn took advantage of every opportunity we were able to afford her.

Our important festival this season was Made in America, Part 2. Since leaving Music Today in New York in 1989, I had somewhat lost touch with the younger composers. Sam Jones and I reached out to all the major composition teachers at the conservatories and universities, asking them to recommend their best students. We also contacted

ASCAP, BMI, and anyone else we thought might help. We studied over 200 works and from them made four interesting programs that were very successful. From among the established composers we chose John Adams, Ken Benshoof, William Bolcom, Michael Colgrass, John Corigliano, George Crumb, Lukas Foss, Philip Glass, John Harbison, Samuel Jones, Libby Larsen, Cindy McTee, George Perle, Bernard Rands, David Schiff, Joseph Schwantner, Bright Sheng, David Stock, Augusta Read Thomas, Joan Tower, and Ellen Taaffe Zwilich. From the younger group we selected Derek Bermel, Daniel Brewbaker, Janice Giteck, Jennifer Higdon, Pierre Jalbert, Daniel Kellogg, James Matheson, Eric Moe, Bruce Ruddell, Yevgeniy Sharlat, and the ensemble Affinity. We also had a day of music dedicated exclusively to American composers.

The event of this season was the Music of Central Europe festival. We called it "Bridging the 48th Parallel"—Hungary, Poland, Romania, Bulgaria, and the Czech Republic. The major works we programmed were by Bartók, George Enescu, Karel Husa, Janáček, Kodály, Ligeti, Lutosławski, Martinů, and Panufnik, but we also did music by twenty-two other composers from these areas, most of them still living. We engaged the whole artistic community with recitals, chamber music, folk music, choral music, and lectures. The brilliant writer and critic Bernard Jacobson had recently moved to the Seattle area, and he participated in a number of lectures.

The most important concert in the festival was a semistaged performance of Bartók's opera *Bluebeard's Castle*, with a set by Dale Chihuly. Dale constructed seven tall wooden columns, which would be turned to expose the stunning multicolored organic glass sculptures he created for each door in the castle. We had two great singers, Sally Burgess and Charles Austin. Charles Simonyi narrated the opening in Hungarian, and Sharon Ott did the staging. It was one of the most significant events in the Seattle Symphony's long history. The other works during the festival that I thought were especially remarkable were Martinů's Double Concerto, Janáček's *Glagolitic Mass*, Levente Gyöngyösi's *Verkündigung* (*Annunciation*), Panufnik's *Autumn Music*, and Grażyna Bacewicz's Concerto for String Orchestra.

We did a second television show featuring music of Kodály and Kernis, as well as the Brahms Second Piano Concerto with André Watts. That week we were using only seven of the eight services for the orchestra the contract allowed (a service is a concert or rehearsal), so on the morning after the Thursday night we did it again in full dress but without the audience so that John Forsen, our executive producer, could get all the shots he wanted without infringing on the audience's concert experience. The visuals were even better than they had been for the first show, and we won another Emmy. This was the event that inspired the idea of my doing another television project without an audience—a project which became the All-Star Orchestra a few years later.

After the success of our two television shows, Leslie Jackson Chihuly, Dale's wife and business partner, wanted to film the performance of *Bluebeard's Castle*. The orchestra had been amenable to the idea of getting more exposure on television, and I hoped they would agree to do the live recording for a reasonable fee. The orchestral leadership told Leslie that they would be happy to do it—for $1 million! I was surprised that this did not antagonize Leslie and Dale forever. Thank goodness it didn't.

This season we began a wonderful relationship with John Lill, a wonderful pianist with a wicked sense of humor. He began the season by performing all five Beethoven concertos in two concerts. Yo-Yo returned with his Silk Road project, and I received the Mayor's Arts Award for my contribution to the arts in Seattle.

We released four new recordings, including the long-awaited live recording on Naxos of Hanson's *Merry Mount*. We did our second installment of the William Schuman series and released Shostakovich's Symphony No. 5 on Artek. We also did a special recording for Starbucks, which had recently formed a company called Hear Music with the Concord Music Group. I wanted to bring contemporary classical music to a new and larger audience, not to mention generate some income for the orchestra. Together the director and I settled on a series of CDs with a group of American composers. We planned to do popular, audience-friendly works first, so we asked the composers to do arrangements of music they loved of the past; the next CD would present short original works by the same composers. The first CD, *Echoes*, was released in the western Washington market as a test for an international release. David Schiff did a jazz version of the "Infernal Dance" from Stravinsky's *Firebird*, Bright Sheng based his piece on a Brahms Intermezzo, David Stock used Jeremiah Clark, John Harbison used Thelonius Monk, Sam Jones used Peter Lutkin, and Aaron Jay Kernis used Hildegard of Bingen. I wrote a piece, too, based on Handel. Although we sold more than ten thousand in the Seattle market, the project of Starbucks doing original material died. Happily, Naxos released that CD a few years later under the same title.

This season brought many changes in leadership, ideas, and challenges. Carolyn Kuan's wasn't the only new artistic face. Our choral director, George Fiore, decided to retire, so Joseph Crnko, director of the Northwest Boychoir, took over as director of chorale activities. I had worked with Joe a great deal with his Northwest Boychoir and other choruses. He had all the needed qualities, both personal and musical. Carolyn Kuan completed her first year as our assistant conductor. Like Crnko, she has it all—great energy, intelligence, and talent. Carolyn was a real joy to work with, and I felt she got everything available from her association with the orchestra.

After a two-year search for a new concertmaster, I decided to follow the model of major European orchestras and appointed four concertmasters. Each would do about a quarter of the subscription season and a few other concerts as their schedules permitted. Of course we were very lucky to have Maria Larionoff in residence, and she was supportive of the idea. One of the problems with finding someone was that Maria was so excellent. She didn't want the position because the concertmaster in our contract did not have tenure. It is very unusual for a new music director to fire the concertmaster, but without tenure it certainly could happen, and Maria was happy with her associate position. It worked out beautifully. Each of the four made a unique contribution to the orchestra, and the first violin section was on its toes each week. My private time with each was very gratifying, and for the moment we had a wonderful artistic solution. The three other outstanding violinists were Emmanuelle Boisvert, concertmaster of the Detroit Symphony Orchestra; Frank Almond, concertmaster of the Milwaukee Symphony Orchestra; and Ani Kavafian, who taught at Yale.

On the managerial front, Susan Hutchison became the chair of the board, and my friend Tom Philion, who had worked with me at the Eastern Music Festival, came in as executive director. Susan is a great leader, has great instincts about people, and was well connected in the community. After the long and productive tenure of Ron Woodard and MaryAnn Champion, this was a terrific choice.

We had a new work by Aaron Jay Kernis on the schedule, as well as a new horn concerto by Sam Jones, to be played by our remarkable solo horn, John Cerminaro. And although we had not worked with a dance company for years, I thought it would be a great idea to do one week a year with the choreographer and Seattle native Mark Morris and his company; for this first year I agreed to conduct. Continuing with the American theme of our festivals, we did a festival called Coming to America of great composers who had immigrated to our country, most of them to escape persecution in the 1930s and 1940s. The highlight of the festival was the performance of the *Genesis Suite* by Arnold Schoenberg, Igor Stravinsky, Alexandre Tansman, Mario Castelnuovo-Tedesco, Nathaniel Shilkret, Darius Milhaud, and Ernst Toch. Dale Chihuly created remarkable abstract video visuals to go along with the music.

A CD I recorded for Milken in Berlin with the Berlin Radio Symphony Orchestra, which included extensive highlights from Kurt Weill's *Eternal Road*, was released at the same time as the *Genesis Suite*. Recording both works was an important major achievement because of the extensive and thorough historical work of the great scholar and intellectual Neil Levin, who was especially knowledgeable about Jewish music.

A few years later we completed *Eternal Road*, which is yet to be released.

The *New York Times*, 2007

In the midst of all these events I ran into a serious problem. As an artist, all my firsts were in New York, and most were reported in the *New York Times*. I had one major piece in the Magazine section, and one in the Arts and Leisure section and generally received excellent reviews. I even wrote an article for Arts and Leisure about programming orchestral concerts. Even though I had I left Mostly Mozart in 2002, reviews for the festival's opening concerts usually included a slight on my past leadership. One reason I decided to leave the festival was that I felt it could use a new direction. Yet for a number of years the *Times* applauded the new direction while criticizing me.

In Seattle some of the players wanted a new conductor, completely understandable in light of my long tenure there. As I mentioned earlier, when I had appointed Maria Larionoff associate concertmaster, two first violins who had also auditioned for the position became very upset and hostile. One of them threatened me, saying that he would do everything in his power to undermine my role as music director, and that I would "rue the day" I appointed Maria. The second became a vocal leader of the members of the orchestra, who spoke out against me. One of them even sued the orchestra for not being sensitive to his mental disability, which was unknown to the organization. After that lawsuit was thrown out of court he sued me personally, and that too was thrown out of court. His lawyer caught the interest of the *New York Times*, and in December 2007 the paper published a very long article about my time in Seattle. It mentioned many of my accomplishments, including the orchestra's tremendous artistic growth during my tenure, our recordings, the building of our incredible Benaroya Hall, and the increase from five thousand to forty thousand subscribers. However, the reporter interviewed only the unhappy Seattle players, and in the end it was a very critical and harmful piece.

Marty Segal, the chairman emeritus of Lincoln Center, told me that Jane Moss, the director of presentations at Lincoln Center, had been making false allegations about me, especially to the writers at the *New York Times*. Jane and I had disagreed when she tried to eliminate the Mostly Mozart Festival, but after that we worked well together, and I believed Marty was mistaken about Jane. After twenty-four years in Seattle, I certainly understood the desire of some of the musicians for a change. I was surprised by the length of the *Times* article, as well as by all the misinformation in it, but there was no way to undo it. I found it interesting that they interviewed only the few musicians who did not advance, including the two violinists, and others who for varying reasons had been let go during my tenure.

When one is a public figure in a leadership position––whether a politician, a business leader, or in my case, an artistic leader––hiring and firing and making critical decisions is part of the responsibility. That said, we learn from every important decision we make, and as I did in Seattle, I always tried to do what was best for the art form, the orchestra, and the community.

The Academy of St. Martin in the Fields

Around the time of this article, I broke my ankle and leg while skiing. As I lay on the couch recovering in our home, I received a call from the Academy of St. Martin in the Fields, asking if I could conduct a tour with them in January in Germany with what they called their full orchestra. Neville Marriner was unable to go, and I jumped at the chance. I had worked with them in London at the Barbican Center a number of years before in an all-Mozart program and loved the orchestra. I explained that I would have to walk with crutches and sit while conducting. Because I was unable to be at the first rehearsal, I asked my Liverpool assistant conductor, Mathew Coorey, to conduct it in my stead. We discussed what needed to be covered, and Mathew did an excellent job.

Neville's two programs included either Dvořák's Symphony No. 8 or Mendelssohn's Symphony No. 3, Beethoven's *Leonora Overture* No. 1, and Beethoven's Piano Concerto No. 3, with Jonathan Biss as soloist. The orchestra was sensational. The players' musical attentiveness to one another was remarkable, and our rapport was, for me, inspiring; it was like conducting a large chamber ensemble. Lars Wallerang wrote in the *Westdeutsche Zeitung* after a concert in Düsseldorf: "Gerard Schwarz achieved a miracle with the clarity and precision of Antonín Dvořák's Eighth Symphony. The Academy performs its magic, as always, through the unity of its silky sound, agility and esprit. Dvorak could not be enjoyed more exquisitely. A celebration in the sold-out hall." The critic in the *Hamburger Abendblatt* wrote, "The conductor and orchestra quite obviously had fun finally being able to show how much one can still pull out of that 'golden oldie.' Full of zest and enjoying the loud risks, it was like off-roading through the Bohemian forests and meadows." And the critic of the *Kölner Stadt-Anzeiger* opined: "Under the guest's (Schwarz) energetic and sparkling direction, the orchestra performed its finest. The typical inclination to the superficial sheen of a neutral, satisfying sound was conspicuously absent this time."

Working around my cast and crutches presented its own set of challenges. Many of the German concert halls were not equipped for people with mobility aids and had a number of stairs to climb. Each time I would enter the stage, the applause, which had already begun, would fade to silence as I hobbled my way to the platform and then up onto the podium. The Academy provided me with a swiveling stool, which was a first for me. It made me think of the challenges my late friend James DePreist must have had during his conducting career.

Mahler's Eighth and a New Contract

There were two works that I had always wanted to program in Seattle: Arnold Schoenberg's *Gurre-Lieder*, a massive cantata for five singers, and Mahler's Symphony No. 8. The problem was the cost of the immense orchestra and the large cast of soloists. I had done it in Los Angeles with the Philharmonic in 1989. André Previn was in his last season as music director then, and it was the major event of that season. By this time André's relationship with Ernest Fleischmann, the executive director of the orchestra, had greatly deteriorated. He became ill and was unable to conduct. I was contacted by my manager at Columbia Artists, Judie Janowski, asking whether I could go to San Diego to replace the conductor being considered for André's replacement. The manager of the San Diego orchestra said he would release his conductor, but only if I could replace him.

It was a Sunday and I was skiing with a friend, Bill Champion, at Crystal Mountain in the Cascade Range of Washington State. Jody received the call and told Judie I was free but wondered whether, instead of going to San Diego, I could do the *Gurre-Lieder* in Los Angeles. Judie said they wanted someone who had conducted the work before. Jody told her I had done it at Juilliard, and Judie relayed that information to Ernest Fleischmann. She then contacted Crystal Mountain and had them put up a notice at the top of the chair lift for me to call home ASAP. Bill, who was a physician, always looked out for such notices, and it was he who saw this one. We quickly skied down the mountain, and I called Jody on the pay phone in the lodge. I told her I had done a small part of the work "The Wood-Dove," at Juilliard but didn't have a full score. I asked her to call Judie back and withdraw my willingness to do the complete work. Jody said it was a long shot anyway, since Jessye Norman had to approve any conductor change, and she and I had never worked together.

It was a snowy, icy Sunday, unusual weather for Seattle. Jody packed up our five-month-old daughter, Gabriella, made it out to the University of Washington library, found someone to help her, and checked out the *Gurre-Lieder* score. In the meantime Judie Janowski was able to turn the situation around, and Ernest got in touch with Jessye Norman.

When I arrived home I started studying the score, still thinking that it wouldn't work out. The first rehearsal was with the massive chorus on Monday night. The soloists' rehearsal would be on Tuesday afternoon, with the rehearsal for chorus and soloists that night. The first orchestra rehearsal would take place on Wednesday morning, continuing until the first performance on Friday night. I was studying the sections with chorus when I got the call that Jessye approved. Finally I was going to conduct this huge, terrific work.

From the choral sections I moved to the sections with soloists. I stayed up all night on Sunday and then flew to Los Angeles on Monday morning, continuing to study nonstop until the chorus rehearsal. The combined choruses were magnificent, and the rehearsal went very well. On Monday I also studied all night so that I could be prepared for

Tuesday's rehearsals. Jody and Gabriella joined me that day, and by then I was starting to feel more comfortable. I managed to get a few hours' sleep that night. The rest of the week was like a dream. I deeply love the *Gurre-Lieder*, and everyone played and sang magnificently. In addition to Jessye Norman, the cast included Florence Quivar, Hans Hotter, Gary Lakes, David Gordon, and James Johnson. In his review of February 26, 1990, Martin Bernheimer wrote in the *Los Angeles Times*: "He exerted fine technical control and demonstrated a keen understanding of the inherent structural problems. He savored the cumulative tensions of the piece, appreciated the crucial differences between pathos and sentimentality, between power and bombast. . . . He offered enlightened, essentially authoritative music-making on a properly heroic scale. He coaxed brilliant playing from a decisively sympathetic, eminently cooperative orchestra."

I had tried to program this masterpiece in Seattle, but unfortunately it never happened due to cost. We did program Mahler's Symphony No. 8 to kick off the tenth anniversary of Benaroya Hall and planned a live recording as well. The recording was a real testament to the greatness of the orchestra. We did not require a single touch-up session—there were no mistakes. Our stellar soloists included Lauren Flanigan, Jane Eaglen, Jane Giering de Haan, Nancy Maultsby, Jane Gilbert, Gary Lakes, Vinson Cole, Clayton Brainerd, and Harold Wilson.

In the spring of 2008 I signed a new three-year contract. These contracts had become simple extensions, and there were never any issues. In August I had a meeting with the board chair, Susan Hutchison. Jody and I had some heart-to-heart talks about continuing after the 2010–2011 season. Gaby was in college, and Julian would enter college in the fall of 2009. We would be empty nesters, and if we were going to have another chapter in our artistic lives, this was the time to make that move. I had a wonderful conversation with Susy. We decided that three more seasons would give the board time to look to the future of the institution. She asked me if I would accept the title of conductor laureate, in which case I would continue to conduct as a guest for the foreseeable future. Of course I agreed, and we started to make plans for the announcement.

The 2008–2009 season was important in many ways. We appointed my close friend Marvin Hamlisch as our principal pops conductor. This idea originated with Larry Tucker and was supported by Marvin's manager, Andrew Grossman. Andrew and I have been friends since our high school years. An extremely gifted horn player, he played first horn in the New York Youth Symphony when I was first trumpet. After high school Andrew joined the Cleveland Orchestra and later became an important vice president of Columbia Artist Management. Today he is one of the most remarkable managers in the business. Marvin stayed with the Seattle Symphony until my departure. He did wonderful work for the pops series and was loved by the community.

For this season I appointed Maria Larionoff as our concertmaster. The four concertmasters we had engaged previously were artistic successes, but the orchestra contract permitted only one concertmaster, and the orchestra committee asked that I appoint a single person. I understood their wishes and happily appointed Maria. She had said earlier that she did not want to be considered, but this time she accepted. I was very pleased that she changed her mind.

I wanted to have a season spotlighting American conductors, so we engaged JoAnn Falletta, David Robertson, Leonard Slatkin, James DePreist, André Previn, and my associate conductor, Carolyn Kuan. We also did our second season with Mark Morris with an all-Mozart program conducted by Jane Glover, with Garrick Ohlsson as piano soloist.

I had always wanted to be able to present chamber music in the Illsley Ball Nordstrom Recital Hall, but because of the smaller number of seats, it was very hard not to create a deficit with such programs. My dear friend Mel Kaplan and his wife, Ynez, would visit Seattle almost every year. As an excellent manager, he always wanted to do business with the orchestra, and his specialty, so to speak, is managing string quartets. He proposed doing all the Beethoven quartets over six concerts with six different quartets. If the concerts sold out, we wouldn't lose money. They did, and the musical results were terrific. Next Mel wanted to do a series of concerts with four quartets, with one work on each program featuring a principal of the orchestra—such as Mozart's Clarinet Quintet, or his Horn Quintet. I thought it was a wonderful idea to build on the success of the Beethoven cycle, but I failed to convince the orchestra management that it would be worthwhile.

A remarkable member of our community, Charlie Staadecker, and his wife, Benita, had recently commissioned a very successful play, *Becky's Car*, and were now interested in commissioning something in honor of their twenty-fifth wedding anniversary. I loved Samuel Jones's Concerto for Tuba and Concerto for Horn and thought that we should now have a trombone concerto. At first Charlie and Benita were not thrilled about the idea, but they eventually warmed to it, and we premiered it in the spring with Ko-ichiro Yamamoto, our principal, as the soloist. It is a terrific work, and the performance was a sensation. When Charlie sent out the live performances to promote the concerto, he included Ko-ichiro's name. When perfectionist Ko voiced fears about his performance, Charlie removed his name from the promotional DVDs. Jay Freeman, principal trombone of the Chicago Symphony, received one of them and wrote a very complimentary letter praising the piece along with the remarkable "anonymous" trombone player. I forwarded this to Ko, who was pleased. He asked Charlie to start putting his name on the DVDs again.

The Aaron Jay Kernis symphony that was to be premiered in the spring of 2008 had been postponed, and the premiere took place in the 2008–2009 season. Aaron's first concept was to do a work with an early music–style sixteen-voice chorus that would be amplified. I had premiered Aaron's Double Concerto for Violin and Guitar at Alice Tully Hall and had some real issues with amplifying the guitar. Generally, I do not like any kind of amplified sound for classical symphonic concerts. Aaron changed the concept entirely, and the new version of the symphony featured soprano and baritone soloists with the chorus and orchestra. However, although he chose two excellent singers, their voices were too light; we needed huge voices to rise above the orchestra, but Aaron always preferred light ones. The singers had to be amplified, and I felt that, great though the piece was, the amplification did it a disservice.

This season we also did a Stephen Albert premiere. He had written his *Anthems and Processionals* for us in 1988 and revised it a year later. That revision was never played, and it seemed I was the only one who remembered it existed. Stephen's publisher didn't remember the revised version at all. The orchestra's principal librarian Pat Takahashi and I had to do some research, but we found it. It was so meaningful to revisit this work with Stephen's excellent changes.

In the spring I was given the Seventy-first First Citizen Award from the Seattle–King County Association of Realtors. This was a great honor for me, and I was asked to perform something at the banquet. Since I had not played the trumpet in over thirty years and my piano playing is not worthy of being heard in public, I either had to find something to conduct or compose a new work. I wrote two duos for violin and cello to be played by our son, Julian, and Maria Larionoff. One was dedicated to Becky Benaroya, the other to Gladys Rubinstein. The other work that we played at the banquet was my *Human Spirit*, performed by the Northwest Boychoir with seven players and conducted by Joe Crnko. Besides Julian and Maria, our daughter, Gabriella, played second violin, Mara Gearman viola, Mark Robbins horn, Barry Lieberman bass, and Ron Johnson vibraphone.

Susan Hutchison was the emcee, and there were tributes by Ralph Palumbo, Susan Hutchison, Sam Jones, Bonnie McElveen Hunter, Becky Benaroya, and all four of my children. Bonnie, who had flown to Seattle from North Carolina to be at the event, was sitting next to me, and with each tribute she whispered in my ear, "And you're still alive!"

I have always admired the glass sculptor Dale Chihuly. He is one of Seattle's treasures, and his work is known worldwide. My first musical collaboration with Dale was on the Seattle Opera's production of Debussy's *Pelléas et Mélisande*. I wanted the orchestra to have a long-term relationship with Dale, so we created a new position for him, Artist in Association. I think we are the only orchestra to have this kind of a relationship with a visual artist, and it was my hope that Dale would work with us to create one new work each year.

This season was my twenty-fifth anniversary with the orchestra, and Mark McCampbell, our vice principal for development, made it memorable. The highlights were a performance of Bernstein's Symphony No. 2 (*The Age of Anxiety*), with the pianist Misha Dichter; Richard Strauss's *Alpine Symphony*; Ernest Chausson's Symphony in B-flat; and Schoenberg's arrangement of the Brahms Piano Quartet in G Minor. I started my weekly radio series *Musical Moments* on Classical King FM, highlighting recordings that I had made over the years as they related to upcoming concerts. And I persuaded Kurt Masur to guest conduct the orchestra for a week.

Mark McCampbell commissioned Melinda Bargreen to do an article for the program booklet, which she has graciously allowed me to reproduce below.

Fans and friends of the Seattle Symphony who heard Gerard Schwarz's very first concert with the orchestra in 1983 will never forget the occasion. It was a remarkable program featuring the swan song of the orchestra's great principal clarinetist Ronald Phillips, who soloed in the Mozart Clarinet Concerto so beautifully that even Symphony insiders were amazed. It was the last concert attended by Schwarz's predecessor as music director, Rainer Miedel, who had only a few more weeks to live. And it was a concert in which Schwarz himself first discovered the possibilities of this orchestra, still relatively little known and on the opposite coast from Schwarz's New York home. No one, Schwarz least of all, could have imagined that he would later celebrate 25 years as the Seattle Symphony's music director, a tenure that has seen not only the creation of a major concert hall but also the rebirth of 20th-century American music as a staple of the orchestral genre. CONTINUED ON NEXT PAGE

THE SEATTLE YEARS

"I'm blessed to have been part of changing the concept of symphonic repertoire," Schwarz said recently, as we considered just the tip of a 25-year musical iceberg.

"We did this through recordings of symphonies by composers such as Howard Hanson, William Schuman, David Diamond, Walter Piston, Paul Creston and several others. Those recordings were able to make an impact. Now, people know these pieces. Creston might have been an asterisk in music history otherwise. For David Diamond, having this relationship with us in our city, where he came regularly, was life-changing."

Indeed, the image of the elderly Diamond beaming as he rose to receive another Seattle audience ovation only a month before his death at 89 (in 2005) is an enduring one. So is the recorded legacy of his works, and those

"Those first couple of years before I became music director, I had to really think about the future. Three orchestras had offered me a music directorship," Schwarz recalls. "My manager at the time said, 'Whatever you do, don't go to Seattle. It's a disaster and it'll never amount to anything.'

"I changed managers."

For years after Schwarz's Seattle appointment was announced, there was a constant litany of "We'll never keep him here" in the community and in the press. Already busy running several orchestras and festivals, Schwarz also was a media darling, appearing on several magazine covers and in the pages of *People*. Nobody figured he'd settle in. But he did, and has raised his family in the city the Schwarzes have made home.

here was more about making it better than about firing a lot of people. I also saw the partnership with Seattle Opera [which jointly employs the Symphony musicians] as a huge advantage for the orchestra." Schwarz himself has also had a close relationship with Seattle Opera, conducting several of its productions.

"There were lots of problems when I first arrived, of course, and the big issue was finances. The orchestra was paid very badly. We didn't even have an education department. Community support for the orchestra was not adequate."

The finances were put in order by a memorable duo of board leaders: Richard P. (Dick) Cooley and Samuel N. Stroum, financial heavy-hitters whose acumen and standing in the community suddenly made the Symphony a blue-chip investment instead

"MY MANAGER AT THE TIME SAID, 'WHATEVER YOU DO, DON'T GO TO SEATTLE.' I CHANGED MANAGERS."

of dozens of other composers in the Seattle Symphony's discography of the Schwarz years: more than 100 CDs on the Naxos, Delos, International, Koch, JVC Classics, Artek, MMC and Crystal labels.

The recordings might never have existed without Schwarz's connections with the first label, Delos International, with which he had recorded during his phenomenal earlier career as a trumpet soloist. The late Amelia Haygood, Delos' founder and president, told him when he arrived at the Seattle Symphony, "When you're ready, we'll start recording." And they did.

"Those were exciting times," he says of his first few years here. "I just got married [to the former Jody Greitzer], and was in a new city with a new wife and an orchestra that was hungry for leadership and artistic success. Those were the years when Seattle became Seattle: Microsoft, Starbucks, Amazon.com, an unprecedented endowment campaign that really boosted the UW."

Maybe it was the cello section, headed then by principal Ray Davis, that first wooed Schwarz here: "They sounded spectacular," he remembers, "and I thought, if they can play like this, everyone can play like this. There were some terrific players: coming

of a liability. This is not to say, however, that financial woes didn't later reappear: as Schwarz puts it, "It's never a good time financially. It's never the right time to launch a major project. Sometimes you have to do it anyway."

The biggest major project, of course, was Benaroya Hall, whose way was paved by nearly two decades of feasibility studies, mayoral panels, steadfast support from the Kreielsheimer Foundation, the visionary advocacy of the late ArtsFund president Peter Donnelly, and finally the landmark gift of $15.8 million from longtime philanthropists Jack and Becky Benaroya – close personal friends of the Schwarz family – in 1993. It's hard to overstate the impact of that gift, which was then the largest ever given to a Washington State nonprofit. Arts watchers reeled ("They gave how much?"). Suddenly the logjam at the Opera House, where the orchestra jockeyed with Seattle Opera and Pacific Northwest Ballet (among other organizations) for available dates, would end, and the Seattle Symphony would have a home designed exclusively for symphonic music, rather than an all-purpose acoustic that didn't really serve the orchestra. But it was going to take a lot more money, and the hall had to be done right. Mindful of the disastrous acoustical outcomes of several other new halls, Schwarz was determined to engage Cyril Harris as acoustician – a choice that proved providential, as visiting orchestras and soloists alike have attested.

The hall, Schwarz believes, has made possible the orchestra's notable artistic growth in the past decade. And what are the highlights? Too

forces of 600 in an epic performance of the last movement of Beethoven's Ninth, before His Holiness the Dalai Lama.

And then there are all the times you never hear about, when Schwarz dons full concert dress and grabs his baton to help a bunch of percussionists who want to set a Guinness World Record, or when he arrives at a school to preside over a concert featuring young people with professional musicians – or all the panels, speeches, fundraising calls, interviews, radio features on the Symphony's radio partner KING-FM, and other events that don't show up on the official Symphony calendars. That's what goes with the territory, when you hold the responsibility of being "Mr. Music" in Seattle.

Schwarz has always been a conductor who looks forward, rather than backward. And much as he enjoys thinking over the high points of a 25-year tenure thus far as music

PHOTOS: Ben Lamond, Jack Mitchell, Yuen Lui Studio

numerous to mention, though Schwarz will happily single out several of them: conducting Deems Taylor's *Peter Ibbetson*; the great Mahler Eighth Symphony; programming and conducting an array of festivals whose variety extends from the Silk Road Project to the two-part *Made in America*; the dazzling, unforgettable collaboration with artist Dale Chihuly in *Bluebeard's Castle*; the orchestra's centennial celebrations and East Coast tour, culminating in a standing ovation at Carnegie Hall. And more recently, the two Emmys from concert broadcasts, the naming of Chihuly as the orchestra world's first Artist in Association, and presiding over combined

director, there's always something new on the horizon.

It's too early to get specific about the projects Schwarz has in mind for 2010–11, his final season as music director here. But it's not hard to guess that they will be imaginative, involving new works and Americana – those two threads that have inspired him ever since he picked up a baton.

"They are complicated ideas," Schwarz says of the master plan: "they'll need a lot of work." His eyes light up at the prospect: for Gerard Schwarz, the best concert is always the one that lies just ahead.

My Farewell Season

Mark McCampbell was appointed interim executive director of the Seattle Symphony, and he led the orchestra with vision and creativity. After the success of Kurt Masur's guest week the previous season, Mark asked me whether I thought Kurt might be a candidate for the position of music advisor. I wasn't involved in the search for my successor, but I was happy to try to help. Kurt had felt a strong connection with the musicians and thought he could do the job for two or three years while the orchestra searched for its next music director. The situation reminded me of when George Szell was the New York Philharmonic's music advisor after Bernstein and before Boulez. To Mark's disappointment, however, the search committee wasn't interested in hiring Masur.

Mark told me he was looking for a large endowment gift to support my new position of conductor laureate and wondered if I had any ideas. I felt the first opportunity should go to the Benaroya family and said he should call Larry Benaroya. Mark later told me that during that very brief conversation Larry and his family agreed to make a substantial gift to the orchestra.

During these last few seasons we continued to record a great deal. One recording that I am especially proud of, featuring the four Brahms symphonies, was released at the beginning of the season. These recordings are a testament to the excellence of the orchestra and were beautifully recorded by Dmitriy Lipay. Dima is a remarkable engineer, producer, and musician, and a great gentleman besides. I trust him completely when we record together because his standards are extremely high. Many orchestras spend twenty or thirty minutes just on sound checks, but ours last only one or two minutes. Dima also has done all my All-Star Orchestra recordings.

The most exciting programming ideas for my final season were the Gund-Simonyi Farewell Commissions. I asked some of my closest composer friends to write short works that would be premiered on each program I conducted during the season. Since our programs were already set, the pieces would be like little gifts to the audience, usually placed at the beginning of the concert. It made them feel a bit like encores and would not alienate those in the audience who didn't care for new music.

The best way to kill any idea is to wait until it's too late to make it happen, then apologize. This is what happened at first. I told Mark that Jody and I were willing to fund it ourselves and then told him my assistant, Anna Brodie, and I would put the whole project together ourselves. Later on Aggie Gund became interested and made a significant gift. Aggie is among the most remarkable people I know, a brilliant woman with superior artistic taste and a deep understanding of the importance of the arts in our society. Her gift for this commissioning project inspired two other remarkable individuals, Lisa and Charles Simonyi, to do the same. We began working on the commissions in February.

Anna contacted twenty-one composers, eighteen of whom—Robert Beaser, Daniel Brewbaker, Richard Danielpour, Philip Glass, Daron Hagen, Samuel Jones, Aaron Jay Kernis, Bernard Rands, David Schiff, Paul Schoenfield, Gunther Schuller, Joseph Schwantner, Bright Sheng, David Stock, Augusta Read Thomas, George Tsontakis, Chen Yi, and Ellen Taaffe Zwilich—signed on. Since I was conducting only sixteen weeks of programs, two works would have to be scheduled for the same program for two of those weeks. We had a remarkable twenty-two world premieres that season. The performances were each incredibly meaningful and personal for me, each work a sparkling distillation of its composer's voice. I continue to program these jewels to this day and have recorded nine of them so far on my All-Star Orchestra series.

My final opening night was very important to me, and I programmed it very carefully. We began with the world premiere of the orchestral version of my work *The Human Spirit*. We had three children's choirs join us. As a gift, Samuel Jones wrote a cello concerto for Julian and me to premiere at this opening celebration. A week before the concert Julian left school and came home to stay with us. I hadn't heard him practice the piece and was starting to worry, so I decided to have a rehearsal early in the week with Julian, Sam, and a pianist. Just before the rehearsal, as he and I were walking downstairs, he asked me whether he should use the music or play the piece from memory. That was the last time I ever doubted Julian's preparation!

I also included Mahler's *Songs of a Wayfarer*, with Denyce Graves as the soloist. I wanted to end the program with my arrangement of a suite from Strauss's *Rosenkavalier*. Tom Philion, our executive director, approved the first half, but he wanted Midori to play Tchaikovsky's Violin Concerto on the second half. That would have been wonderful, but for my final opening night I did something I had never done before: I insisted. Tom was afraid the program wouldn't attract a large audience, but the concert was a sell-out. Sam's piece was so successful that I programmed it on the first season of the All-Star Orchestra recordings for television.

Hovhaness Gets a Boost

The Seattle Symphony often celebrates the anniversaries of major composers. This is especially important for lesser-known composers such as Alan Hovhaness. His music is rarely played at the professional level, and it was part of the reason I felt it was important to celebrate the 100th anniversary of his birth, which was in 2011. That season we also recorded other works of his and presented a short festival. We began recording Hovhaness's music in the early 1990s. In a review of our first Delos release, which included the Symphony No. 2, "Mysterious Mountain," Donald Vroon, chief editor and co-owner of *American Record Guide*, wrote:

> A comparison to the Reiner recording is required of the critic. It was a great recording, and has served us well for 35 years, but perhaps it is time to retire it. First of all, the sound here is just beautiful. The Reiner sounded good but not this good. The Chicago strings don't have the sweetness of Seattle's and I think that is more than sound engineering: I think it's Seattle's superior strings. They certainly sound ethereal in this music, and that makes the Chicago ones seem even more earthbound. The faster tempos seem to serve that music, making it speak whole sentences instead of stream-of-consciousness. None of the mystery of the opening movement is

lost, but a certain rapt fascination is added. There's never been anything wrong with the Reiner, but it can't stand up next to something this good. Delos has filled the rest of the disc with some of this composer's best music. Certainly Delos and Seattle have made a wonderful thing of their continuing partnership. They are now producing discs like this one, on the highest possible artistic and technical level. I wish Delos a lot of sales so they can double their Seattle recording schedule. What they are doing is a lot more interesting than what is being recorded in Boston, New York, or Philadelphia.

Hovhaness was always true to himself musically. Intellectuals never accepted his work, but he made a good living from composing. When I was seventeen Keith Brion, the director of the West Caldwell High School band and later the Yale Band, introduced me to Alan, who at the time was living in a hotel at Fifty-second Street and Broadway in Manhattan. That year, 1964, Keith and I recorded a piece of his called *Return and Rebuild the Desolate Places*, for trumpet and wind ensemble. In 1970 Alan moved to the Pacific Northwest, married the Japanese-American soprano Hinako Fujihara, and became deeply influenced by Japanese music. He loved nature and was a gentle, sensitive soul. Their house in the South of Seattle had a beautiful view of Mt. Rainier, and it must have inspired many of his works. It was wonderful to have him in our community for all those years. Hinako still lives in Seattle and advocates tirelessly for her late husband's music. For the Seattle Symphony's Hovhaness festival in March 2011, I combined three ideas. My dear friend the cellist Lynn Harrell played Dvořák's Cello Concerto on one program and Edward Elgar's Cello Concerto on the second. We had two Gund-Simonyi commissions, by George Tsontakis and Chen Yi. We programmed the Symphonies Nos. 2, 7, 14 by Hovhaness, as well as his Prelude and Quadruple Fugue. The University of Washington Wind Ensemble participated in one of the programs.

Klaus Heymann, Naxos, and Russian Music
Naxos Records and its president, Klaus Heymann, have done so much

to expand the repertoire, and their pricing has made classical CDs available to many music lovers. I first began to record for Klaus in 1998 as part of a series for the Milken Archive of mostly twentieth-century repertoire. In 2010 Klaus asked me to do three albums of the music of Nikolai Rimsky-Korsakov. One featured *Scheherazade* and *Tsar Sultan*, another had opera excerpts and suites such as *Coq d'or* and *Sadko*, and still another was of overtures—the *Russian Easter Overture*, the *May Night Overture*, the *Overture on Russian Themes*, and so forth. I studied these works as if I were conducting them for the first time and gained new respect for the composer. After the critical success of these three CDs, Klaus asked me to record Alexander Borodin's three symphonies. These works are a revelation, charming and energetic, and the First Symphony is an absolute jewel. The Second Symphony is the one everyone knows, and the never-completed Third Symphony is also fantastic. I immersed myself in these works, many of them new to me. I had conducted the Second, and I knew the Third because Boulez conducted it once when I was in the New York Philharmonic. The First I had never heard.

When I conducted Borodin's Symphony No. 1 with the Seattle Symphony, a work by Gunther Schuller was also on the program. Gunther was amazed at how imaginative the Borodin symphony was. He told me he thought Borodin was the precursor of many innovative works that were written twenty-five years later.

My next project for Naxos was a recording of the symphonies of Rimsky-Korsakov.

I wanted to end the season with Strauss's *Alpine Symphony*. Our new board chair, Leslie Chihuly, let it slip that such a large work, with its twelve extra offstage horns, could bankrupt the orchestra. Rather than explain that we would only need three extra horns, I decided to suggest Mahler's Symphony No. 2, which was agreeable to all. The season was a tremendous send-off for me and my family. For the next three years I conducted my concerts as conductor laureate. I hoped I would have an ongoing relationship with the orchestra, like the one Bernstein had had with the New York Philharmonic. After Boulez became its music director, Bernstein continued to tour, record, and play concerts with us each season. It was a wonderful relationship for everyone, especially the audience. I never felt that Boulez was threatened by Bernstein, and it was always an inspiration when he returned to work with us.

The former chair of the Seattle Symphony's board of directors, Susan Hutchison, wanted me to stay involved after stepping down as music director. As part of my conductor laureate role, the board wanted me to conduct a few weeks each season. I love Seattle and the orchestra, and I was happy to do as they wished.

Some highlights of the next three seasons included my new arrangement of excerpts from Engelbert Humperdinck's *Hansel and Gretel* and working with two of my dear friends: John Lill, playing Mozart's Piano Concerto No. 24 in C Minor, and Alexander Toradze, doing Prokofiev's Piano Concerto No. 3. Once again we played Mahler's Symphony No. 1, a work the orchestra and I had performed at many important junctures. We premiered Daron Hagen's Five Sky Interludes from his opera *Amelia* and performed Shostakovich's Symphony No. 8. The Shostakovich was on one of our Emmy–winning television programs from 2006. Joined by two extraordinary singers, Nancy Maultsby and Charles Austin, we repeated Bartók's *Bluebeard's Castle* with Dale Chihuly's sets, which had been so memorable in 2007. We did the world premiere of Michael Hersch's work for piano and orchestra *Along the Ravines*. Michael's language has changed a great deal since I first performed his music many years ago with the New York Chamber Symphony. In 2011 we did his work *A Sheltered Corner*, for horn and orchestra, at the Eastern Music Festival. It is a remarkable but very difficult work. One of the fine musicians in the orchestra said he was not sure he liked the piece, but he knew it was a very important one. Michael Hersch's Piano Concerto is the same way. Michael has a very distinctive voice, perhaps hard to absorb yet, I think, an important one.

The other premiere was an orchestration of some of the soprano arias from David Diamond's 1971 opera *The Noblest Game*. It is a remarkable story, with an excellent libretto by Katie Louchheim. It had never been produced, and David had not orchestrated it. I found it very powerful and asked David if he could orchestrate some of the great arias for the main character, a soprano. He agreed, and a performance was scheduled for the 1997–1998 season; but the soprano fell ill, and the performance had to be canceled.

We did the world premiere of the Six Arias. Finding a soprano who could handle the difficult arias was challenging, but Jennifer Zetlan, with whom I had worked in Daron Hagen's *Amelia*, was sensational.

CHAPTER FOURTEEN

Operas

Though I have conducted more than fifty operas, I am not known as an opera conductor. I love opera, but it is the most difficult of all art forms to make a complete success. There are so many elements: cast (vocally and as actors), direction, sets, costumes, lighting, orchestra, and the theater itself. But when everything comes together, the experience is extraordinary. During my time in Seattle I did twenty-one productions with the Seattle Opera with music by Wagner, Janáček, Johann Strauss, Richard Strauss, Bizet, Mozart, Verdi, Weber, Daron Hagen, Beethoven, and Debussy. I had such great experiences with so many wonderful singers, and of course my orchestra in the pit. The Seattle Opera is different from the Seattle Symphony, though they share the same orchestra. I am extremely grateful to Speight Jenkins for all the opportunities he gave me, and for being such a thoughtful and serious leader of the Seattle Opera during my tenure with the orchestra. Our personal and professional relationship was very special.

My operatic debut came in 1978 at the invitation of Martin Feinstein of the Washington (D.C.) National Opera. I conducted Mozart's *Abduction from the Seraglio* in fourteen performances at the Terrace Theater, which worked well for the small-scale Mozart opera. It was a great introduction for me, and I had some important help from Frank Rizzo. Martin subsequently engaged me to do *Fidelio* and *Salome* in the big house. I always believed that part of my job was to make the singers comfortable, so if we disagreed about a tempo, I always yielded to them. The tenor in the *Abduction* cast wanted to do his big aria somewhat slower than I did. I asked him to try it faster, but he wasn't comfortable, so we did it at his tempo. At one point in the run I had to miss a performance because of a previously scheduled concert at the Y, and the choral director conducted in my place. Before the next performance, the tenor came to me and asked if we could do the aria faster: they had done it like that when I was away, and it was much better. It was an important lesson for me. I should have insisted during the rehearsal period that he do my tempo, and if, by the dress rehearsal, he really couldn't, we could revert to his preference.

Maria Ewing was the remarkable Salome in the Washington National Opera's Peter Hall production of Strauss's opera of the same name. She had done the production a number of times, so her cover (understudy) did some of the rehearsals. Jody and I were staying at the Watergate Hotel with our two-year-old daughter, Gaby, and occasionally they would go to one of the staging rehearsals with me. The cover had a slow, pronounced vibrato—in fact, a wobble. Gaby was sleeping when the rehearsal began, but when she woke up she began to sing, imitating the cover, wobble and all. Jody snatched up our little angel and ran from the room. Later, Jody brought Gaby to one of the performances, though she slept soundly for most of it. At the conclusion of Salome's dance, Maria was nude. Gaby woke up, looked at the stage, and yelled, "Mommy, she's naked!"

During that run my mother died. I went back to New York on a Sunday between performances to see my mother for the last time. My mother looked at Jody, who was pregnant with Julian, and said, "Wolfie!" Neither of us knew what she was talking about. She repeated it, then said, "Wolfgang Mozart." She wanted us to name our son Wolfgang, after Mozart. She said he was going to be a great musician, and that should be his name. I tried to explain that in the United States "Wolfgang" would not go over well. It reminded me of my mother's first choice of a name for me: Rudolf. When she was pregnant with me, she was convinced that I was going to be a conductor. I resisted until I was twenty-eight, but in the end she was right. Jody and I named our son Julian, and he is indeed a great musician.

I knew that my mother would have been very angry with me if I had canceled the Tuesday performance, so I went through with it. It all seemed like a dream to me, and when it ended I didn't even realize it. As we were taking our bows, the stage covered in blood, Maria leaned over to me and said the performance was for my mother.

The next excellent production I took part in was in Washington, D.C.: *Fidelio*, with the outstanding tenor James McCracken.

I've mentioned all the early Mozart operas that I did at Mostly Mozart. I was very happy to accept Joseph Polisi's invitation to do the two William Schuman operas at Juilliard and record them for Delos. One of the last operas I did in Seattle was the world premiere of Daron Hagen's *Amelia*. Gardner McFall, the librettist, was with us for the whole rehearsal period. It was a joy to spend so much time with her, working with her wonderful text. In many ways this was Stephen Wadsworth's production: he wrote the story and directed the production. We had a great cast, and as always Stephen was inspirational artistically. I find him to be one of the greatest directors working today. This was the only opera that Speight Jenkins commissioned and premiered while directing the Seattle Opera. As always, he sat through all the rehearsals, made insightful contributions, and helped create a lovely atmosphere.

In the summer of 2000 I was conducting Weber's *Der Freischütz* in Seattle with Deborah Voigt, Gary Lakes, and Ute Selbig. Julian was nine, and he sat next to me at every rehearsal with a baton and a piano score on his stand. When we started rehearsing in the theater, I continued to let him sit next to me until the orchestra rehearsals began. At the piano tech rehearsal I let him conduct the waltz and aria in the first act. The cast didn't mind, and he did wonderfully. Afterward I asked him why he did the waltz differently from me, and he said, "Daddy, you do it in one and I do it in three!"

There were many memorable productions with the Seattle Opera, but one that stood out was Debussy's *Pelléas et Mélisande*, primarily because of the magnificent sets by Dale Chihuly, the great direction by Neil Peter Jampolis, and the exceptional cast. Dale created seven scenes for the production. Many people came to the production because of Dale's involvement, though they may not have been opera lovers. I found that a little odd since the opera is almost three hours long, and generally we look at works of visual art for about a minute each. Dale made seven sets that in a museum would probably have been viewed for less than ten minutes in all.

In 1998 Seiji Ozawa was to do a tour in Japan of *Pelléas* with the New Japan Philharmonic but had to withdraw. He asked me if I could do the rehearsals and performances for him. I was honored and adjusted my schedule. The cast was sensational: Teresa Stratas, José Van Dam, Dwayne Croft, Robert Lloyd, and Jane Henschel. David Kneuss directed, and Pierre Vallet did some great work as the French language advisor. Ozawa set a really unusual schedule. What usually happens while preparing an opera is that we begin with a daylong musical rehearsal. Then come weeks of staging and a few rehearsals with the orchestra. Ozawa did just the opposite: most of the rehearsal time was spent with the cast and the orchestra, and we spent only one week on staging. With such an experienced cast and director, the result was wonderful. The score was beautifully played by the New Japan Philharmonic.

Summer 1997: My Fiftieth Birthday

The summer of my fiftieth birthday was one of my most enjoyable. I was in Seattle conducting my favorite opera, Strauss's *Der Rosenkavalier*, and I was also performing Mozart at the Mostly Mozart Festival in New York. The *Rosenkavalier* cast included Angelika Kirchschlager as Octavian, Nadine Secunde as the Marschallin, Jane Giering-De Haan as Sophie, and Helmut Berger-Tuna as Baron von Ochs. The beautiful production was designed by Bruno Schwengl and directed by Dieter Kaegi. Trying to work out the schedule between Mostly Mozart and the opera wasn't easy. Except for one opera performance on August 19, everything worked out. Speight Jenkins allowed me to miss that one performance, and all was in order.

However, we had a problem: none of our regular members of the symphony flute section were available that summer, and the flute part is very demanding. Jody and I had always tried to keep her flute playing separate from my conducting, but the personnel manager, Ron Simon, asked if she would consider making an exception just this once. We discussed it at length and Jody agreed to play, which she did magnificently.

The one Seattle Opera performance that I missed was the night of my fiftieth birthday. I had a concert that night in New York at Lincoln Center and then went back to our apartment to celebrate alone. I didn't really mind, because Jack and Becky Benaroya had given me a bottle of Dom Perignon and eight ounces of beluga caviar. Whenever we had caviar in the house, Julian would find it and eat most of it. That was one time I had it all to myself!

CHAPTER FIFTEEN

———

Composing

My focus is now on education, composition, and conducting. Is it more important for me to conduct ten orchestras or to write a twenty-minute piece? If I conduct ten orchestras, is that more important than coming up with one really phenomenal educational television show that might have a positive influence on many more people?

On the one hand, you have to look at what is practical. I have expertise in a certain area, as a conductor, and I think I have something to offer interpretively. I love my profession, and though it can be very difficult, it is extremely rewarding. On the other hand, this new world of television, online education, and composing is one in which I am less comfortable. I have been conducting Brahms symphonies for forty years, and though that is always challenging, it is also very comfortable. I do not write music with that kind of facility. Maybe no one does because of the inspirational and creative element needed. I work very hard at each piece, and I find such work very gratifying. At this time in my life, I even enjoy the solitude that I did not in my twenties. I returned to writing music in 2005. Will it get easier? It might.

I am composing a lot these days. I actually dream music, wake up, and rush over to my study to write it down. The music comes to me most when I'm driving, when I'm in the shower, and when I'm watching movies (the little thirty- or forty-second gems created by film composers are amazing and sometimes inspirational). I then sit down at the piano and start improvising. To start, I write a melody. My main composition teacher, Paul Creston, had me write fifty melodies a week when I first began studying with him, and then we'd discuss them. All those weeks ensured that I became quite good at writing melodies. Melodies lead to harmonies, and harmonies lead to pieces. Once you have something on paper, it starts to evolve and take on a life of its own.

In 1998 Mina Miller, a fine pianist and organizer, started a concert series in Seattle called Music of Remembrance that honored the Holocaust through music. Her ensemble was made up of some of Seattle's finest players, including the cellist David Tonkonogui. I had helped David come to Seattle from Russia to join the symphony, and he also became our son Julian's wonderful cello teacher. He was a remarkable musician and man who unfortunately died very young. Mina wanted to honor his memory with a new work and asked me to write something for Julian to perform. That 2005 experience led me to compose *In Memoriam*, which exists in three versions: solo cello with piano, with string quartet, and with string orchestra. It was named the best new work of 2005 by the *Seattle Weekly*. Julian premiered it and recorded it at the age of fifteen for Naxos records in the version with an open grave. Rudolf was sixty and Jeanette was fifty-four. My work is called string quartet. *Fanfare* described it as "poignant and deeply moving," and *Gramophone* called it "an affecting blend of tender and disquieting utterances." My wonderful principal cellist in Liverpool, Jonathan Aasgaard, recorded it a few years later in the orchestral version. In 2007 Mina commissioned me to write another work for her series. My maternal grandparents lived in Vienna and in 1942 applied for a visa to come to the United States. The application was denied, and with that their fate was sealed. They were sent to the concentration camp in Riga, Latvia, where they were shot into an open grave. Rudolf was sixty and Jeanette was fifty-four. My work is called *Rudolf and Jeanette* and was originally scored for a chamber ensemble of fourteen players. I revised it slightly for a large orchestra and premiered it in Zagreb with the Zagreb Philharmonic in 2008. More recently, I have written two works for concert band, both for the President's Own Marine Band.

Under the excellent leadership of Lieutenant Colonel Jason Fettig, this remarkable music institution plays like a string quartet. Fettig is a superb conductor, and these musicians are inspired. My first work for the Marine Band was *Above and Beyond*, which they premiered when I guest conducted them in 2012. A live recording was later released on the Naxos label. In 2015 Maestro Fettig conducted a very moving performance of a new version for band of *Rudolf and Jeanette*. Eugene Corporon recorded his wonderful performance in 2015 with the North Texas Wind Symphony.

Toby Saks commissioned me to write a trio for horn, violin, and piano for the Seattle Chamber Music Society in 2010. Toby was music director of the festival and an excellent cellist. We were in the New York Philharmonic together before she left the orchestra to settle in Seattle and teach at the University of Washington. In 2010 the Society premiered the piece, described by MusicWeb International as "ingeniously constructed within its thoroughly accessible romantic idiom." The music critic Bernard Jacobson told me that in it I had referenced a theme from the *Four Last Songs* of Strauss. I hadn't even realized it. It was just a few notes, and it did not matter because those notes went in a different direction in my piece. It is interesting to me how we absorb and rework, often unconsciously, the music of composers who influence us. When Sam Jones was writing his Cello Concerto for Julian, he asked me if he could quote a theme of mine from my cello work, *In Memoriam*. I was touched and honored. He used it so imaginatively and made it his own.

A commission by Dave Gannett for a major orchestral work from me for the Eastern Music Festival in 2012 resulted in *A Journey*.

When I was honored as First Citizen of Seattle in 2009, I was asked to perform during the evening ceremony. My trumpet days had long passed, and I thought it might be a little difficult to invite the Seattle Symphony so that I could conduct something. I decided to write two works for the occasion: a pair of duos for violin and cello performed by the orchestra's concertmaster, Maria Larionoff, and Julian; and a work for children's choir and small ensemble to words by Aaron Copland titled *The Human Spirit*. The duos have been played all over the world, and I made an orchestral version of *The Human Spirit* that the Seattle Symphony performed at the opening concert of my final season as music director in 2012. I have now made a version for full choir and expanded the work somewhat. In recent years I have written *Poem* (2015) for the Hartford Symphony and their music director, Carolyn Kuan, as well as another tone poem titled *Abraham and Isaac*.

Ever since my early days in the American Brass Quintet, I have loved making arrangements. To date I have made orchestral arrangements of four movements from Bach's *Art of the Fugue* as well as suites from Strauss's *Der Rosenkavalier*, Humperdinck's *Hansel and Gretel*, Debussy's *Pelléas et Mélisande*, and some holiday works; Handel's *Water Music* (complete); a brass quintet concerto (after Handel); and a string orchestra version of Webern's *Langsamer Satz*. In 2016 the superb horn player Leslie Norton, together with the outstanding violinist Carolyn Huebla and pianist Melissa Rose, recorded my horn trio. I'm surprised I so enjoy the solitude of composing. In a sense you are alone with music that hopefully will have a life of its own.

CHAPTER SIXTEEN

The Eastern Music Festival

W hen I resigned from Mostly Mozart, my intention was to do some guest conducting in July of each year and leave August for composition. However, I now spend July as music director of the Eastern Music Festival at Guilford College in Greensboro, North Carolina. My association with the festival began in 2003, when Tom Philion, the executive director, invited me to guest conduct for a week. At that time pretty much all I knew about it was that it had been founded in 1961 by Shelly Morgenstern, who had been its music director for many years.

I enjoyed my week in Greensboro very much, and I returned in 2004. I became EMF's music advisor in 2005, principal conductor in 2006–2007, and music director in 2008. The festival and school have two hundred students and a faculty of eighty. The faculty members make up the Eastern Festival Orchestra, with each member teaching and coaching the students. We have two student orchestras that play weekly concerts, as well as chamber music concerts for students and faculty, a weekly piano recital, and other special musical events. The festival runs from the last week of June through the month of July. All the events are indoors, and orchestra concerts are performed in the acoustically outstanding Dana Auditorium. The support from the community and board are excellent: the mayor gave me the key to the city in 2012. We have also started to make some very fine recordings.

Tom left to become the executive director in Seattle; I am grateful to him for his guidance. He was succeeded by Stephanie Cordick, an extraordinary leader and an especially warmhearted person. After the

2014 season Stephanie resigned for health reasons, and Chris Williams took over. My son Julian joined the faculty in 2013.

The most exciting thing that has happened to the festival is a ten-year American Works commission by Bonnie McElveen-Hunter, a former ambassador to Finland, the chairperson of the American Red Cross, and the founder and CEO of Pace Communications. She's a remarkable leader and philanthropist. Each season the festival orchestra premieres a new work. I cannot think of another example of a patron making this kind of long-term commitment to new American works. Bonnie chooses the composers, and so far EMF has worked with Richard Danielpour, John Corigliano, Lowell Liebermann, and André Previn. These five weeks in Greensboro are a very happy time for Jody and me, with regular visits from our other children.

Our programming is just the kind I like—some new works, some by distinguished American composers, traditional works, and visits by guest artists. In 2011, to celebrate our fiftieth anniversary, we commissioned five young American composers—Peter Boyer, Vivian Fung, Michael Hersch, Pierre Jalbert, and Philip Rothman—to compose pieces for that summer's festival. They all turned out wonderfully, and the audience was very supportive.

Eastern Music Festival is primarily an orchestral instrument teaching program, with the addition of an important piano program. The piano department is led by two extraordinary musicians and teachers, Awadagin Pratt and Bill Wolfram. In 2015 we added a guitar program and a comprehensive conducting program. Although I have taught conducting and given master classes elsewhere, EMF's is the first extended program for the teaching of conducting that I have been involved with, so it became a very important department for me. We accepted nine students and gave them many opportunities to conduct. Together we really delved into the essence of the scores and focused on the technique needed to create a superb musical result.

CHAPTER SEVENTEEN

The Milken Archive

O f all the extraordinary people and organizations I've been
fortunate to be involved with, the Milken Archive of Jewish
Music has been among the most significant. The composer Sam Adler
recommended me to Neil Levin, the artistic director of the project,
and I was invited to become a member of the board in 1996. That
began a fantastic journey as I learned new repertoire and became
acquainted with new composers.

The Milken Archive, which Neil has described as "an exploration
of the rich variety of musical expression born of, inspired by, associated with, or reflecting the full spectrum of Jewish life in the US,"
was started in 1990 by the philanthropist Lowell Milken to "document, preserve and disseminate the vast body of music that pertains
to the American Jewish experience." Neil became the artistic director
in 1993. Lowell is quite a visionary, and he found in Neil one of the
world's most knowledgeable authorities on Jewish-influenced music.
He also has exceptionally broad knowledge in many areas of music,
religion, and the world. Most important to the success of the project is
the archive's artistic administrator, Paul Schwendener. His sensitivity
and thoughtfulness, not to mention his deep artistic and administrative background, led me to invite him to become the executive director
of the All-Star Orchestra, a position in which he has flourished.

The archive has recorded over five hundred works by more than
two hundred composers. Before I became involved in this project, I
thought that Ernest Bloch and Leonard Bernstein were almost the only
composers who wrote music with Jewish themes. Beginning in 1998

I began recording for the archive. Some of the works and composers were familiar, but others were completely new to me. In Seattle I started recording works by Bruce Adolphe, Herman Berlinski, David Diamond, Paul Schoenfield, Elie Siegmeister, Sheila Silver, Ernst Toch, and Hugo Weisgall.

In 2000 we recorded the remarkable *Avodat Shabbat* by Berlinski with the Berlin Radio Orchestra. The recording took place in the Jesus Christus Kirche, a church near Berlin that Karajan would often use for recording. Berlinski was born in Leipzig in 1910. When he was ninety, one year before he died, he attended our recording of his Shabbat service. It was so moving to hear him explain to the young members of the Ernst Senff Chor Berlin the meaning of the work while translating both the English and Hebrew texts for them. At the recording sessions he sat in the back of the church, and whenever I would turn to him to ask if some tempo was correct or the phrasing was to his liking, he would always say yes. There was only one exception. After completing a movement, I heard the sound of very slow steps coming up behind me. When Herman finally arrived at the podium he said to me, "Maybe this movement could be a very little bit slower," and with that he turned and walked to the back of the church.

That same year we recorded the *Genesis Suite* by Schoenberg, Stravinsky, Milhaud, Toch, Castelnuovo-Tedesco, Shilkret, and Tansman. This was another great achievement by the Milken Archive. Five of the seven movements were thought to have been lost in a fire soon after the premiere in 1945. Through some remarkable research by Neil and Paul, much of it was found and reconstructed from the piano scores, and the private recording was made shortly after the premiere.

We did a special concert with the Czech Philharmonic featuring Milhaud's *Sacred Service*, Toch's *The Bitter Herbs*, and Joseph Achron's *The Golem*. The two other most memorable recordings were Bernstein's Symphony No. 3 (*Kaddish*) and *Chichester Psalms*, recorded in Liverpool, and Kurt Weill's opera-oratorio *The Eternal Road*, recorded in Berlin. We did highlights and a concert version of the Weill in 2001, and in 2006 we completed it. The complete version has yet to be released.

CHAPTER EIGHTEEN

The All-Star Orchestra

J ust before the beginning of the 2008–2009 season, I met with
the Seattle Symphony board chair, Susan Hutchison to tell her I
wasn't going to extend my contract beyond the 2010–2011 season. We
always like to say that these are difficult decisions, but when they are
the correct decision they seem natural rather than difficult. I remember
that when I left the New York Philharmonic and stopped playing the
trumpet, those decisions simply seemed a natural path to the future.
I felt the same way about leaving my position in Seattle. It was time
for me to begin the next chapter in my life. Jody and I were so lucky
to have our children grow up in one place and have a normal family
life. I remember my friend Leonard Slatkin telling me over dinner
one evening how lucky I had been to be able to raise my family in the
way Jody and I did. After all is said and done and all the concerts are
played, family is the most important thing in any of our lives.

Susan had decided to run for the chairmanship of the county
council and therefore had to resign her post on the board. She chose
Leslie Chihuly as her successor. I told Leslie that I would cooperate
in any way that the board would like over the next three years. It
was decided that I would do my regular work as music director for
the first year and focus on my own programs after that. So for the
last two years of my contract, I was able to design my own transition
and think about my artistic plans for the future. Jody and I had often
talked about the need to expose more people to great music, to make
it affordable and accessible, and at the same time to give the audience
a chance to be educated. This is what I have worked for all my life. I

believed that great performances and a strong educational component would be the best way of accomplishing that, but I knew that television and the Internet would play critical roles.

I thought that our 2007 and 2008 Emmy Award–winning Seattle Symphony KCTS broadcasts, "Live from Benaroya Hall," music-based shows with educational content and fast-paced camerawork, could be a prototype for future programs. Jody and I eventually came up with the idea of an All-Star Orchestra program featuring top players recording made-for-television shows that would then be used for in-depth education.

Most classical music television shows come from New York via *Live from Lincoln Center* and are performed by the New York Philharmonic. It seemed to me that a better model would be to represent the whole country and to create shorter, one-hour shows, without the restrictions of a live concert audience. I felt that besides my normal guest conducting and my work with the Eastern Music Festival, my future should be focused on composing and on developing the All-Star Orchestra education project.

First, we had to form a small board and apply for nonprofit status, and I asked our dear friend Marlys Palumbo, a flutist and singer as well as a lawyer, to see if she would like to be president. She always kids me about calling it a small venture. She accepted, and Susan agreed to be vice president, as long as it didn't take too much time.

Although Jody had never participated in the foreground of any of my numerous projects (while making significant contributions behind the scenes), she agreed to be on the board at the urging of Marlys, Susan, and me. The rest of the board included at first Tom Firman, Athena Kennedy, Ralph Palumbo, and Charles Staadecker, with Jay Cantor, Jerry Farley, Ernie Kafka, Michelle Gerber Klein, Frances Lawrence, Lynn Loacker, Fred Miller, Sharon Mosse, and Ted Parker added later. We began by setting by-laws, becoming a 501(c)(3), deciding on a name, and addressing the other issues that pertain to an artistic start-up.

Jody and I wanted the name to sound as popular as possible. Some of us felt "All-Star Orchestra" was exactly right, because of the phrase's association with sports teams. Others thought it didn't describe who or what we were. In the end, though, everyone agreed on the All-Star Orchestra, and we were off.

My assistant from the Seattle Symphony, Anna Brodie, and their education director, Nancy Gosen, became our volunteer staff. Marlys's law firm, Van Ness Feldman, became our support in all legal matters. The mission of the All-Star Orchestra was clear—to bring music to a large audience, help educate that audience, and make it affordable. Public television was the perfect outlet: the potential audience was immense, we could do shows with some educational content, the shows would be free to the audience, and we could add to the material for our educational website. The musicians would be chosen from as many orchestras around the country as possible, and we would record in New York because of the large pool of great players available in the northeast.

We asked Paul Schwendener to be our executive director and began working on the details. There were so many decisions to be made: our recording team, the orchestra personnel, the repertoire, the venue, our stage clothing, the contractor for the musicians, how to pay for everything, how much to pay, who should help with education, how the musicians' union should be involved, whether the local public station would agree to present it. We knew that, as wonderful as public television is, they generally limit the amount of classical music they program. If we were going to present the material to PBS, we needed a local public station to be the presenting station. The questions to be answered seemed to be endless but always interesting and stimulating. We were a small organization with no history, but a thrilling level of openness.

I had some experience from starting the Waterloo Festival and the NYCS, but they were traditional organizations with many prototypes. The nearest thing to a prototype for the ASO series we could find was the *Omnibus* television series with Leonard Bernstein in the 1950s—the last time made-for-television orchestral shows were produced, as far as I knew. The advantages of such a format were that our cameras wouldn't interfere with the audience, we could program for television, and we could treat the performance less like a concert and more like a recording session.

Funding of such a new and untested venture can be difficult. Why should someone invest in a project without a track record? Fortunately, Lisa and Charles Simonyi believed in this project and understood its potential. Without their help this would never have happened, and I am beyond grateful for their vision and commitment.

A handful of remarkable friends also became early supporters: Dave Gannett, Agnes Gund, Gladys Rubinstein, Bruce and Jeanne McNae, Betty Lou Treiger, Becky Benaroya, Alan Benaroya, Bonnie McElveen-Hunter, Ken Hollingsworth, Faye Sarkowsky, Joan Watjen, Sally Gerber Phinny, Judi Flom, Patrick Park, Gideon and Sarah Gartner, the Hearst Foundation, the Sorel Foundation, the M. J. Murdock Foundation, the Jerome L. Greene Foundation, Ralph and Marlys Palumbo, Microsoft, Michele and Giuseppe Torroni, Jerry Farley, Benita and Charles Staadecker, Susan Hutchison, David and Amy Fulton, Bernice and Sanford Grossman, Bob and Clodagh Ash, David and Jane Davis, Robert Wallace, Chris McInerney, Judy and Bob Rubin, Bernard Osher, Vivian Serota, Karen Brenner, Curtis Wong, the Seattle Foundation, Nadine Asin, the Lapkin Foundation, David and Nancy Rossmiller, Jan and Ronnie Greenberg, Nicolas and Jeanne Rohatyn, Robert Ted Parker, Fred Miller, and Sharon Mosse.

I have made many recordings over the years without a performance preceding the session. I thought that I could approach the All-Star Orchestra sessions in the same way, and that if I chose the repertoire carefully and was able to get experienced players, the sessions could go quickly. First came the repertoire. The idea was to do standard pieces that could be useful for future educational work. I also wanted to play works by living American composers to show that classical music was a living art form.

For me this was to be a long-term project, and I wanted to have a single work from the one hundred most important composers in history, along with living composers. After that we could do some repeat works by Beethoven, Mozart, and so on, and start to include a more international group of composers. I was able to choose the new repertoire from the short works written for my farewell season in Seattle.

The time frame was fifty-six minutes, so we started with the idea of about forty-six minutes of music and the rest talk. I could do the basic discussion about each piece, but I wanted to have others as well. Making the list of traditional composers' works was especially fun. Beethoven's Symphony No. 5 is only about thirty-four minutes long, leaving twelve minutes for a new work or a more in-depth discussion. Schumann's Symphony No. 3 coupled nicely with Brahms's *Academic Festival Overture*, and we could discuss the relationship between the two composers. We also chose Tchaikovsky's Symphony No. 4 and Shostakovich's Symphony No. 5; Stravinsky's *Firebird Suite* with Ravel's *Daphnis et Chloé*, both showpieces for the orchestra; the Adagio from Mahler's Symphony No. 10; and Dvořák's Symphony No. 9. We also wanted to include a program featuring young soloists.

Most classical music television shows, in the attempt to win a large audience, highlight a famous soloist. But I wanted the music and the orchestra themselves to be the attraction. Besides, if the series lasted (as we hoped), we would quickly run out of star soloists.

One of the problems with Bernstein's Young People's Concerts was that there were only three a year, and it was easy to miss them. I wanted to do eight shows a year, every year, and broadcast them either weekly or monthly. I asked my friends Neil Balm and Jon Haas, from Gemini Productions, to contract the players and also play in the orchestra. Neil, Jon, and Paul described our vision to the American Federation of Musicians, which was very receptive. We were paying double television scale, but we needed to be able to carve the material up so we could use it for educational purposes, and the union had never set a fee for that. In the end it all worked out.

We decided to tape our shows during the last week of August, since most orchestras are on vacation then. During our first recording season in 2012, the only orchestras not available were Cleveland, which was on tour; St. Louis, which was preparing for a European tour; and the Los Angeles Philharmonic, which was playing at the Hollywood Bowl. With my extensive recording experience, an experienced and well-prepared orchestra, and Adam Stern as producer and Dmitriy Lipay as engineer and producer, I knew I could do one show per three-hour recording session. John Forsen was our executive video producer, and Habib Azar was our video director.

I had done many recordings at the ballroom of the Manhattan Center on Thirty-fourth Street. A carpet had been put down many years ago that hurt the acoustics for recording, but they had a wooden floor that they could put down to bring it close to where it had been prior to the carpeting. John Forsen, Paul, and I had to check every detail against the requirements of a television show. Some of the stands needed to be upgraded, the floor needed to be replaced with a better-looking one, and the chairs seemed all right, but the lighting was not sufficient.

We scheduled eight sessions, two a day for four days, with possible overtime on the last day. Money was being raised, and Jon and Neil started hiring the musicians. Mark Facci, from the Eastern Music Festival, was our librarian. The great advantage of this was that he and I could work on all the parts for the ASO taping during the festival in July.

Except for the musicians who recorded with me in Seattle, no one believed we could do two shows a day—especially with an orchestra that had never played together. I felt that the level of musician that I was seeking not only would know the pieces, but would listen and play together like a chamber ensemble, and that the sound would be magnificent. In addition, the parts would be meticulously marked with my musical ideas, and I would follow that with my gestures. Of course, I would give lots of leeway to the solo players and in general try not to micromanage the performance. As far as the sound of the orchestra, I felt if we chose the players well and everyone was really focused, it could be magnificent.

We had to choose a concertmaster, or perhaps more than one. I thought that we should have one from each of the big-budget orchestras—New York, Cleveland, Chicago, Boston, and Philadelphia. Cleveland was out, so I thought that if I could get concertmasters from the other four, we could fill the first two stands of first violins and then rotate them each day. I quickly came to realize that my plan would never work. Instead, we chose David Kim from the Philadelphia Orchestra as our concertmaster. David was perfect in every way. He is not only an exquisite musician and violinist, but also a great leader, in a gentle, positive way. Furthermore, he excelled at the educational work.

I wanted another great violinist to sit on the first stand with David, and I needed someone who had worked with me a great deal and knew both my style and the sound I was looking for. I was lucky to get Jeff Multer, my concertmaster at the Eastern Music Festival and the concertmaster of the Florida Orchestra, to sit with David. I chose Marc Ginsberg, the principal second violin in the New York Philharmonic, to lead the seconds. Marc and I had played together with Stokowski in the American Symphony as youngsters, and we were in the Philharmonic together. Marc is not only a brilliant musician with a gorgeous sound, but also a strong and experienced leader. I always have the second violins to my right, and you need a strong leader if that setup is going to work. Marc was interested but didn't know the new music we were doing, so he wanted to see all the parts before he would agree. He questioned the schedule, but the only piece that he mentioned as possibly being too difficult was the Adagio from Mahler's Tenth Symphony. Our discussion persuaded me to drop the Adagio for the first movement of Mahler's Symphony No. 2.

One of the ideas of these programs was to play complete works as much as possible. I felt that the most important programmatic element was the music itself. The music would be our star and would draw people into our world. The first movement of Mahler's Symphony No. 2 was originally a separate work called *Totenfeier*, so that seemed a legitimate exception to me. All the other Mahler orchestral works were too long for this format.

I also wanted Kim Fisher, the principal second in Philadelphia. I knew, though, that it would be almost impossible to get her to sit next to Marc rather than be in the first position. In the end she agreed, I think out of curiosity also because Marc was many years her senior. They were both fantastic, and I think they enjoyed themselves very much that week. In the end we had players from thirty major American orchestras and an orchestra full of stars.

'The contemporary works were a little more difficult to select. I needed shorter pieces, and they had to be relatively easy to record since none of the members of the orchestra—except for the few from Seattle—had played them. I chose works by Robert Beaser, Richard Danielpour, Philip Glass, Samuel Jones, Bernard Rands, Bright Sheng, Joseph Schwantner, David Stock, Augusta Read Thomas, and Ellen Taaffe Zwilich. With the exception of Bright, each one wrote a short version of their essence as composers. Bright's piece was a simple orchestration of a beautiful Brahms Intermezzo for piano. Before the music was distributed, while the names of the composers were still unknown, the principal trumpet of the Philadelphia Orchestra, Dave Bilger, called Neil Balm and said that he knew Bright's work and would need an assistant to help out with the first trumpet part. Neil called me and I agreed, as I always do in situations like that, but I suggested that Dave first look at his part in the piece. Knowing that this very simple part would not need an assistant, I thought both Dave and Neil would enjoy my little joke.

As we got closer to the recording date, people became concerned about the recording schedule. Could we really make top-notch recordings of so much music in such a short time? Some people in the music industry were saying that one could not throw an orchestra together and immediately create an ensemble sound. I believed I could, but I had a Plan B to do fewer shows if things didn't go well. I told no one of this because I wanted to give the impression of confidence in my team and the musicians. Even Paul became concerned. He is a great support for me and trusts my judgment, but he called me a few weeks in advance and suggested that I make plans for as few as four shows. I told him that I had but asked him not to mention it to anyone. I worked out the schedule very carefully.

I decided that we would start with the finale of Shostakovich's Symphony No. 5. That movement was generally fast and loud, a little challenging, but well-known by all. The end is taxing for the brass players, and since we were recording everything, they couldn't take it easy even for a moment. I planned to go through the finale twice and then pick up any problem sections afterward. Next we would do the third movement, which has no brass but is full of subtleties. The second is quite straightforward, and we would do the difficult first movement last. With any luck we would have most of the symphony completed by the end of the morning session, and if necessary we could start with anything left over in the afternoon.

We found a floor that looked presentable. As for concert clothes, I decided that the men should wear the same black suit and the same tie. Paul and I chose a style and bought a hundred ties. The women would wear long black skirts or dresses. It was delightful to see the players arrive. Some saw colleagues they hadn't seen since their conservatory days. It felt like a real reunion.

Part of the excitement was that no one in the room had ever made classical orchestral television programs without an audience. Nor had they played together in sections. Everyone was anxious to prove themselves. They all shared one goal: a series of extraordinary made-for-television orchestral performances by some of the finest players in the world. At moments like this, when I have ventured into risky new territory, I always wonder if this is going to be my folly. It happened when I commissioned Dale Chihuly to help with a concert performance of Bartók's *Bluebeard's Castle*. So far I've avoided catastrophe, and this new venture—thank goodness—was no exception.

The first note of the last movement of Shostakovich's Symphony No. 5 is a trill in the woodwinds starting *forte* (loud) and crescendoing. It is often played too softly so that a bigger crescendo can be made, but that was not the composer's intention. A few weeks after the sessions Jody and I were having dinner with Jeff Khaner, our principal flute. He told me he knew everything would be fine once he heard that first note with everyone playing *forte*.

One amazing thing about the All-Star Orchestra was that everyone was listening so intently. The second movement, Andantino in modo di canzone, of Tchaikovsky's Symphony No. 4 begins with a long and very beautiful oboe solo. During a short break I asked our magnificent oboe soloist from the Boston Symphony, John Ferrillo, what tempo he preferred. "Nicht schleppen," he replied—not too slow. He sang a little of it; it was exactly as I would have done it. He played with very sensitive rubato, and the accompanying string pizzicatos were perfectly with him, the players intuiting what he was going to do. It was magical, and we did it only once.

During the next break, however, Dima Lipay asked me if I could do this oboe solo again. He was concerned that when we listened to the recording, we might hear some noise that we might have missed. When I asked John about it, he said simply, "I'd rather not, Jerry." What we hear on the recording is that single version.

While we were making television shows, I was always thinking about what we might need for the educational part of our mission. We interviewed all the principal players on camera. The idea was to present their lives, their instruments, and their relationship to the repertoire we were recording. I interviewed David Kim and asked John Goberman to interview the other twenty principals. John Forsen made the short introductions meaningful and compelling.

We also talked to musical experts, including Michael Beckerman from New York University and Leon Botstein from Bard College and the American Symphony. I did my own interviews with Forsen when we returned to Seattle in September. For the most part we divided our talks into history and analysis. I also did a conducting lesson, planning to do one per show as time permitted.

I had pushed John to have the small HD cameras focus on each section so that a show could be viewed from a particular section. A flutist could watch the whole show or any part of it with only the flute onscreen. John and I disagreed on how to do this. In the end he placed GoPro cameras around the orchestra.

I wanted WNET to be our presenting station and bring the shows to the American Public Television network. We had interest from the CEO, Neal Shapiro, and from Stephen Segaller, who passed the hands-on work to Julie Anderson. When we finally had a completed show to send to WNET, they said they loved the musical content and the imaginative way in which Habib and John had presented the orchestra, but they thought that the focus of the shows, besides the music, was really the All-Stars, and that we needed more musicians talking about the pieces. We did more editing to change the direction of the interviews somewhat.

Now that we were ready to go, we needed fund-raising help. WNET agreed to air a promotional broadcast in June, and we alerted all our potential donors. This test broadcast was only partially successful because of the many versions of the sound that public television required, including normal stereo and surround sound. I had had similar problems with the classical radio station in Seattle. Some radio stations compress the sound so that it isn't too loud or too soft, but of course this distorts the dynamic range. We were having the same issue and others with television, and it was a lesson for us. We were determined to have better control of the sound when the broadcasts of the whole series aired in September.

We had to drop the idea of recording again in August 2013. Without the broadcasts, people didn't know what we were up to, and this would compromise our ability to raise the approximately $1.5 million necessary to continue.

When I showed the series to my friends at KCTS in Seattle, they wanted to broadcast them for eight weeks in July and August, before the general release, and chose a ten o'clock time slot on Friday nights. I was concerned about the time of year and the time slot, but with the approval of WNET, all was agreed. We also thought it might be a good test run for the shows. In the end these turned out to be eight of the ten most successful shows for KCTS in that time slot that year. Everyone was thrilled.

I was afraid few students would be watching public television at that time during the summer, so KCTS agreed to broadcast our series a second time on Sunday afternoons beginning in January. The shows were so successful in Seattle that KCTS asked me to take part in their next on-air fund drive, with our recording of Tchaikovsky's Symphony No. 4 as a gift for a certain level of donation. The shows aired all over the country, mostly in September and October, with each station choosing its own air date. We received some excellent press, two Emmy Awards, and the ASCAP Deems Taylor Award for Outstanding Television Broadcasting. Naxos released four DVDs, with two programs on each disc.

The Most Important Work I Do

We began working hard on the educational component. I wanted the material to be featured online at the Khan Academy, a nonprofit educational organization that produces excellent micro-lectures which began with mostly math and science. I was so impressed by this institution and its educational vision that I asked Paul to see if they would consider including music in their offerings. They looked at our All-Star Orchestra material and listened to my Musically Speaking CDs, which I had done ten years earlier—a series of educational CDs profiling thirty-four composers that had one disc with a discussion of the music with musical examples and a second disc with the complete performance. My dear friend Gilbert Scherer and I tried to do a continuity series with them. In the end it wasn't profitable, so we stopped producing the CDs. They are still available, however, and I am very proud of them.

After Paul met with Steven Zucker and Beth Harris, who do the visual art segments for Khan, they wanted very much to include our All-Star Orchestra content. Thus far we have reached more than four million students, and the program is still growing. I write and record each lesson for the Khan Academy, then email these to our video editor in San Diego, Andrew Mayatskiy, who puts the content together with the video graphics. We are not paid for the material we produce for Khan, so we fund-raise. I believe if every student studied music, some of the problems we see in our educational systems would be greatly ameliorated. This isn't just my fantasy; there are many studies that support this idea. It can change people's lives for the better and teach important lessons and skills. My work for Khan and the All-Stars is probably the most important I have ever done.

The All-Stars, Season 2

We now had to focus on season 2 of the All-Star Orchestra, to be recorded in August 2014. In the end, we had enough money to do four shows. The recording venue changed to New York State University at Purchase, whose concert hall had acoustics even better than Manhattan Center's; it also allowed better camera shots. The team at Purchase

Julian's bar mitzvah, 2004. These religious occasions were very important for our family. *Left to right*: Jody, Dan, Alysandra, Julian, Gabriella, and me. Photograph by Robin Layton.

Left to right: audio engineer Al Swanson, conductor Christian Knapp (then my assistant), and composer Bright Sheng during a recording session of Bright's music, 2004. Photograph by Larey McDaniel.

Lang Lang, Seattle, 2006. I first heard about this remarkable musician when Gary Graffman, Lang Lang's teacher at Curtis, told me of his extraordinary talent. I always trusted Gary's judgment and taste. I started working with Lang Lang at the very beginning of his career. It is always a joy when I have the opportunity to make music with him. Photograph by Larey McDaniel.

With my dear friend Dave Gannett in my studio in Benaroya Hall. Dave commissioned the Montana artist Con Williams to create this bronze. Dave had twenty-five copies cast and gave them to members of my family and to others who had made a major contribution to musical life in Seattle. On the wall on the right is a painting that Dale Chihuly made for me as a gift for the opening of the hall. He asked what I would like him to paint, and I suggested one of his chandeliers that hang in the Boeing Gallery. Next to it are a photograph of Beethoven (a gift from Otto Lang) and a metal sculpture by my son Daniel. Photograph by Ben VanHouten.

All-Star Orchestra team, 2016. Left to right: Paul Schwendener (executive director), me, Dmitriy Lipay (recording engineer/producer), and Habib Azar (director). With their extraordinary talents, this remarkable team of individuals makes this project work at the highest level. Personal collection.

Our Seattle family home. Our house was built by the Kerry family in 1903. When we first purchased the house in 1995, Albert Kerry, then ninety-eight years old, took us through it and shared some of his memories. Our home was the location for many symphony parties, galas, and dinners. It is also where our whole family lived together and celebrated many happy occasions and holidays. It will always be in our hearts. Photograph by John McKinney.

In Rogaška Slatina, Slovenia, my paternal grandmother's birthplace, in 2008, when I conducted the Zagreb Philharmonic in the premiere of my tone poem *Rudolf and Jeanette*. We made the short trip to see the family home. Personal collection.

James Ehnes, Seattle, 2009. James is a wonderful musician and a fantastic violinist. I remember thinking, the first time I heard him play the Mendelssohn Concerto, that rarely had I heard such deep and perfect musical understanding. Photograph by Larey McDaniel.

Seattle Symphony gala concert, 2009. *Left to right*: Elmar Oliveira, Vinson Cole, Garrick Ohlsson, Jane Eaglen, me, Gary Graffman, and Lorin Hollander. Photograph by Larey McDaniel.

With Gabriella and Julian at the Debutante Ball at the Olympic Hotel, Seattle, 2009. Gabriella was a debutante in 2006, and Julian was an usher in 2009 and the lead usher in 2010. Photography by Michael Rosenberg.

Midori, 2009. Midori was a joy to work with. As a very young soloist she was outstanding, and now she is deeply involved with education as well as performing all over the world. It is wonderful to see such an important artist giving so much of herself to the next generation. Photograph by Larey McDaniel.

Paul Schoenfield and me discussing the score of his *Sinfonietta*, Benaroya Hall studio, 2010. The *Sinfonietta* was one of the Gund-Simonyi commissions in 2010. I have recorded his *Klezmer Rondos* in Seattle and performed his Viola Concerto with the Los Angeles Philharmonic. Photograph by Ben VanHouten.

Among the most memorable concerts that I conducted in Seattle was Bartók's *Bluebeard's Castle*, staged with towering and extraordinary sets by the incredibly creative Dale Chihuly, 2010. *Onstage, left to right*: Jill Heerensperger, Marlys Palumbo, Jeanne McNae (the three former wives), Charles Austin (Bluebeard), Dale Chihuly, me, and Sally Burges (Judith). Photograph courtesy of Chihuly Studio.

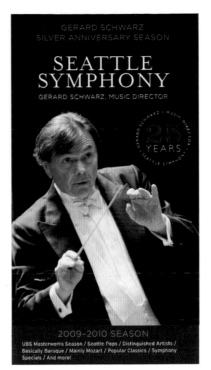

Throwing out the first pitch at a Seattle Mariners game. I loved baseball and our team. Chuck Armstrong, the president of the team at that time, and his wonderful wife, Susan, are close friends, and it was because of them—and our shared love of both music and baseball—that I met Craig and Joan Watjen, who became so important to the symphony. Photograph by Ben VanHouten.

The cover of the season brochure celebrating my twenty-fifth anniversary as music director in Seattle. Our acting executive director, Mark McCampbell, was responsible for making this a very memorable year for me in Seattle. Photograph by Ben VanHouten.

This was taken in 2011 during my last season as Music Director in Seattle. It shows the full orchestra at that time. Photograph courtesy of Yuen Lui Studio.

Conducting a premiere of Gunther Schuller's (in plaid jacket) "Bagatelle: with Swing," with the symphony's composer-in-residence Sam Jones, January 2011. This concert was part of the Gund-Simonyi commissioning project during my last season as music director, which resulted in eighteen new works by some of our finest composers premiered during the 2010–2011 season. On the same program I was conducting Bright Sheng's "Shanghai Overture." Photograph by Ben VanHouten.

Jody and me visiting Dale Chihuly's boathouse with Gladys Rubinstein, 2012. Dale is a dear friend, and Gladys, who is especially close to Jody, was like family to us during our years in Seattle. Gladys and her husband, Sam, were the godparents of Gabriella and Julian. Personal collection.

The recording of the Sam Jones Cello Concerto with the All-Star Orchestra in 2012 with my son Julian. Sam wrote this as a gift for my last season as music director of the Seattle Symphony; it was premiered on opening night in 2010. Photograph courtesy of the All-Star Orchestra.

I was overwhelmed and so appreciative when the city council named a street in downtown Seattle for me. Personal collection.

The whole family at Thanksgiving 2013 in New York City at the home of our dear friends, Misha and Cipa Dichter. *Front row, left to right*: Alysandra, Layton, Aidan, and Daniel. *Middle row*: Gabriella and Jody. *Back row*: Dave, me, and Julian. Personal collection.

At the opera house in Budapest with the Budapest Philharmonic, October 2013. The concert was arranged by the brilliant and remarkable United Nations ambassador from Hungary, Katalin Bogyay, to perform Bernstein's Symphony No. 3 (*Kaddish*), with narration by Sam Pisar. Dignitaries from Hungary, including the president, were in attendance. On one night the program included the Schubert "Unfinished" Symphony, and on the other, the Fauré *Requiem*. Personal collection.

Celebrating Bella Davidovich's eighty-fifth birthday at Jody's and my New York apartment, 2013. I first met Bella when she made her New York orchestral debut with the Los Angeles Chamber Orchestra in 1980 at Carnegie Hall. We played many concerts together and also recorded the Schumann and Grieg Piano Concertos in Seattle. I first became friends with her son, the violinist Dmitry Sitkovetsky, when he was a student at Juilliard. Since then we have played many, many concerts together in Europe, Asia, and the United States. Personal collection.

Jody and I with two of our closest friends, Charles and Lisa Simonyi, hiking in Norway, 2014. Without the Simonyis' trust and support, the All-Star Orchestra would never have come into being. Now that educational project is reaching millions of students through the Khan Academy. Personal collection.

My dear friend Alan Benaroya and I during our family Thanksgiving in 2016. Alan is like a member of our family and he celebrates most family holidays with us. He is a remarkable man with a very sophisticated taste in music. Alan has inspired me to believe in the power of great music. Personal collection.

Jody and me in New York celebrating our thirtieth wedding anniversary, 2014. Personal collection.

Wynton Marsalis was a student at Juilliard when I was on the faculty. Although his talent was blazingly obvious, I was not aware of his remarkable jazz background; I thought he would be the next great orchestral trumpet player. This photograph was taken in 2016 at the Juilliard graduation of my son Julian, who received his masters' degree. Personal collection.

All-Star Orchestra, 2014. With principal second violin Marc Ginsberg, whom I've known since we both played with Stokowski in the American Symphony in the late 1960s; later we both joined the New York Philharmonic. The principal viola is Becky Young, whom I have known since she was a student of my father-in-law, Sol Greitzer, at the Waterloo Festival. Photograph courtesy of the All-Star Orchestra.

In the rehearsal room that the Seattle Symphony had to use when we played in the Opera House. Since the opera house was used by the opera, the ballet, and the symphony, we were unable to expand our offerings or properly rehearse on the stage. This terrible overcrowding helped make a case for a new hall for the orchestra. Photograph © 2016 The Milken Family Foundation, courtesy of the Milken Archive of Jewish Music.

was extremely helpful, and we had the perfect atmosphere in which to create great programs.

We did two huge blockbuster works from the standard repertoire, Richard Strauss's *Ein Heldenleben* and Rimsky-Korsakov's *Scheherazade*, each of which featured one of the most important concertmaster solos in the repertoire. We also did an American show with the original version of Gershwin's *Rhapsody in Blue* (played by Lola Astanova), Aaron Copland's *Music for the Theatre*, and Robert Beaser's *Ground "O."* We had recorded the Beaser, a gorgeous and important work, in 2012 but didn't have a place for it.

We also did the world premiere of Samuel Jones's Violin Concerto, originally written for Nadja Salerno-Sonnenberg. So far as I know, only two works have ever been premiered on television in the United States—Gian Carlo Menotti's *Amahl and the Night Visitors* on NBC in the 1950s and Stravinsky's *The Flood* on CBS in the '60s. Of course, concerts were broadcast that featured premieres, but they were concerts, not specific television shows.

Nadja said that she would do it if necessary, but she really needed to rest after a taxing season, so we got the brilliant violinist Anne Akiko Meyers. She and Sam conferred by phone and Skype, and at the session she played as if she had been doing it all of her life. I also wanted to include some Mozart, so I scheduled four movements from the Serenade in D Major, K. 320 ("Posthorn"), adding the posthorn movement to Mozart's three-movement suite of this work to create a "Posthorn Symphony."

David Kim and I arrived in Purchase the day before the sessions to go over all the repertoire, as we had done in 2012. David suggested that we go over the most difficult work first. I agreed: *Heldenleben*. He disagreed. So you want to do *Scheherazade*, I said. He disagreed again. What *did* he want to go over? I asked. He said the most difficult piece was Copland's *Music for the Theatre*. He had never performed it, and it is very tricky. It turned out to be a quite extraordinary performance. Everyone shone, especially Jon Manasse on the E-flat clarinet solos.

As much as we loved working with WNET, we decided to move our host station to Oregon Public Broadcasting (OPB). My very good friend Steve Bass, a fine musician who is the CEO of OPB, supported the idea, and Dave Davis, the vice president for television production, and his team have been fantastic. Our basic team for all the post-production, besides Paul and me, included Habib Azar, Dmitriy Lipay, and Andrew Mayatskiy, to whom in particular we owe much of the success of the Khan Academy material.

In the spring of 2015 we won our third Emmy, and all twelve programs were broadcast in the fall of 2015 and into 2016. Naxos has released the new programs on DVD, and all our efforts are now focused on creating more material for the Khan Academy. We are all inexpressibly grateful to the Khan Academy and to our four million viewers and listeners. We hope next year to reach ten million students.

At the moment we have three platforms on the Khan Academy: fundamentals (note reading and rhythm); literature (analysis and history); and orchestral-instrument demonstrations. I plan to add a fourth: piano technique and literature. Lang Lang is a wonderful artist who has made a real effort in the area of music education and will be leading this fourth platform for us.

In 2016 we won our fourth Emmy and prepared our third season, recorded in August 2016, with music by Sibelius, Britten, Hovhaness, Elgar, and Mussorgsky, as well as a set of variations on a theme of Eugene Goossens by Copland, Taylor, Hanson, Piston, Schuman, Harris, Fuleihan, Rogers, Bloch, and Creston.

CHAPTER NINETEEN

The Mozart Orchestra of New York

My dear friend Mel Kaplan approached me with the idea of a chamber orchestra made up primarily of members of his New York Chamber Soloists. The instrumentation of this ensemble, which has played impressive concerts for years, is dictated by the repertoire being performed. Mel has a gift for knowing what kinds of programs would appeal to audiences. This chamber orchestra is made up of regular members of the New York Chamber Soloists, with others engaged as necessary from their pool of extra players. He asked me to become their music director, and I agreed. Mel wanted first to do the last three Mozart symphonies on one program. This was a program that I had done a number of times, and it always works so beautifully. He also wanted to do an all-Mendelssohn program, including Mendelssohn's Violin Concerto, and an all-American program. For the American program he wanted to do Samuel Barber's Cello Concerto. This marvelous work is rarely played and needs a big cellist to make it successful. I had recently sent Mel a DVD of my son Julian playing Elgar's Cello Concerto with me in Australia. After hearing it, he thought Julian would be the perfect soloist for that concerto.

Our first concert took place at the Tilles Center on Long Island in 2015. The program consisted of the last three Mozart symphonies, and Elliot Sroka, who has programmed for the Tilles Center for many years, did the first presentation. It turned out sensationally. The orchestra was what one would expect when great chamber music players come together to play in an orchestra. It was certainly a wonderful experience for me, and the second concert, in Troy, New York, was just as good. We have now added an all-Mendelssohn program to our touring offerings. Mel and his partner in the management, John Zion, are moving full speed ahead, and I predict great success for the future of what is now known as the Mozart Orchestra of New York.

CHAPTER TWENTY

What Is a Conductor?

Conductors have to be consummate musicians. They have to know the repertoire they are conducting intimately—every note, every part, every phrase, every nuance, every marking in the score. They also should understand the piece's social and historical context. For instance, if you are conducting Beethoven's Fifth Symphony, you should know what was happening in Beethoven's life during that period, and you should study the first four symphonies to see how they relate to it. If you are conducting the Symphony No. 2, look at the piano trio version of the work arranged by Beethoven.

Then you have to be able to communicate your ideas to the musicians. You have to do it physically, with your arms, your face, your eyes, your whole body. On occasion you have to instruct verbally, so it is important to know how to craft your words without insulting people. You hope to be able to encourage them. The conductor's job is to get the musicians to do their best, and to have them buy into the interpretation the conductor is putting forward. Sometimes it takes time for an orchestra to understand and embrace an interpretation. Sometimes there is not enough time, but you strive for their involvement in the process.

The Podium, the Baton, and Concert Dress
On occasion, with a small group, I have chosen not to use a podium. Over the years I have reduced the height of my podium to lessen the distance from the players. But always conducting with no podium at all isn't feasible, since the musicians in the back of a large orchestra may have trouble seeing you. Also on occasion I have dispensed with a

baton, which can be freeing. In some ways you can be more expressive, if perhaps not as clear. It can be very elegant.

Proper concert attire is a frequent topic of conversation. Some believe that more formal wear such as tails are off-putting for the audience. But I think that any uniform, including tails, allows the audience to focus on the music and not be distracted by what the players are wearing. It does not seem to me that the audience would feel more comfortable if members of an orchestra wore their street clothes. A concert is a special occasion, and I believe the audience wants to feel that as well. The uniform can be anything, but I feel that uniformity is preferred.

Orchestral Disposition

From the beginning of my professional conducting career in the mid-1970s, I have arranged the orchestra in what I call a historically traditional way, with the first and second violins split on the conductor's left and right respectively, the cellos next to the first violins, the basses behind them, and the violas between the cellos and second violins. This was generally the arrangement until around 1950, when it became common for the violins to sit together on the conductor's left, with the cellos and violas on the right and the basses behind them.

The difficulty with my traditional setup is the ensemble between the first and second violins. *Any* group that sits opposite the first violins will have some difficulty playing perfectly together with the firsts. If the second violin section has a strong and demonstrative leader (which is why I refer to my principal second violinist as the second concertmaster), much of this problem disappears, but most seconds do not like the arrangement. The other issue with the second violins sitting to the conductor's right is that their F holes face away from the audience, they may need to give a little more volume in order to be as "present" as the firsts. That said, when the violins are divided it is the cellos that have their F holes facing out, and sitting next to the firsts creates a very strong ensemble between the top and bottom string voices.

One advantage of the split violins sections is that historically most works were written with this disposition in mind. Much of Mahler's and Tchaikovsky's music, for example, does not make sense unless there is some separation between these sections. Another advantage is that the distribution of the sound of the strings is even, with the treble voice spread throughout the front of the stage. The effect of having all the violins on one side is that all the treble is on the conductor's left and all the bass on his or her right. Finally, this arrangement allows us to hear the second violins as a distinctive voice, adding marvelous texture to the string section and thus the entire orchestra. It is especially interesting to hear my recordings of the Mahler symphonies with the Royal Liverpool Philharmonic seated in this way.

As a guest conductor, however, I usually do not try to change the orchestra's normal position. I don't believe in coming into someone else's home and rearranging the furniture.

I'm Just Conducting the Fifth

Who are the conductors I respect? I feel that if you can go out onstage and get from the beginning of a concert to the end, that in itself is a great accomplishment. You should not take anything for granted. Sometimes a player or conductor will say, "Oh, I'm just doing the Tchaikovsky Violin Concerto [or the First Piano Concerto, or the Fifth Symphony]." Well, those great masterpieces are all extremely difficult and challenging works that cannot be taken lightly. I know a superb violin soloist who recently told me that she was not going to do concertos anymore, even though she is playing better than ever. She said it was simply too difficult, and I understand.

How to Become a Conductor

A youngster I met in Los Angeles recently asked me, "How do you become a conductor?" It's simple: by being a great musician. You must be a knowledgeable musician with a strong idea of how you feel works should be performed. And you must believe you have the ability to be a musical leader. The very basic technique of conducting is quite simple, but it becomes very detailed and complex as you grow. The idea is to be able to express your musical ideas with physical movement and facial expressions only. Then you must focus on the all important study of what the composer wrote and intended. In addition learning and focusing on the musical period in which any work is written is paramount. Expose yourself. Listen. Train your ear. I told this young man: "You will have opportunities, and then it is your job to do well. If you do well, you will have more opportunities. If you do not do well, you will have to wait until the next chance—so be prepared. Sometimes it is better if you begin conducting when you are a little older, because you are less likely to make the juvenile mistakes young conductors often make."

The Paradox of the Profession

When young conductors audition for an assistantship or to study at a festival or school, they are usually required to submit DVDs of their work. When I receive such a recording I put it on and watch with the sound off. This lets me know quite quickly what information besides the beats I'm getting from that conductor: the mood, a phrase, some kind of expression, the dynamics. The physical movements should not be distracting, but helpful; you have to be at the service of the music. Stay out of the way when you are not needed, and be present when you are. At those moments—a transition, a ritardando, any kind of tempo fluctuation or mood change, the musicians look to you. Much of the rest of the time they can play without you.

If you watch a video of Bernstein with the sound off, his motions may sometimes be distracting, but at the same time he is extremely expressive, and you can see what he wants musically. His gestures became part of his technique: holding his arms out as if God were telling him something, or holding his baton with two hands to make a gesture more powerful. When he wanted the orchestra to play very soft, he would bend down so far that the orchestra could hardly see him. Every conductor has his or her little idiosyncrasies.

Flamboyance is the paradox of our profession. It is usually unnecessary for the orchestra but entertaining for the audience. When I attended Peter Eros's conducting classes at the University of Washington in Seattle, he said, "When you're conducting for the board of trustees, or for the audience, you may want to jump around and become entertaining. That's your business. I am not going to teach you that. I am going to teach you what you need to do to be a fine conductor."

Are Conductors Egomaniacs?

If you're going to stand in front of an orchestra and instruct them in how you think the music should be played, you need a healthy ego. If you are insecure—I do not mean personally, I am only talking musically—the musicians will know it immediately. Every moment of a work can be played in many different ways, and it is the conductor's responsibility to make decisions and communicate them to the orchestra. Yet conductors must be flexible, not only with respect to mistakes, such as dealing with an incorrect entrance, but also with respect to new ideas from the players. What a musician does with a certain passage might lead you to rethink your ideas about a phrase. If it works with your overall concept, fine. If not, you must ask the player to change his or her approach.

You sit in your room and look at the notes. How fast should they go? How should they be phrased? How long should the phrase be? How loud? What's the balance? What should it sound like? If you have an idea of what something should sound like, and the brass section plays it but the middle voices are missing, you must respond to what you hear and then make the necessary correction. So: big ego, I'm not sure; healthy ego, yes. Your decisions should be based on knowledge, experience, intuition, and artistry.

As you study a score you can easily anticipate problems. I have often taken conductors through scores and explained what the problems are likely to be. At the same time, it is important for all conductors to respond only to what they hear rather than what they think they're hearing. I once worked with a fine conductor at the New York Philharmonic who insisted I was playing too loudly in the last movement of the Beethoven Seventh. He kept insisting on it, and when he finally looked over at the trumpet section, he noticed that we were not even playing! Conductors make mistakes, but we try to make as few as possible.

Being a Music Director Is More than Conducting

In Seattle I was the representative of classical orchestral music to the community. It was an important responsibility. As a music director of an arts institution in a city like Seattle, you become a public person whose responsibility it is to let people know that the orchestra and classical music are relevant and important to the image of the community, as well as the broader artistic mission.

When I first arrived, many in the community did not think the Seattle Symphony was relevant at all. "Why do we need a great symphony orchestra instead of just a good one?" they wondered. After all, a good orchestra is cheaper and easier to manage. To make the case for what we do, and its importance to the city, we reinstated and greatly expanded our educational programs. We wanted to reach every age group, beginning with programs for four- and five-year-olds and going all the way up to adults. We did Tiny Tots (four-to-seven-year olds), Discover Music (eight-to-twelve-year-olds), Meet the Beat (thirteen-to-seventeen-year-olds) and Musically Speaking (fifteen and up). We began playing free lunchtime concerts in the business and political community, places like City Hall and the Starbucks headquarters. Our recordings have brought national notice to our orchestra and city, and we had a great deal of support from our two daily papers and the mayor's office. As a result, the last time anyone asked about the orchestra's relevance was years ago.

And That's How That Goes

Playing an instrument is very different from conducting. You can attain a certain level of perfection as a player. You can play a concert and feel afterward it was perfect—that every attack and every sound were just the way you wanted them. But a conductor never has that kind of satisfaction. As perfectionists, we try to micromanage the performance, but musicians need to have some freedom. Give and take can lead to a far greater performance. When something went really well, I would say to Joe Cook, the Seattle Symphony stage manager, "Well, Joe?" And he would answer with Leonard Bernstein's line: "And that's how that goes!" But you do not often get that as a conductor. You can feel that it was a great performance and be very proud of the result, but there is so much that will not be perfect. A player is under tremendous pressure to play well, but he or she does not have that big-picture pressure. Will people like it? Is the whole thing musically excellent? Are you getting through to the orchestra? Is the pacing correct? Will the audience embrace your interpretation? When I first began conducting major works at the Waterloo Festival, I simply did not have time to feel the pressure I should have because I was studying so hard.

Making musical decisions is always challenging but extremely exciting. It is part of why we conduct: to create a convincing performance through a lot of study and then, at the concert, to be one with the music and the musicians, and to try to bring the performance to an inspiring level.

I had a little taste of this when I played with the American Brass Quintet, because playing chamber music requires a conductor's level of decision making. You have to work with your colleagues in the ensemble, but you produce the sound and have more control over the results. As a conductor you feel the pressure of the orchestra's perception of you, your approach, your personality, and your style of music making, rehearsing and performing. There are two things to remember: you can't be loved by everyone, and the whole orchestra will never completely agree with your interpretation. Once you realize that, you can just do the best performance of which you are capable. I reached a certain comfort level when I was playing in an orchestra because of all the experience I had had as a young musician. I have achieved that comfort level now as a conductor, but it took many years.

Music with Text

When I was in the New York Philharmonic, we performed Shostakovich's Symphony No. 14 with Bernstein conducting. There is no trumpet in the piece, so during rehearsals I sat in the back, watching and listening. For the first forty-five minutes of the first rehearsal Bernstein read aloud the four poems on which the piece is based. I'm a believer in knowing the text; I think it adds musical depth, even if it does not make a difference in the individual musician's performance. But I'm not convinced that having musicians sit and listen to poetry is the best use of the player's rehearsal time. When I first started doing vocal works, I asked the library staff to put the text (and the translation, if needed) on all the music stands or someplace else where the players could read it if they chose.

The Rehearsal Process

I begin rehearsals by going through a piece once so that everyone knows what I'm doing and what lies ahead. You have to make sure the musicians feel comfortable, and they have to know the music well. If it is a Brahms symphony, they know it already, but if you're doing something interpretively unusual, it is important that the musicians be comfortable with your choices. I play through the movement to evaluate the tradition of the orchestra. Then I go back, start again, and stop to correct trouble spots. I do not try to fix everything. Many things will take care of themselves, and you must think about the flow of the rehearsal. I find it very important not to talk too much.

There are exceptions. I was doing a piece with the Philadelphia Orchestra by George Perle. It was a difficult work, commissioned by the orchestra, and we were preparing the first performance with George in attendance. It is the kind of piece that does not make sense unless it is meticulously rehearsed, but I decided to do my regular routine: run through the twelve-minute work and then go back and begin to work. The reading had little to do with what the end result would be, but it was their first exposure to the work. At the end of the reading the orchestra hissed. Imagine the sound made by so many musicians hissing!

Were they right to hiss? No. But the piece did sound terrible. They had previously premiered some very difficult, severe, and inaccessible music, and here they were faced with more of the same. The way that rehearsal unfolded was a mistake on my part. I should have done eight or ten bars, tried to make them make sense, and then moved on. By the end I think they enjoyed the piece, but it took a little work for them to realize what was actually there. Just reading it through was of no value. I learned that you should not always just read through the piece, especially if it's modern. My advice with new music is to rehearse it section by section. Give the music a chance, and give the players a chance to absorb what is in the piece.

Make the Score Come Alive

I try to be faithful to the score, but I also have to make the score come alive. So what does "faithful to the score" mean?

To take one example: Beethoven's metronome marking in the Funeral March from his 3rd Symphony is that an eighth note should be played at eighty beats per minute. Is that how fast it should be? Well, maybe that's how fast the first bar should be, or maybe it's the tempo of the middle of the work. You can change tempo all the time, which I do. But you have to do so fluidly so that the audience doesn't hear it as getting faster here and getting slower there. If you are unsuccessful, the piece won't sound seamless. It is usually the fault of the conductor. Perhaps the musical ideas are not good ones, or the orchestra has not had an opportunity to become part of the interpretation.

I try to be true to the score—to a point. What is most important to me is that the piece come alive for the audience. The listeners are not sitting there with scores waiting to see if I am doing something other than what is written. I do what I can, and then I interpret, and, on occasion I rewrite. Sometimes I change orchestration, change dynamics, vary tempos. Few people have ever noticed. Only sophisticated musicians will on occasion hear these subtle changes. If you decide to double the clarinet in a place where it only calls for one clarinet, no one is going to notice. In a Dvořák symphony I conducted recently, there was one woodwind section that began with oboe and bassoon and then continued with the clarinet and flute. Neither version had enough power or depth, so I had all the woodwinds play the whole passage. It is only three bars, but this subtle change made the whole section more successful. No one said a word, no one even noticed, because it made good musical sense.

These are not decisions that need to be advertised. If you're careful, and if you make such changes only for musical reasons, performances can be enhanced. Do exactly what the composer wrote, and if it does not work and you feel you have to make a slight change, do so. But you first have to give it your all and try to make it convincing just the way it is written.

Just Play the Notes

Schumann once said, "Don't interpret my music. Just play the notes, please." I don't think he was right. Music needs to be interpreted. In fact, Schumann's scores in particular have notation problems, for example when he writes a crescendo. At times he doesn't tell you whether the crescendo should be for a particular note, for a bar, or for twenty bars. Sometimes he writes poco a poco crescendo, little by little, but very often he does not make that indication. As an interpreter, you have to make some sense out of these markings. I've heard performances of Schumann symphonies where conductors do what I consider to be absolutely the wrong dynamics because they have not thought through these issues. I once met with Erich Leinsdorf during a lunch break when he was conducting the Los Angeles Philharmonic and I was conducting the chamber orchestra. He was doing Schumann's Symphony No. 2 in the version by Mahler, which I was first exposed to when I played it with him in the New York Philharmonic. Mahler dealt with the question of dynamics by adding many new markings that Schumann did not indicate, changing the whole feeling of the direction of the work—especially in the last movement. I made my argument to Leinsdorf—and against Mahler. Leinsdorf said that I had convinced him, but that he was still going to do the Mahler version.

The Weight Is Off My Shoulders

When I stepped down from the Seattle Symphony, a huge weight was lifted off my shoulders. I used to worry about everything. I worried about the musicians' schedules and whether they were happy musically and professionally. I worried about whether they were paid enough and whether we were raising enough money. I worried about the audience, the programming, the soloists, the costs, and everything else. But during that last season I didn't worry anymore, and it was wonderful.

The board had begun to look for my successor and, together with the orchestra's administration, took over most of the music director's responsibilities. My only concern was to do excellent concerts. I used to think that the music director's job was 60 percent conducting, and 40 percent administrative. But during that last season in Seattle I realized that it was more like 75 percent administrative and 25 percent conducting.

Memory versus Reality

During my farewell season in Seattle I did my last *Messiah*. Members of the audience came to me and said; "Oh, it's the best *Messiah* ever." You often hear such remarks, but they may not reflect reality. Sometimes the memory of a performance is much greater than the reality, and at other times it's the opposite. It has to do with the individual listener. In 1975 I was touring with Bernstein doing Mahler's Fifth, one of the great thrills of my playing career. Years later, I listened to a tape of the performance we did in Australia—one that for me was especially memorable. Some aspects of it were quite remarkable, but there were others, particularly of the actual orchestral playing, that were not on the highest level. I was more focused on my own contribution and on watching Bernstein. Sometimes memories are better than reality, and sometimes reality is more wonderful than memory.

Try, with Intelligence

I do not like to focus on things over which I have no control. My ideas about a performance, a work, a relationship are ones I have thought about and feel will be successful. There were times when I had ideas that did not come to fruition because I did not get support from others around me. I am a great believer in being allowed to fail, and I strongly believe in always trying. Of course, if you fail too many times you will not be allowed to try again, or at least not very often; your track record matters. But so many people are afraid to try. If you try something and it isn't successful, fine; but if you refuse to try it at all, you'll never know whether that new idea would have been a dud or a smashing success. During my years in Seattle I was allowed to try out a number of new ideas, and in most cases there was an artistic reason for them, such as the many festivals I initiated. Other reasons included bringing the orchestra more into the community, educating the audience, or bringing the orchestra more national attention. Everything I did in all my years there was based on what I thought was best for the orchestra, for the community, for the audience, and for the art.

Nerves

My nerves have never affected my performance. Of course, I get nervous, but I am more nervous before a first rehearsal than I am before a concert. I study hard and am strongly focused on the works to be rehearsed. Are my decisions the correct ones? Are the tempos right? Did I make the right choices? Do I know the piece well enough? For me the most anxious moments are before the first rehearsal.

Tuning

Tuning is a very touchy area for most orchestras, especially the woodwind section. As a music director my approach is quite simple: I ask the oboe to use 440 cycles per second as the frequency for the tuning A, and I make sure that the player uses a machine to check the A to make sure it's consistent for each section of the orchestra. When I was in the New York Philharmonic, Harold Gomberg would give a lower A for the strings, so they basically ignored him. When I first came to Mostly Mozart, I asked our first oboe, Leonard Arner, to use a tuning device to give a consistent A. He objected, and I had to insist, even buying the tuner for him.

After Randall Ellis took over as first oboe in the Mostly Mozart orchestra, we would check to make sure that the pianos were being tuned to 440 as well. Sometimes they were actually tuned higher. When we installed the organ in Benaroya Hall, the organ maker wanted to tune the organ to 441, since he felt the orchestras always played sharp. However, if you are adamant about keeping the pitch down, the orchestra will follow your lead. Sometimes the oboe sounds flat at the end of a movement or a work—because the orchestra has started to raise the pitch. In that case I remind the orchestra to tune carefully and observe the 440 A. With a consistent A, the players can tune by themselves, and the A onstage will not be that crucial. This is especially important for the double basses, since it takes much longer to tune them than the other instruments.

Some orchestras prefer a higher pitch, but I love the consistency of the 440 A. We once did a joint concert in Tokyo with Mostly Mozart and the Tokyo Philharmonic. One of my first requests was to be sure we tuned to the same A. The Tokyo Philharmonic tuned to 442, and neither of the two first oboes wanted to make new reeds to adjust their pitch. In the end we made a compromise to 441: a little higher for the Mostly Mozart orchestra, a little lower for the Tokyo Philharmonic.

CHAPTER TWENTY-ONE

Vignettes

Grimthorpe

In 1977 I was asked by my good friend Elgar Howarth to guest conduct the Grimthorpe Colliery Band at the National Brass Band Championship of Great Britain at the Royal Albert Hall in London. Gary gave me a history lesson in British brass bands. I'd known Gary since the first European tour of the American Brass Quintet, when we met after the quintet's Wigmore Hall recital ten years before. Gary was a superb trumpet player—a member of the Philip Jones Brass Ensemble and principal trumpet of the Royal Philharmonic. He left trumpet playing to become an excellent conductor and composer and in the 1970s was changing the repertoire of the British brass band to include music by such important composers as Hans Werner Henze and Harrison Birtwistle. His request led me to a wonderful adventure. I spent a week in English coal-mining country, staying in the attic home of a wonderful cornet player in the band, Fred Partlett, and his wife, Mary.

All the members of the ensemble were amateurs and had to work in the mines, so our rehearsals were limited by their work schedule. I lived as they did and was touched by their dedication to the band and their tremendous work ethic, even though we could rehearse only early in the morning and in the evenings. The contest composition was a work by Edward Gregson called *Connotations*. Like the other bands that were competing, we had one week to prepare it.

The band was excellent and the preparation was very intense. Gregson's work was challenging, with difficult rhythms, tricky balances and technical passages, and some beautiful music that needed to be thoughtfully phrased. I was also practicing for the gala concert to be given after the competition, in which I was the featured soloist, with Gary conducting the Grimthorpe Band. Gary scheduled difficult pieces to be played on the trumpet, cornet, flugelhorn, and piccolo trumpet. Of course, I rehearsed the band thoroughly and with great intensity. I also tried to deal with the pressure of the contest, hoping to give the band the confidence they needed.

We traveled to London on Friday night for the Saturday competition. The first order of business was to draw for our performance starting time. Each band played the same ten-minute work, beginning around eight in the morning and lasting until mid-afternoon. Unluckily, we drew 8:30 A.M. Everyone was terribly worried, but once again I gave my pep talk, and they all played their best.

I returned to the Royal Albert Hall with the band at five in the afternoon to hear the results. They only announced the top ten bands, starting with number 10. As the list moved toward the top three, we became more and more nervous. I had so hoped to be among that elite group, but I knew that the starting time had worked against us. In the end we came in second, and Black Dyke Mills Band, which had been favored, came in first. A little disappointing, but we were very proud of our playing. By the end of the week I felt very close to these marvelous musicians, their town, and their dedication to this world of brass band repertoire. I think of that week often.

Vibrato in Baroque and Classical Repertoire

I recently attended a concert of the music of Mozart and Beethoven played by a fine orchestra. Both violin sections did not use any vibrato during their performance, and the resulting tone of those sections was, in my opinion, harsh, dry, and lacking in warmth. There was also no personality in the string sound. The idea of a Russian, French, or German sound was nowhere in evidence. This "international" style in baroque and classical music has become the norm, yet if you asked most conductors and instrumentalists why they chose it, they would say that it is the accepted style of performing music from these periods.

I am sure there are some performers, and certainly some critics, who prefer this kind of sound, and that would be a fine reason for playing in that way. During this period, historically, there certainly was no consistency of approach to performance or pitch. If we read the two most important books for the study of the violin, we get a varying prospective. As early as 1687, a treatise by Jean Rousseau says, "The batement (vibrato) imitates a certain sweet agitation of the voice: this is why it is used on all notes long enough to permit it, and must last as long as the note." Francesco Geminiani's *Art of Playing on the Violin* was published in London in 1751. This excellent book, with many musical studies, deals with most aspects of violin playing at the time.

Writing about vibrato, Geminiani says: "It only contributes to make their sound more agreeable and for this reason it should be made use of as often as possible." Leopold Mozart, Wolfgang Mozart's father, wrote in his *Violinschule*, published in 1756, that vibrato (or tremolo) should not be used on every note, though some performers do so. In his musical examples he suggested that vibrato should not be used on short notes but should be heard on longer ones. The proportion in one musical example was one-quarter without vibrato and three-quarters with vibrato. Another example was one-third without and two-thirds with vibrato. For me, the other big issues are what kind of vibrato to use and how wide or heavy or how fast it should be. I personally like a generally continuous vibrato, except on short notes. In the baroque and classical periods I prefer a lighter vibrato, with the speed varied according to the work's musical needs. I find criticism of performances from the baroque and classical periods that complain about using vibrato at all a bit peculiar.

Let the Orchestra Decide

Music directors are constantly making decisions, usually with the guidance of the orchestra's collective bargaining agreement. Most American orchestras stay very close to that agreement, even if it is not in their best interest. In 1974 I was playing with the New York Philharmonic on a tour of New Zealand and Australia with Leonard Bernstein. We had our final rehearsal the morning of our first concert with Mahler's Symphony No. 5 and a Mozart piano concerto played by

Bernstein. The contract rule was that we had to have a break no later than ninety minutes after the start of a rehearsal. At the appointed time we still had about six minutes to go to conclude the Mahler. Then there would be a break, and after the break only the Mozart, utilizing a much smaller orchestra and making it possible for most of the players to enjoy some extra time off.

The orchestra steward stood and stopped the proceedings. Bernstein protested, but the only way we could continue and finish the last few minutes of the symphony was with a vote by the orchestra. Bernstein was instructed to turn his back on the players, and we voted. John Cerminaro and I were the only ones who voted to continue and finish the Mahler. Most of us would have more time to see the city or rest. A friend of mine who had been on the negotiating committee for many years explained how hard they worked for that provision and how incorrect my vote was. I explained that this slight adjustment would have been best for all, and certainly not precedent setting. Too often orchestras are not as flexible as they could be, even when it is to their benefit.

In 2004 we had an opening for two spots in the viola section in Seattle. Two musicians were chosen, and it was my job to put one on the third chair and the other in the section. I suggested to the audition committee that we have each player sit in the third chair for a month, and then the section and I could decide together. The committee agreed with the idea, but not with the method I had put forth. I could not suggest a better one, so I asked them to come up with a way forward, to which I would agree. After a few days they said that my process was fine, and everything worked out very well.

Teaching

I had just turned twenty-nine when I left the New York Philharmonic, but I continued to play and teach. When I turned thirty I stopped playing the trumpet, and I have not played it since. To continue to play at a high level while studying so many scores became increasingly difficult, especially with the level of commitment I was taking on as a conductor. I continued to teach trumpet for a while, and then I stopped that too. I could not keep up with my students. I left Juilliard last, as it was my alma mater and my favorite, but in the end my travel schedule, especially to Los Angeles for the chamber orchestra, interrupted my responsibilities to my students. It was a great loss for me, because I truly loved teaching.

I have now begun teaching conducting in a new conducting program I created at the Eastern Music Festival. When I have the time and opportunity, I conduct at universities and conservatories with honor high school and honor ensembles around the country. In the Pacific Northwest I have worked with the All-Northwest Orchestra, and in Washington State with the All-State Orchestra. It is always exciting to work with these talented students, but the real teaching is being done by their private and classroom teachers. In 2006 I was asked to be the president of a support group for the Washington Music Educators Association called Young Musicians Excelling. I continued there until 2014, when I became the honorary president. The group was led by two dedicated educators, Jo and Bruce Caldwell, and the WMEA leadership. Such great and inspirational music teachers are the real educators of our country.

Diamond's *Rounds*

David Diamond's *Rounds for Strings* is his most popular work. He wrote the piece in 1944, in the midst of World War II, when the conductor Dimitri Mitropoulos wrote to him asking if he would compose a "happy" piece: "These are distressing times. Most of the difficult music I play is distressing. Make me happy." Most of the major conductors have performed *Rounds*, including Mitropoulos, Bernstein, Koussevitzky, and Copland. David said Copland envied him and wished he had written it himself.

Rounds was a favorite of mine. As a young trumpet player, whenever I bought a recording of Copland's *Quiet City* or Barber's *Capricorn Concerto*—two works with prominent trumpet parts—David's *Rounds* was often on the same LP. I had programmed it both in New York with the NYCS and in Los Angeles with LACO, and was going to record it with LACO on our first recording for Nonesuch, titled *Ameri-*

can String Music. The recording also included Barber's *Serenade,* Irving Fine's *Serious Song,* and Elliott Carter's *Elegy.*

One afternoon, as we were leaving Juilliard after teaching, I told David I planned to record *Rounds* with LACO. He was not pleased: Bernstein was going to do it with the full New York Philharmonic string section, and he preferred a large string group—the large orchestra having about fifty strings versus about half that number in a chamber orchestra. For him, big was wonderful, and he wanted that big sound.

I did the recording anyway with LACO, and in the end David was very pleased. I programmed *Rounds* a number of times in Seattle and eventually recorded it again with the big string complement he had always wanted. As it turned out, David was right: larger numbers of strings created a magnificent sound.

Perception versus Reality

There are three levels of perception: one, what you think is real; two, what others think is real; and three, what is actually real. Ideally we bring these three perceptions together. It would be best if reality were the same as what I think, and the same as what the world thinks. You may think you are the greatest pianist in the world, others might disagree, and the reality might be somewhere in between. What we all should try to do in our lives is to meld those three levels of perception. I hope that the way I think of myself as an artist is the way the public thinks of me as an artist, and that this is also close to reality.

Of course, the question remains: who decides what reality is? Very often that information is given to you. If someone tells you, "You're the greatest trumpet player in the world," but you can't get a job, there is some kind of disconnect. In that case you have to rein in your evaluation of yourself and work harder to change that reality.

Nadja's First Recording

Patty Larson, of Angel Records, contacted me to ask if the NYCS could be a part of Nadja Salerno-Sonnenberg's first recording. We recorded Mendelssohn's Violin Concerto, two works by Camille Saint-Saëns, and the Meditation from Jules Massenet's opera *Thaïs.*

We went to Purchase, New York, where there is an excellent hall for recording. As always, Nadja was serious and thoughtful, and her performances were unreservedly committed and heartfelt.

At the time some people thought her performances were too emotional, too free, too personal. Yet I feel that these qualities embody what making music is all about. Yes, we try to represent the composers properly, but in a personal way. Nadja did that on this recording, and she does it to this day. It was very meaningful to me that I was there supporting my dear friend during this important moment for her. It is interesting that she still plays in this very personal way and is no longer criticized but praised for it.

The Marketing Gurus

Orchestras are generally much more conservative now in terms of what they program than in the past. For instance, Serge Koussevitzky's programs in the 1930s and 1940s with the Boston Symphony were extremely imaginative, and he programmed an incredible amount of new music—Bernstein, Chávez, Copland, Diamond, Hanson, Hindemith, Martin, Martinů, Piston, and Surinach, among others, at the early stages of their careers. He also programmed less well-known French repertoire. How often do you hear the Vincent d'Indy *Symphony on a French Mountain Air*, or, for that matter, *any* of the d'Indy symphonies? I often hear people in charge of programming say, "We have to do Tchaikovsky, Beethoven, or Brahms." Even Schumann symphonies are difficult to program: "Schumann doesn't sell!" It is very difficult to determine why people attend a concert. Certainly if Lang Lang or another star appears, the sales will be excellent, but will programming a Schumann symphony really be a deterrent?

I recently programmed two concerts, one Russian and the other Austro-German. The Austrian concert was Mozart and Mahler: the Overture to Mozart's *Marriage of Figaro*, a Mozart piano concerto, and Mahler's Symphony No. 1. The Russian program was Prokofiev's Piano Concerto No. 3 and Shostakovich's Symphony No. 8. The Eighth is a little unusual, but it's not hard to market.

I received word that the marketing department did not like the idea of all-Russian and all-Austrian programs and wanted to switch the first halves. I didn't think that was a good idea. You can play a Mozart piano concerto and then a Shostakovich symphony, but they're worlds apart—there's no connection. And though that might not matter, subliminally you are much better off doing a Mozart piano concerto with the Mahler symphony. The language of Prokofiev and that of Shostakovich work very well together. In the end I was able to convince the marketing department of my choices. Both programs sold extremely well.

About Religion

When Jody and I were first married, we came to Seattle and joined Temple de Hirsch Sinai, a Reform temple. I know most of the prayers in Hebrew and love prayer through song, but I also appreciate having some of the service in English. I am always curious to hear what people think, so I am interested in every sermon. When I go to temple, though, I long to be spiritually touched. It is not a question of believing or not believing; it is a question of having a hallowed place for thought and reflection.

A favorite time of mine in the service is the silent prayer, and I often wish it would last longer. After we moved back to New York, Jody and I began going to Central Synagogue. We have a special northwest musical connection with Angela Buchdahl, the rabbi and also the former cantor at Central: she was raised in Tacoma and played flute in the Tacoma Youth Orchestra. As a rabbi she continues the spiritual tradition of ingenuity and forward thinking, but she adds a great deal with her beautiful voice and emphasis on music as a conduit to prayer.

Who Has Time for Music?

I believe it's crucial to reach young audiences in their formative years, between the ages of seven and fourteen. If young people are exposed to music and that exposure resonates with them, they might want to have music in their lives. This increases the likelihood they will attend an orchestral performance when in college or at least that they will feel comfortable attending at an older age. The classical music world seems obsessed with attracting a young audience. Serious music lovers will certainly attend, but most people in their twenties are interested in developing their careers, having a social life and network, and finding a partner. Attending a concert does not afford much interaction because the involvement is private rather than social; also, it is often expensive. My goal has always been to make concerts as affordable as possible, understanding that involvement may come at later stages for many. Classical music lovers are not dying off, but many may find classical music when they have more time later in life.

As a longtime music director in Seattle, I did my best to promote education, exposure, and affordability. I am now focusing on online exposure through the All-Star Orchestra and the Khan Academy. This medium affords a huge variety of possibilities and allows listeners and viewers to experience complete performances of the greatest masterpieces, to be introduced to the musicians, and to discover the context in which the pieces were written. Many organizations, including the All-Star Orchestra, work hard to supplement existing arts education in school systems across our country. It is not easily achieved, but it should be a goal of all school systems to integrate the arts back into our schools. My small public grade school in New Jersey had a band, an orchestra, a chorus, and a jazz band. Every young person should have that level of exposure.

I also believe that it is extremely important to include music as a core subject in general education. It helps with all subjects and increases success even in non-music-related courses of study. To ensure the future of concert attendance, we must educate our young people. It is not about marketing or making the concerts less formal, but simply about education and exposure.

American Music

American audiences don't appreciate American music the way the English appreciate English music. The English are wonderfully supportive of their own artists—their conductors, their instrumentalists, and especially their composers. England is a great musical country where the art form is embraced. There are six professional orchestras in

London alone, and the works of Benjamin Britten, William Walton, and Ralph Vaughan Williams are well loved and often played. A few American pieces have been accepted as part of the classical canon—Gershwin's *An American in Paris* and *Rhapsody in Blue*, Copland's *Billy the Kid* and *Appalachian Spring*. But the works of other composers—William Schuman, David Diamond, Walter Piston—are not part of the fabric of our musical life.

In the nineteenth century, musical culture was dominated by German and Austrian composers. French, English, and Russian composers came to the fore in the first part of the twentieth century. In mid-century the greatest musical strides were made in the Soviet Union and the United States. The remarkable American works this era produced deserve to be known worldwide, and the best place for this process to begin is in our own country. It is our responsibility to lead the way.

Publications and Politics

Sam Lipman was a fine pianist and writer, often a tough music critic, and a friend of mine. His writing on music was always thoughtful and well researched.

In the 1980s Lipman agreed to write a profile of Leonard Bernstein for the *New York Times Magazine*. He listened to many of his recordings, watched his Young People's and Omnibus television shows, read his books, studied his compositions and lectures, and researched his political activism and involvement with the Black Panthers and left-wing organizations. The resulting article was truly positive, filled with praise for this gifted and accomplished musical leader. However, the *New York Times* had hired Lipman because they thought, on the basis of Lipman's conservative political views, so much at odds with Bernstein's, that they would receive a controversial and critical piece. The *Times* asked if he would change it. He refused, and the *Times* rejected it. The newspaper even went so far as to attempt to deny him payment for the unpublished article.

A Hindemith Premiere

One of my last recordings with the Seattle Symphony was the complete *Nobilissima Visione*, by the German American composer Paul Hindemith. I consider this forty-five minute ballet to be one of Hindemith's greatest works. It had been commissioned by the Russian impresario Sergei Diaghilev in 1929, but Diaghilev died that year and the ballet was not finished. In 1938 the choreographer Léonide Massine restructured the Ballets Russes in Monte Carlo and asked Hindemith to resume work, which he did, scoring it for a small orchestra rather than the large one used in the suite.

The piece is about St. Francis of Assisi's intense and personal transformation from a wealthy, womanizing bourgeois into a deeply devout man of religion. Along his road to salvation, Francis faces intense criticism from his father but is ultimately guided by three female figures representing poverty, chastity, and obedience. My favorite scene is when St. Francis is attacked by the town wolf, represented in the score by a wild trombone solo, which has frightened the public for many years. St. Francis tames the wolf in a beautiful chorale played by the winds.

Seven years after conducting the piece's New York premiere, as described earlier, I programmed it for the NYCS again. As far as I know, at that time those were the only two U.S. performances of the work.

It was a dream of mine to record this piece—a dream that came true when I recorded the complete ballet for Naxos with a small orchestra of Seattle Symphony musicians in the Nordstrom Recital Hall. Ko-ichiro Yamamoto played the important trombone solo, and our engineer Dmitriy Lipay captured the brilliance of the performance. When I spoke to Klaus Heymann about releasing this piece, he pointed out that although he himself loved Hindemith, the sales would not be strong. I will never understand why this great composer has never found a place in the hearts of audiences. Klaus said he would release the CD, which he did, and I am grateful to him for this support.

Junctures

In my life there have been certain significant junctures. My decision to become a musician was the first one. I decided at age twelve that it was what I wanted to do with my life. Becoming a member of the New

York Philharmonic was the next moment for me. Just a few years after I failed my orchestra audition at Juilliard, I was teaching there and playing in the New York Philharmonic.

I had a kind of crisis when I left the New York Philharmonic. I worked all my life for a certain position, but after a few years I started thinking that: maybe this was not what I wanted to do for the rest of my life. To quit playing, to stop doing something that was part of my soul, something I had always done, and become a conductor? It was a momentous decision for me.

The next juncture of importance was coming to Seattle. I was a New Yorker, recently married to another New Yorker. Yet I had always liked the idea of going somewhere else, just to see what life would be like. Seattle turned out to be the perfect place for both of us.

Making the decision to leave the Seattle Symphony was the next major change. Your whole identity is tied up in who you are as the music director in a particular city. In a sense, coming home to New York made that transition much easier—I was moving on to the next chapter in my life.

Many people thought I was retiring. During my last season with the Seattle Symphony I was in a store when a woman came up to me with her husband and son. They were very sweet, and her husband said, "What are you going to do in your retirement?" I said, "Conductors don't retire, we die on the podium!" I have often been asked that question, and now I simply say that I will continue to conduct. Which is true.

Composers and Their Egos

Temperamentally, composers vary a great deal. When a composer has written a work but hasn't heard it yet, he or she can become unpredictable, nervous and tense. Did someone make a mistake? Are there wrong notes in the parts? Will the conductor rehearse it properly? What will happen during the rehearsal process? Will the musicians like it?

Some composers are obsessive about details and will tell you exactly how to play every note; others are very happy to have you interpret their work. David Diamond was always thrilled when I interpreted his music. I would say that composers are not egomaniacs, but are insecure. The work is their baby, and they love it just as it is. If a composer is a close friend, I can certainly speak more or less freely, and as I have gotten older, composers have become more willing to listen to me.

I once worked with the composer Hugh Aitken. He was extremely demanding, and I spent a tremendous amount of time on his piece, which I programmed with a Schubert symphony. Finally I said, "Hugh, I will do anything you want, but I have not even played a note of the Schubert yet." He said, "Who cares about Schubert? Schubert's dead."

Always Under Fire

When you are a performer, you are constantly being evaluated. A person goes to a concert and asks the person sitting in the next seat how he or she liked the performance. We performers are always being criticized. It comes with the territory. Performers are always judging everything that happens onstage: How was the conductor? Did you like the piece? What did you think of the soloist? Very few professions are constantly being evaluated, but when you are a performer, you are always evaluating everything—yourself, others—and they are evaluating you.

When our son wanted to become a musician, what upset me was knowing that he would be criticized. So far he has received nothing but rave reviews, but that will not last forever. It can be a great life, but it can be a tough one as well.

The Future

I am a great lover of what we do in our art form, and I want everyone in the world to experience it. I am doing everything I can in my life to make it as accessible to as many people as possible. If they are not touched by it, so be it. But I do not want that to be because they have not had an opportunity to hear the music.

Why do some people dislike classical music? I can only tell you what I think: they were not exposed to it when they were young, they were not educated, and the works weren't repeated for them. If you hear a piece of music every day for a few weeks, all of a sudden it becomes yours; you own it. How does a pop singer become successful? He or she gets the radio stations to play the song over and over again, until it becomes part of listeners' memories.

Classical music has an esoteric, elitist reputation because most pieces are relatively long, and all you do is sit there and listen. You don't get to interact with it. Interaction comes with hearing, feeling, and intellect. If you play an instrument, however, you become involved, and music will be with you forever. If you don't, getting to the point where it resonates with you is a little harder.

So many young people are not being educated the way we would like, even in the basics. Where does music fit in? I believe music is fundamental, and that most students will perform better in other courses of study if they also study music. I have never met anyone who studied music seriously in high school who did not go on to college. There are some exceptions, but very few. Only about 4 percent of students who study music in high school pursue it professionally, and many stop playing after graduation; but the ones who get involved in classical music in high school are going to excel. They will associate with people who are excelling and will become involved in a world that has more depth and understanding than what popular culture alone can offer. I think music instruction is a crucial part of the larger project of education.

CHAPTER TWENTY-TWO

A Conductor's Guide to the Orchestra

Generalizations can be problematic. That said, here's my take on the roles of the orchestra musicians and their instruments.

Concertmaster

This one player can affect the sound of the whole orchestra. If the concertmaster has a bright sound, the first violins will have that same sound, and the whole orchestra will be set in that direction. People are often amazed that a conductor giving a downbeat can change the sound of an orchestra just by the way that beat is given. The concertmaster has the same effect.

Principal Second Violin

I often call this individual the second concertmaster, especially in the orchestral configuration that I prefer: with the first and second violins playing from opposite sides of the conductor. This person must play with strength, independence, and leadership.

Viola

There are two basic types of viola sounds: a brighter one, leaning toward the violins, and a darker, leading toward the low strings. My personal preference is for the latter. This section can often become lost in a texture, and like the seconds, it needs to be independent in sound and execution while still playing with good ensemble.

Cello

The biggest general problem with this section is the use of harmonics. So often I hear these sounds emanating from the cellos without any musical rationale. Sometimes they're needed because of extreme technical difficulties, and sometimes they can make a lovely musical effect—but those should be the reasons for using harmonics, rather than laziness and convenience. I also often find cellists hover over the fingerboard when it is not appropriate.

Basses

The basses too often play off the string and not close enough to the bridge. I prefer a brighter bass sound facilitated by playing closer to the bridge. Playing more on the string and stopping the bow adds clarity to fast passages. I also prefer an extension for the E string. This usually opens up the sound of the instrument, but, more important, it also makes it possible to play down to low C.

Strings in General

Performing pizzicato is often a problem. Many players tend to accent the last note of a pizzicato passage and to take less care with ensemble. Also, players need to think about vibrating the little notes. An inconsistent vibrato can hurt the musical phrase.

Flute

The following are some problems I have recently been hearing on the flute: some players are unable to taper the final notes of a phrase, while others can't seem to play short, well-articulated notes. At times I like a click at the beginning of the notes, but I rarely hear that. Players also often begin the vibrato late. That can be a lovely effect, but generally if one uses vibrato it should last the whole note, from beginning to end. Many players, when playing short notes, tend to have undertones, which sound an octave lower and make articulated passages sound sloppy.

Piccolo

Intonation can be very tricky, and tone quality in the low register can often be problematic. The ability to taper notes is more problematic than on the flute.

Alto Flute

The biggest issue here is the ability to be heard.

Oboe

Some players make swells on all long notes, trying either to play bigger or to be expressive, but this is an affectation. I strongly believe in an A of 440 cycles per second. This uniformity of approach helps the orchestra's general intonation and allows all the players to tune their instruments offstage on their own. For greatest accuracy, I prefer that the oboist use a tuner.

English Horn

The biggest problem here is the dynamic range necessary. Some players try to play very loudly all the time, and others don't have a full range from very soft to very loud.

Clarinet

The two biggest issues here are general intonation and tone quality. Players should be careful not to play too sharp and to make sure that the bridge notes have a consistent pitch. Bridge notes need to sound even, like all the others, and there needs to be a balance between bright and dark. Lately I've been hearing players who play with such a dark sound that there are no highs to give the sound life. Then we sometimes have the opposite, with players feeling that they have to play quite brightly so that they will be heard.

E-flat Clarinet

The main issue here is always intonation.

Bass Clarinet

I've had no issues here.

Bassoon

Players need to be especially careful that the F on the fourth line in bass clef isn't sharp, and that the low register isn't sharp. At times I've found that the players with the most beautiful sounds can have trouble playing softly while maintaining that beautiful quality.

Contrabassoon

The big issue is the quality of the sound. At times I have found players with an unpleasant buzz in the tone and a slight crack in the attack.

French Horn

Players need to be careful not to play on the high side of the pitch. If a player is used to playing sharp, he or she will have to get used to playing with a different center of pitch. Until that happens the player may try to lip down the notes, which causes them to crack. And players who are used to playing flat—which is rare—will have the same problem when correcting this issue by lipping up. I have found that most cracks by players who are technically secure come from intonation issues.

Wagner Tuba

The Wagner tuba is an instrument that combines tonal elements of the French horn and the trombone. Special care must be taken to tune these instruments as an ensemble before the work's first rehearsal.

Trumpet

The player must always work on his or her dynamic range. Most players play too loudly and have trouble playing at a soft dynamic level. And they can have difficulty maintaining a beautiful tone quality when playing loudly. Furthermore, few players study vibrato, which can be a major problem.

Piccolo Trumpet

This instrument is used too often. The quality of sound is inferior to that of a normal-sized instrument. It is sometimes specifically called for, but in simpler works such as Handel's *Messiah*, it is used unnecessarily.

Trombone

Having uniform articulation in legato passages between natural slurs, natural breaks, and legato tonguing is the main issue.

Tuba

I have no issues here.

Brass in General

The biggest issue with the brass section is balance. Generally the first trumpet and tuba will predominate. The inner voices need to play louder to balance the top and bottom.

Timpani

I personally like the sound of the calfskin head.

Cymbals

Very often a rich sound is missing. I find that a dark cymbal sound for cymbal crashes is usually better.

————

2016: Emmy Award for the All-Star Orchestra

2016: Lifetime Achievement Award, National Society of Arts and Letters, Florida East Coast Chapter

2014: Emmy Award for the All-Star Orchestra

2013: ASCAP Foundation Deems Taylor Television Broadcast Award

2013: First Honorary Member of the Washington Music Educators Hall of Fame

2013: Emmy Award for the All-Star Orchestra

2011: Title of Honorary General presented by the Association of Washington Generals, for Many Contributions to the City of Seattle and to the State of Washington

2011: Seattle street named "Gerard Schwarz Place" in Honor of Service to the City of Seattle

2011: Paul Harris Fellow from the Rotary Club of Seattle, for Many Contributions to the City of Seattle

2011: Seattle Sounders Football Club Golden Scarf Award for Impact on the State of Washington

2010: Seattle City of Music Outstanding Achievement Award

2010: ArtsFund Award for Outstanding Achievement in the Arts, Seattle

2009: Key to the City, Greensboro, North Carolina

2009: First Citizen of Seattle Award

2008: Grammy Nomination: Best Musical Album for Children

2007: Emmy Award for *Seattle Symphony: Live from Benaroya Hall* (Brahms, Kernis, and Kodály)

2006: Mayor's Arts Award from the Seattle Arts Commission for Contribution to the Arts (presented by Mayor Greg Nickels)

2006: Emmy Award for *Seattle Symphony: Live from Benaroya Hall* (Sibelius, Bruch, and Shostakovich)

2006: ASCAP Award for Adventurous Programming

2005: Honorary Doctorate of Fine Arts, Cornish College of the Arts

2004: Appointed to the National Council of the Arts

2004: ASCAP Award for Programming of Contemporary Music

2003: IMPACT Lifetime Achievement Award from National Academy of Recording Arts and Sciences, Pacific NW Chapter

2002: ASCAP Concert Music Award

2001: ASCAP Award for Adventurous Programming

2001: Prime Time Emmy Nomination, *Mostly Mozart*

2000: Honorary Fellowship, John Moores University, Liverpool

1998: Emmy Award for *Opening of Benaroya Hall* (KCTS)

1997: Society for American Music Honorary Membership

1996: Honorary Doctorate, Juilliard School

1996: ASCAP Award for Programming of Contemporary Music

1995: Metropolitan King County Council, Honor for Educational Outreach

1995: Phi Beta Kappa-Pathfinder Award

1994: First American conductor to be named Conductor of the Year by Musical America

1994: ASCAP Award for Adventurous Programming

1993: Honorary Doctorate of Humanities, Seattle University

1993: Grammy Nomination, Best Engineered Album and Classical Producer of the Year

1992: Grammy Nomination, Best Classical Album

1991: ASCAP John S. Edwards Award for Strongest Commitment to New American Music

1991: Grammy Nomination, Best Classical Album

1991: Honorary Doctorate of Music, University of Puget Sound

1990: Juilliard School, Master of Music

1990: ASCAP Award for Adventurous Programming

1990: Emmy Nomination

1990: Grammy Nomination, Best Orchestral Performance

1990: Grammy Nomination, Best Classical Performance

APPENDIX I: LIST OF AWARDS

1990: Grammy Nomination, Best Solo with Orchestra

1990: Grammy Nomination, Best Contemporary Composition

1989: Ditson Conductors Award from Columbia University

1989: Grammy Nomination, Best Classical Album

1989: Grammy Nomination, Best Orchestral Performance

1989: Grammy Nomination, Best Engineered Album, Classical

1987: Arts Service Award from King County Arts Commission

1987: National Arts Club Award for Distinction in Music

1985: Grammy Nomination, Gerard Schwarz, New York Chamber Symphony, and Teresa Stratas

1983: Honorary Doctorate of Fine Arts, Fairleigh Dickinson University

1980: Grammy Nomination, Best Classical Performance

1978: Ford Foundation Award for Concert Artists

1977: *Stereo Review*'s Record of the Year

1974: *Stereo Review*'s Record of the Year

APPENDIX II: LIST OF RECORDINGS

—

COMPOSER	REPERTOIRE	LABEL
Achron, Joseph	*The Golem* Czech Philharmonic *Belshazzar* Barcelona Symphony Orchestra	Naxos 8.559408
Adolphe, Bruce	*Mikhoels the Wise* Seattle Symphony Orchestra	Naxos 8.559413
Aitken, Hugh	*Aspen Concerto; Rameau* *Remembered; In Praise of Ockeghem* Seattle Symphony Orchestra	Artek AR-0004-2
Albert, Stephen	*In Concordiam* Seattle Symphony Orchestra *TreeStone* New York Chamber Symphony	Naxos 8.559708
Albert, Stephen	*Into Eclipse* Juilliard Orchestra	New World 381-2
Albert, Stephen	*Flower of the Mountain* New York Chamber Symphony	Nonesuch 79153-2
Albinoni, Tommasso	*Concerto in C Major* Baroque Chamber Music of Telemann, Hertel, Albinoni	Desto 6438
Altenburg, Johann	*Concerto for 7 Trumpets* New York Trumpet Ensemble	Delos 3002
Avshalomov, Aaron	*Four Biblical Tableaux*	Naxos 8.559426
Bach, C. P. E.	*Harpsichord Concertos* Malcolm Hamilton, harpsichord; Los Angeles Chamber Orchestra	Nonesuch 79015

APPENDIX II: LIST OF RECORDINGS

Bach, J. S.	*Arias* Mostly Mozart Festival Orchestra	Delos 3026
Bach, J. S.	*Orchestral Transcriptions by Respighi and Elgar* Seattle Symphony Orchestra	Naxos 8.572741
Bach, J. S.	*Brandenburg Concertos 1–6* Los Angeles Chamber Orchestra	Sesophin 69015
Bach, J. S.	*Suite No. 2* Los Angeles Chamber Orchestra	Sesophin 69016-2
Bach, J. S.	*Musically Speaking—Bach* Academy of St. Martin in the Fields	Musically Speaking, ASIN: B001G2LX5M
Ballet for Martha	*Making Appalachian Spring* Sarah Jessica Parker, narrator; Seattle Symphony Orchestra	Brilliance Audio
Barber, Samuel	*Serenade for Strings* Los Angeles Chamber Orchestra	Nonesuch 79002-2
Barber, Samuel	*Overture to "The School for Scandal"* Seattle Symphony Orchestra	Naxos 8.559709
Barber, Samuel	*Commando March* United States Marine Band	Naxos 8.573121
Barber, Samuel	*Medea's Dance of Vengeance* United States Marine Band	Naxos 8.573121
Bartók, Béla	*The Miraculous Mandarin* Seattle Symphony Orchestra	Delos 3083
Bartók, Béla	*Concerto for Orchestra* Seattle Symphony Orchestra	Naxos 8.571201
Bartók, Béla	*Musically Speaking— Bartók* Seattle Symphony Orchestra	Musically Speaking, ASIN: B000YYAY6C
Bassett, Leslie	*Concerto Lirico; Concerto for Orchestra* Seattle Symphony Orchestra	MMC 2090

APPENDIX II: LIST OF RECORDINGS

Beethoven, Ludwig van   *Overture to "Prometheus"; Symphony No. 5; Piano Concerto No. 4* Carol Rosenberger, piano; London Symphony Orchestra   Delos 3013

Beethoven, Ludwig van   *Symphony No. 6* New York Chamber Symphony   Delos 3016

Beethoven, Ludwig van   *Symphonies No. 1 and No. 8* Los Angeles Chamber Orchestra   Delos 3027

Beethoven, Ludwig van   *Symphony No. 9* Various artists; Seattle Symphony Orchestra   Seattle Symphony 2010

Beethoven, Ludwig van   *Musically Speaking—Beethoven* London Symphony Orchestra   Musically Speaking, ASIN: B0000B383B

Bell, David   *Andromeda* Symphony No. 1   MMC 2142

Berlinski, Herman   *Avodat Shabbat* Berlin Radio Symphony   Naxos 8.559430

Berlinski, Herman   *From the World of my Father; Shofar Service; Symphonic Visions for Orchestra* Seattle Symphony Orchestra   Naxos 8.559446

Berlioz, Hector   *Musically Speaking—Berlioz* New York Philharmonic Orchestra and the Royal Philharmonic Orchestra   Musically Speaking, ASIN: B001FLIEGU

Bernstein, Leonard   *Symphony No. 3; Chichester Psalms* Royal Liverpool Philharmonic   Naxos Spring 2005

Bernstein, Leonard, and Bright Sheng   *Arias and Barcarolles* Seattle Symphony Orchestra   Naxos 8.559709

APPENDIX II: LIST OF RECORDINGS

Biber, Heinrich	*Sonata for 8 Trumpets* New York Trumpet Ensemble	Delos 3002 Naxos 8.572743
Bloch, Ernest	*America; Concerto Grosso No. 1* Seattle Symphony Orchestra	
Bloch, Ernest	*From Jewish Life: "Prayer";* *Schelomo Kaddish*	AV 2149
Diamond, David	*In Memoriam*	
Schwarz, Gerard	*Kol Nidre*	
Bruch, Max	Jonathan Aasgaard, cello; Royal Liverpool Philharmonic	
Borodin, Alexander	*Symphonies 1–3* Seattle Symphony Orchestra	Naxos 8.572786
Bozza, Eugene	Caprice	Delos 1047
Brahms, Johannes	*Hungarian Dances Nos. 3, 6, 11, 16* Seattle Symphony Orchestra	Delos SSLE
Brahms, Johannes	*Serenade No. 1, Op. 11* Los Angeles Chamber Orchestra	Nonesuch 79065-2
Brahms, Johannes	*Violin Concerto* Elmar Oliveira, violin' Seattle Symphony Orchestra	Artek 0003-2
Brahms, Johannes	*Complete Symphonies* Seattle Symphony Orchestra	Seattle Symphony 2010
Brahms, Johannes	*Musically Speaking—Brahms* Boston Symphony Orchestra	Musically Speaking, ASIN: B000YXZ576
Brant, Henry	*Concerto for Trumpet* Gerard Schwarz, trumpet; Berlin Radio Symphony	PHCD 115 Naxos 8.559452
Braun, Yehezkel	*Sacred Services from Israel* Berlin Radio Symphony	
Brouwer, Margaret	*Concerto for Clarinet and Orchestra* Seattle Symphony Orchestra	MMC 2149

APPENDIX II: LIST OF RECORDINGS

Brouwer, Margaret	*Aurolucent Circles; Mandala; Sizzle* Royal Liverpool Philharmonic Orchestra	Naxos 8.559250
Bruch, Max	*Kol Nidrei* Royal Liverpool Philharmonic	AVIE 2149
Bruch, Max	*Violin Concerto No. 2* Nai-yuan Hu, violin; Seattle Symphony Orchestra	Delos 3156
Busoni, Ferruccio	*Concertino for Clarinet* David Shifrin, clarinet; Los Angeles Chamber Orchestra	Nonesuch 79077
Carbon, John	*Notturno*	MMC 2166
Carter, Elliott	*The Minotaur* New York Chamber Symphony	Nonesuch 979248
Carter, Elliott	*Canon for Three*	PHCD 115
Chopin, Frédéric	*Musically Speaking—Chopin*	Musically Speaking, ASIN: B000YY4FJY
Copland, Aaron	*Fanfare for the Common Man;* *Lincoln Portrait* Seattle Symphony Orchestra	Delos 3140
Copland, Aaron Creston, Paul	*Concerto for Piano and Orchestra;* *Appalachian Spring (Suite);* *Symphonic Ode* *Symphony No. 3* Seattle Symphony Orchestra	Naxos 8.571203
Copland, Aaron	*Dance Panels* New York Chamber Symphony	EMI/Angel 3 97727
Copland, Aaron	*An Outdoor Overture; Canticle* *of Freedom* Seattle Symphony Orchestra	Delos DE3140
Copland, Aaron	*Clarinet Concerto; Quiet City* David Shifrin, clarinet; New York Chamber Symphony	HMV 5728442
Copland, Aaron	*Emblems* United States Marine Band	Naxos 8.57312

APPENDIX II: LIST OF RECORDINGS

Copland, Aaron	*Musically Speaking—Copland* Seattle Symphony Orchestra	Musically Speaking, ASIN: B01G6633AK
Creston, Paul	*Symphony No. 3; Partita for Flute,* *Violin, and Strings;Invocation* *and Dance; Out of the Cradle* Seattle Symphony Orchestra	Delos 3114
Creston, Paul	*Celebration Overture* United States Marine Band	Naxos 8.57312
Creston, Paul	*Toccata, Op. 68; Choreographic* *Suite; Symphony No. 5* Seattle Symphony Orchestra	Delos 3127
Crusell, Bernhard	*Clarinet Concerto* Emma Johnson, clarinet; English Chamber Orchestra	AVS 659
Danielpour, Richard	*First Light;Symphony No. 3* Seattle Symphony Orchestra	Naxos 8.559712
Davies, Peter Maxwell	*Sonata* Gerard Schwarz, trumpet; Ursula Oppens, piano	Nonesuch H-71275
Diamond, David	*Symphony No. 3; Psalm for Orchestra;* *Kaddish for Cello and Orchestra* János Starker, cello; Seattle Symphony Orchestra *Romeo and Juliet* New York Chamber Symphony	Delos 3103
Diamond, David	*Kaddish* Royal Liverpool Philharmonic	AVIE 2149
Diamond, David	*Symphony No. 1; Violin Concerto* *No. 2; The Enormous Room* Ilkka Talvi, violin; Seattle Symphony Orchestra	Delos 3119
Diamond, David	*Symphony No. 8; Suite from the* *Ballet TOM;This Sacred Ground* Seattle Symphony Orchestra	Delos 3141
Diamond, David	*Elegy in Memory of Ravel* Seattle Symphony Orchestra	Naxos 8.559709

APPENDIX II: LIST OF RECORDINGS

Diamond, David	*Symphony No. 2; Symphony No. 4* Seattle Symphony Orchestra *Concerto for Small Orchestra* New York Chamber Symphony	Delos 3093
Diamond, David	*Hommage à Satie* Seattle Symphony Orchestra	Koch 3-7358-2
Diamond, David	*Symphony No. 3; Psalm; Kaddish* *for Cello and Orchestra* *Romeo and Juliet* János Starker, cello; Seattle Symphony Orchestra	Naxos 8.559155; Delos 3103
Diamond, David	*Violin Concerto No. 2; The* *Enormous Room; Symphony No. 1* Ilkka Talvi, Violin; Seattle Symphony Orchestra	Naxos 8.559157
Diamond, David	*Rounds for Strings* Los Angeles Chamber Orchestra	Nonesuch 79002-2
Debussy, Claude	*Trois gymnopédies, Nos. 1, 3* Seattle Symphony Orchestra	Koch 3-7358-2
Debussy, Claude	*Danses sacrée et profane* Los Angeles Chamber Orchestra	EMI DS-37339
Debussy, Claude	*Musically Speaking—Debussy* BRT Philharmonic Orchestra	Musically Speaking, ASIN: B000YY5GFG
Dlugoszewski, Lucia	*Tender Theatre Flight Nageire*	CRI 388
Dlugoszewski, Lucia	*Space Is a Diamond*	Nonesuch G-71275
Dohnyáni, Ernst von	*Konzertstück* Seattle Symphony Orchestra	Delos 3095
Drattell, Deborah	*Sorrow Is Not Melancholy;* *Clarinet Concerto; Lilith;* *The Fire Within; Syzygy* David Shifrin, clarinet; Seattle Symphony Orchestra	Naxos 8.571204

Dvořák, Antonín	*String Serenade; Silent Woods; Notturno* Los Angeles Chamber Orchestra	Delos 3011
Dvořák, Antonín	*Czech Suite; Serenade for Winds* Los Angeles Chamber Orchestra	Nonesuch 79044
Dvořák, Antonín	*Symphony No. 6* Seattle Symphony Orchestra	Naxos 8.572698
Dvořák, Antonín	*Musically Speaking— Dvořák* London Symphony Orchestra	Musically Speaking, ASIN: B000YXV4GC
Echoes	*Echoes: Classic Works Transformed* Seattle Symphony Orchestra	Starbucks/Seattle Symphony 2007
Echoes	*Echoes: Classic Works Transformed* Seattle Symphony Orchestra	Naxos 8.559679
Elmer, Howie	*Panoramas* Royal Liverpool Philharmonic	MMC 2143
Falla, Manuel de	*Nights in the Gardens of Spain; The Three Cornered Hat* London Symphony Orchestra	Delos 3060
Falla, Manuel de	*Musically Speaking—Falla* London Symphony Orchestra	Musically Speaking, ASIN: B0000B383I
Finck, Mildred	*Concerto for Clarinet* Richard Stolzman, clarinet; New York Chamber Symphony	MMC 2137
Fine, Irving	*Serious Song* Los Angeles Chamber Orchestra	Apex 0927494212
Fontana, Giovanni	*Sonatas* Gerard Schwarz, trumpet; Julie Feves, bassoon; Helen Katz, harpsichord	Desto DC 6481
Foote, Arthur	*Francesca da Rimini; 4 Character Pieces after "The Rubáiyát of Omar Khayyám"; Serenade, Air, and Gavotte; Suite in E Major* Seattle Symphony Orchestra	Naxos 8.559365

APPENDIX II: LIST OF RECORDINGS

Frescobaldi, Girolamo	*Canzoni*	Desto DC 6481
Froom, David	*Serenade* Seattle Symphony Orchestra	MMC E 3187
Gershwin, George	*An American in Paris*	Naxos 8.571205
Grofé, Ferde	*Grand Canyon Suite* Seattle Symphony Orchestra	
Glass, Philip	*The Concerto Project, Vol. 1: Concerto for Cello; Concerto for Two Timpani* Jonathan Haas and Evelyn Glennie, timpani; Royal Liverpool Philharmonic Orchestra	Orange Mountain Music 0014
Goldmark, Karl	*Violin Concerto No. 1* Nai-Yuan Hu, violin; Seattle Symphony Orchestra	Delos 3156
Gould, Morton	*The Music of Morton Gould* Seattle Symphony Orchestra	Naxos 8.559715
Grainger, Percy	*Lincolnshire Posy* United States Marine Band	Naxos 8.573121
Grieg, Edvard	*Piano Concerto in A Minor; Lyric Suite; Holberg Suite* Bella Davidovich, piano; Seattle Symphony Orchestra	Naxos 8.571206
Griffes, Charles	*The White Peacock; Bacchanale; The Pleasure Dome of Kubla Khan; Poem for Flute and Orchestra*	Naxos 8.559724
Taylor, Deems	*Through the Looking Glass* Scott Goff, flute; Seattle Symphony Orchestra	
Handel, George Frideric	*Arias* Arleen Auger, soprano; Mostly Mozart Festival Orchestra	Delos 3026
Handel, Georg Frideric	*Concerto Grossi, Op. 6, Nos. 1, 6, 9* *Flute Concerto Op. 10*	Naxos 8.571208
Vivaldi, Antonio C. P. E Bach	*Flute Concerto in D Minor* Scott Goff, flute; Seattle Symphony Orchestra	

APPENDIX II: LIST OF RECORDINGS

Handel, George Frideric	*Acis and Galatea* Seattle Symphony Chorale; Seattle Symphony Orchestra	Naxos 8.572745-46
Handel, George Frideric	*Aires and Arias* Judith Blegen, soprano; Columbia Chamber Ensemble	CBS 76636
Handel, George Frideric	*Musically Speaking—Handel* Los Angeles Chamber Orchestra	Musically Speaking, ASIN: B0000B383H
Hanson, Howard	*Symphony No. 1; Symphony No. 2; Elegy in Memory of Serge Koussevitzky* Seattle Symphony Orchestra	Delos 3073
Hanson, Howard	*Symphony No. 3; Symphony No. 6; Fantasy Variations on a Theme of Youth* Seattle Symphony Orchestra	Delos 3092
Hanson, Howard	*Symphony No. 4; Lament for Beowulf; Suite from Merry Mount* Seattle Symphony Orchestra *Serenade for Flute, Harp, and Strings; Pastorale for Oboe, Harp, and Strings* Randall Ellis, oboe; New York Chamber Symphony	Delos 3105
Hanson, Howard	*Mosaics; Piano Concerto in G Major; Symphony No. 5; Symphony No. 7* Carol Rosenberger, piano; Seattle Symphony Orchestra	Delos 3130
Hanson, Howard	*Symphonies 1–7* Seattle Symphony Orchestra	Delos 3150
Hanson, Howard	*The Mystic Trumpeter; Lux Aeterna; Lumen in Christo; Dies Natalis* James Earl Jones, narrator; Seattle Symphony Orchestra	Delos 3160
Hanson, Howard	*Merry Mount* Various artists; Seattle Symphony Orchestra	Naxos 8.669012-13
Hanson, Howard	*Complete Symphonies*	Delos DE 3150

Hanson, Howard	*Symphonies* Seattle Symphony Orchestra	Naxos 8.559700 Naxos 8.559701 Naxos 8.559702
Harbison, John	*Rubies* Seattle Symphony Orchestra	Naxos 8.559679
Harris, Roy	*American Creed; When Johnny Comes Marching Home* Seattle Symphony Orchestra	Delos 3140
Haydn, Franz Joseph	*Trumpet Concerto* George Vosburgh, trumpet; Seattle Symphony Orchestra	Four Winds 3021
Haydn, Franz Joseph	*Symphony No. 22; Symphony No. 104; Piano Concerto in D* Carol Rosenberger, piano; Scottish Chamber Orchestra	Delos 3061
Haydn, Franz Joseph	*Symphony No. 21; Symphony No. 96; Cello Concerto in C* János Starker, cello; Scottish Chamber Orchestra	Delos 3062
Haydn, Franz Joseph	*Symphony No. 61; Symphony No. 103; Cello Concerto in D* János Starker, cello; Scottish Chamber Orchestra	Delos 3063
Haydn, Franz Joseph	*Symphony No. 51; Symphony No. 100; Piano Concerto in G* Carol Rosenberger, piano; Scottish Chamber Orchestra	Delos 3064
Haydn, Franz Joseph	*Trumpet Concerto* Gerard Schwarz, trumpet; Y Chamber Symphony of New York	Delos 3001
Haydn, Franz Joseph	*Trumpet Concerto in E Flat Major* Gerard Schwarz, trumpet; The Philharmonia Virtuosi of New York	Turnabout QTV-S 34646
Haydn, Franz Joseph	*Musically Speaking—Haydn* Scottish Chamber Orchestra New York Chamber Symphony	Musically Speaking, ASIN: B0000B383J

APPENDIX II: LIST OF RECORDINGS

Hellermann, William	*Passages 13* Gerard Schwarz, trumpet; Ursula Oppens, piano	Nonesuch H-71275
Herbert, Victor	*Serenade for Strings; Three* *Compositions for Strings; Suite* *for Cello, Op. 3* Doug Davis, cello; Los Angeles Chamber Orchestra	Nonesuch H-79107
Hertel, Johann Wilhelm	*Concerto A Cinque* Baroque Chamber Music of Telemann, Hertel, Albinoni	Desto 6438
Hindemith, Paul	*Kleine Kammermusik, Op. 24, No. 1* Los Angeles Chamber Orchestra	Nonesuch 79077
Hindemith, Paul	*Nobilissima Visione; 5 Pieces for* *String Orchestra* Seattle Symphony Orchestra	Naxos 8.572763
Holiday Classics	*Holiday Classics* Seattle Symphony Orchestra	Seattle Symphony 2008
Holiday Classics	*Holiday Classics* Seattle Symphony Orchestra	Naxos 8.572673
Honegger, Arthur	*Symphony No. 2* Seattle Symphony Orchestra	Naxos 8.572748
Honegger, Arthur Lazarof, Henri	*Intrada* *Icarus; Poema* Seattle Symphony Orchestra	Delos 1047
Honegger, Arthur	*Concerto da camera* Los Angeles Chamber Orchestra	Nonesuch 79018
Hoose, Alfred	*Symphony No. 2*	MMC 2189
Hovhaness, Alan	*Symphony No. 50; Symphony No. 22* Seattle Symphony Orchestra	Delos 3137
Hovhaness, Alan	*Symphony No. 2; And God Created* *Great Whales; Prayer of St. Gregory;* *Prelude and Quadruple Fugue;* *Celestial Fantasy; Alleluia and Fugue* Seattle Symphony Orchestra	Delos 3157

APPENDIX II: LIST OF RECORDINGS

Hovhaness, Alan	*Prelude and Quadruple Fugue; Concerto for Soprano Saxophone and Strings; Symphony No. 48* Greg Banaszak, saxophone; Eastern Music Festival Orchestra	Naxos 8.559755
Hovhaness, Alan	*The Rubaiyat; Exile Symphony; Meditation on Orpheus; Fantasy on Japanese Woodprints* Seattle Symphony Orchestra	Delos 316
Hovhaness, Alan	*Armenian Rhapsodies Nos. 1, 2, and 3; Concerto No. 10, Op. 413* Seattle Symphony Orchestra	Koch 7422
Hovhaness, Alan	*Symphony No. 2; Symphony No. 66; Symphony No. 50; Storm on Mount Wildcat* Royal Liverpool Philharmonic Orchestra	Telarc 80604
Hovhaness, Alan	*Symphony No. 60; Guitar Concerto* Khrimian Hairig, guitar; Berlin Radio Symphony	Naxos 8.559294
Hovhaness, Alan	*Symphony No. 1, "Exile"; Fantasy on Japanese Woodprints; Symphony No. 50; Mt. St. Helens* Seattle Symphony Orchestra	Naxos 8.559717
Hummel, Johann Nepomuk	*Trumpet Concerto* George Vosburgh, trumpet; Seattle Symphony Orchestra	Four Winds 3021
Hummel, Johann Nepomuk	*Trumpet Concerto* Gerard Schwarz, trumpet; New York Chamber Symphony	Delos 3064
Ibert, Jacques	*Impromptu* Gerard Schwarz, trumpet; Kun Woo Paik, piano	Delos 1047
Janáček, Leoš	*Idyll for String Orchestra* Los Angeles Chamber Orchestra	Nonesuch 79033

APPENDIX II: LIST OF RECORDINGS

Jolivert, André	*Air de bravoure* Gerard Schwarz, trumpet; Kun Woo Paik, piano	Delos 1047
Jones, Samuel	*Symphony No. 3, "Palo Duro Canyon"; Tuba Concerto* Chris Olka, tuba; Seattle Symphony Orchestra	Naxos 8.559378
Jones, Samuel	*Benediction* Seattle Symphony Orchestra	Naxos 8.559679
Kernis, Aaron	*Symphony in Waves* New York Chamber Symphony	Argo 436 287-2
Kernis, Aaron	*Musica Celestis* Seattle Symphony Orchestra	Naxos 8.559679
Khachaturian, Aram	*Piano Concerto* Dickran Atamian, piano; Seattle Symphony Orchestra	Delos 3155
Kodály, Zoltán	*Háry János* Seattle Symphony Orchestra	Delos 3083
Kodály, Zoltán Dohnányi, Ernst von	*Háry János* *Konzertstück* Seattle Symphony Orchestra	Naxos 8.572749
Kolb, Barbara	*Chromatic Fantasy* Music Today Ensemble	MMC 2143
Korneitchouk, Igor	*Triptych* Royal Liverpool Philharmonic	New World 80422-2
Korneitchouk, Igor	*Everything That Rises Must Converge* Royal Liverpool Philharmonic	MMC 2116
Krása, Hans Laitman, Lori	*Brundibár* *I Never Saw Another Butterfly* Music of Remembrance	Naxos 8.570119
Lancino, Thierry	*Prélude et mort de Virgile* Orchestre National de France	Radio France

APPENDIX II: LIST OF RECORDINGS

Lazarof, Henri	*Symphony No. 3, "Choral";* *Encounters with Dylan Thomas* Seattle Symphony Orchestra	Centaur 2519
Lazarof, Henri	*Symphony No. 4; Symphony No. 5* Seattle Symphony Orchestra	Centaur 2657
Lazarof, Henri	*Second Concerto for Orchestra* Seattle Symphony Orchestra	Delos 3069
Lazarof, Henri	*Symphony No. 2; Violin Concerto* Yukiko Kamei, piano; Seattle Symphony Orchestra *Clarinet Concerto* David Singer, clarinet; New York Chamber Symphony	Delos 3133
Lazarof, Henri	*Violin Concerto; Tableaux for Piano and Orchestra; Symphony No. 2* Takiko Kamei, violin; Seattle Symphony Orchestra	Naxos 8.559159
Liadov, Anatoly	[Various works] Seattle Symphony Orchestra	Artek 0056-2
Liszt, Franz	*Musically Speaking—Liszt* London Philharmonic Orchestra	Musically Speaking, ASIN: B000YY8INI
Mahler, Gustav	*Symphony No. 1; Symphony No. 4* Royal Liverpool Philharmonic	Classico 1503
Mahler, Gustav	*Symphony No. 5* Tokyo Philharmonic Orchestra	Fun House 2002
Mahler, Gustav	*Symphonies No. 1 and No. 9* Royal Liverpool Philharmonic	Artek AR-0041-2
Mahler, Gustav	*Symphony No. 7* Royal Liverpool Philharmonic	Artek AR-0043-2
Mahler, Gustav	*Symphony No. 6* Royal Liverpool Philharmonic	Artek AR-0046-2
Mahler, Gustav	*Symphony No. 4* Royal Liverpool Philharmonic	Artek AR-0052-2
Mahler, Gustav	*Symphony No. 8* Royal Liverpool Philharmonic	Seattle Symphony 2009

APPENDIX II: LIST OF RECORDINGS

Mahler, Gustav	*Symphony No. 10: Adagio* Seattle Symphony Orchestra *Symphony No. 3* Royal Liverpool Philharmonic	Artek AR-0057-2
Mamlok, Ursula	*Constellations for Orchestra* Seattle Symphony Orchestra	CRI 806
Massenet, Jules	*Méditation from "Thaïs"* New York Chamber Symphony	EMI 49276
Mayer, William	*Inner and Outer Strings* Various artists	Albany 068
McKinley, William Thomas	*Concerto for Orchestra No. 2* Seattle Symphony Orchestra *Tango, Intermezzo, and Dance* New York Chamber Symphony	MMC 95016
McKinley, William Thomas	*The Mountain; Flying Home* Seattle Symphony Orchestra	MMC 95016
McKinley, William Thomas	*Wild Stallion* Royal Liverpool Philharmonic	MMC 2143
McKinley, William Thomas	*Concerto Domestica* Czech Radio Symphony	MMC 2066
Mendelssohn, Felix	*Symphony No. 2* Seattle Symphony Orchestra	Naxos 8.571209
Mendelssohn, Felix	*Son and Stranger* Seattle Symphony Orchestra	Delos SSLE
Mendelssohn, Felix	*Violin Concerto* Nadja Salerno-Sonnenberg, violin; New York Chamber Symphony	EMI 49276
Mendelssohn, Felix	*Musically Speaking—Mendelssohn* New Philharmonia Orchestra	Musically Speaking, ASIN: B000YY0W9G
Mennin, Peter	*Moby Dick; Symphonies No. 3 and No. 7* Seattle Symphony Orchestra	Naxos 8.8.559718
Milhaud, Darius	*Service sacré* Czech Philharmonic	Naxos 8.559406

APPENDIX II: LIST OF RECORDINGS

Milhaud, Darius	*Sacred Service* Prague Philharmonic Chorus; Czech Philharmonic	Naxos 8.559409
Milhaud, Darius	*Jewish Music of the Dance* Berlin Radio Symphony	Naxos 8.559439
Moryl, Richard	*Das Lied* New England Contemporary Ensemble	CRI 397
Moryl, Richard	*Salvos* Gerard Schwarz, trumpet	PHCD 115
Mozart, Wolfgang Amadeus	*Four Horn Concertos* John Cerminaro, French horn; Seattle Symphony Orchestra	Crystal 515
Mozart, Wolfgang Amadeus	*Symphonies Nos. 40 and 41* Los Angeles Chamber Orchestra	Delos 3012
Mozart, Wolfgang Amadeus	*Clarinet Concerto* David Shifrin, clarinet; Mostly Mozart Orchestra	Delos 3020
Mozart, Wolfgang Amadeus	*Piano Concertos K. 467 and 491* Eugene Istomin, piano; Seattle Symphony Orchestra	Reference 68
Mozart, Wolfgang Amadeus	*Musically Speaking—Mozart* Los Angeles Chamber Orchestra	Musically Speaking, ASIN: B0000B383D
Nelson, Mary Barker	*Symphonic Fantasy on Orpheus Lex* Seattle Symphony Orchestra *The Rocky Mountains* New York Chamber Symphony	MMC 2103
Nelson, Mary Barker	*Culinary Concerto for Clarinet* Richard Stoltzman, clarinet; Seattle Symphony Orchestra	MMC 2103
Nytch, Jeffrey	*Concerto for Clarinet and Orchestra* Richard Stoltzman, clarinet; New York Chamber Symphony	MC 2080
Orff, Carl	*Carmina Burana* Czech Philharmonic	P 006-2 Czech Autumn

APPENDIX II: LIST OF RECORDINGS

Panufnik, Andrzcj	*Symphonies No. 3 and No. 10;* *Autumn Music; Heroic Overture* Seattle Symphony Orchestra	JVC 6511
Pasatieri, Thomas	*Letter to Warsaw* Music of Remembrance	Naxos 8.559219
Pascal, Claude	*Capriccio* Gerard Schwarz, trumpet; Kun Woo Paik, piano	Delos 1047
Pergolesi, Giovanni Battista	*The Music Master* Los Angeles Chamber Orchestra	EMI 37344
Perle, George	*Serenade No. 3* Music Today Ensemble	Nonesuch 79108
Perle, George	*Sinfonietta No. 2; Piano Concerto* *No. 1; Adagio for Orchestra* Richard Goode, piano; Seattle Symphony Orchestra	TROY 292
Piston, Walter	*Symphony No. 2; Symphony No. 6* Seattle Symphony Orchestra *Sinfonietta* New York Chamber Symphony	Delos 3074
Piston, Walter	*Symphony No. 4; Capriccio for Harp* *and String Orchestra; Serenata;* *Three New England Sketches* Seattle Symphony Orchestra	Delos 3106
Piston, Walter	*The Incredible Flutist; Fantasy for* *English Horn, Harp, and Strings;* *Suite No. 1 for Orchestra; Concerto* *for String Quartet* Glenn Danielson, English horn; Juilliard String Quartet; Seattle Symphony Orchestra	Delos 3126
Piston, Walter	*Suite for Orchestra; Psalm and Prayer* *of David; Concerto for String Quartet* Juilliard Quartet *Ballet Suite, "The Incredible Flutist"* Seattle Symphony Orchestra	Naxos 8.559160

APPENDIX II: LIST OF RECORDINGS

Piston, Walter	*Symphony No. 2; Symphony No. 6* Seattle Symphony Orchestra	Naxos 8.559161
Piston, Walter	*Three New England Sketches;* *Symphony No. 4; Capriccio for* *Harp and String Orchestra* Seattle Symphony Orchestra	Naxos 8.559162
Prokofiev, Sergei	*Classical Symphony* Los Angeles Chamber Orchestra	Delos 3021
Prokofiev, Sergei	*"Romeo and Juliet" Suites 1 and 2;* *Pushkin Waltz No. 2* Seattle Symphony Orchestra	Naxos 8.571210
Prokofiev, Sergei	*Piano Concerto No. 3* Dickran Atamian, piano; Seattle Symphony Orchestra	Delos 3155
Prokofiev, Sergei	*Symphony-Concerto for Cello* *and Orchestra* Lynn Harrell, cello; Royal Liverpool Philharmonic	AV 2090
Prokofiev, Sergei	*Violin Concertos No. 1 and 2* Jennifer Frautschi, violin; Seattle Symphony Orchestra	Artek AR 0020-2
Prokofiev, Sergei	*Peter and the Wolf* Jim Dale, narrator; Seattle Symphony Orchestra	Brilliance Audio
Prokofiev, Sergei	*Musically Speaking—Prokofiev* Los Angeles Chamber Orchestra and the Seattle Symphony Orchestra	Musically Speaking, ASIN: B000YYAPTS
Rands, Bernard	*Canti dell'Eclisse* Philadelphia Orchestra	New World 80392
Rands, Bernard	*Ceremonial* United States Marine Band	Naxos 8.573121
Ravel, Maurice	*Le tombeau de Couperin* Seattle Symphony Orchestra	Koch 3-7356-2h1
Ravel, Maurice	*Daphnis and Chloe* Seattle Symphony Orchestra	Delos 3110

APPENDIX II: LIST OF RECORDINGS

Ravel, Maurice	*Daphnis and Chloe*	Naxos 8.571211
Hovhaness, Alan	*Meditation on Orpheus* Seattle Symphony Orchestra	
Richards, Stephen	*Songs of a Survivor* Royal Liverpool Philharmonic	MMC 2143
Richter, Margo	[Various works] Czech Radio Symphony	MMC 2066
Rimsky-Korsakov, Nikolai	*Russian Easter Overture* Seattle Symphony Orchestra	Delos 3054
Rimsky-Korsakov, Nikolai	*Scheherazade; "Tale of Tsar Saltan" Suite; Flight of the Bumblebee* Seattle Symphony Orchestra	Naxos 8.562793
Rimsky-Korsakov, Nikolai	*Capriccio espagnol;May Night;* *"The Tsar's Bride" Overture;* *Overture on Three Russian Themes;* *The Maid of Pskov; Russian Easter* *Festival Overture* Seattle Symphony Orchestra	Naxos 8.572788
Rimsky-Korsakov, Nikolai	*Suite from "The Snow Maiden";* *Sadko; Mlada; Le coq d'or* Seattle Symphony Orchestra	Naxos 8.572778
Rimsky-Korsakov, Nikolai	*Symphonies 1 and 3* Berlin Radio Symphony Orchestra	Naxos 8.573581
Rossini, Gioachino	*Grand Overture; Sinfonia* *"al conventello"* Los Angeles Chamber Orchestra	Nonesuch 79023
Rouse, Steve	*The Avatar* Seattle Symphony Orchestra	MMC 2108
Saint-Saëns, Camille	*Violin Concerto No. 3* Elmar Oliveira, violin; Seattle Symphony Orchestra	AR-0003-2
Saint-Saëns, Camille	*Havanaise; Introduction and* *Rondo Capriccio* Nadja Salerno-Sonnenberg, violin; New York Chamber Symphony	EMI 49276

APPENDIX II: LIST OF RECORDINGS

Satie, Erik	*Passacaille* [arr. Diamond]; *Trois gymnopédies; Messe des pauvres* [arr. Diamond] Seattle Symphony Orchestra	Koch 37358-2
Scarlatti, Alessandro	*Cantata* Columbia Chamber Ensemble	CBS 76636
Schiff, David	*Jewish Operas, Vol. 2* Seattle Symphony Orchestra	Naxos 8.559450
Schiff, David	*Infernal* Seattle Symphony Orchestra	Naxos 8.559679
Schoenberg, Arnold	*Chamber Symphony, Op. 9; Five Pieces, Op. 16* Los Angeles Chamber Orchestra	Nonesuch 79001
Schoenberg, Arnold	*Concerto for String Quartet and Orchestra* American String Quartet; New York Chamber Symphony	Nonesuch 275031
Schoenfield, Paul	*Klezmer Rondos* Seattle Symphony Orchestra	Naxos 8.559403
Schreker, Franz	*Chamber Symphony* Los Angeles Chamber Orchestra	Nonesuch 79077
Schubert, Franz	*Symphonies No. 5 and 8; German Dances* New York Chamber Symphony	Delos 3067
Schubert, Franz	*Musically Speaking—Schubert* New York Chamber Symphony	Musically Speaking, ASIN: B0000B383G

APPENDIX II: LIST OF RECORDINGS

Schumann, Robert	*Konzertstück for 4 Horns*	Naxos 8.572770
Mendelssohn, Felix	*Overture [to] "Heimkehr aus der Fremde"*	
Schumann, Robert	*Symphonic Etudes Nos. 11 and 12* [arr. Tchaikovsky]	
Brahms, Johannes	*Hungarian Dances Nos. 5, 6, 11, and 16*	
Webern, Anton von	*Langsamer Satz* [arr. Schwarz]	
Pfitzner, Hans	*Symphony in C Major* Seattle Symphony Orchestra	
Schumann, Robert	*Symphonies Nos. 1 and 2* Seattle Symphony Orchestra	Naxos 8.571212
Schumann, Robert	*Symphonies Nos. 3 and 4* Seattle Symphony Orchestra	Naxos 8.571213
Schumann, Robert	*"Manfred" Overture; Piano Concerto; Overture, Scherzo, and Finale* Bella Davidovich; piano; Seattle Symphony Orchestra	Naxos 8.571214
Schumann, Robert	*Symphony No. 1; Symphony No. 2; Symphony No. 3; Symphony No. 4; "Manfred" Overture; Piano Concerto; Overture, Scherzo, and Finale; Konzertstück for Four Horns; Symphonic Etudes* [arr. Tchaikovsky] Seattle Symphony Orchestra	Delos 3146
Schumann, Robert	*Musically Speaking—Schumann* Seattle Symphony Orchestra	Musically Speaking, ASIN: B000QRHY4C
Schuman, William	*The Young Dead Soldiers* Various artists	CRI 439
Schuman, William	*The Mighty Casey; A Question of Taste* Juilliard Orchestra	Delos 1030

APPENDIX II: LIST OF RECORDINGS

Schuman, William	*New England Triptych; Symphony for Strings*	Delos 3115
Ives, Charles	*Variations on "America"* [orch. Schuman] Seattle Symphony Orchestra	
Schuman, William	*Symphony No. 4; Symphony No. 9; Orchestra Song; Circus Orchestra* Seattle Symphony Orchestra	Naxos 8.559254
Schuman, William	*Symphony No. 7; Symphony No. 10* Seattle Symphony Orchestra	Naxos 8.559255
Schuman, William	*Symphonies Nos. 3 and 5; Judith* Seattle Symphony Orchestra	Naxos 8.559317
Schuman, William	*Symphony No. 6; Prayer in a Time of War; New England Triptych* Seattle Symphony Orchestra	Naxos 8.559625
Schuman, William	*Symphony No. 8; Night Journey*	Naxos 8.559651
Ives, Charles	*Variations on "America"* [orch. Schuman] Seattle Symphony Orchestra	
Schuman, William	*The Symphonies* Seattle Symphony Orchestra	Naxos 8.685728
Schwarz, Gerard	*Above and Beyond* United States Marine Band	Naxos 8.573121
Schwarz, Gerard	*Concerto for Brass Quintet and Orchestra* Seattle Symphony Orchestra	Naxos 8.559679
Schwarz, Gerard	*Rudolf and Jeanette* Music of Remembrance	Naxos 8.559641
Schwarz, Gerard	*In Memoriam* Royal Liverpool Philharmonic	AVIE 2149
Schwarz, Gerard	*In Memoriam* Music of Remembrance	Naxos 8.559379
Schwarz, Gerard	*Variations on "Greensleeves"* Seattle Symphony Orchestra	Naxos 8.572673

Schwarz, Gerard	*We Three Kings* Seattle Symphony Orchestra	Naxos 8.572673
Schwarz, Gerard	*Silent Night* Seattle Symphony Orchestra	Naxos 8.572673
Senee, Henri	*Concertino* Gerard Schwarz, trumpet; Kun Woo Paik, piano	Delos 1047
Shchedrin, Rodion	*"Carmen" Ballet* Los Angeles Chamber Orchestra	EMI ASD 4194
Sheng, Bright	*H'un (Lacerations)* New York Chamber Symphony	New World 80407
Sheng, Bright	*Black Swan* Seattle Symphony Orchestra	Naxos 8.559679
Sheng, Bright	*The Phoenix; Red Silk Dance;* *Tibetan Swing; H'un (Lacerations)* Seattle Symphony Orchestra	Naxos 8.559610
Shostakovich, Dmitri	*Symphony No. 6; Violin Concerto* *No. 1* Elmar Oliveira, violin; Seattle Symphony Orchestra	Artek 0017-2
Shostakovich, Dmitri	*Symphony No. 11* Seattle Symphony Orchestra	Koch 3-7414-2
Shostakovich, Dmitri	*Piano Concerto No. 1* Carol Rosenberger, piano; Los Angeles Chamber Orchestra	Delos 3021
Shostakovich, Dmitri	*The Execution of Stepan Razin;* *October, Op. 131; Five Fragments,* *Op. 42* Seattle Symphony Orchestra	Naxos 8.557812
Shostakovich, Dmitri	*Cello Concerto No. 2 in G Major,* *Op. 126* Lynn Harrell, cello; Royal Liverpool Philharmonic Orchestra	AV 2090

APPENDIX II: LIST OF RECORDINGS

Shostakovich, Dmitri	*Symphony No. 5; Suite from "The Golden Age"* Seattle Symphony Orchestra	Artek AR-0037-2
Shostakovich, Dmitri	*Symphony No. 8* Seattle Symphony Orchestra	Artek AR-0044-2
Shostakovich, Dmitri	*Cello Concerto No. 1; Symphony No. 9* Lynn Harrell, cello; Seattle Symphony Orchestra	Artek AR-0056-2
Silver, Sheila	*Shirat Sara* Seattle Symphony Orchestra	Naxos 8.559426
Sondheim, Stephen	*Johanna; Not While I'm Around* Seattle Symphony Orchestra	Delos 3187
Spohr, Louis	*Clarinet Concerto No. 1* Emma Johnson, clarinet; English Chamber Orchestra	ASV 659
Starer, Robert	*Invocation* Seattle Symphony Orchestra	Delos 3187
Starer, Robert	*Concerto a Quattro* Seattle Symphony Orchestra	MMC 2048
Starer, Robert	*K'li Zemer*	Naxos 8.559403
Stock, David	*Plenty of Horn* Seattle Symphony Orchestra	Naxos 8.559679
Stock, David	*American Accents* Seattle Symphony Orchestra	Innovo 586
Stock, David	*Symphony No. 2* Seattle Symphony Orchestra	Innovo 586
Stock, David	*A Little Miracle* Berlin Radio Symphony Orchestra	Naxos 8.559422
Stock, David	*Tekiah* Seattle Symphony Orchestra	Naxos 8.559422
Strauss, Richard	*Symphonic Fantasy on "Der Rosenkavalier"* [arr. Schwarz]; *"Der Rosenkavalier" Waltzes, Suites 1 and 2* Seattle Symphony Orchestra	Naxos 8.571217

APPENDIX II: LIST OF RECORDINGS

Strauss, Richard	*Also Sprach Zarathustra; Four Symphonic Interludes from "Intermezzo"* Seattle Symphony Orchestra	Naxos 8.571215
Strauss, Richard	*Symphonia Domestica; "Die Liebe der Danae"—Suite* Seattle Symphony Orchestra	Naxos 8.571216
Strauss, Richard	*Also sprach Zarathustra; Dance of the Seven Veils; Four Symphonic Interludes from "Intermezzo"* Seattle Symphony Orchestra	Delos 3052
Strauss, Richard	*Symphonia Domestica; Josephslegende* Seattle Symphony Orchestra	Delos 3082
Strauss, Richard	*Serenade for Winds; Ein Heldenleben; Macbeth* Seattle Symphony Orchestra	Delos 3094
Strauss, Richard	*Der Rosenkavalier; Die Frau ohne Schatten; Burleske for Piano and Orchestra* Seattle Symphony Orchestra	Delos 3109
Strauss, Richard	*Also sprach Zarathustra; Waltzes from "Der Rosenkavalier"; Dance of the Seven Veils from "Salome"; Burleske for Piano and Orchestra; Music from "The Loves of Danae"; Metamorphosen for 23 Strings* Seattle Symphony Orchestra	Delos 3707
Strauss, Richard	*Metamorphosen* Seattle Symphony Orchestra	Delos 3121
Strauss, Richard	*Divertimento, Op. 86* New York Chamber Symphony	Nonesuch 79145
Strauss, Richard	*Duet-Concertino* Los Angeles Chamber Orchestra	Nonesuch 79018
Strauss, Richard	*Le bourgeois gentilhomme* New York Chamber Symphony	ProArtek Y88

APPENDIX II: LIST OF RECORDINGS

Strauss, Richard	*Alpine Symphony; Suite for Wind Instruments, Op. 4* Royal Liverpool Philharmonic	RLCD 401P
Strauss, Richard	*Don Quixote* Royal Liverpool Philharmonic	RLCD 403
Strauss, Richard	*Symphonia Domestica; Oboe Concerto; Alpine Symphony; Duet-Concertino* Jonathan Small, oboe; Royal Liverpool Philharmonic	AV 2071
Strauss, Richard	*Musically Speaking—Strauss* Seattle Symphony Orchestra	Musically Speaking, ASIN: B013Q7GS9A
Stravinsky, Igor	*The Firebird; Song of the Nightingale* Seattle Symphony Orchestra	Delos 3051
Stravinsky, Igor	*Petrouchka; Fireworks; Scherzo fantastique* Seattle Symphony Orchestra	Delos 3054
Stravinsky, Igor	*The Rite of Spring; Pulcinella* Seattle Symphony Orchestra	Delos 3100
Stravinsky, Igor	*The Firebird* [complete ballet] Seattle Symphony Orchestra	Delos 3702
Stravinsky, Igor	*The Soldier's Tale* Los Angeles Chamber Orchestra	Delos 3014
Stravinsky, Igor	*Musically Speaking—Stravinsky* Seattle Symphony Orchestra	Musically Speaking, ASIN: B013Q6ZQX0
Taylor, Deems	*Peter Ibbetson* Various artists; Seattle Symphony Orchestra	Naxos 8.669016-17
Telemann, Georg Philipp	*Concerto for Trumpet* George Vosburgh, trumpet; Seattle Symphony Orchestra	Four Winds 3021
Telemann, Georg Philipp	*Concerto for Trumpet in D* Gerard Schwarz New York Chamber Symphony	Delos 3002

APPENDIX II: LIST OF RECORDINGS

Telemann, Georg Philipp	*Concerto in D Major* Baroque Chamber Music of Telemann, Hertel, Albinoni	Desto 6438
Tchaikovsky, Pyotr Ilyich	*Symphonies Nos. 1 and 2* Seattle Symphony Orchestra	Delos 3087
Tchaikovsky, Pyotr Ilyich	*Rococo Variations* Royal Liverpool Philharmonic	RLCD 403
Tchaikovsky, Pyotr Ilyich	*Musically Speaking— Tchaikovsky* Polish National Radio Symphony Orchestra and the Royal Philharmonic Orchestra	Musically Speaking, ASIN: B000S6OGYM
Toch, Ernst	*Cantata of the Bitter Herbs* Czech Philharmonic Orchestra *Jephta (Symphony No. 5)* Seattle Symphony Orchestra	Naxos 8.559406
Torelli, Giuseppe	*Sonata in D* New York Chamber Symphony	Delos 3002
Villa-Lobos, Heitor	*Harmonica Concerto* Robert Bonfiglia, harmonica; New York Chamber Symphony	RCA 7986-2-RC
Vivaldi, Antonio	*The Four Seasons* Los Angeles Chamber Orchestra	Delos 3007
Vivaldi, Antonio	*Concerto for 2 Trumpets in C* Gerard Schwarz and Norman Smith, trumpets; New York Chamber Symphony	Delos 3002
Vivaldi, Antonio	*Musically Speaking—Vivaldi* Los Angeles Chamber Orchestra	Musically Speaking, ASIN: B0000B383F
Wagner, Richard	*Wagner* [box set] Seattle Symphony Orchestra	DE 3040, 3053, 3120
Wagner, Richard	*Orchestral Excerpts from "Rheingold," "Tannhäuser," "Götterdämmerung," "Die Meistersinger"* Seattle Symphony Orchestra	Delos 3040

APPENDIX II: LIST OF RECORDINGS

Wagner, Richard	*Excerpts from "Tannhauser,"; "Die Meistersinger," "Tristan und Isolde"* Alesssandra Marc, soprano; Seattle Symphony Orchestra	Naxos 8.572769
Wagner, Richard	*Overture to "The Flying Dutchman"; Orchestral Excerpts, "Lohengrin" and "Parsifal"* Seattle Symphony Orchestra	Delos 3053
Wagner, Richard	*"Siegfried," Forest Murmurs; "Lohengrin," Elsa's Dream; Suite from "Tristan und Isolde"; "Die Walküre," Wotan's Farewell; Faust Overture* Scattle Symphony Orchestra	Delos 3120
Wagner, Richard	*Faust Overture; Excerpts from "Lohengrin"; Excerpts from "Parsifal"* Seattle Symphony Orchestra	Naxos 8.572768
Wagner, Richard	*Overture to "The Flying Dutchman"; Orchestral Excerpts from "Rheingold"; "Die Walküre," Wotan's Farewell; "Siegfried," Forest Murmurs; Orchestral Excerpts from "Götterdämmerung"* Seattle Symphony Orchestra	Naxos 8.572767
Wagner, Richard	*Musically Speaking—Wagner* Seattle Symphony Orchestra	Musically Speaking, ASIN: B000JLHQZC
Wagner, Walt	*The Miracle* Seattle Symphony Orchestra	Semaphone 79312
Weber, Carl Maria von	*Clarinet Concertos* Emma Johnson, clarinet; English Chamber Orchestra	Apex 0927 49421-2
Webern, Anton	*Langsamer Satz* [arr. Schwarz] Seattle Symphony Orchestra	Delos 3121
Weill, Kurt	*The Eternal Road* Berlin Radio Symphony	Naxos 8.559406
Weill, Kurt	*Stratas Sings Weill* Teresa Stratas, soprano; New York Chamber Symphony	Nonesuch 7931

APPENDIX II: LIST OF RECORDINGS

Weinberg, Jacob	*The Maypole; Canzonetta* Berlin Radio Symphony Orchestra	Naxos 8.559403
Weisgall, Hugo	*Tkiatot* Seattle Symphony Orchestra	Naxos 8.559425
Whittenberg, Charles	*Polyphony*	PHCD 115
Wolpe, Stefan	*Solo Piece*	PHCD 115
Zamont, Judith	*Sacred Service* Ernst Senff Choir; Berlin Radio Symphony	Naxos 8.559444

ACKNOWLEDGMENTS

———

I t was a pleasure to write this memoir, but it would not have been possible without the help of many friends and family. Most important is my wife, Jody. Of course she guided me as I was writing with thoughtful and sensitive advice. When it was complete, she did the first editing which was remarkable, and she pushed me to delve into many areas more deeply. My life wouldn't be what it is without her, and I can easily say the same for this book. My daughter Gabriella also helped with the editing of the vignettes section. The book came into existence because of the original work, through interviews, that Maxine Frost did. She was an on-air announcer for KING-FM in Seattle and often interviewed me. She had the idea of making a book out of these interviews and made the initial proposal to Amadeus Press. That was the start, and her continued support and research helped make the book a reality. Barbara Norton was a fantastic editor and helped not only with making everything as clear as possible, but helped reduce an overly long book into something manageable. As a musician, I can feel a sense of confidence about my work, but my world is not a literary one. I am so grateful to John Cerullo of Amadeus Press for all his guidance and extraordinary support. Also from Amadeus Press, Lindsay Wagner, who kept me focused on the task and made the reality of doing something of this magnitude possible and moving forward. Finally, I would like to thank my remarkable manager, Jenny Rose. Our world of classical music is in many ways a very difficult one and having someone like Jenny on your team is essential. She has been with me throughout the whole process of writing this book as she has in my professional life and I am very grateful to her for all her many talents and her constant support and guidance.

INDEX

INDEX

INDEX

INDEX

INDEX

INDEX

INDEX

INDEX

INDEX

INDEX

INDEX